MAWSON

MAWSON

A LIFE

Philip Ayres

MELBOURNE UNIVERSITY PRESS

MELBOURNE UNIVERSITY PRESS
An imprint of Melbourne University Publishing Ltd
PO Box 1167, Carlton, Victoria 3053, Australia
mup-info@unimelb.edu.au
www.mup.com.au

First published 1999
Paperback edition 2003

Text designed and typeset in 11.5/14 Bembo by Sandra Nobes
Cover designed by Ruth Gruener
Cover photograph: Sir Douglas Mawson, Mawson Collection,
South Australian Museum
Printed in Australia by BPA Print Group

National Library of Australia Cataloguing-in-Publication entry
Ayres, Philip.
Mawson: a life.
Bibliography.
Includes index.
ISBN 0 522 85078 2 (pbk.).
1. Mawson, Douglas, Sir, 1882-1958. 2. Australasian Antarctic
Expedition, (1911-1914). 3. Explorers-Australia-Biography.
4. Antarctica-Discovery and exploration. I. Title.
910.92

CONTENTS

Contents

ILLUSTRATIONS

COLOUR PLATES

between pages 226 and 227

BANZARE: geopolitics in process
Hurley/MAC

BANZARE: scientific activities consume time
Hurley/MAC

Mawson with some of the scientific personnel
Hurley/MAC

Mawson about to ascend in the Gipsy Moth
Hurley/MAC

With daughters Jessica and Patricia, at home
MAC

Mawson with American trans-Antarctic flyer Lincoln Ellsworth
and Sir Hubert Wilkins
Sydney Morning Herald/Author Collection

Same day, same people
Sydney Morning Herald/Author Collection

Mawson in the field in South Australia, 1948
Alan Spry Collection

Members of the University of Adelaide's Department
of Geology
MAC

The Mawsons in the family car, early 1950s
MAC

With Soviet Antarctic personnel from the *Lena*, 1956
MAC

Phillip Law, Mawson, General Hjalmar Riiser-Larsen,
and Captain J. K. Davis
A. Campbell Drury/Phillip Law Collection

Mawson with Sir Raymond Priestley and J. K. Davis
MAC

MAPS

ACKNOWLEDGEMENTS

THIS BIOGRAPHY IS indebted to many generous people. Foremost among them are members of the Mawson family, who gave of their time and provided access to their private collections of relevant documents and photographs, and to documents held in Adelaide's Mortlock Library but not generally accessible to the public. In this regard I particularly thank Sir Douglas Mawson's daughters, Patricia Thomas and Jessica McEwin, and two of his grandsons, Gareth and Alun Thomas.

For their care in reading and commenting on the manuscript I thank Phillip Law, former director of ANARE; David Corbett, the outstanding authority on Mawson's geological work; R. A. Swan, Antarctic historian; Mark Pharaoh, curator of the Mawson Antarctic Collection; Nancy Flannery, biographer of Paquita Mawson; Jessica McEwin; Gareth and Alun Thomas; and Michael Casey.

People who knew Mawson, most of them closely, granted me interviews, face-to-face, by telephone or correspondence, so that this book could contain memories of him all the way from the 1920s to the 1950s: Bryan Forbes, Alf Howard, Phillip Law, Jessica McEwin, Robin Oliver, Lee Parkin, the late Eric Rudd, Ralph Segnit, Alan Spry, R. A. Swan, Patricia Thomas, and Allan Wilson. Others who shared their memories of Mawson and J. K. Davis with me include the late Sir Robert Southey (Davis), Geoffrey and Ann Blainey (Mawson), Don Hossack (Davis), and Paul Hackforth-Jones (Mawson).

I also thank Tim Bowden for drafts of his interviews with Harold Fletcher and Alf Howard; Ian Fletcher for access to his father's BANZARE diary; Edward Fletcher of the Aviation Heritage Museum of Western Australia for the flight logs of Gipsy Moth VH-ULD; Iris Hanna for information on Mawson's home in Plumpton near Sydney; Marg McPherson, History Information Officer of the NSW Department of School Education; Dion Makowski, aviation historian, for his file on the REP monoplane; John Rowley for taking me over Mawson's farm, and Charles Phillipson for granting access; Stephen Williams, Manager of the Adelaide Club for the Club's records on Mawson; and Andrew Wilson.

This book draws on a vast array of unpublished material including the diaries of men who served with or under Mawson during the BAE, the AAE and the BANZARE cruises. By far the largest archival source is the Mawson Antarctic Collection (archival successor to the Mawson Institute for Antarctic Research), at Urrbrae House on the University of Adelaide's Waite campus. The curator, Mark Pharaoh, was unsparing in his assistance, enabling me to go through the vast bulk of materials with maximum efficiency. Yvonne Routledge, in charge at Urrbrae House, was also extremely helpful. A number of other archives hold relevant material. Within Australia I record the co-operation of archivists at the Mortlock Library in Adelaide, the Mitchell Library in Sydney, the University of Sydney Archives, the La Trobe Library in Melbourne, the National Library of Australia in Canberra, the Australian National Archives in Canberra, the Adolph Basser Library at the Australian Academy of Science in Canberra, the University of Melbourne Archives, the Archives of the Royal Historical Society of Victoria, the Archives of the University of Adelaide, the Adelaide Club and the Melbourne Club. In the United States I was assisted by librarians of the National Archives at College Park in Maryland, the Byrd Polar Research Center at Ohio State University, Columbus, Ohio, and the University of Michigan Archives at Ann Arbor. For the United Kingdom I record the co-operation of the Scott Polar Research Institute at Cambridge and its Curator, Robert Headland, and the Cambridge University Library. The Royal Geographical

Society in London, the Turnbull Library in Wellington and other archives and institutions, by sending photocopies of their Mawson-related materials to the Mawson Antarctic Collection in Adelaide, also contributed indirectly to this book. I thank them all.

The largest collection of photographic images from Mawson's Antarctic expeditions is held by the Mawson Antarctic Collection (there is also a large collection of negatives and photographs at the Mitchell Library). These include the majority of the colour Autochrome and Paget plates, and the stereoscopic plates. Images in this book have also been provided by members of the Mawson family, including the Kodachrome of Mawson at Mt Stromlo (Kodachromes of Mawson are extremely rare). Mr R. A. Swan generously gave me contemporary photographs from his collection, including ones from the 1920s and 1930s of Mawson with Byrd, Ellsworth and Wilkins reproduced here, and contemporary photographs of J. K. Davis and the *Aurora*, as well as original correspondence from Mawson on Antarctic geopolitics. And Mrs A. Campbell-Drury allowed me to publish one of her late husband's professional photographs.

I am particularly grateful to my mother for accommodating me on numerous trips to Adelaide, and to my brother Bronte and his wife Mandy for allowing me to use their country house in the Adelaide Hills as an occasional place of work. For her suggestion, several years ago, that an objective biography of Mawson was long overdue I thank Karen Lamb. And finally, I thank Ev Beissbarth, and the staff at Melbourne University Press, especially Teresa Pitt and Gabby Lhuede, for the efficient manner in which this book was put into production, and for the decision to include it in the Miegunyah series.

ABBREVIATIONS

A SEPARATE LIST of abbreviations is given at the beginning of the Bibliography. Abbreviations have generally been avoided in the text and notes, with the following exceptions:

AAAS   Australasian Association for the Advancement of Science
AAE   Australasian Antarctic Expedition 1911–14
ADB   *Australian Dictionary of Biography* (Melbourne, 1966–)
ANARE   Australian National Antarctic Research Expeditions
            (1947–)
ANRC   Australian National Research Council
ANZAAS   Australian and New Zealand Association for the
            Advancement of Science
BAE   British Antarctic Expedition 1907–9
BANZARE   British, Australian and New Zealand Antarctic Research
            Expeditions 1929–31
BHP   Broken Hill Proprietary Limited
CSIR   Council for Scientific and Industrial Research
CSIRO   Commonwealth Scientific and Industrial Research
            Organisation
FRGS   Fellow of the Royal Geographical Society (London)
FRS   Fellow of the Royal Society
MAC   Mawson Antarctic Collection, Waite Campus, University
            of Adelaide
RGS   Royal Geographical Society (London)
RN   Royal Navy
TRSSA   *Transactions of the Royal Society of South Australia*

Note on Measurement

Mawson did not use the metric system in his published work or correspondence although he advocated it's introduction. To avoid unpleasant anachronism, and in the interests of authenticity and contemporary atmosphere, as well as for the convenience of American readers, measures have not been metricated. Readers may readily make their own conversions according to the following guidelines:

Length

1 inch (in)	=	2.54 centimetres		
1 foot (ft)	=	30.48 centimetres		
1 yard (yd)	=	91.44 centimetres		
1 statute mile	=	5280 feet	=	1.61 kilometres

Weight

1 pound (lb)	=	16 ounces (oz)	=	0.454 kilograms
1 ton	=	2240 pounds	=	1.016 tonnes

Volume

1 gallon = 4.546 litres

Temperature

−50°F (82 degrees of frost)	=	−45.5°C
−40°F (72 degrees of frost)	=	−40°C
−30°F (62 degrees of frost)	=	−34.5°C

−20°F (52 degrees of frost)	=	−29°C
−10°F (42 degrees of frost)	=	−23.5°C
0°F (32 degrees of frost)	=	−18°C
32°F (freezing-point at sea-level)	=	0°C

CURRENCY

The pound (£) was divided into 20 shillings of 12 pence each. Sums in pounds, shillings and pence are represented thus: £5 7s 6d. The British pound sterling during Mawson's lifetime was generally worth somewhat more than the Australian pound, though they were comparable.

1 South

LONDON DOCK OCCUPIED a stretch of the north bank of the
Thames, just down from Tower Bridge and other landmarks, but
views of the metropolis from here were hazed by smog, mangled
by cranes, the masts and stacks of steamers, the shrouds and rigging
of the clippers which still ran out to China and down to Australia
by the Great Circle route for the wool. Such a clipper, the *Ellora*,
1727 tons, Captain William Clayton, lay by this dock on the hazy
summer morning of Friday, 20 June 1884, readying for departure.
She lay low, for she carried 72 000 slates for the roofs of Melbourne,
200 tons of pig iron, 500 casks of cement, 200 cases of galvanised
iron, and five cased billiard tables. Built in 1855, *Ellora* had declined
to a down-at-heel hack, convertible on demand. Last year it was
Indian coolies for Guyana, and immigrants from Plymouth to
Sydney, up to 460 on a trip, packed like animals into her unventilated between-decks where lice and fleas ran riot. This year it was
cargo. A week ago she had arrived here from Iquique loaded with
nitrate. Now she was south-bound with her slates and her pig iron,
and fewer than fifty passengers, most in steerage, some in the saloon.

They included a small family from Yorkshire, Robert and
Margaret Mawson with their two boys, William, not yet four, and
Douglas, just two. These were well-dressed, fine-featured people
with the money to travel first-class. Like innumerable restless others
in that age of empire, they were doing what empire is for, following
fortune, defining destinies, leaving the land of forefathers whose
lives had been defined by place, class and the past.[1]

For Robert Mawson that place had been the green Wharfe valley in Yorkshire where his family had lived for centuries as yeoman farmers, in the vicinity of the villages of Stainburn, Kirkby Overblow and Rigton, on the Harewood estates. In the years 1911–17 Joseph Mawson of Hampstead laboriously traced the Mawsons of the Wharfe valley all the way back to 1290 and believed that the name originated there. In Northumberland he followed it back to 1312, in Durham to 1336, in Lincoln to 1338, in Ripon to 1356, but there were relatively few Mawsons outside the valley and most of the ones he traced lived in the three villages just mentioned. They gave their name to local landmarks—Mawson's Field, Mawson's Well. There is a legend in these villages that a Mawson was steward to the monks of nearby Fountains Abbey, the great Cistercian monastery destroyed by Henry VIII but still magnificent in its ruins. The farms of the valley are mixed—dairying, sheep and crops. One of them belonged to Robert Mawson's father, William, who died in 1862, just six years after his father, Robert, who was born in 1787 and to whom a line of traced names descends from the seventeenth century.[2]

When Robert Mawson's father died, his farm was managed by his widow Mary, who sent her 8-year-old boy to Dr Kerr's Grammar School in York. Robert's ambitions lay beyond the farm and he became a draper, buying and selling cloth, his fickle fortunes, like his partner's, up and down to bankruptcy, then up again with another partner. During a visit to the Isle of Man he met Margaret Ann Moore, daughter of James Moore, plumber. She was twenty and he was twenty-five when they married on 7 October 1879.[3] The marriage certificate gave Robert's address as 'Frizinghall near Bradford' (on the Shipley side) and this was where William and Douglas were born, Douglas on 5 May 1882, a day that augured well in Yorkshire, with showers moving off, becoming fine. This same year Robert's mother died. After months of deliberation, flirting with romantic notions of a life in the South Pacific, and with ways to make money there, he compromised and chose the raw, new world of Australia, partly for the sake of the boys' education. Some months into 1884 he sold the farm and any business interests he had, farewelled his disapproving sister Sarah

Ann, and took his family by direct express on the Great Northern, from Bradford through Leeds to King's Cross. He had places to go.

Anchors weighed, *Ellora* cast off and hauled out of dock, the tug swung her round till the bowsprit pointed seawards and she set sail, past Deptford and Greenwich, Gravesend and Tilbury, the last of England, down the estuary to the sea. It was the standard route to Australia for sailing ships, by the west coast of Africa, then round into the Southern Ocean where, south of latitude 40°, the cold westerlies rarely moderate and the mountainous waves, the biggest in the world, roll ceaselessly on, unimpeded by continents. Three hundred miles a day down here was not exceptional in these heavy following seas. The only danger was in carrying too much sail, a mistake made by the record-breaker *Ariel* in 1872 when, hurrying to Australia, the westerlies drove her bow under water, sending her straight to the bottom. The children were kept inside the warm saloon, from the windows of which they watched the albatrosses, Cape hens and sea hawks that follow the ships in these high latitudes.

This was one of the fastest passages *Ellora* ever made to Australia. On Tuesday, 26 August 1884, she sailed into Port Phillip Bay in squally weather, the seas chopped by westerlies and the rain hard against the port windows of the saloon. At Melbourne the Mawsons disembarked along with the other passengers and three days later they sailed on the fast coastal steamer *Gabo* for Sydney, arriving within two days.[4]

Robert ploughed some of his capital into a farm at Woodstock–Rooty Hill, west of Sydney (now suburban) where he grew fruit trees and ran pigs, at the same time making jam and pioneering fruit-canning at a plant he set up with a partner. By 1888 Douglas Mawson was of school age. His first formal education was in a small building almost 4 miles' walk from home. When Douglas was six his father wrote a petition to the Minister of Education for New South Wales asking that a National Public School be erected 'in the vicinity of the Woodstock Fruit Preserving Company's Factory as the distance our children have to walk to the present building is far too great to admit of them doing so with comfort to themselves, causing them to arrive at their destination in so exhausted a condition as to admit of their doing but little work'. The petition is in Robert Mawson's hand and signed by himself and those of his neighbours or employees who had children of school age.[5] As a result the Woodstock (later Plumpton) School was erected. The house in which the Mawsons lived still stood in 1997, greatly reconditioned, in Hyatt Road, Plumpton, a few hundred yards from Jersey Road.[6]

Unfortunately none of Robert Mawson's ventures prospered and he finally sold the farm and took a secure job as an accountant with a Sydney timber merchant, the family moving to Glebe and living from 1893 in Glebe Road (285, 345 and 351), then later, from 1902 to 1905, at 28 Toxteth Road between Mansfield and Bell Streets, in a large house where they took in boarders to supplement the father's income. In Glebe Douglas attended a first-rate school, the Forest Lodge Superior Public School, opened in 1883 on the corner of Bridge Road and Ross Street.

At the beginning of 1895 he progressed to Fort Street Model Public School for his secondary education. No records from Fort Street survive from the 1890s aside from the school's magazine, the *Fortian*, which begins on 7 August 1899, eight months after Mawson left. However, the magazine gave a great deal of space to him in 1909 on his return from Ernest Shackleton's British Antarctic Expedition (BAE), and provides early retrospective views. His headmaster was J. W. ('Boss') Turner, a strong figure who inspired loyalty, though his enthusiasm for sports never rubbed off onto Mawson. J. A. Klein, who taught at the school from 1896 to 1899, gave Mawson his first lesson in geology, as Klein pointed out to the Old Boys' Union on 28 August 1958. In 1909 the tall and lean young Mawson was remembered by one of his former schoolmates as modest and unprepossessing, 'just an ordinary lad of manly disposition'.[7] The headmaster was more impressed, asking with uncanny prescience at the Speech Night of 1898, 'What shall we say of our Douglas as an acknowledged leader and organiser? This I will say— that if there be a corner of this planet of ours still unexplored, Douglas Mawson will be the organiser and leader of an expedition to unveil its secrets.' Mawson himself is the source—on his return from his Australasian Antarctic Expedition (AAE) in 1914, Klein reminded him of Turner's extraordinary words.[8] In these years Mawson and his brother William sang in the choir of St Andrew's Cathedral, although William was the more musical and also the more studious at this stage.

At the beginning of 1899 William entered the Faculty of Medicine at the University of Sydney, going on to practise in Campbelltown where he later owned a cinema.[9] Douglas, only sixteen, passed the University's entrance examination at the same time as his brother and chose engineering—the mining and metallurgy division. His overall performance in the three-year degree was solid but not outstanding. In 1899 he studied conics, chemistry, physics, physiography, applied mechanics and descriptive geometry (a usefully wide range), gaining second-class honours in physics.

The following year he studied chemistry, physics, geology, mineralogy, surveying and applied mechanics, and gained first-class honours in geology and mineralogy, second-class honours in chemistry, and Professor T. W. Edgeworth (later Sir Edgeworth) David's Prize for Geological Microscope Slides. David, in his forties, with high cheekbones and a weathered and wizened face, gentle by disposition, always courteous, was an inspiring teacher much loved by his students, and the prize is significant—Mawson's subsequent geological work would be backed up by much solid microscopic analysis. During this second year, according to Mawson's friend and fellow student T. Griffith Taylor, he helped David sink a test shaft on the Maitland Coal Seams, which suggests the closeness of professor and protégé at this early stage.[10]

In 1901 he studied mining, metallurgy, materials and structures, gaining second-class honours in mining and qualifying for the degree of Bachelor of Engineering, conferred on 19 April 1902.[11] Meanwhile, during his second year (1900), along with Professor Edgeworth David, Mawson had been one of the founders of the University Volunteer Rifle Corps. Mawson served with the Corps for three years and was rated 'Marksman',[12] and helped to found the University's Science Society.

He now applied for the position of Junior Demonstrator in the Department of Chemistry at the age of just nineteen, with Edgeworth David as referee, and was appointed with effect from

11 April 1902 at an annual salary of £100.[13] The Professor of Chemistry and Dean of Science, Archibald Liversidge, had a strong interest in chemical geology and reinforced David's influence. At the same time Mawson undertook further studies in geology, working towards the B.Sc. degree and teaming up with Griffith Taylor to conduct a field survey of the area around Mittagong, in the Southern Tablelands of New South Wales, resulting in his first major publication.[14]

Then in early 1903 he was offered an adventure that could contribute to the discipline in a more impressive fashion. Edgeworth David suggested he spend the winter on a geological expedition to the New Hebrides under the auspices of Captain E. G. Rason RN, Britain's Deputy Commissioner there, and Mawson seized the opportunity. On Friday, 3 April 1903, in company with Rason and W. T. Quaife, the expedition's biologist-cum-botanist, he left Sydney on the steamer *Ysabel*. On the way up he got to know Rason reasonably well. There was nothing to do for ten days but eat and drink, lounge on deck chairs in their whites, smoke Rason's cigars and listen to him talk. He had entered the Royal Navy in 1865 and commanded HMS *Ready* in the Egyptian War and at the capture of the Suez Canal. His most recent achievement was putting down the restive natives of the New Hebrides, in conjunction with the French Commissioners there. Rason admitted, however, that he had not made a thorough enough fist of it, and resistance was continuing, particularly on Malekula, the biggest island in the group after Espiritu Santo. 'Unsettled' was the word. The Malekulans were still cannibals, and the Presbyterian missionaries shied away. There was also a war going on between the inhabitants of Rano and Wala. But Rason was confident—he had the cruiser *Archer*, and he and its commander, J. P. Rolleston, knew exactly where and how to use it. They would spend the next few months taking it around the island group, partly for 'punitive' purposes, and Mawson and Quaife could use it as a mobile base camp.

On 13 April the *Ysabel* arrived in Vila, the commercial centre on the island of Efate, and after settling in Mawson began the first-ever extensive geological survey of the island group.[15] He started by examining the raised coral reefs around Vila and the foundation rocks beneath them, proceeded to Havannah Harbour, still on Efate, where he traced the uplifted reefs in rising terraces to the top of Mt Erskine, 1270 feet, then proceeded to the south of Undine Bay. Frequent earthquakes were *leit-motifs* to this patient activity, tectonics-in-process. These excursions occupied the second half of April and most of May. His diaries and field notes are almost exclusively geological in focus but contain evidence that he was already succumbing to bouts of fever, which never entirely left his system during the rest of the expedition—gaps in the entries of up to six days are frequent.

Satisfied with his work on Efate, during the night of 25 May he left with Rason on the *Archer*, feeling feverish, as he noted. They worked their way up the east coast of Malekula and the off-lying islands. This was the most dangerous part of the expedition. Geologically the island is important, and older than the more southerly islands, consisting of dome-shaped mountains with denuded cores to 3000 feet and thick-bedded alluvial valleys. 'On account of the prohibitive savagery of the natives', Mawson noted in his full report, 'explorations in this island are necessarily limited; we were, however, able to examine the east coast', as well as 'making several excursions well into the interior'.[16] These excursions were almost certainly conducted under guard, courtesy of Rason. On 3 June they were back on *Archer*, 'which had just returned from a punitive expedition to the west coast', as Mawson noted.[17] This punitive expedition would have drawn warriors away from the east of the island where Mawson was working, which may have been a factor in Rason's mind. With her six 6-inch guns, eight 3-pound quick-firers and two machine guns, *Archer*'s shelling would have been heard for many miles around and must have had considerable impact.[18]

She now disembarked Rason at Malo Island where he had business to attend to, and Commander Rolleston took Mawson and Quaife on to the Presbyterian mission settlement of Tangoa on the south coast of Santo from where they made deep incursions into the hinterland and across to the west coast. The highest mountain on Santo is Losumbunu, 5520 feet, one of a series of mountains

rising in ridges from the coast that had never before been crossed
or even closely approached by Europeans. Mawson and Quaife
determined to climb Losumbunu and set out in continuous
drizzling rain on 11 June with three native guides supplied by the
Rev. F. Bowie. These guides lived on the southern slopes of
Losumbunu and were reputed to have climbed to the summit in
quest of flying-foxes, one of their delicacies. They were misunder-
stood—it was another, lesser peak these natives had ascended,
further south. The party hacked their way through valleys and
ravines and across the ridges, Quaife collecting species of orchids
never before recorded. Their first approach to the summit had to
be abandoned; their second took them to 4300 feet on the morning
of 13 June, just a mile and a half south of their goal, but was also
abandoned. Mawson's large notebook, with entries made *en route*,
tells why:

> Stopped at 11 O'Clock as natives would go no further. reasons
> 1. Seemed to be as far as ever
> 2. Ravine in front
> 3. Mist came up so we could not see
> 4. Very cold wind
> Collected a few species coming back.[19]

Mawson's expedition to the New Hebrides took him to all
the significant islands in the group, clearly demonstrated that they
constituted a fold-chain of Alpine age, and indicated the application of similar geological principles to other island groups in the
South Pacific. Previous geological work in the New Hebrides had
been piecemeal—Mawson's was the first systematic account. It
almost cost him a leg. While hammering into a rock for a specimen
he was pierced in the knee by a splinter which lodged under the
kneecap, and serious swelling ensued. The *Archer* was many miles
away, and by the time Mawson and Quaife had rowed back to it
the leg was black to the groin. The ship's doctor considered ampu-
tation, but after opening up the knee and releasing the dark fluid
Mawson's condition improved and within a week or two he was
out of danger.[20]

Back home again, he undertook with T. H. Laby the first study of radioactivity in Australian minerals. The footnotes to the ensuing publication, which appeared towards the end of 1904, show how up-to-the-minute this study was. Aside from predictable citations such as Mme Curie, Mawson and Laby drew on a swathe of articles just a few months old in the most recent 1904 volumes of American, British, French and German scientific journals.[21] With such wide experience and significant publications behind him, his B.Sc. was assured. He qualified at the end of 1904 and graduated early in 1905, while his reputation as an adventurer was celebrated in the University's Commemoration Day Procession when, in black-face and dressed as a New Hebridean cannibal, he stood on one of the floats beside a large pot with a cowering 'missionary' on the other side.[22]

Even before qualifying for the B.Sc. he had applied for a lectureship in mineralogy and petrology at the University of Adelaide, in mid-1904, and been successful. The salary was to be £300 initially, and he would be working with Walter Howchin, who had made his name internationally by proving the existence of a period of glaciation in South Australia in Cambrian times (500 million years before the present, by modern dating) or even late Precambrian times (570 million years or more before the present) —a vastly earlier ice-age than any previously known.

Mawson took up his appointment on 1 March 1905 and quickly settled in, staying initially at the Newmarket Hotel on the corner of North and West Terraces, and subsequently in rooms at the seaside suburb of Glenelg and on the corner of Angas Street and East Terrace in the centre. His early Adelaide friends included William (later Sir William) Henry Bragg who, with his son William Lawrence (later Sir Lawrence) Bragg, would win the Nobel Prize for Physics in 1915 for work on X-ray crystallography; Sir Charles Todd, Government Astronomer and the 'father' of the Overland Telegraph from Adelaide to Darwin; the historian George Henderson, who also lectured on English literature; and William (later Sir William) Mitchell, the Hughes Professor of English Literature and Mental and Moral Philosophy. Todd's daughter Lorna, who arranged for Mawson to be partnered to a ball on his arrival, later recalled him at this time as 'most attractive. He often came to supper at the Observatory'.[23] In addition to his lecturing responsibilities, in 1908 he was appointed Honorary Curator of Minerals at the South Australian Museum on North Terrace, and his association with this institution would last for the rest of his life (at his death he was chairman of its board).[24]

He devoted 1905 to writing a course of lectures and settling in to his teaching responsibilities, but whenever time permitted he made field trips, including one to Kangaroo Island and the lower Eyre Peninsula with friends from Sydney during the Congress of the Australasian Association for the Advancement of Science (AAAS, or as its members wrote it, the A3S) in early 1907, and others through 1906 and 1907 to the region west of Broken Hill. Meanwhile his reputation as a pioneer in radioactive minerals was enhanced in May 1906 when he identified as carnotite the radio-active constituent of a rock sample found by A. J. Smith at the subsequently-named Radium Hill, 70 miles south-west of Broken Hill. Smith then pegged the area and came to Mawson with an offer: half a share in whatever might develop in return for Mawson's footing all expenses and attending to investigation and exploitation of the find. Mawson agreed, subsequently identifying and naming the primary mineral there as davidite after Edgeworth David but finding that as a source of radium it was at that time uneconomical. The lease expired.[25]

His most interesting South Australian field work from 1906 to 1907 was in the Broken Hill area, from Olary on the railway line, west-south-west of Broken Hill, to Menindee on the Darling River in New South Wales, an east–west stretch of 125 miles with a maximum north–south depth of 55 miles from Euriowie in the northern Barrier Ranges to Thackaringa south-west of Broken Hill. His investigations in this region gained him his D.Sc. at the end of 1909.[26] The outstanding features here are the Boolcoomata Hills and the Barrier Ranges, with intervening alluvial plains.

In 1906 this country, dry and very remote, was difficult for a geologist to work. Horse-drawn coaches radiated out from Broken Hill to the distant, lonely settlements, on primitive roads, but coaches were useless to Mawson, who could hardly confine himself to roads. He began by hiring a horse, sometimes a gig as well. Then he bought a motor-bicycle that he could take on the train to Broken Hill—an example of his commitment to technological advance, like his purchase in February 1906 of the first Zeiss camera, expensive and of advanced design, which he used on these excursions and into the 1940s.[27] He made traverses in several directions but was hampered by the sheer hostility of the country. Summer temperatures ran to 125°F in the shade, in winter the nights were frosty, and water supply was always a problem. Often he was reduced to finding a rock hole or soak, pushing aside dead rabbits floating on the surface or straining green slime through calico, then boiling up the 'water' to make tea.[28] On 28 September 1907, from a cheap hotel in dusty Broken Hill, he wrote to his mentor, Edgeworth David, whom he had just learned was to go south with Ernest Shackleton on his polar expedition later that year. 'I should have dearly loved to have gone myself', he confided, and then sketched his past few weeks' activities:

> I took my motor bicycle and many times wished I had not as the roads were too bad and was continually having mishaps . . . I went N. & S. of Silverton—Cockburn to B. Hill via Thackeringia [sic] and the Pinnacles—several excursions E of B. Hill, including one to Menindee—one trip through the hills N.E. of Stephen's Creek—and a week in the vicinity of Tarrowangee stopping at Poolamacca Station. Am leaving for a final fortnight in the Olary to Mingay country including 50 miles N & S of the line.[29]

These dry landscapes, in which Mawson read the evidences of ancient glaciation, were not as remote from Antarctica as they seem.

Following his return to Adelaide he met Shackleton who came ashore for half a day when the mail steamer RMS *India*, on which he was travelling out, docked briefly there. Mawson found the bluff, dapperly dressed Anglo-Irishman 'an attractive and interesting personality', as he later told Shackleton's biographer Margery Fisher, and offered his services without cost if he could sail from New Zealand down to Antarctica and back on Shackleton's ship, the old 300-ton sealer *Nimrod*, a well-worn but handsome barquentine with auxiliary steam power (that is, a three-masted ship, square-rigged on the foremast, fore-and-aft-rigged on the mainmast and mizzen). Shackleton said he would think it over and let him know in a few days' time. 'My idea', Mawson later explained to Fisher, 'was to see a continental ice-cap in being and become acquainted with glaciation and its geological repercussions. This especially interested me for in glaciological studies in South Australia I was face to face with a great accumulation of glacial sediments of Pre-Cambrian age, the greatest thing of the kind recorded anywhere in the world. So I desired to see an ice age in being.'[30]

Following his arrival in Sydney Shackleton saw Edgeworth David who sang his old student's praises, and shortly afterwards Mawson received a telegram—he was appointed Physicist for the length of the expedition. As he was not a physicist and had only volunteered for the round trip on *Nimrod*, this was a surprise, but he accepted and the University granted him the necessary leave. He wrote off to David, thanking him 'for achieving my inclusion' and seeking his help in finding a *locum* whom he could pay to deliver his lectures, the normal procedure.[31] Shackleton was even more indebted to David, who persuaded his friend Alfred Deakin, the Prime Minister, to provide the expedition with a grant of £5000 from the Treasury, one of Shackleton's backers having failed him.

Antarctica was the last frontier, a vast, undefined continent, perhaps two continents, or a number of islands covered and cemented by ice, the coasts and interior entirely unknown except for fringes to the south and west of the great bight named the Ross Sea, and one or two other spots on its enormous circumference (see map, between pages 17 and 18). The first landing on the mainland, at Cape Adare directly south from Dunedin, had been made as recently as 1895 under Leonard Kristensen. Carsten Borchgrevink had spent a winter in that area in 1899 and sailed down the coasts of Victoria Land and along the edge of the Great Ice Barrier (or Ross Ice Shelf) south of the Ross Sea. Lieutenant Robert Falcon Scott RN, organiser and leader of the National Antarctic Expedition of 1900–4, had established a base in McMurdo Sound at the south-west corner of the Ross Sea, manning it with scientific and naval personnel who had made incursions in several directions, but Scott had not got far south— only to 82°17' in fact, over 500 miles short of the Pole, with a group including Shackleton, who had to be invalided home on his return to base.

These expeditions had aroused great interest in Australia. Now Shackleton, a born leader with entrepreneurial drive, was running his own show, the British Antarctic Expedition (BAE), a privately funded enterprise with a publicly stated goal: 90° south.

2 MAGNETIC SOUTH

MAWSON SAILED TO New Zealand in late December 1907 on the *Wimmera*, with Edgeworth David and Leo Cotton, one of David's students who was just along for the ride down and straight back, as David professed to be. The *Nimrod* awaited them at Lyttelton, the port of Christchurch, her departure scheduled for New Year's Day. Here they met their fellow expeditioners.

Two of them, like Shackleton, had been south with Scott: Ernest Joyce, an ex-Naval petty officer in charge of the sledge dogs, and Frank Wild, a wiry 34-year-old in charge of provisions, of great resource with an on-shore penchant for whisky. 'The first time I met him', Mawson later told a correspondent, 'he was being carried out of the Christchurch Club'.[1] None of the others had polar experience. Aside from Mawson, David and the free-rider Cotton, there was another Australian, the likeable but diffident Bertram Armytage, Cambridge-educated, a fine oarsman and a cavalry veteran of the South African War. A few months after this expedition, unsuccessful in seeking employment at the War Office in London, he would return to Australia without his wife. On the evening of 12 March 1910, in his room at the Melbourne Club, he would put on full dress and decorations, spread the counterpane on the floor, lie down with a pillow on either side of his head, and shoot himself through the temple.[2]

When *Nimrod* sailed on the afternoon of 1 January 1908 her Plimsoll line was well below water and her freeboard a mere 3 feet 6 inches. On board were ponies, dogs, sheep, a motor car, the materials for a large wooden hut, equipment and sufficient supplies for two winters, and as much coal as could be carried with doubtful safety. To conserve it, Shackleton had arranged for *Nimrod* to be towed to the pack-ice by an old steamer, the *Koonya*. Over 30 000 people, and ships of Britain's Australian Squadron, saw them off. Not long out of harbour, Frank Wild shot an albatross, the winds picked up, the seas turned heavy.

Mawson found himself consigned to Oyster Alley, a tight-packed, unventilated though not watertight section of *Nimrod* where he was literally up against other members of the shore party, including the blunt-spoken, self-assured Jameson Boyd Adams (meteorologist, former merchant mariner, a lieutenant in the Naval Reserve), Eric Marshall (chief surgeon, censorious and arrogant), tough and wilful Alistair Forbes Mackay (second surgeon), James Murray (biologist), the quiet Raymond Priestley (geologist, twenty-one, a future Vice-Chancellor of the University of Melbourne), the young baronet Sir Philip Brocklehurst (assistant geologist, just twenty, here for adventure on his own bank account, the others being paid by Shackleton), Bernard Day (motor mechanic), George Marston (artist), William Roberts (cook), as well as Armytage, Wild and Joyce. David was more fortunate—he had his own cabin.[3]

Oyster Alley was no place to vomit, and as the gales rose Mawson was wretchedly sick. Eric Marshall despised him as 'useless & objectionable, lacking in guts and manners', lying about 'in a sleeping bag at one end of the bridge vomiting when he rolled to starboard, whilst the cook handed up food from the galley beneath him. He did no watches'.[4] *Nimrod*'s first officer, the tall, gaunt, humourless, red-headed John King Davis, two years Mawson's junior, found him lying in a lifeboat not having eaten for days and persuaded him to have some pears. That evening he was still there but looking better and asking for more of the same, which Davis supplied, taking him into the galley where he dried himself off and took some hot cocoa. He was soon cheerful and talkative.[5] This marked the beginning of a lifelong friendship resilient enough to survive severe tests, albeit not unscathed.

Released from *Koonya* on 15 January near the Antarctic Circle, *Nimrod* under Lieutenant Rupert England continued south through heavy pack that gave way to looser floes and 'pancake ice' before thickening up again. By now Edgeworth David had announced he was staying on for the full expedition, having sent a letter by the *Koonya* to the University of Sydney requesting the leave he was in any case taking. Shackleton told England to make for Barrier Inlet towards the eastern end of the Great Ice Barrier, knowing it from the Scott expedition, but it was no longer there—vast sections of the Barrier had calved off here, radically altering the geography of the Barrier face. The inlet had been replaced by a large bay, the Bay of Whales, they called it, after its satisfied inhabitants.

In retrospect Shackleton should have landed here, where Roald Amundsen would land in less than four years' time, but he was alarmed at what he saw as the calving propensities of this stretch of the Barrier and finally decided to proceed westward to McMurdo Sound, despite his promise to Scott not to impinge on his 'territory' there, and despite the fact that the Bay of Whales was 60 miles closer to the Pole. In fact the new face of the Barrier at the Bay of Whales was more stable as a result of the massive calving-off. Shackleton's biographer Roland Huntford notes that his decision was backed by David, but Mawson knew it to have been more strongly influenced by Ernest Joyce, who like Shackleton had been down before. Neither David nor Joyce, of course, knew anything about the structural characteristics of Barrier ice.[6]

Having decided for McMurdo Sound, Shackleton was forced to choose Cape Royds on Ross Island for his base, twenty miles north of Scott's old base at Hut Point where Ross Island at its southernmost point meets the Barrier face. This was because the southern end of McMurdo Sound was still solidly iced up. The stores were landed and a hut constructed. Just a few miles to the east sat Mt Erebus, 13 280 feet of active volcano, its glacial southern reaches cutting off Cape Royds from any land access to the Barrier and the continent. The only path south from Cape Royds was by the sea-ice of McMurdo Sound which soon melted away, leaving the hut isolated. The winter would keep them hut-bound until August. Meanwhile no depots could be laid to the south in advance of Shackleton's polar journey. With everyone settled in and *Nimrod* gone, there was little to do.

Mawson and David shared a compartment, named the Pawn Shop for its vast assortment of instruments, notebooks and geological specimens in packing cases ranged as tiered shelves. Here they contrived to sleep on boxes and kerosene cases.[7] Nearby was Mawson's darkroom where he generally worked. Other sleeping compartments ranged down either of the two long sides of the rectangular hut. There was a narrow central area reserved for dining and, with the table hoisted to the roof, for working on sledging equipment and other jobs. Shackleton realised, however, that the sense of adventure so strong in these men must be fed, and readily accepted David's proposal for an ascent of Mt Erebus. This would not be difficult, would exercise some of the men and train them in the use of equipment, and would rank as a significant achievement for the expedition. He selected David, Mawson and Mackay as the summit party, with Adams, Marshall and Brocklehurst as support party with the option—which they exercised—of continuing to the top if provisions allowed.

The men set out on the morning of 5 March under Adams's command, with ten days' provisions and equipment packed onto an 11-foot sledge pulled by the men in their harnesses and wearing improvised crampons (detachable, spiked footgear) worn over finnesko (reindeer-skin boots with the fur outside, often stuffed with dry sennegrass to absorb moisture) or cowhide ski-boots (skis were not taken). Erebus, and Mt Terror beyond it, had been named after his ships by Sir James Clark Ross, discoverer of the Ross Sea, in 1841. Erebus in particular is an impressive sight from any direction, its long slopes draped in snow and ice, rising to an old inactive crater and then, more steeply, to two more craters, one inactive, the other at the summit, issuing clouds of steam and sometimes ash in tremendous volumes. There is a good description in Edgeworth David's diary: 'Immense masses of steam rushed upwards to at least 2000 feet above the summit in about half a minute, and spread out to form a vast mushroom shaped cloud'; three days later 'Mawson came rushing down from Anemometer ridge to say that an eruption had broken out from a new quarter' with clouds 'of great volume . . . to probably at least 5000 feet'.[8]

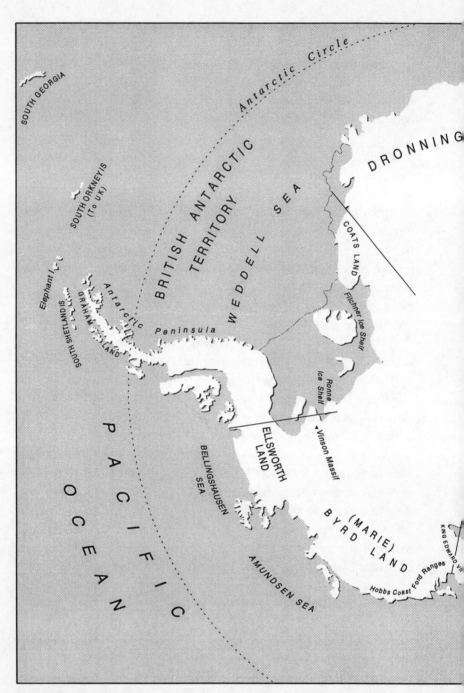

General map of the Antarctic regions, with some of the major features of the Australian quadrant marked

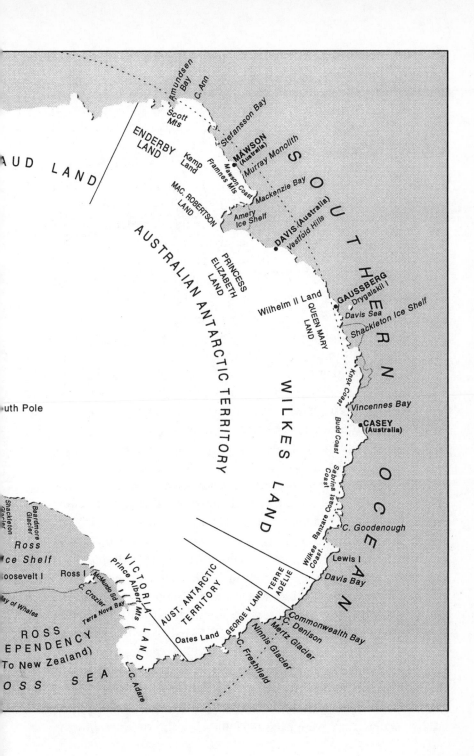

The initial going was not too difficult despite having to cross sastrugi—long, sharp ridges in the snow, often several feet high, furrowed by the prevailing winds and best sledged 'across the grain'. The first day took them 7 miles towards Erebus and up to 2750 feet, but from there the gradient rapidly increased, complicating negotiation of sastrugi and causing frequent capsizing of the sledge. As they ascended the temperature dropped. The evening of the second day saw them just 3 miles further on but at 5630 feet. Night temperatures were now down around 30° below zero Fahrenheit (62° of frost). Here, beneath the lower crater, they depoted their sledge and some of their food and equipment, even their tent poles, proceeding on 7 March with three days' provisions, minimal cooking equipment, and tents to be used merely as covers over sleeping bags. Hazards increased with the angle of attack, Mackay sliding a hundred feet down the ice at one point. That evening, camped at 8750 feet, they were hit by a blizzard from the south-east which continued through the fourth day, 8 March, finally blowing itself out that night.

The party set out again at 5.30 a.m. on the 9th, the ascent now 1 in 1½, using their ice axes to cut steps in the névé (compacted snow) or, where possible, keeping to bare rock. By now they were well above the clouds. Just after midday Mackay impulsively chose to axe his way up a particularly steep névé slope rather than go with the others by a roundabout route across bare rocks, but in the rarefied atmosphere he rapidly tired and then fainted, fortunately on a ledge, having to be rescued by David and Marshall. This was typical behaviour from Mackay, who a few years later would meet his death leading members of Vilhjalmur Stefansson's Beaufort Sea expedition off in a doomed direction of their own, in mutiny.[9]

Meanwhile Brocklehurst was losing feeling in his feet because, foolishly, he was still wearing ski-boots rather than the warmer finnesko with which all had been issued. Marshall and Mackay had to work fast to restore circulation to the blackened, frost-bitten toes, one of which would be amputated some weeks later. By mid-afternoon Brocklehurst was sufficiently improved to be left in his bag while the rest explored the rim and interior of the higher inactive crater. They were now at 11 400 feet, and on the following morning, 10 March, set out for the summit 2½ miles away, reaching it around 10.00 a.m. Mawson, the party's photographer, was having trouble with his camera's focal plane shutter jamming in the frosty conditions, but managed to take excellent shots down into the steaming, hissing, booming crater, which smelt of burning sulphur. He also took angular measurements of the crater's 900-foot depth and half-mile width, and Marshall took barometric and hypsometer readings of the altitude. (The small, tubular hypsometer, containing distilled water, works on the principle that water's boiling point decreases with altitude.)

On the way down Mawson and David made a traverse of the active crater, took levels for constructing a geological section, and collected specimens of felspar crystals, pumice and sulphur. Rather than retrace their cautious ascent they chose to glissade down névé slopes hundreds of feet long, using their ice-axes as brakes. Between 3.00 and 7.00 p.m. that afternoon they descended 5000 feet, continuing to the depot they had left on the morning of the 7th. After a short sleep they resumed the return at 5.30 a.m. and reached the hut that same morning at 11.00, having left their sledge several miles behind to be picked up later, concerned at an approaching blizzard. Exhausted and famished, they were feasted and toasted in champagne.[10]

As winter closed in Mawson occupied himself taking wind-speed readings at his anemometer on a nearby ridge, carrying out structural analyses of varieties of ice and snow, studying the Aurora Australis and building up his geological collections. He would later supply important scientific appendices for Shackleton's account of the expedition, *The Heart of the Antarctic*. Shackleton had brought along a printing press, and the men amused themselves writing chapters for a book they printed, *Aurora Australis*, to which Mawson contributed a dream fantasy titled 'Bathybia', about an expedition which discovers an alternative Antarctic world of exotic plant life and giant insects. Entertainment ranged from amateur theatricals to the latest gramophone records and readings from Dickens by 'the Prof' as David was known—'the only man I ever enjoyed listening to', Wild noted.[11] Then on 12 August Shackleton took David and Armytage on a depot-laying trip to the south, though in fact they laid no depots, merely tidied up Scott's old quarters at Hut Point, to which they subsequently sledged stores and equipment each week. On 22 September Shackleton led another party that laid a depot 100 miles south of Hut Point. Meanwhile he had selected David to lead the Northern party and David had eventually invited Mawson to join it. Their goal was the South Magnetic Pole, estimated to lie some 400 miles to the north-north-west, deep inside Victoria Land.

Shackleton's instructions, dated 19 September 1908, were clear, but he read them aloud to the party. First priority was to take magnetic observations at all suitable points to determine the dip and position of the Magnetic Pole, which they should reach if possible. Secondly, they should make a geological survey of the eastern coast of South Victoria Land, but not at the expense of the primary goal. Related to this, Mawson should spend at least a fortnight prospecting for valuable minerals at Dry Valley, on the other side of the Sound from Cape Royds—this was of 'supreme importance' but should be undertaken on the way *back* from the Magnetic Pole. In the event of David suffering an accident, Mawson would be leader.[12] Mackay, a Scots surgeon four years older than Mawson, was included because such an extended expedition required a medical officer. A depot was laid by motor car 10 miles out on the ice of McMurdo Sound in late September and other supplies taken further out on 3 October, the expedition finally departing Cape Royds on the 5th. This epic journey (see map, between pages 27 and 28) will be described here from three points of view, through the eyes of the participants, using their private journals (two of them, Mackay's and David's, unpublished), with David's extended but heavily sanitised account in *Heart of the Antarctic* in the background.

The first task was to haul their two sledges, together weighing over a ton, across the frozen southern reaches of McMurdo Sound to Butter Point in South Victoria Land, from where they proposed to sledge some 150 miles north, over the sea-ice fringing the coast, to the Drygalski Ice Barrier Tongue, whence they would proceed far inland to the north-west until reaching the Magnetic Pole. Because of the weight of their sledges, however, they were compelled to relay them—drag one forward and go back for the other, thus walking 3 miles for every mile of advance. It took them nine days just to reach Butter Point, not much more than 30 miles distant. At this rate they would never make their goal and return to Dry Valley, near Butter Point, by the first week of January as Shackleton wanted. He had given them the option, if worst came to worst, of being picked up by *Nimrod* anywhere along the Victoria Land coast south of Cape Washington in early February following the ship's return to Cape Royds. Even that might be problematical.

To make matters worse, Mawson and Mackay found their 50-year-old leader had peculiar ways: 'Prof finds it necessary to change his socks in morning before breakfast', Mawson observed, 'also has to wear 2 [pairs] per day. And comes in late for bag and sits on everybody. God only knows what he does'.[13] In the large sleeping bag they shared, David invariably took the warm central position, and more than his share of it, as he was always over-dressed.

On reaching Butter Point, their first contact with the Antarctic mainland, on 13 October, they depoted a quantity of food and gear, lightening their load. The next day they started north, past New Harbour towards the low promontory of Cape Bernacchi, and on the 15th, in fine weather, had stunning views of the Ferrar Glacier on their left and a cloud-topped Erebus 50 miles away on the right horizon.

Mawson and Mackay rigged sails on both sledges using the floor-cloth of their tent and other material, taking advantage of southerly winds, but on most days they were still relaying, the two Australians 'geologising' as they went. At Cape Bernacchi they hoisted the Union Jack and David took possession of Victoria Land for the Empire. Advancing a mere 4 miles per average day, they dragged their way north past Granite Harbour and the mountains above the Mackay Glacier. As the weather became daily warmer the snow on the sea-ice turned sticky, and by 1 November, at what they called Depot Island, they made a decision: to depot a large weight of food, geological specimens and other material, and travel on half rations to the Drygalski Glacier, 100 miles to their north, supplementing their food stores by taking seal meat along the way. Mackay improvised a cooker that would burn seal blubber to save kerosene. They left messages at a cairn they constructed on this island, with a black flag over it, informing *Nimrod*'s commander that because of slow progress they now planned to be picked up on the north side of the Drygalski Ice Barrier Tongue at the beginning of February. Determined to reach the Magnetic Pole, David had had to force his authority on Mawson, who already by 23 October had consigned the Pole to impossibility and was advocating they merely carry out geological reconnaissance and geographical and magnetic survey work along the coast, returning to Dry Valley to prospect by New Year's Day. In other words, just two and a half weeks into the expedition Mawson had given up on the main goal. David had won the argument with Mackay's strong support.[14]

By early November they were sledging at night, when the surface was a little harder, reaching the Nordenskjöld Ice Barrier Tongue on the 10th and living on one plasmon biscuit each for breakfast, one in the evening, and hoosh—a hot soup of pemmican (fine, powdered beef with 60 per cent added fat) crushed with plasmon biscuit and boiled up with water, a Mawson speciality. He did a delicious crumbed seal in its own blood, too. Even with the occasional seal meat, however, they were generally hungry, Mawson noting bitterly, 'We don't seem to be able to save what we should in the way of provisions accruing by unforeseen circumstances as the Professor gives any such away to Mac whenever he thinks to please him'.[15]

They made ever-slower progress, taking twenty days to cover the 40 miles between the Nordenskjöld and Drygalski Barrier Tongues. As they inched north Mawson continued making geo-logical, magnetic and geographical observations, including a trigonometrical survey of the entire stretch of the coast along which they passed. In the heavy under-foot conditions each man watched the others, wondering whether they were pulling in harness or faking it. 'The Prof is certainly a fine example of a man for his age', Mawson admitted to himself, 'but he is a great drag on our progress . . . it is difficult to judge but seeing that he travels with thumbs tucked in his braces, and general attitude, one concludes he lays his weight on harness rather than pulling. Several times when we have been struggling heavily with hauling he has continued to recite poetry or tell yarns'. In camp he was slow in doing things, fiddling about, taking three hours to divide a week's rations in two.[16]

At the vast and daunting Drygalski Barrier Tongue they found themselves faced with rounded ridges of ice to 100 feet running north-south, absurdly crossed by snow ridges running east-west. Further in it turned ever rougher, a mass of pale green ice-embankments and deep chasms, and they were forced to proceed east along the edge of the Tongue before cutting north across it. Even then the going was extremely tough. Mackay spent a sleepless night on 2 December worrying that the others might be inclined to give up.[17] He took a lot of seal meat here and an Adélie penguin; Mawson killed another whose curiosity had drawn it into their camp. Half-way across the Tongue they had glorious views of Mt Nansen and other peaks to the north-north-west, while 65 miles due north Mt Melbourne appeared to be issuing smoke. But every-where they were confronted by precipitous chasms and sharp blue ridges of glacier ice, while treacherous crevasses, often of vast depth and generally covered with deceptive snow-lids, lay waiting like hidden graves around them. Daily advance was minimal. Then on 9 December Terra Nova Bay came into view and three days later they had crossed the Tongue and laid a depot near what would later be called Relief Inlet, on the edge of the Drygalski Glacier. Here they slaughtered more seals and Emperor penguins, cooking the meat for the long inland journey ahead of them.

After sitting out a two-day blizzard they prepared to break camp on the morning of 16 December with just one sledge now, weighing over 650 lb, and Mackay, at least, optimistic: 'Writing letters. These are the last adieus, so they ought to be tragic, but I cannot make mine so, I feel we have such a good chance of reaching the pole'.[18] Mawson wrote to his brother, conveying his 'most affectionate remembrance' to him and their parents.[19] The route they initially chose to the plateau was up the glacier between Mts Nansen and Larsen, but they soon struck problems, including a network of crevasses down one of which Mawson fell, clear out of sight, held by his worn sledge rope, swinging between glassy walls. While David was getting some alpine rope from the sledge, the rope holding Mawson cut back further through the edge of the lid, dropping him several feet lower. 'I'm going', he called, but then, seeing that the rope still held, he coolly detached ice crystals from the walls of the crevasse and threw them up for examination. With the alpine rope lowered to him, he secured himself a looped foothold and was gradually hoisted out, his head and shoulders initially coming up against the underside of the lid through which his rope had sliced like a knife. A little later the entire sledge skewed into a crevasse opened by its great weight, wedged there at an angle fortunately, or it would have taken all three men with it to the unseen bottom.

A change in plans was demanded, so they swung south and then west towards the Larsen Glacier that runs down between Mts Gerlache and Bellingshausen. This was a spectacular landscape. From high above them in the mountains came the roar of avalanches, 'like the booming of distant artillery' as David observed.[20] Another blizzard descended, crevasses and pressure ridges still had to be negotiated, but by Christmas Day they had dragged their sledge close to the Larsen Glacier, and over the next two days were able to follow a smaller glacier running parallel to it directly up onto the plateau.

Age was increasingly telling on David—'Prof getting flat-footed', Mawson noted, 'very doggo', seeming 'to have lost all interest in the journey', and constipated to boot.[21] They left a small depot near the top of the glacier, 4050 feet above sea level, before heading out north-west across the steadily rising, largely featureless ice plateau. Up here 10 miles a day was standard for them but they needed to cover more, Mackay admonishing David for not pulling his weight, and Mawson concurring:

This morning I told him he was keeping us waiting as he was not attempting to get ready and we were all packed after working. He looked very angry at my saying this and started packing up loose impedimenta, then went out of tent, had rear [defecation], and did up his finneskos. In meantime we had tent down and sledge strapped. He never, or seldom, helps pack a sledge—even at lunch time he is content with looking on. Something has gone very wrong with him of late as he [is] almost morose, never refers to our work, shirks all questions regarding it, never offers a suggestion. Well anyway, he is getting the value of our blood as we (Mac and I) do our level best at pulling and generally pushing on the expedition.[22]

By New Year's Day, which broke delightfully calm, they were 60-odd miles out on the plateau which had now risen to 7200 feet, the temperatures generally mild, sometimes over 20°F (12°F below freezing). The bad news was that by Mawson's calculations the Magnetic Pole was further away than expected, and that their tent had become so thin 'it tore with the least touch', as David noted. 'Mac botched it this morning, and at lunch time today Mawson tore it again.'[23] Although they were on full rations now, their work produced tremendous appetites and they fantasised over food: 'Mac would like to drink a gallon of buttermilk straight off', David recorded, 'Mawson a big basin of cream.'[24]

They now planned to go on at 10 miles per day until 15 January and then turn, hoping to do 15 per day on the return. Unfortunately the weather deteriorated and they were forcing their way against blizzards on 8 and 9 January, 9000 feet up, the rarefied air making the going hard. 'I never felt in lower spirits', Mackay wrote on the 8th. Frost-bite attacked Mawson's right cheek, David's nose, Mackay's hands, and by the 11th Mawson was snow-blind in the right eye.[25] At noon on 13 January his readings of the magnetic dip circle, with the needle at 89°10' from the horizontal, suggested that they were still 50-odd miles from their goal, but on the other hand they were now covering more ground —13 miles on the 13th, 12 on the 14th, 14 on the 15th with a strong cold wind behind. That evening the dip circle registered a dip of 89°48'. Given that the Pole is in constant swing, Mawson estimated that they were now about 30 miles from its mean position. They agreed that the 16th would be their last day of advance, and his diary for that day reads:

Up early (4.15 true)—cold. Temp −16° at 7.15 true. A light wind from south.

We did 2 m, dropped everything we could, then every 2 m left signal post to 8 miles total. Lunched, walked 5 m, hoisted flag and

Prof took possession of this region containing Mag Pole. I arranged
camera and Prof pulled string [for shutter release]. 3 cheers given for
King.[26]

It was a glorious day, with a hot sun. The three cheers were the
suggestion of Mackay, who observed, 'At the pole, the [ordinary]
compass still pointed, very sluggishly, towards the N.W.'.[27] When
Mawson's detailed instrument readings were analysed in New
Zealand two years later, as will be seen, they showed that the men
had not in fact reached the Magnetic Pole 'Area' or sphere of
oscillation, which lay still further to the north-west.

If they were to return to the edge of the Drygalski Glacier,
now over 200 miles away, by 7 February, which was the latest they
could expect to be picked up by *Nimrod*, they would need to
average 13 miles a day. In fact they routinely did 16 a day.
Navigation was no problem, they simply followed their out-bound
tracks, collecting their used tea bags (regular issue on expeditions,
even then) at the old camps and reusing them.[28] Rations could be
increased. Mt Larsen was sighted on 27 January, 50 miles off, with
striking views of Mts Nansen, Baxter and Queensland out to the
north-east. With a sail on the sledge and a blizzard behind they
were now covering up to 20 miles a day, downhill on the glassy
surface to their depot at the head of the glacier they had ascended,
then down the flank of its neighbour, the Larsen Glacier, to the vast
Drygalski Glacier to the left, reaching this at the end of January.

The final stages were fraught with difficulty in almost impassable sérac ice—masses of icy pinnacles, jammed confusedly
together, barred the party's way to the sea. So close to safety,
desperate lest they miss their ship, their patience with one another
was fraying and the weakest became the victim. As David stumbled
along, endlessly falling into crevasses, Mackay roundly vilified him.
To mollify Mackay, David proffered additional biscuits and
chocolate. 'Why shouldn't *Mawson* have it?' Mackay demanded,
perversely. Mawson noted,

Prof's burberry pants are now so much torn as to be falling off. He
is apparently half demented, by his actions—the strain has been too

great. . . . Mac, it seems, got on to the Prof properly at one halt during afternoon whilst I was reconnoitring. He told the Prof also that he would have to give me written authority as commander or he would, as medical man, pronounce him insane.[29]

During 2 February David's boots were found to be frozen on, and one foot gone numb. Mackay thought his own feet were becoming gangrenous. 'During most of day the Prof has been walking on his ankles', Mawson observed. 'He was no doubt doing his best this way, and Mac appears to have kicked him several times when in the harness.'[30]

During the day they spotted their depot flag, on the other side of an enormous, impassable fissure in the ice, and had to travel inland for 1½ miles to cross it, only to find other fissures cutting across their way. David by this time seemed 'certainly partially demented', Mackay again threatening to pronounce him insane unless the leadership were passed to Mawson. The Professor, according to Mawson,

> said he would draw it up in writing and get me to sign it. I said I did not like it and would think on it. Whilst Mac was away killing seal [David] drew out his pocket book and began writing out my authority as leader of expedition and asked me to sign it. I again said I did not like the business and stated he had better leave matters as they were until the ship failed to turn up.[31]

In Mackay's view, though, the *coup* was complete and Mawson was now definitely the leader:

> I have deposed the Professor. I simply told him that he was no longer fit to lead the party. . . and that he must officially appoint Mawson leader, or I would declare him, the Professor, physically and mentally unfit. He acted on my proposal at once.

By the evening of the 3rd they were camped near what was later named Relief Inlet. 'We are now, of course, expecting the ship', Mackay wrote. 'The Professor says that Shackleton promised to send her to look for us on the 1st, but one can't believe a word he says.'[32]

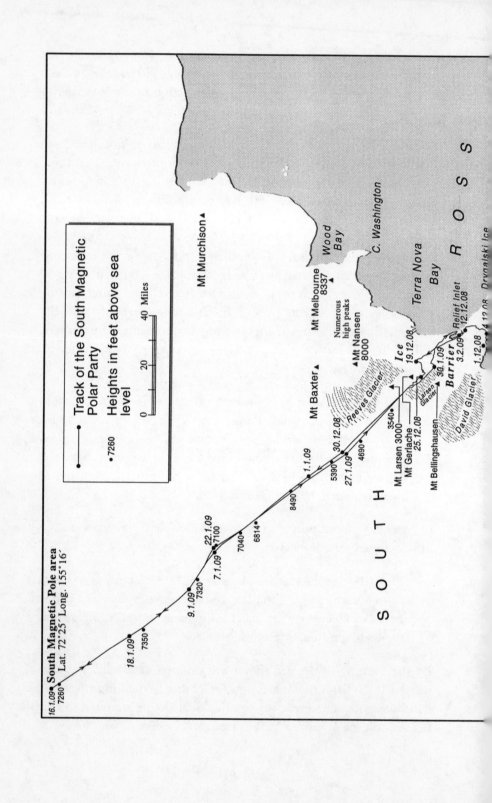

South Magnetic Pole area
Lat. 72°25´ Long. 155°16´

16.1.09
7260

18.1.09
7350

9.1.09
7320

22.1.09
7.1.09   7100

7040

6814

8490

Track of the South Magnetic
Polar Party

•7260   Heights in feet above sea
level

0   20   40 Miles

1.1.09

5390   30.12.08
27.1.09

4690

Mt Baxter ▲

Reeves Glacier

▲ Mt Nansen
8000

Numerous
high peaks ▲

Mt Melbourne ▲
8337

Mt Murchison ▲

Wood
Bay

C. Washington

Mt Larsen 3000•
3540•
Mt Gerlache
25.12.08

Mt Bellingshausen

Larsen
Glacier

Ice

19.12.08

Terra Nova
Bay

Barrier

30.1.09

David Glacier

Relief Inlet
12.12.08

3.2.09

1.12.08

4.12.08 Drygalski Ice

S O U T H

R O S S

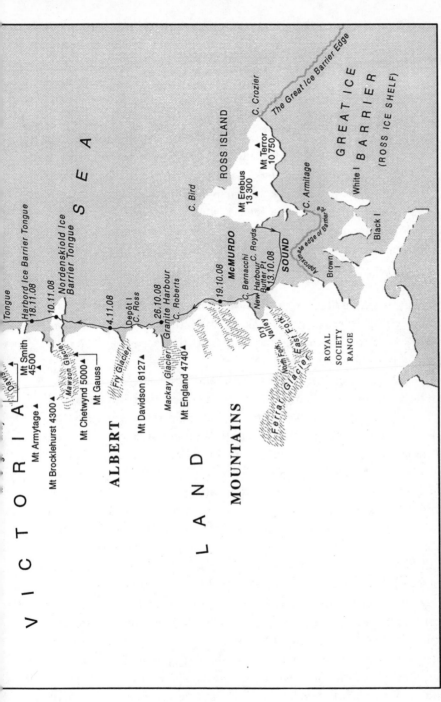

Route of the South Magnetic Polar Party, British Antarctic Expedition, 1908–1909. In most of its details this is essentially the map Mawson himself provided for Shackleton's *Heart of the Antarctic* (1909).

They did not have long to wait—*Nimrod* found them at 3.30 p.m. the following day. Mawson's diary records the event and the near-disaster that then befell him:

> Mac was just having a final fill up of blubber and we were discussing immediately shifting camp to higher depot when a shot rang out. In a second I had overturned the cooker and was through the door where the bow of the *Nimrod* was just appearing round a corner in the inlet. A second shot rang out and we hurried, one after the other, to the beach. Just as I was descending to the lower shore the snow gave way and down I went some 18 ft on to the middle of my back, almost breaking it on the hard snow ridge in the crevasse. After some trouble I was hauled up safely by the crew, Davis jumping down on rope to give me a hand.[33]

Mackay seems to have found the experience transforming: 'the whole thing is enough to make a man turn religious'.[34] Like Mawson he resolved never to venture to the Arctic or Antarctic again, a resolution neither would keep.

Nimrod sailed for Cape Royds and then anchored further south, awaiting Shackleton's party. He had left instructions that if the ship had to depart before his return, a relief party led by Mawson should stay behind for another winter and make a search at the earliest opportunity. Following Shackleton's return with Wild on 1 March, Mawson, Mackay and McGillan, a stoker, accompanied the leader on a short journey south to bring in Marshall and Adams whom Shackleton had left behind, Marshall having been unable to continue. Though some now dispute his precision, by Shackleton's calculations he and his party had reached 88°23' south, just 97 miles from the Pole, one of the most inspiring journeys ever made. As for the Northern party, they had travelled about 1260 miles, 740 of this in relay work, without the assistance of dogs or ponies, dragging at first a ton and later something under half a ton, diminishing, of provisions and equipment, on a 122-day expedition with no supporting party, the longest unsupported, man-hauling journey ever undertaken in the south. Detailed and extensive geological, glaciological and magnetic work, together with a valuable geographic survey of the coast of South Victoria Land, was carried out, Mawson producing the most detailed and accurate map of the region to that time, based on his own triangulation and traverses, and published as a supplement in the back-cover pocket of the second volume of *Heart of the Antarctic*.

On their return to Sydney at the end of March, Mawson and David were fêted as heroes in a new nation seeking its own icons. The *Sydney Morning Herald* gave almost an entire page to their exploits, with most of the focus on David. There was a magnificent reception for them at the University, where David paid a special tribute to his student: 'Just as Shackleton was the general leader, so, in all sincerity and without the pride that apes humility, I say that Mawson was the real leader and was the soul of our expedition to the magnetic pole. We really have in him an Australian Nansen, of infinite resource, splendid physique, astonishing indifference to frost.'[35] Mawson had also been fêted by his old schoolmates, who had turned up at the wharf. Reticent in the extreme, he was almost literally dragged to a reception at Baumann's Café where an assembled throng awaited him. 'He had an expression of surprise—almost consternation for the moment—on his face at the roar of applause that greeted him', the *Fortian* reported. On demand, he made a short speech, but he was 'decidedly uncomfortable'.[36] The Old Boys' Union elected him an honorary life member. In Adelaide too there was a great reception, this time for him alone. When he arrived at the Railway Station on North Terrace, a few blocks down from the University, a hundred students rushed his carriage, then bore him shoulder-high to a commandeered trolley on which he was pulled up the ramp and along North Terrace (a policeman in pursuit) to the University, where a further two hundred students awaited him.[37]

He soon resumed his teaching and field work, travelling again to Broken Hill where, in August, at the home of Adam Boyd, underground manager of BHP, he met Francisca ('Paquita') Adriana Delprat, the dark-haired, ivory-skinned, patrician-looking youngest daughter of G. D. Delprat, BHP's General Manager. Nine years younger than Mawson, she had been born in England, the sixth child of her well-to-do Dutch parents. The family had followed Delprat to Spain where he had re-opened ancient Roman silver mines, then to London, and out to Australia in 1898 where he took up the position of Assistant General Manager at BHP. His great achievement was to move the company from silver into steel. From 1902 the family had a house in Tynte Street, North Adelaide, and soon another at the seaside suburb of Brighton. Mawson was attracted to the young girl but for the rest of 1909 had no opportunity of pursuing his interest. Unbeknown to him, she had seen him once before, at a University sports function, and been struck by his smile and his looks, though the smile had not been for her.[38]

In any case his mind was preoccupied with other things during the second half of 1909, principally a trip to Europe at the end of the year. Its main purpose was to meet prominent scientists in his field. David wrote to him in September, 'Delighted to hear that you are getting leave that you have so well earned so as to admit of your taking a trip to Europe . . . Confident that you will get an excellent reception from the scientific world in the old countries'. Letters of introduction, David said, would follow.[39] With the Shackleton expedition behind him, his doctoral thesis submitted by November, and these entrées, Mawson was probably now flirting with the idea of a lectureship in England or the United States.

3 GOLD-DIGGERS
OF 1910

WEST-BOUND AND second-class, Mawson left Adelaide on the
SS *Mongolia* on 9 December 1909.[1] He was unimpressed by his
fellow passengers but met a few congenial professors in first class.
One of them told him that Edgeworth David had been asked by
Scott to nominate a man for his forthcoming polar expedition. This
little piece of intelligence preoccupied Mawson all the way across
the Great Australian Bight, and on arrival in Fremantle, the port of
Perth, he cabled Scott in London asking to meet him in January to
discuss Antarctic matters.

The ship stopped for a day in Colombo on 22 December. He
bought a few curios, looked over the museum and a Buddhist
temple, then caught a train to Kandy, with its famous temple and
botanic gardens. Here he took out his Zeiss camera and exposed a
few plates on the sights, then had dinner at the Queen's Head Hotel
before the run back down to Colombo. The *Mongolia* proceeded to
Aden, up the Red Sea, through Suez. They went by Sicily. 'Mt
Aetna is a fine sight, reminds me of Mt. Terror', he recorded. This
was because, as he wrote to Edgeworth David a few days later, 'the
recent blizzard had whitened it to sea level'.[2] At Marseilles he
visited a cinema, at Gibraltar he explored the town. *Mongolia* struck
heavy weather through the Bay of Biscay, then a dead calm on
approach to the fog-bound English coast, only the dull sea horns
of invisible channel traffic breaking the early-morning silence as the

ship passed the shrouded Eddystone Light and slipped into Plymouth Harbour, just after breakfast, on 14 January 1910.

This was Mawson's first return to the unremembered land of his birth. He accompanied his baggage in a hansom cab to the railway station, finding that instead of travelling on the express to London he had to go via Bristol.[3] Nevertheless he was at Paddington Station by 7.15 p.m., where he took a cab to the Kingsley Hotel, Bloomsbury Square, close by the British Museum and the University of London. 'Bed-and-breakfast arrangement', he recorded, 'dinner and lunch *en pension*'.[4] Then, before turning in, he went for a stroll along Oxford Street.

Next morning, by prior arrangement, he met J. K. Davis for whom England was still home, and after calling (again by previous arrangement) at Crown Chambers, 9 Regent Street, Shackleton's BAE offices, to collect his mail, he allowed Davis to guide him around. The sights were predictable—Tower of London, Mme Tussaud's—and Davis introduced him to the Lyons Cafés he frequented, middle-class establishments for teas and snacks, with laid tables and attractive waitresses. But Mawson was not here for the sights or the waitresses. This trip, he had decided, would be professional and Antarctic in focus, though he did see relatives at Harrogate in Yorkshire, and visited York and Derby. There was a dinner and meeting of the Geological Society to attend in London, and he visited leading geologists at Cambridge and Oxford to whom he had *entrées*—T. G. Bonney (*Story of our Planet*, 1893, *Volcanoes*, 1898), J. E. Marr (*Scientific Study of Scenery*, 1900), Alfred Harker (*Natural History of Igneous Rocks*, 1909) and others. These were important connections for the young geologist from Adelaide, who knew the value of travel—these men would never sail out to meet *him*. Heading south, however, might establish his name more securely than any number of connections with Oxbridge dons, and that was why one of the first things he did in London was to see Scott.

This was in spite of a cable from Shackleton urging 'On no account see Scott till I return'. Mawson chose to ignore this. As he wrote Edgeworth David, 'I have no connection with Shackleton in any way, and he is foolish to write me so. I shall act here with a free hand and try and make up some of the ground in scientific prestige which he is <u>rapidly</u> loosing [*sic*] on account of most foolish anti-Scott tactics'.[5] Scott was at his offices preparing for his assault on the South Pole, and had received a cable from David advising him to take Mawson.[6] Scott assumed that the Australian was coming to enlist, certainly not to do deals. 'Have you thought of exploring the uncharted coast west of Cape Adare?' Mawson asked. Scott had not. Mawson pointed out the geographic value of extended reconnaissance in that direction. Nobody had explored it since John Biscoe, John Balleny, Dumont D'Urville and Charles Wilkes had sighted the odd spots of coast seventy and eighty years earlier. 'I'll join you', he added, 'if you'll land me and a party of three on that coast'. Scott said it was an interesting idea and he would think it over. Meanwhile he would put Mawson down as a member of the expedition and give him three weeks in which to confirm his participation. 'He offered me not less than £800 for the two years and that I should be one of the three to form the final pole party provided nothing unforeseen happened before the final dash', he later wrote in reviewing the three-hour interview.[7] Scott had been impressed. However, Mawson was not strongly tempted. Unromantic by disposition, to him there seemed little of scientific value in a dash to the Pole. In any case, he must have asked himself, why should a man who had failed to get beyond an unimpressive 82°17' south on his last expedition be so much more successful this time? Mawson, with David and Mackay, had covered vastly more ground down there, in immensely tougher terrain.

After giving Scott time to consider his proposition, he revisited him. This time Edward Wilson was there. 'I did not like Dr. Wilson', Mawson recorded, without elaborating.[8] He would have detected the strong influence which the evangelical Wilson had over the agnostic Scott, dating from Scott's previous expedition, and may have interpreted a look as supercilious, or it could have been physical (Wilson was consumptively thin), or the Cambridge manner, or a whiff of sanctimony. Scott had decided against Mawson's proposal—not enough men. In reply Mawson said he would go to the north coast himself, and Scott turned defensive:

He stated that it had always been his intention to do what he could around the north coast but could promise nothing—In fact he had now set his mind on picking the plums out of the north coast by a boat reconnaissance on the return of the ship. I said finally that as I could not be landed on the north coast I would go in no other capacity than as chief scientist and that as Wilson had been appointed to that position I would not dream of making the suggestion nor indeed would I henceforth accept a part on the expedition.[9]

This was a disappointment to Scott and Wilson, the latter telling David, 'We both of us liked what we saw of Mawson—he is obviously capable and keen on his work'.[10] Mawson had accepted an invitation to dine with Scott and his wife Kathleen on 26 January, at 174 Buckingham Palace Road, when he was again urged to join the expedition, but Mawson said his 'no' was definite and that he was planning to mount his own expedition.

To this end he now turned to Sir Ernest Shackleton, knighted in the previous Birthday Honours for his southern achievement, meeting him in late January at Dover on his return from lecturing on the Continent. In Budapest Shackleton had heard about a group of Hungarian gold mines at Nagybanya which, properly developed, might make a man rich very quickly indeed, but though his conversation on the train to London was full of gold he also listened carefully to Mawson's increasingly ambitious schemes. By now these involved a three-year expedition with three or four bases. 'You ought to go yourself!', Shackleton exclaimed. 'I could get you support.'[11] This was what Mawson wanted to hear. In Shackleton's presence, everything seemed possible. The man was instinctively generous and expansive, committed to the bold private initiative, totally unlike the reserved and cautious, officially-funded and officially-minded Scott.

Mawson was regularly in and out of 9 Regent Street, where one morning an ebullient Shackleton came in, lit up a cigarette and declared that he had decided to go to the coast west of Cape Adare himself. Mawson was to be his chief scientist. 'I hope you'll agree to this', he added. 'I can get the money, and that'll be your trouble were you taking the expedition yourself.' Mawson decided to fall in with this—after all, where was he to find £70 000, which was what Shackleton claimed to be able to get?[12] The latter now told Mawson to put his ideas on paper, use the office typist, make himself at home. A few days later Shackleton sent a telegram from out of town, saying that three years was too long. Mawson therefore built into his scheme a justification of the three-year concept. This document, with its accompanying manuscript map, sent off post-haste to Shackleton, is of great interest.[13] Undated, typed up on BAE stationery, it belongs to February 1910. The ideas were forming as the document was composed. 'Have just figured out details of work as it could be done along the unknown coast South of Australia', he wrote. The plan involved chartering a ship from mid-1910 to mid-1913. Through the 1910–11 summer the ship would reconnoitre the Adélie, Clarie and Sabrina Land coasts, locating a suitable site for a hut and assessing the best stretches for sledging. A team of three (presumably led by Mawson) would erect a hut, train and breed dogs, and make meteorological records as well as laying a few outlying depots—the Australian Government to foot the bill for this. Coastline surveyable from the ship, which would also do hydrographic work, would not need to be sledged along later. Shackleton would then go down with the rest of the men in late 1911. The following merits quoting in full:

> On carefully going into the coast details, it seems to me that 4 men should winter at N. Cape or C. Adare—9 men at Adelie Land— 3 men at Sabrina Land—none as far as Gaussberg.
>
> 1. The C. North–C. Adare party to pay special attention to Geology and Economic Minerals, and probably to keep a magnetic record, even possibly to penetrate to the Magnetic Pole. Robertson Bay offers special opportunities to Biologists— dredging in summer.
> 2. A main party of 9 wintering on Adelie Land as far E. as the ship can take them. Work: Geology, Meteorology, Biology, Magnetic, Sledging to C. North and possibly to Magnetic Pole (alternative with preceding party). Another three to sledge W. towards Sabrina Land.
> 3. A party of 3 to winter at Sabrina Land. Sledging E. and W.

(a short E. journey and a long W. journey). A party of 6 would be better here if afforded.

This party might even get as far as Gaussberg; in any case they would get very near it.[14]

This is a more grandiose scheme than Mawson finally adopted. His map, with its dramatic arrows (between pages 40 and 41), shows great boldness. A 2000-mile arc of coast from Cape Adare west to Gaussberg is to be explored, each of the three teams striking east and west, and one of them south as well. No expedition on this scale had ever been conceived for Antarctica. Alongside this, the Pole seemed a conventional goal. Shackleton was inspired by this letter and its map, and it could all be done, Mawson's figures showed, for £41 000.

Shackleton returned to London and they set to work. Money was needed. Mawson suggested the 86-year-old millionaire philanthropist Robert Barr Smith of Adelaide, the 'Smith' in Elder Smith & Co. which opened up the South Australian outback. Mawson knew him. He had sat on the University's Council and endowed its Library, but was in the opening stages of senile dementia, so the cable went to his son. It carried a recommendation from (Sir) William Bragg FRS, who had left the University of Adelaide for the Cavendish chair of physics at Leeds. The request was for £10 000 to £15 000. The reply was short: 'Sorry cannot.'[15] A similar cable went to Roderick Murchison at the Melbourne Club (President, 1899), requesting £5000. He cabled back pledging £1000—the first contributor to what would become the Australasian Antarctic Expedition (AAE). These results were not encouraging.

So Shackleton took Mawson down to Plymouth to see the steel magnate Gerald Lysaght, who had backed the BAE. They travelled on the Cornish Riviera Express which did the 226 miles from Paddington in 247 minutes—a thousand tons of rolling steel, lined with walnut, upholstered in velvet and strung with chandeliers. Shackleton left Mawson alone with Lysaght, and for five hours the Australian summarised the history of Antarctic exploration and laid out his plans. The next day Shackleton asked Lysaght's support and he promised £10 000. There was slippage in Shackleton's own commitment, though, as he was talking about exploring Alaska and other places, hinting that his wife was unhappy about a return to Antarctica. On 18 March an outline of the proposed expedition appeared in the *Daily Mail*.[16]

Mawson was now in Shackleton's debt, and on the latter's request (and account) he travelled by the Orient Express (running Ostend to Constantinople) as far as Hungary to assess the potential of the Nagybanya mines. Davis went too, as did Aeneas Mackintosh, second officer on *Nimrod* during the BAE. Mawson would be able to meet geologists while on the Continent, and carried Antarctic rock samples as presents. As Davis would later observe, the Europe through which they travelled 'was a continent that had been at peace for nearly forty years, where cities and towns, moulded by time, still wore their old, historical and well-remembered aspect. It was the old Europe ... where Englishmen travelled without passports—a Europe wealthy, sophisticated and seemingly wise'.[17] Shackleton, meanwhile, sailed for New York and a lecture tour, to clear BAE debts, writing from the *Lusitania* before departure on 19 March, 'Do not see Scott about the new Expedition. I will dictate a letter to him on board'.[18]

At Nagybanya Mawson soon determined the best mines by assay.[19] In the first half of April, his assessment complete, he drew up terms, 'but such low terms', he told Shackleton, 'as, if they accept, they are bargains seldom to be met with'.[20] Negotiations were started with the owners, one of whom was an enriched peasant, Mr Pokol, who inhabited an extraordinary edifice, the 'Pokol Kastely'. Generous with his mobile cocktail cabinet and cigars, Pokol was a slippery dealer. If you agreed to his price he would raise it—an auction where the seller does the bidding.[21]

Leaving negotiations to be pursued later by others, Mawson went to Berlin. (By now Davis had returned to London, while Mackintosh was still in Hungary.) He booked in at the Central Hotel, Friedrichstrasse, and visited the director of the Natural History Museum, Professor Vanhöffer, biologist on the *Gauss* during Professor Erich von Drygalski's scientifically brilliant 1901–3 expedition, which put Kaiser Wilhelm II Land on the map of Antarctica along with the mountain they named Gaussberg, to which they sledged. Von Drygalski had left for the country, but Vanhöffer proudly showed Mawson the geological specimens brought back by the expedition. The next stop was Stockholm, to see the Antarctic collection brought back by Otto Nordenskjöld's 1901–3 expedition on the *Antarctic* to Graham Land. Among other places visited on this tour were Leipzig, Hamburg, Bonn and Heidelberg.

On 23 April Mawson returned to London where a letter awaited him. It contained another get-rich-quick scheme, this one devised by his father at Orokolo, British Papua, on the island of New Guinea. Robert Mawson had spent a lot of time in recent years in British Papua, where he was convinced that the fortune which had seduced him from his homeland, but then perversely eluded him, was to be found. As soon as Mawson saw the handwriting on the envelope he could guess the contents. It would be the same £10 000 scheme for a rubber plantation on his 3000 acres there, already mentioned in a somewhat calculating letter of the previous June, also from Orokolo, which had put Mawson in an embarrassing position with its unsubtle suggestion that 'No doubt Lieut. Shackleton could, if so disposed speedily raise the amt & properly managed and developed such a Company would realise financial success'. Mawson's father had speculated on whether Shackleton was a Yorkshire man—'If so we have some connection with the Bingley branch. I had an Aunt Shackleton of Yeadon old family'.[22] Though Anglo-Irish, Shackleton's family had indeed migrated from Yorkshire in the eighteenth century. Still, Mawson had been reluctant to ask 'the Boss', as Shackleton's men referred to him, for such capital when he was already being so helpful on the Antarctic front. The new letter was a blunter and heavier weapon. What his father desperately needed was *capital*, he reminded his son, capital to clear and develop his 3000 acres, for

> unless the development conditions are fulfilled the land will be forfeited to the Govt. and all paid thereon and expended on a/c of it will be lost—You will see therefore the need to get along with development work & that can only be done by a certain capital ... Remember that if the whole 3000 acres was cleared & planted it wd return a good £30 000 a year, if not more. So that it is worth

a good struggle to get it through—If you think of it the return to you would mean a lot more than any Professorship beside the probability of further extensions here.

Hope you have enjoyed yourself in Europe—

Yours truly R E Mawson

In the margin was a postscript: 'If the thing can be carried through you will be the biggest benefitor by it eventually—'.[23] The man was impossible! Then again, just maybe he had something... Mawson put the letter away and tried to forget it.

He had baggage to pack and a steamer to catch, for New York, where he arrived in early May. From there he travelled on the Pennsylvania Railroad to Chicago, then the Union and Central Pacific to meet Shackleton in Omaha, where his lecture tour had run out of steam. For three full days, from 13 to 16 May, they discussed Hungarian gold mines, Antarctica and money. Mawson had already recommended that the six best mines, including Pokol's, be purchased and consolidated.[24] By this time, as he later noted, Shackleton 'had many get-rich-quick schemes in view and I felt that the chances of his going to the Antarctic were lessening'.[25] Mawson had learned by experience that it paid to get certain promises in writing. He still had not been paid his full salary from the BAE, nor had he received anything aside from expenses for his work in Hungary. Shackleton must have had cash from his lectures, probably in a suitcase up in his room. Mawson on the other hand was practically cleaned out. Finally, through the night of 16 May, in some hotel lounge redolent with brandy and Shackleton's ten-cent cigars, Mawson tied him to a three-point guarantee, wrote it all out on a couple of sheets of BAE stationery in 'Shackleton's' words, and pushed it across the table for him to sign. Shackleton engaged to pay £400, covering Hungary and the unpaid BAE salary, £30 of it in United States bills now, £70 by 20 May, telegraphed to await him in Vancouver, with the remaining £300 to be sent to Australia at the end of July. He also engaged to assign to him a block of 2500 fully paid shares each to the value of £1 in a company, nominal capital £200 000, to be formed to exploit the mines. The third part read:

I intend to proceed with the arrangements for an antarctic expedition to commence in the latter half of 1911, and shall appoint D Mawson as director of the scientific work with power to make all necessary arrangements in that respect compatible with the funds at the disposal of the expedition. In the event of my not accompanying the expedition as commander, D Mawson will be in charge and I shall still use my influence with my supporters in regard to raising the necessary funds for equipment.

Nobody witnessed the document, but it was enough to make a public liar of Shackleton should he renege.[26]

Through the southern winter of 1910 Mawson gave public lectures on polar discovery (in addition to teaching at the University), trying to arouse enthusiasm and hoping that Barr Smith would come good. At the same time he began to court Paquita Delprat on regular visits to the family's homes at North Adelaide and Brighton until, one warm evening in early December 1910, on the verandah of the Brighton house, *El Rincon*, he proposed marriage and she accepted.[27]

Meanwhile in London Shackleton had given the *Sphere* a story on the planned expedition and spoke to the Royal Geographical Society (RGS). As Mawson recorded, 'During this time I understood that he had abandoned the idea of going himself, so that these notices were very confusing and prevented my asking in private for funds for an expedition of my own. He did not write to me and failed to answer directly my enquiries regarding money matters.'[28] During July, perhaps pressed again by his father, or himself seduced by the idea, Mawson had forwarded the rubber proposal to Shackleton. Sir Ernest showed it to a friend, director of six rubber companies, who warned that the market was saturated. Mawson also cabled (in late August) asking whether Lysaght's offer still stood. Shackleton replied, 'Hungary satisfactory Lysaght definite 10,000 rubber impossible overloaded here'.[29] Soon after, Mawson wrote to Thomas Laby,

I have not started pushing the antarctic expedition but it is now about time ... The latest thing over here is oil—people are oil

Margaret and Robert Mawson, Douglas Mawson's parents, early 1880s

Thought by the family to be Douglas Mawson, *c.* 1884, though it
may be his older brother William, *c.* 1882

Douglas (left) and his older brother William Mawson, late 1880s

Mawson, David and Mackay ascended to the Antarctic plateau up a walled glacier just like this one, but a little further south, on their way to the South Magnetic Pole in December 1908. This is the Priestley Glacier, Victoria Land.

Geologists in the field, turn of the century. T. W. Edgeworth David, who
taught Mawson at the University of Sydney, is second from left. Walter
Howchin, the University of Adelaide's senior geologist when Mawson was
appointed lecturer, is second from right.

Mawson in 1902, aged twenty, Junior Demonstrator in
Chemistry at the University of Sydney

Mawson at a camp-site in New South Wales, *c.* 1902

'South Magnetic Pole', 16 January 1909. From left, Alistair Forbes Mackay, Edgeworth David (triggering shutter with cord), Mawson

In front, Mawson with Shackleton, following their return from the BAE, 1909. Aeneas Mackintosh and J. B. Adams behind, the former with glass right eye following an accident during the expedition

Shackleton's offices, 9 Regent Street, London, early 1910.
Mawson's thoughts run on an Antarctic expedition of his own,
but Shackleton is more interested in gold mines.

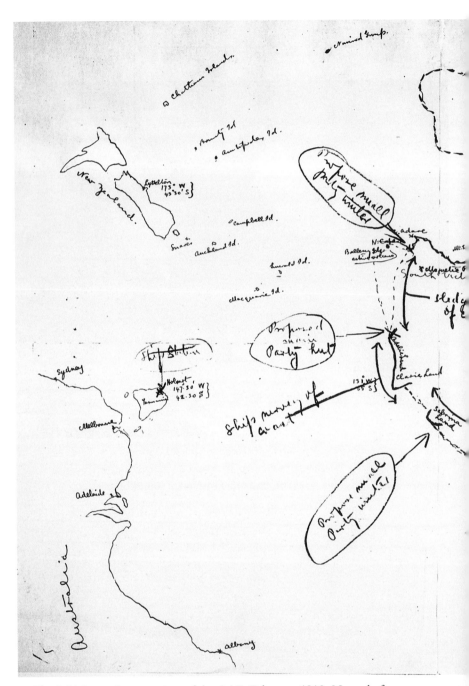

The initial grand conception of the AAE, February 1910. Never before made public, Mawson's first hand-drawn plan of action, with its dramatic arrows, shows great boldness.

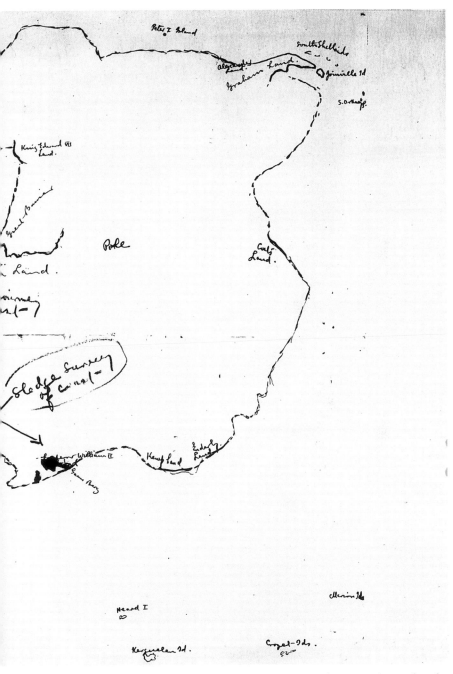

A 2000-mile arc of coast from Cape Adare to Gaussberg is to be explored,
each of the three teams striking east and west, and one of them south as
well. No expedition on this scale had ever been conceived for Antarctica.

Douglas Mawson
27/7/11

London, 1911. Preparation for the AAE intensifies,
and portraits are part of the publicity.

G. F. Ainsworth, leader of the AAE party at Macquarie Island.
Paget-process colour plate

H. Hamilton and Frank Hurley at Macquarie Island.
Paget-process colour plate

Boat and barrels at Macquarie Island. Paget-process colour plate

Winter noon at Cape Denison, 1912. Lumière Autochrome

Sun above the northern horizon, Cape Denison, 1912. Lumière Autochrome

AAE Main Base locality, Cape Denison. The boat harbour, half iced–up
(this is 1 November 1998), cuts in at the left. The main hut,
to the right of the boat harbour, is circled.
North is to the top left.

mad—I have just reported on a proposition on Kangaroo Island—
this with some profit to myself (providing I receive my fee) though
there is not a trace of oil on the Island. Have got a number of papers
almost complete for publication but am so busy that they are being
seriously delayed.[30]

A more promising prospect turned up in October. He wrote
to J. K. Davis (in London) on the 19th, 'Things look good out
here—I shall make a public appeal for funds in latter part of
November when Scott has gone. I am in great haste as it is now
early morning and I leave tomorrow for the far north. I have
induced the Govt. to let me have a camel equipment [*sic*] and
am making a run out into the arid country to look after a radium
and sapphire show—it may mean a good deal to me.'[31] He was
heading for Mt Painter in the northern Flinders Ranges with
a prospector, G. A. Greenwood, who had shown him some torbernite he had found up there and which the South Australian
Mines Department had dismissed as worthless iron phosphate.
Mawson recognised it as a uranium mineral. Up on Radium Ridge,
1000 feet above the creek in which Greenwood had found his
torbernite, Mawson located the lode.[32] It was the Radium Hill
story all over again.

Back in Adelaide they registered the Radium Extraction
Company of South Australia Ltd., a paper company with nominal
capital of £5000 in 1000 £5 shares, the search licences giving
Mawson 4 square miles, Greenwood 3, with 1 for the company.
They found, unfortunately, that to exploit the find would require
more capital than they could raise, and were soon trying to sell their
rights and titles to a larger company in return for their expenses
(said to be £3500) and a quarter share in a company of 30 000
£1 shares.[33] After World War II Mawson would feel understand-
ably 'sore' that 'considering I was fundamental in establishing the
presence of uranium in the Mt. Painter and Radium Hill fields and
had spent so much money and time thereon the Government
(when uranium did become a commercial proposition) closed the
door for exploitation by anybody else'.[34] He was thinking of the
mid-to-late 1940s when rationing ruled, and Canberra was hungry

for anything on the ground (especially the banks) and whatever was bankable beneath it.

Shackleton meanwhile was continuing his attempts to buy the Nagybanya mines, but the price kept going up and he finally had to withdraw, having earlier sunk £5000 just to secure the options.[35] In early December he received a cable from an increasingly desperate Mawson—was Shackleton still leading the expedition? If not, *he* would. Sir Ernest replied that he could not now go, but would give his wholehearted support.[36] This was the cable Mawson needed. Now he could move.

4 AUSTRALASIAN ANTARCTIC EXPEDITION

AT THE END of the first week of January 1911 Mawson boarded
the Melbourne Express *en route* for Sydney and the thirteenth
meeting of the AAAS. It would be a grand affair—a garden party at
Government House, a *conversazione*, dinners, a Harbour excursion.
Here he would launch his expedition, to which he hoped the
AAAS would contribute £1000. He was in touch with the
President, David Orme Masson FRS, Professor of Chemistry at the
University of Melbourne, who did the ground work.

At 11.30 a.m. on Wednesday, 11 January, Mawson addressed a
packed hall in the Geology Department at the University of
Sydney, backing his three-base, Cape Adare-to-Gaussberg scheme
with dramatic maps projected from lantern slides, and arguments—
economic ('whale and sea products . . . guano . . . mineral wealth'),
scientific (Argentina, no richer than Australia, already had 'two
permanent meteorological stations in Antarctic waters'), and
nationalistic ('the spirit of maritime enterprise . . . is an indispensable element of national greatness'). No time was to be lost, lest
'foreign nations . . . step in and secure this most valuable portion of
the Antarctic continent for themselves, and forever from the control
of Australia'. The expedition's work would take at least seventeen
months, and the results would be on display at 'one of the greatest
scientific events in the history of Australia, namely, the meeting of
the British Association for the Advancement of Science in 1914'.[1]

The amount of £1000, a third of the Association's liquid assets, was voted three days later, with the proviso that Masson get Shackleton's agreement that Mawson was 'supreme commander'. A cable went off that afternoon.[2] The AAAS set up a committee, with Edgeworth David as chairman, Masson acting chairman pending David's return from overseas, and sub-committees in all states and New Zealand. The committee would assist in preparations and oversee the appointment of the expedition's scientific staff, Mawson having power of veto.

At New Year he had written to Robert Barr Smith, who this time gave £1000, hoping that forty Australians would do the same. Letters were then sent off to others, and before the Sydney meeting closed Mawson had promises of £1000 each from Hugh Dixson and Hugh Denison (uncle and nephew, noted philanthropists with interests in tobacco) and Sam Hordern (owner of the Italianate Palace Emporium in Sydney—he later increased his donation to £2500). With Lysaght's and Murchison's money, this made £16000, not a bad start. It was to be a private enterprise expedition, like Shackleton's BAE and unlike the 'official' expeditions of Scott, but Mawson would need at least £40000 and he was counting on support from state and federal governments. To this end he saw Andrew Fisher, the Australian Prime Minister, in January. Although Fisher was enthusiastic he made no promises.[3] The Committee, however, would follow up on this interview after Mawson's departure for England on 27 January—he needed to be in London, where Shackleton's support was promised, where equipment and a suitable ship could be purchased,[4] and where, during the first half of 1911, Australia's richest families would be congregating for the most magnificent event of the London season, the coronation of George V.

He arrived in London towards the end of February to find that Shackleton was in Hungary and J. K. Davis, whom he wanted as second-in-command, in Canada. Establishing himself in Shackleton's offices, he cabled Davis to return to London, and through early March used connections to make connections. From the Committee in Australia there was silence. Masson had promised that they would see Fisher about a grant of £10 000. That was six weeks ago. Frustrated, he wrote to Thomas Laby, 'You should have been on the Committee to push things.'[5] During March Scott's ship *Terra Nova* returned to New Zealand with the news that Scott had established his second base at Cape Adare instead of near the eastern end of the Barrier, where they had found Amundsen ensconced at the Bay of Whales. Scott had been furious in 1908 when circumstances forced Shackleton to break his word and use 'Scott's' McMurdo Sound, yet now he recognised no proprietorial rights where Mawson was concerned. It is true that Scott had told Mawson in London that he was contemplating doing something on the north coast around Cape Adare, but Mawson felt double-crossed all the same, because the previous October Scott had been in Australia and had asked Mawson for his plans, which had been sent to him.[6] The grand concept, Cape Adare to Gaussberg, was compromised on its eastern flank and would have to be trimmed at that end. Worse was to come.

When Shackleton returned from Hungary in March, Mawson asked whether Gerald Lysaght's £10 000 was firm. Shackleton hedged. He and Lysaght had rather fallen out of late, and Shackleton doubted whether there would be anything doing on that front. His heart in his mouth, Mawson dashed off a desperate letter to Lysaght. 'Shackleton tells me very little', he wrote, 'but I understand that you are not on the best of terms with him now— no doubt judging that he has too many irons in the fire. I shall be awfully disappointed if your attitude has changed . . . Surely I can rely on you for £1,000 anyway—this would give you a good interest in the results'.[7] (Mawson lured prospective donors with pro-rata participation in 'economic discoveries'.) Lysaght was in hospital, but on 26 March his wife replied: 'All that he could afford—indeed more—he did for Sir Ernest Shackleton this time last year. Sir Ernest can, and will no doubt, tell you what that was.'[8] The money had simply disappeared into one or more of Shackleton's many schemes. Mawson, in his own words, felt 'double-crossed'.[9] As he put it in a letter to H. R. Mill, 'When it comes to the moral side of things, S. and I part brass rags'.[10] The £16 000 was now £6000. Yet he could not afford to break with Sir Ernest.

It was through Shackleton that he had met Campbell Mackellar, who idealised polar explorers and had assisted the BAE. Mackellar introduced him to Lady Hart whose husband Sir Robert had made his career in the British administration in China, along with his friend Charles George ('Chinese') Gordon, hero of Khartoum. On 9 March Lady Hart gave a luncheon for Mawson where the guests included Lady Stanley, widow of Sir Henry Morton Stanley, who had found Dr Livingstone, and whose explorations (and massacres) had opened up central Africa. The significant guest was Sir Robert Lucas-Tooth, a wealthy Australian brewer, though in the end he was only good for £1000. At the luncheon he radiated caution: 'am afraid he won't give much', Mawson wrote to Laby, 'though he has just bought the largest estate [Holme Lacy near Hereford] in Great Britain. Lady Stanley (African) was sitting next me—she is tremendously broadly educated—is a cousin of Asquith—am beating up influential people all day'.[11]

Mawson was due to address the RGS on the evening of 10 April. He decided to ask them for £1000, more than they had given Scott, and backed his request by sending his plans to influential RGS Council members in the days leading up to the Council meeting, to be held a few hours before his address.[12] These plans include motor sledges. The Wolseley Company of Birmingham sent Mawson photographs and blueprints of their mid-engined, tracked snow vehicles, resplendent in white as supplied to Scott's current *Terra Nova* expedition and Oberleutnant Wilhelm Filchner's forthcoming *Deutschland* expedition.[13] Hand-built, low-slung prototypes, they were expensive, and probably rejected by Mawson for that reason.

On 3 April a cable finally arrived from Orme Masson. He had led a delegation to the Minister for External Affairs, Egerton Batchelor, seeking £20 000. Batchelor thought £10 000 likelier. Cabinet would decide by 3 April. On April Fool's Day it was announced that Cabinet had deferred consideration of any Antarctic grant to September, following their return from the Coronation. Masson advised Mawson to use the good offices of the Australian High Commissioner in London, former Prime Minister

Sir George Reid, and approach Batchelor and Fisher following their arrival in London on 15 May.[14] Under such pressure it is no wonder Mawson came down with influenza that week. And yet he continued to expect £20 000 from Fisher, as he wrote to his prospective mother-in-law, Mme Delprat, the very next day.[15] His determination to win through is evident at every step, though as he later noted, 'the whole of my stay in London was about as distressing a time as could be imagined'.[16] 'It is most soul destroying work', he told a certain Mr Biedermann whose assistance he sought, 'begging money for a large undertaking of this kind'.[17] Biedermann gave nothing.

When Mawson laid his plans before the RGS on the evening of 10 April he was joining the ranks of Dr David Livingstone, Sir Richard Burton and John Hanning Speke. For over eighty years the Society had thrived on and driven the imperial idea. In 1911 it still occupied its elegant Regency building, 1 Savile Row. From here, with the applause of its Fellows ringing in their ears, went forth 'the men who were to wipe "unexplored" from the maps of the world'.[18] For Mawson exploration was intimately connected to the imperial idea: 'Along the whole 2,000 miles of coast between Cape Adare and Gaussberg', he reminded them, 'a landing has been made once only and then but for a few hours, by D'Urville's expedition in 1840. Only few vessels have ever come within sight of this coast, and practically none since the days of D'Urville and Wilkes. We desire to receive authority to raise the Union Jack and take possession of this land for the British Empire.'[19] Afterwards the President, Major Leonard Darwin, announced a grant of £500. Sir George Reid, Lord Lamington and Shackleton all spoke in praise and encouragement. The great authority on Antarctica, Hugh Robert Mill, who was staying with Mawson at the Royal Societies Club during this period, spoke of Mawson's expedition as 'the special work for which he came into the world', giving it a divine aspect. R. N. Rudmose Brown pointed to 'something undeniably heroic in his programme, in that he has left out the pole'; money would consequently be harder to find.[20]

Mawson now travelled to France to discuss with Dr Jean Baptiste Charcot the purchase of the *Pourquois Pas?*, in which

Charcot had explored the west coast of Graham Land in 1908–10. (While in Paris he had dinner at the Travellers' Club with William Heinemann, who offered a loan of £1000 in consideration of a promised book on the AAE.[21]) Charcot had earlier donated his ship to a maritime museum in Rouen, and Mawson now learned that the French Government were unlikely to agree to any sale. Negotiations finally fell through. However, Norwegian, Newfoundland and Dundee ships were under offer, *Nimrod* was a possibility, and Donald Alexander Smith, Lord Strathcona, the ninety-year-old High Commissioner for Canada, was trying to get *Discovery* for Mawson from the Hudson's Bay Company. Mawson was also interested in W. S. Bruce's old ship, the *Scotia*, but finally, on Davis's advice, he settled on *Aurora*, a Dundee whaler with the Newfoundland fleet, built in 1876, registered tonnage 386 net, capacity 600 tons gross. She had compound engines of 98 HP, and was square-rigged on the foremast, schooner-rigged on the main and mizzen.[22] In 1883 she had assisted in the rescue of Lieutenant A. W. Greely and other survivors of his 'farthest north' expedition which had ended in shooting and cannibalism (see Chapter 8).

Just prior to his RGS address Mawson had been to see Kathleen Scott at 174 Buckingham Palace Road. Later, it seems, she destroyed his letters to her.[23] However, hers to him survive. In her autobiography she records a diary entry, meant to be read by her husband on his putative return:

> April 8th. Mawson came to lunch. He came in a bad frame of mind, as you will see from the newspapers, having firmly persuaded himself that you had 'done him in the eye' and had always intended to land a party at Cape Adare, and hadn't made a fair try for King Edward's Land, and so on. I explained to him, and when he went he said he was very much happier. We parted excellently good friends.[24]

She does not say she invited him to live at her house, but Mawson does: 'Mrs Scott had asked me to live at her house in London if it would assist in any way.'[25] Kathleen Scott was high-spirited, independent, artistic, adventurous, high-bohemian, and definitely not a feminist. She preferred the company of men, who should be *real* men. It would very probably be a mistake to read anything sexual into her friendship with Mawson, though (as will be seen) he would sign a letter of condolence to her from the Antarctic with 'Love'. Kathleen Scott had numerous male friends. Her very openness about them tends to disarm suspicion.

Her current passion was flight, about which she knew a lot. Mawson had been toying with the idea of an aeroplane—it could conceivably reconnoitre in advance of sledging journeys and would generate publicity. Even if not flown in Antarctica it could serve as an air-tractor hauling sledges. But what type of aeroplane? The science of flight was in its infancy. Everything was trial and error, all types essentially prototypes. Biplanes were more stable and manoeuvrable but slower than monoplanes, which were more 'state-of-the-art'. To her credit, Kathleen Scott preferred mono-planes. Mawson having mentioned his idea and the name 'Blériot', she passed this on to her friend at Vickers Ltd., Hugh Evelyn Watkins. Vickers had just acquired the English production rights to the advanced French REP monoplane. Captain Herbert F. Wood was about to go to France to fly a French-built REP back. Lieutenant Watkins wrote to Mawson on 18 April, 'Mrs Scott tells me you are taking an aeroplane to the Antarctic and suggests that I should call on you'.[26]

A week later Kathleen wrote from her cottage on the beach at Sandwich in Kent to remind Mawson of the 'Yorkshire Dinner' on 17 May—she had the tickets if he could go (he accepted). 'Do you think you could slip down here?', she added. 'We are on the phone and almost any morning would suit'.[27] The next day she followed this up with another:

Dear Dr Mawson—

I believe I can help you about aeroplanes. I think you can do far better than a Bleriot . . . There is a machine that the Vickers people have bought which is infinitely more stable, heavier and more solid and will carry more weight. Its cost is £1000, but I think it could be worked to get it for £700 or even less. . . . It's got a very much more satisfactory engine than the gnome.* It is not rotary and has five cylinders . . . A man I know who had only before driven biplanes, drove it and stayed up half an hour, which speaks very well for its stability. . . . If you think it's worth considering, I can let you meet the man concerned early next week and he can show you the machine and take you up in it . . .

I am just off to Brooklands though I expect it will be too windy for much flying—very sincerely yours, Kathleen Scott—suggest yourself for lunch any day or dinner if you let me know before.

(*I think if you took a gnome you'd have to take a gnome mechanic.)

Mawson took her advice and negotiated for an REP. The letters stood for Robert Esnault-Pelterie, notable for his tapered, tubular-steel fuselages, generally triangular in section but lozenge-shaped on the latest D-type (for which Vickers had bought the British rights), as contemporary French sources show.[28] Vickers incorporated Esnault-Pelterie's latest innovation, a single control for pitch and roll. Wing control was on the warp principle. The D-type had a five-cylinder REP engine, fan-shaped, developing 60 HP, wingspan of 47 feet, length of 36 feet, and a cruising speed of 48 knots.[29] It was available as a single-seater or (as with Mawson's) a two-seater, tandem arrangement. With one spare ski undercarriage the cost to Mawson was £955 4s 8d.[30] This, as we will see later, remained an unpaid bill. Lieutenant Watkins was to accompany the machine to Australia and on to Antarctica to fly it there.[31] It is interesting to note the disingenuous way Vickers publicised Mawson's machine. They told a reporter from *Flight* that 'Lieut. Watkins shall pilot the machine in the final dash for the Pole', belying the nature of the expedition.[32] The REP left for Adelaide on the *Macedonia* at half the usual rate of freight, courtesy of P&O.

Mawson had negotiated the purchase of a ship and an aeroplane without the money to buy either. 'Sorry!' letters were arriving in droves, some from very notable Australians or former residents including Sidney Kidman, the world's biggest landowner, Walter Hall ('Not in sympathy with expedition'[33]), Sir Winthrop Hackett and others. On 2 May he was reduced to asking P&O for help with his return passage. They offered a 25 per cent discount and he used it in purchasing a first-class ticket.[34] This was reasonable. He may have had to solicit and sweat for his funds, but they would not then be spent travelling steerage.

Shackleton now made good his promise of assistance. He saw his friend Alfred Harmsworth, Lord Northcliffe, owner of the *Daily Mail*, and Northcliffe agreed to publish an appeal for funds under Shackleton's name. This was launched on 8 May, infuriating Scott's supporters, though not Kathleen Scott who had earlier been apprised of it by Mawson. Within four days some £12 000 had been subscribed in cash and goods, enabling Mawson to purchase *Aurora* for £6000 and, with Davis's help, to load her to the gunwales with most of what he required.[35] According to a statement submitted to the Australian Government in August there was £7760 in cash donations alone from this appeal.[36] Cash donors numbered over 140.[37] They included Sam Hordern (an additional £1500), Lord Strathcona (£1000), W. A. Horn, mining magnate formerly of South Australia (£1000), and Eugen Sandow (£1050—1000 guineas). Dame Nellie Melba gave £100. Sandow, 'the strongest man in the world', was 'the King's Professor of Scientific Physical Culture' and ran a school for physical fitness. Suave, with dark curly hair, thin lips and brushed-up moustaches, he now patronised Mawson as an ideal type, taking him on 17 May to the royal command performance of Bulwer Lytton's *Money*, where Sandow's box was close to the King's, in which sat George V, Queen Mary and Kaiser Wilhelm II.

Much of Mawson's time was spent organising the supply of equipment. He ordered twenty Norwegian sledges of ash and hickory (nine 12-foot, nine 11-foot, two 7-foot) and seventeen Australian (thirteen 12-foot, four 7-foot); twelve pairs of Norwegian skis, twelve pairs of Australian; thirty one-man reindeer-skin sleeping bags (fur turned inside), three three-man; 250 'special finskoo'—not just ordinary finnesko but finnesko specially cut from the leg of the reindeer stag where the fur was hardest wearing; and eighty-six pairs of wolfskin mitts (fur turned outside) to go over woollen gloves. On Shackleton's recommendation the fur-wear was ordered from W. C. Møller of Drammen, near Christiania (now Oslo). Their 'special finskoo' was very hard to get because the Lapps preferred to keep the best fur for themselves. Shackleton had only been able to buy twenty-four (twelve 'pairs' as he calls them) for the BAE. Other items of clothing (Burberry gabardine helmets and blouses, both one-piece and individual, woollen suits and balaclavas by Jaeger, and so on) were bought or donated in England. Most of the food was donated.

For his cameras Mawson went to Newman and Guardia of London who provided everything *gratis*: eight cameras including a 5"x 4" 'Reflex' model. All but one came with superb Zeiss Tessar lenses, and there was a supplementary Busch Bis-Telar telephoto lens for the 'Reflex'. Frank Hurley, subsequently appointed AAE photographer, also took his own cameras including stereoscopic and panorama models. The London office of the Lyon firm Lumière donated four hundred of their colour autochrome plates. This process, which produces permanent colour transparencies of great beauty, had been introduced by the Lumière brothers in 1907. Unfortunately Hurley would later let Mawson down (as so often), failing to send the developed transparencies to him in London in 1914, so that only one autochrome appeared in Mawson's *Home of the Blizzard*, though colour photographs of the less attractive 'Paget Plate' process were included. Scientific instruments came from Negretti and Zambra or on loan from the Admiralty and the RGS. Oceanographical gear was loaned by the Prince of Monaco, whom Mawson saw in Paris on his way home. Wireless equipment was the best, Telefunken, supplied through the Australasian Wireless Company.[38]

The AAE's library was almost equally provided by Campbell Mackellar and Mawson himself. The books from Mackellar included literature of Arctic and Antarctic travel, scientific textbooks and general literature. Mawson's contributions included, besides popular volumes of Antarctic literature like Shackleton's *Heart of the Antarctic* and H. R. Mill's *Siege of the South Pole*, volumes of scientific results from Scott's 1900–4 *Discovery* expedition, W. S. Bruce's 1902 *Scotia* expedition, the BAE, Otto Nordenskjöld's 1901–3 *Antarctic* expedition, and Jean Charcot's first, 1903–5, expedition. He also supplied volumes of popular poets like Rudyard Kipling and Robert Service, anthologies, and other items including the *Meditations* of Marcus Aurelius (which reflect Mawson's austere and stoic credo, above any particular religion). Interestingly, he took *German Self-Taught*, a recognition of Germany's superiority in many scientific and technological fields.[39]

On 21 June, the day before the Coronation, he left England, travelling through Paris to Marseilles where he boarded the *Morea* for Adelaide. Davis and the *Aurora* followed at the end of July with supplies and equipment, two members of the expedition, Dr Xavier Mertz from Switzerland and Lieutenant B. E. S. Ninnis, and their charges, forty-nine Greenland dogs. At Cardiff Davis lost many of his sailors, rebellious over shipboard conditions (heavy weather had seen their bunks drenched) and threatening suit for damages.[40] He appointed a scratch crew, took on coal and headed for Hobart, which he reached early in November.

Through the second half of 1911 Mawson resumed his teaching and by the end of October had appointed most of his expeditionary staff and ordered the rest of his stores. He had substantial government grants from New South Wales (£7000), Victoria (£6000), and South Australia (£5000), £500 from Tasmania and nothing from Queensland, Western Australia or New Zealand. The hoped-for £20 000 from the Commonwealth Government turned out to be £5000 (with another £5000 in 1913). The British Government gave £2000. The high point of this period was reached on the evening of Wednesday, 13 September 1911, at a national fund-raising meeting in the Melbourne Town Hall where Mawson spoke to an audience that included the Governor-General, Thomas, Baron Denman (presiding), Prime Minister Fisher, and Alfred Deakin, Leader of the Opposition. Mawson followed this up with lectures in other states and sought more private donations, but it was clear that the AAE would sail deeply in debt. At this time he estimated the cost of the AAE at £48 000. Not only was he thousands off target, but Heinemann's £1000 had been merely a loan until the anticipated £20 000 came in from the Commonwealth Government. This was also the case with G. P. Doolette and G. Buckley, each of whom had loaned £1000. All this had to be repaid. Mawson was selling shares and putting the money into the AAE. His fiancée noticed that 'he looked thinner and thinner as the months went by'.[41]

Among his Adelaide friends at this time were the Chief Justice
of South Australia and University Chancellor, Sir Samuel Way, and
George Henderson, Professor of History and English, like Mawson
a product of Fort Street Model Public School. Way, a pragmatic-
minded Methodist of high integrity, lived at Montefiore, across the
Torrens from the centre of Adelaide. He was intrigued by polar
exploration and followed with fatherly interest all of Mawson's
plans.[42] With Way and most other friends Mawson kept his
anxieties to himself, like any good leader, but unburdened himself
to George Henderson, now forty-one.

Henderson and Mawson had much in common. Above all,
each was a philosophical stoic. Henderson was widely liked and by
nature idealistic, but his wife was in England, not here, and by now
they had been separated almost ten years. During 1911 he was
divorced. He lived in boarding houses, and when he could sleep,
which was not often, he awoke from his dreams in despair. He
dined at the Adelaide Club, but neither conviviality nor work
helped. He listened to Mawson's problems, silent about his own.
When Mawson sailed for the Antarctic he carried a letter from
Henderson:

> My dear Mawson
>   Just a word of farewell before you sail. Is it any use asking you
> not to worry about that £9000? I really do not think you have any
> reasonable excuse . . . You are, I believe, setting out on one of the
> most important expeditions ever undertaken in this country; you
> and your companions are to make history for the Commonwealth,
> and to acquire knowledge which will make the whole scientific
> world indebted to you . . . May the kind Providence in whom you
> believe keep a watchful eye on your wanderings, and bring you all
> back again.[43]

Henderson once wrote, 'To read order into chaos—this is the
secret of happiness and the source of content.' He continued to
raise money for the AAE after Mawson left, and to throw himself
into historical work in Adelaide and later Sydney, fighting on until
9 April 1944, when, alone in his garden, he triggered his own

expedition to the 'undiscovered country' from which no-one returns.[44]

As if Mawson did not have enough financial worries, his London manager, Alfred Reid, now showed his colours. Reid had worked for Shackleton, who had no complaints, so Mawson paid Reid £50 for several months' work, trusting him. The day after he left England, for instance, he sent Reid a draft letter to Lewis Harcourt, Secretary of State for the Colonies, requesting authority to take possession of discovered lands for the Empire—a request destined to be refused. 'Get this typed and forge my signature', he told Reid.[45] By late September Reid was idle and thinking about how much he had done for the AAE. 'The amount of goods donated', he wrote to Mawson,

> is enormous. When I first gave you and Davis all the names of the best firms you jocularly remarked at the time 'It will pay us to give Reid a commission on the value of all the stuff presented.' Well that alone would amount to about £150 . . . I really think that taking everything into consideration, and the amount of work entailed, your committee might vote me a further sum of £300 (three hundred pounds).[46]

Without Mawson's agreement Reid went ahead and drew £225 from the accounts. Legal action initiated by Mawson would drag on until January 1915 when Reid would finally agree to refund £112 10s 0d.[47]

To cap everything, the REP monoplane, which reached Adelaide in early October, crashed during a fund-raising display at Cheltenham Racecourse on 5 October. Mawson blamed the accident on Lieutenant Watkins, who 'had been very late at the Naval and Military Club the night before'.[48] This is probably unfair. The pilot's detailed account has never before been printed. On 10 October Watkins wrote to Captain H. F. Wood, manager of Vickers' Aviation Department,

> I've done the 'Bus in. We got it here alright, and did quite a good flight the morning before the smash. I was up for about 20 or 30

minutes when the petrol started squirting out of the top tank owing to too much pressure from the large tank. I was nearly blinded and the fumes were awful.

The next morning I took Wild up, (the Chap you lifted) about 200 ft. up. I got into a fierce tremor, and then into an air pocket, and was brought down about 100 ft., got straight, and dropped into another, almost a vacuum. That finished it. We hit the ground with an awful crash, both wings damaged, one cylinder broken, and the Nose bent up, the tail in half, etc.

I've got a cracked chest bone, and any amount of bruises and cuts. Wild got his shoulder sprained and some bruises etc. . . . I tried everything to get her right, but it was no good. The machine was perfect, and the engine was pulling like blazes. It was simply pure rotten luck.[49]

Frank Wild's account, also unpublished, records Watkins's first agonised words from under the wreckage: 'Poor old bus, she's all jiggered up!'[50] Mawson decided to take the repaired machine to Antarctica without its wings, and as a pilot was no longer required, Watkins returned to England. The machine's maintenance would be in the hands of F. H. Bickerton, FRGS, appointed to the AAE in England as engineer and motor expert.

At the beginning of November Mawson travelled to Tasmania, reaching Hobart on 2 November. Two days later *Aurora* arrived. On the way out Davis had formed critical views of the two expedition members on board. Xavier Mertz, twenty-eight, of Basel, was a lawyer and engineer who had climbed Mt Blanc. Almond-faced, with a trim moustache, he was from a rich family and had won the Swiss ski-jumping championship in 1908 with a jump of 31 metres. Belgrave Ninnis, twenty-three, previously Royal Fusiliers, still had traces of puppy fat on his face. Was he as ingenuous as he looked? He had been educated at Dulwich College, Shackleton's old school. Mertz and Ninnis were charged with looking after the dogs on the voyage out and in Antarctica. They were 'idlers', Davis wrote in his private journal. Ninnis was 'lazy and ignorant and appears to think that to boast of being hopelessly incompetent is extremely smart. . . . He is one of those people who go through life always depending on some one else to pull him out of difficulties.' The crew were often left to tend the animals. 'The dogs had a bad time of it in the breeze last night', Davis remarked. 'I wish we had some one on board who could look after them it is a great shame that they should suffer from neglect.' He did not envy Mawson 'his job down South unless he has got some better chaps than we have here at present'.[51]

Aurora's cargo had to be unloaded, sorted, and re-loaded, along with additional supplies and equipment including the pre-fabricated wooden huts for the Antarctic bases and the one at Macquarie Island. As Mawson describes it,

> The exertion of it was just what was wanted to make us fit ... Some five thousand two hundred packages were in the shed, to be sorted over and checked. The requirements of three Antarctic bases, and one at Macquarie Island were being provided for, and consequently the most careful supervision was necessary to prevent mistakes, especially as the omission of a single article might fundamentally affect the work of a whole party. To assist in discriminating the impedimenta, coloured bands were painted round the packages, distinctive of the various bases ... every package bore a different number, and the detailed contents were listed in a schedule for reference.[52]

Archibald McLean, the expedition's chief medical officer and bacteriologist, offers another perspective: 'Mawson was afoot down the fairway between the stores, armed with bundles of typewritten lists, checking here, sorting there, answering enquiries with short shrift, earnest and hurried, comprehending a host of details ... There was a galvanism in it all.'[53]

Helping Mawson supervise all this work was Frank Wild, recovered from his crash injuries, a mine of energy, the chosen commander for the Central (or, as it turned out, Western) Base. Charles F. Laseron, twenty-five, from Sydney, the AAE's taxidermist, recorded that 'At one stage a strike was threatened, as objections were taken to some of our members encroaching on ... trade-union grounds. The grumblers were, however, told that we were quite prepared to do the whole work ourselves, and nothing further was heard of the impending trouble.'[54]

'After a hard day's work in the shed', McLean noted, 'we would crawl home wearily and don respectable garb. Then small and cheery parties would explore the crowded streets and ultimately foregather in a strawberry-and-cream shop.' Mawson and Wild were already legends to McLean and his new friends. 'We had never seen these men before and most of us were boys with the instinct of worship. So life was a very sweet thing as the days of our departure drew on to its consummation.'[55]

There was too much cargo for the *Aurora*, so the small steamer *Toroa* was chartered to carry some of it, along with most members of the continental bases, as far south as Macquarie Island. She followed a few days after *Aurora*, which finally set sail on the afternoon of Saturday 2 December to a rousing send-off from the thousands of spectators lining Queen's Wharf. The Governor of Tasmania, Sir Harry Barron, Lady Barron, and the Premier, Sir Elliot Lewis, had come on board for final farewells, and cabled good wishes arrived from George V and Queen Alexandra the Queen Mother. The *Aurora* flew the pennant of the Royal Thames Yacht Club on her main top-mast and the Commonwealth red ensign at the mizzen. As she slipped her moorings and the town clock chimed 4.00 p.m. the sun still shone, but inside the wardroom the glass was falling.

5 Sacred Anthem

A HEAVY SEA was running as the men on *Aurora* watched Tasmania slowly sink below the north-western horizon, the wind comfortably abaft the beam, but by late the following day the waves were grey and rolling mountains and the wind had swung to a gale-force southerly. Half the bridge was demolished as seas swept the decks, smashing one end of the slim packing case containing the 'air-tractor' and driving the fuselage through the other end 'like a nail', in Francis Bickerton's words.[1] 'It seemed as if no power on earth could save the loss of at least part of the deck cargo', Mawson wrote. 'Would it be the indispensable huts amidships, or would a sea break on the benzine aft and flood us with inflammable liquid and gas?'[2]

Macquarie Island, some 850 miles south-south-east of Hobart, was sighted on 11 December. On the east side of the northern tip of this bleak and windy place *Aurora* was signalled by the sealing crew of the *Clyde*, wrecked a month earlier, to anchor in Hasselborough Bay on the western side, as the prevailing winds, oddly, had been easterly for a month. Wireless masts were landed, then the rest of the gear required by the party selected to man this base, which was to serve as a meteorological and wireless-relay station for the Antarctic bases.

The leader here was to be George F. Ainsworth, a 30-year-old meteorologist. Captain Davis fell out with him at the start by suggesting that when Ainsworth selected the site for the hut 'it would be well to ask the [marooned] islanders their opinion as having lived on the island they would probably know the sheltered spots this idea was ridiculed by this gentleman . . . Well I am glad I shall not be with Ainsworth he is an ass.'[3] Davis's entries in his private journal were composed in the heat of the moment but are interesting as the views of Mawson's trusted second-in-command, best friend, and soon-to-be best man.

Incompetence manifested itself in various ways: '6 am Commenced on wireless gear', Arthur J. Sawyer, appointed wireless operator here, wrote in his diary on 15 December. 'Hannam has opened all the barrels & boxes, therefore exposing almost everything to rain. The generator lying out with only an overcoat over it.'[4] Hannam was to be in charge of wireless at the Main Base—not a hopeful sign.

Davis recorded that during the two weeks it took to establish this base, 'Mawson throughout worked like a Trojan'.[5] This is a constant feature of Mawson's leadership, which was largely based on example. The masts were erected on Wireless Hill using a 'flying fox' supplied by the sealers. Construction of the hut was begun and the *Toroa* arrived safely with seventeen members of the expedition, fifty sheep, coal for *Aurora*, and additional stores for the island base. Left here with Ainsworth were L. R. Blake (geologist and cartographer), H. Hamilton (biologist), C. A. Sandell (wireless operator and mechanic), and Sawyer.

Christmas Day broke calm and clear as *Aurora* made south on the 157th meridian. The celebratory dinner was held in three relays. 'Dr. Mawson sent along Tintara Claret', Dr Archibald McLean noted, '& Capt. Davis cigars—Benedictine Liqueur was broached'.[6] 'The members of the landing parties', Davis recorded, 'have been told off in watches. They assist with the pumping, bracing yards, making or furling sail, steering, hoisting boats in and out, and other miscellaneous duties. I think most of them rather enjoy keeping watch.'[7] This observation, which he later published, contrasts with his view of his own officers, which he did not publish: 'I feel that I have not an officer in the ship that can be trusted to do anything . . . it is too much to find that the officers are too lazy [*sic*] to take the ordinary precautions.'[8] Morton Moyes, a meteorologist slated for the Western Base, formed similar views: 'Crew a rotten lot', he observed after leaving Macquarie Island, and a few days later, 'Never saw such a dirty unshaved crowd Captain Davis dirtiest. Dr M. easy 2nd'. Of the others, 'Hannam awful liar and skite. Laseron [C. F. Laseron, taxidermist, Main Base] childish. Rest A1'.[9] Hannam also thought Davis 'as dirty as it is possible for anyone to be',[10] while McLean's assessment of him was equally, if differently, unflattering: 'fond of meat & drink—gushing if all goes well—irritable & peevish when things go wrong'.[11]

There were boxing contests on 28 December (Boxing Day). On the 29th they entered a zone of fog. Alec Kennedy, a good-looking 22-year-old science graduate of the University of Adelaide, appointed magnetician for the Western Base, was on deck, staring into the grey vagueness:

> Then suddenly out of the fog on the starboard quarter loomed a huge mass, the first iceberg. Coming past it giving it about a half mile berth we saw it in all its beauty. A huge flat-topped mass about a mile long and ½ broad and 180 feet high. A magnificent introduction to the ice to come. The colours were beyond description, all shades of blue. Cracks and crevasses, caves and caverns covered its sides and the water rushing and roaring thro' them gave a sound like 100 locomotives blowing off steam. Then around us were icebergs of all shapes and sizes. We were in the thick of it.[12]

On New Year's Eve Kennedy recorded in his diary that

> The sky was cloudy except towards the south, and the cloud effects and colours were beautiful. At 12 o'clock Webb and I brought most of the crowd in the ward room and in the bunks on deck by pulling 8 bells on the whistle. Tins were banged and revolvers fired. Dr McLean and I went up to the crows nest to see the New Year in and hurried down when we found Hurley was taking a group photo of the 8–12 and 12–4 watches on the quarter deck.[13]

Restless, impulsive, versatile, Frank Hurley would make his name as a photographer on this expedition. His quizzical squint suggested an obscure anxiety behind the grin. Dr Alf Howard remembers him from the 1929–31 BANZARE expeditions: 'He was a born comedian and was the main mover in any party we had such as Christmas or New Year. I recall one occasion in which he startled us all by having smoke come out of his ears—all done by way of rubber tubes.'[14] Kennedy's account of the New Year's Eve fun makes no mention of the leader's presence. Nor do the other diaries consulted including that of George Dovers (cartographer, Western Base) which is detailed on the celebration.[15] Mawson himself nowhere mentions it. Had he come on deck? Or was he in his bunk, asleep or reading? He took a paternal interest in his men but was no hale companion. Charles Harrisson (biologist, Western Base) had observed four evenings earlier, 'N.B. Dr Mawson who is a bad sailor, does not have his meals with us, but in the Captn's cabin on deck with Davis, and sleeps there too'.[16] His men called him *Dux Ipse*, the leader himself, but not to his face. On the BANZARE cruises, too, he preserved a certain aloofness. 'We used to get together in one or other of the cabins for a singsong or a gramophone session', Alf Howard recalls, 'and, if I have any criticism of Mawson, it is that he did not participate in these'.[17] A degree of distance is necessary for successful leadership—even Shackleton, boon companion to his men *and* inspiring leader, reserved such a space for himself. Mawson, unlike Shackleton, was private and self-contained, radiating an existential autonomy, almost visibly repelling familiarity. His contribution to New Year's Day was a lecture on meteorology.[18]

Aurora was now up against the pack-ice, forced to make west before south. Then, on the 6th, a great barrier of land ice loomed ahead, trending south-west. On and on it went, for 60 miles, gradually rising in elevation, the massive shelf-ice tongue of what would later be named the Mertz Glacier. This was well to the east of D'Urville's landfall of 1840 which he had named *Terre Adélie*, but Mawson would refer to the bleak Antarctic coasts along here as Adélie Land too. On the evening of the 6th Kennedy was entering up his diary, glancing out through his port-hole onto the main hatch and bridge. 'The view consists of the officer on watch or "Gloomy" Davis passing up and down, getting whiter and whiter with snow', he noted. He also reported that 'The rumour of the 3rd party merging with the first and second was confirmed today'.[19] Given the iced-up condition of the coasts along here and the likelihood of difficulties and delays in landing three widely-separated parties, Mawson had reluctantly decided on only two.[20]

The party for the second base, under Frank Wild, was selected with care, for Mawson would not be able to keep a watch on them. 'I don't think one could find eight men to agree so well', Kennedy observed of Wild's men. 'Wild likes his team.'[21] It consisted of Dovers, Kennedy, Harrisson, Moyes, Archibald Hoadley (geologist), S. Evan Jones (medical officer), and Andrew Watson (geologist). Mawson's view of Wild, expressed in a letter of 1952, was that 'He was an excellent Petty Officer type and in some respect more than that. With Scott and later with Shackleton he had learned the drill of sledging technique under the worst climatic conditions of the world. I supplied him for the Queen Mary Land [Western] base with a company of seven tough University graduates. He as leader was to train these students also in the ways of Antarctica. He did the job well. He could not be excelled in intrepidity and had a full quota of sound horse sense. A very likeable fellow and a good companion.'[22]

On 8 January a site (named Cape Denison) for the Main Base was chosen within what was called Commonwealth Bay. A boat was lowered and Mawson and a small party examined a locality which, because of its extensive ice-free ground and sheltered boat harbour, seemed suitable for a hut or 'Winter Quarters' as Mawson would refer to it. The day, untypically, was calm. This region, as they would soon discover, is the windiest spot on earth, swept by catabatic gales rushing down from the high Antarctic ice plateau. Landing of equipment and supplies continued until 18 January. Charles Harrisson noted in his diary that it was

> a matter of congratulations, really, that the landing has passed off so well! On some days, rough & dangerous work. Boats tossing wildly—boxes & briquettes flying down a plank that was working with the motion of the boat—One of us catching them & breaking the force of their fall, 2 stowing—& it was 'look out' for heads & legs, mates & boats! Really a mercy there was no mishaps; a boat would be loaded in less than ¼ of an hour—so 1½ tons of boxes of briquettes had to come down in quick succession!—& hard work in the boats while it lasted. Heavy cases slung.[23]

Mawson set the pace, at one point making a strong impression by diving into the water to bring up a case which had fallen in.[24]

There was a farewell party in *Aurora's* wardroom before her departure west. Wild 'came out dressed as Sir Francis Drake in a fancy-dress costume', McLean noted. 'He made a remarkably fine character-portrait. The long purple stockings, scarlet cap with white feathers and tinselled coat were all part of himself.'[25] He even sported a 'pointed beard and twisted moustachios'.[26] Toasts were drunk to D'Urville and Wilkes in Madeira carried on HMS *Challenger*, the first steam-powered vessel to cross the Antarctic Circle, at 78° E., in December 1873. Several bottles of this had been presented to Davis and Mawson by James Y. Buchanan, *Challenger's* physicist and chemist. Mawson made a speech of farewell, everyone shook hands, and the Main Base group climbed into their boat and rowed ashore 'amid cheers and Auld Lang Synes'.[27] Wild, on the forecastle head, sang them an 'anchor song'.[28]

By the end of January, having worked his men from 7.00 a.m. to 11.00 p.m. daily, Mawson had the main hut, designed to his specifications and consisting of living quarters and attached workshop, well on the way to completion. Meteorological observations began on 1 February under the care of Cecil Madigan, a science graduate of the University of Adelaide who had put off his Rhodes Scholarship to Oxford. A magnetograph hut, prefabricated like the main hut, was erected, and observations begun by Eric Webb, from New Zealand. In 1976, as the last survivor of the AAE, he would recall Mawson as 'an intellectual leader with utter motivation and selfless dedication to his objective which he handed out to all of us ... so that, by common consent, it became accepted and promoted as the policy of the expedition. Thus, when we saw how he was completely committed, so each one of us became committed to his own particular discipline.'[29] Through February a stock of fresh penguin meat was laid in and preparations made for autumn sledging. Although Mawson, with Madigan and Lieutenant Robert Bage (astronomer and magnetician), managed to haul a loaded sledge 5 miles up the icy slopes towards the south, they were forced by a blizzard to leave it there and return to the hut, now snugly embedded in drift-snow almost to the tops of the verandahs.

This was in early March. When rare breaks in the weather allowed, anchorages were made for the wireless masts and a hangar constructed against an outside wall for the air-tractor. After the equinox the winds increased beyond Force 12 (hurricane), often averaging over 80 miles per hour. Walking outside to read instruments became impossible without crampons, and even finding one's way back in the endless drift was difficult. It was clear that there would be no autumn sledging or early erection of the wireless masts.

Since he could not occupy his men in these ways, Mawson kept them busy inside adapting gear and clothing to the severe conditions, or outside gathering geological specimens, dredging for marine-biological ones, or reading instruments. All animal and bird life had now departed north. There was the daily ice to be cut for domestic purposes, and the routine duties of the hut. Frank Hurley has described how a typical day began:

> At 7.30 A.M. the night watchman winds up the gramophone and selects a record according to his mood. A towel is thrust into the horn to subdue the tune to pianissimo. Gentle strains fall on the ears of the . . . sleepers [who] stir and turn in their bunks. It is pleasant to play in the day with harmony—it invariably closes with song.[30]

He claimed, for public consumption, that 'those who lived with [Mawson] through long tedious months in the blizzard-smitten South looked up to him not only as a leader but loved him as a comrade and a man'.[31] Perhaps Hurley loved Mawson as a father figure—Mawson seems to have regarded him as a wayward son (see Chapter 8). To most of his men, though, *Dux Ipse* was too distant to be loved. By 18 February 1912 Charles Laseron had decided he was 'a comrade' but 'stern as billy Oh!', admired 'in spite of all his faults of which he undoubtedly has a good many. One of his worst is a nasty sneery way he has of saying things at times, though perhaps he doesn't mean all he says and evidently forgets it soon after.'[32] Xavier Mertz wrote at the beginning of March 1912, 'It is difficult to get to know or judge him. All I know to this point is that he can work hard and has lots of energy.'[33]

Mawson revealed his inner self to his diary. Reading William S. Bruce's view, in Robert Brown's *Voyage of the 'Scotia'* (London, 1906), that 'Isolation among the fastnesses of nature does not bring loneliness', only 'the busy haunts of men', Mawson observed that he had been 'Most humanly lonely in London', but added, 'Lonely with nature on plateau' (21 March 1912). The howling blizzards outside the warmth of the hut were not chaos: 'The Voice of the Great Creator, etc. Sacred Anthem' (26 March). Down here sweet philosophies rang hollow: 'Where Nature is sterner and elements fewer one sees that [Omar] Khayyam's similes are not accurate (p. 59) "I came like water like wind I go, Into this universe and why not knowing, Nor whence like water willy nilly flowing—etc.". Water is flowing to a definite goal—so are we', Mawson wrote (28 March). 'Outside one is in touch with the sternest of Nature— one might be a lone soul standing in Precambrian times or on Mars—all is desolation and hard in the durest [*sic*]. Life opens up to one as it must to the savage. Inside the Hut all is 20th Century civilization. What a contrast' (9 April). He read, in F. A. Cook's *Through the First Antarctic Night* (London, 1900), of the madness and dissidence on the *Belgica*, beset by the pack-ice through the black winter of 1898: 'am shocked by his account' (15 April). Within a year he too would face the madness.

In the evenings, after supper, as the Sacred Anthem shrieked its fury overhead and the 'puffometer' registered blasts of up to 150 miles per hour, a book would be read at the long communal table, often by Mawson himself—Robert Service's poems on Alaska, or Marcus Aurelius, or some other favourite.[34] Much space in *Home of the Blizzard* is devoted to entertainments (including an operatic farce) devised to keep spirits high through the winter, when boredom posed a silent threat to morale and cohesion. Birthdays and key dates such as Midwinter's Day were celebrated with lavish dinners and Hurley's beautifully printed menus. Meanwhile meteorological data were continuously recorded, marine life dredged up and analysed, and two wireless masts erected with an aerial stretched between. During September regular messages in morse code were transmitted, many of them received at Macquarie Island, but no return signals could be heard as gales and drift-snow caused intense static. This was the first use of wireless in the Antarctic.[35] Hannam, the operator, resented Mawson's blaming him for non-reception: 'The Dr informed me that wireless was the biggest failure on the expedition which makes one laugh as he expects a thing to be put up & work without any testing out or anything'.[36] Violent winds tore the masts down in mid-October and they stayed down until the following year.

In August Mawson had led a team south to the abandoned sledge and they had excavated a cosy cave in the ice, filling it with little conveniences including a primus cooker and fuel, and some provisions. They called it Aladdin's Cave. It could accommodate three men and served as a permanently available striking-off point for the summer sledging parties. Two other depots were laid further out on the plateau.

Three reconnoitring parties went out in September but only the south-western party made much progress—50 miles, less than one degree of latitude. Cape Adare to Gaussberg was already an impossibility because of the reduction of the mainland bases from three to two, and as the weather continued wild through October Mawson grew increasingly depressed.

There was definitely something wrong with Whetter—Dr Leslie H. Whetter, twenty-nine, surgeon, from New Zealand—and Mawson jotted his observations down in pencil on a scrap of paper. For a start there was Whetter's cooking—'the pudding tapioca a damned disgrace, only tapioca and butter—and nothing else'. Once when he was rostered cook he failed to bake the bread, and at dinner the soup was 'so badly burnt that [it was] not fit to eat'. He seemed to be hiding poor health: 'Why did he not mention to me at dinner time that he was not well enough?'[37] Then came the explosion. On 6 October Mertz noted, 'First Sunday without work. A few days ago Whetter and Mawson had a drawn-out altercation after he had answered him rudely in front of everyone. In the upshot Mawson acknowledged that he had too often allowed his temper free rein.' Mawson dates this to 3 October.[38] In his diary he does not mention any fault on his part but gives the background and dramatic circumstances. By the time of the blow-up his complaints included, besides general slothfulness, secret drinking.

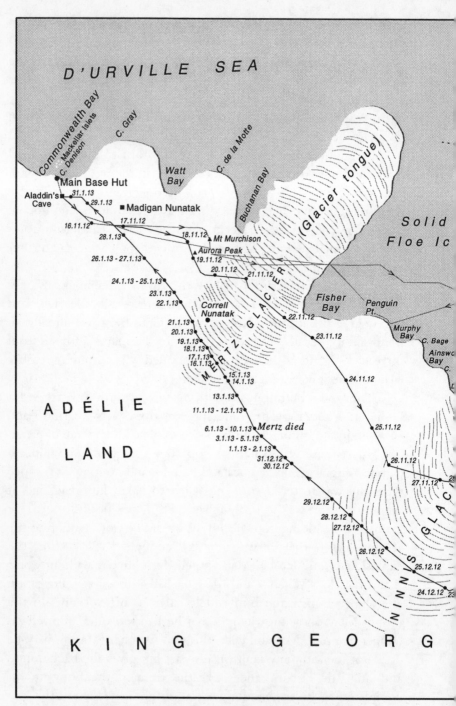

Routes of the Main Base sledging parties of the Australasian Antarctic Expedition during the summer of 1912–1913. This is a simplified version of the map Mawson himself provided for *Home of the Blizzard* (1915).

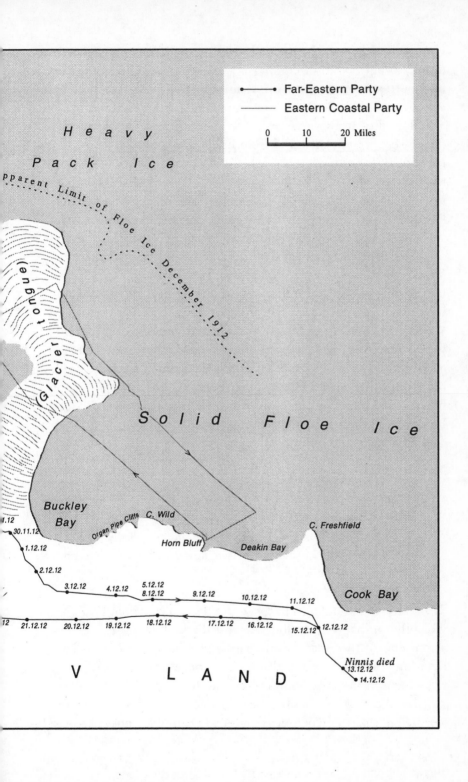

Far-Eastern Party
Eastern Coastal Party

0   10   20 Miles

Heavy

P a c k   I c e

Apparent Limit of Floe Ice December 1912

(Glacier Tongue)

S o l i d   F l o e   I c e

Buckley Bay

Organ Pipe Cliffs   C. Wild

Horn Bluff

Deakin Bay

C. Freshfield

Cook Bay

1.12
30.11.12
1.12.12
2.12.12
3.12.12   4.12.12   5.12.12
8.12.12   9.12.12   10.12.12   11.12.12
12   21.12.12   20.12.12   19.12.12   18.12.12   17.12.12   16.12.12   15.12.12   12.12.12

Ninnis died
13.12.12
14.12.12

V   L A N D

He had noticed on 27 June that 'a bottle of Port (wine) has been drunk, so put a drop of croton oil [strong purgative] in some Port in a bottle. Await results.' On 3 July he observed, 'Whetter has apparently drunk the Port wine containing a drop of croton oil'.[39]

The final straw came on 3 October when Whetter failed to dig out the accumulated drift from inside the 'hangar' as instructed. In front of everyone, he was asked by Mawson (who later wrote the dialogue down verbatim in his diary), 'Why did you come on the expedition?' 'Not to do such kind of work!' Whetter shouted. 'Well then you're a bloody fool to come on the expedition if that was the case!' 'Bloody fool yourself! I won't be caught on another one.' Whetter was then ordered into Mawson's room where the leader cooled down and reasoned with him, though 'it was of little use'. At dinner Mawson made a speech to the men: everyone would henceforth be expected to put in a fair day's work but they could 'knock off at 4 pm except set duties and compulsory scientific work'. Moreover, 'Sundays would be exempt'. Afterwards, Hannam 'came in to me . . . and said he would be damned to such people but would "make them work". He showed a fine spirit by saying he was very sorry for any hasty words he may have ever said, etc. Hurley and others said similar things.'[40]

Mawson's criticism of Whetter went deeper. The man was a surgeon—the expedition depended on him for its very life:

> He appears to have changed since joining the expedition—appeared willing when he arrived first.
>
> According to his own words he came on the expedition so as to have a quiet time for study—I believe he came also for his health.
>
> This is a criminal matter.[41]

Whetter was also hiding a bad case of piles—they would break out violently on the Western Journey with Bickerton and Hodgeman at the end of that year.[42] But Mawson's concession on working hours and Sundays suggests that he was concerned at a build-up of resentment in the expedition on these issues.

By the end of October he had decided that whatever the weather, five parties would set out, four in early November and the fifth in early December: the Southern Party led by Lieutenant Bage, with Webb and Hurley, and initially supported by Herbert D. Murphy, John G. Hunter (biologist), and Laseron, to make magnetic observations in the area of the South Magnetic Pole; the Near Eastern Party to explore the coast between Cape Denison and the Mertz Glacier tongue, under Frank L. Stillwell (geologist), assisted by John H. Close (collector) and (before his departure west) Alfred J. Hodgeman (cartographer), and later by Laseron; the Eastern Coastal Party led by Madigan, with McLean and Percy E. Correll (mechanic, physicist), to explore the coast beyond the Mertz Glacier; the Far Eastern Party, with dogs, exploring the more distant eastern coastline, led by Mawson himself, with Mertz and Ninnis who were here principally to look after the dogs; and finally, setting out in December, the Western Party led by Bickerton, with Hodgeman and Whetter, using the air-tractor (see map, between pages 67 and 68, for the routes of these parties). Hannam would maintain the hut. Back in May Mawson had considered leaving Eric Webb at the hut, along with Murphy who was 'quite unsafe to send on any journey'. He considered Webb 'perky'.[43] Webb, however, as magnetician, simply had to go with the Southern Party as their brief was the Magnetic Pole. Murphy, on the other hand, was merely a member of this party's support team, not going out very far. His greatest talent was summed up by Morton Moyes in a diary entry: 'Murphy's yarns unsurpassable'.[44]

Eric Webb, twenty-two, merits close attention. Before joining the AAE he had worked at the Carnegie Institute in Washington, DC. He was a highly qualified magnetician. On 21 October he told Mawson that the second dip circle, vital in locating the Magnetic Pole, needed work and he did not have time to do it—Bage perhaps could do it. As Mawson recorded it,

> He states that Madigan is weak in his astronomical work. I say things to egg him on to say his mind and more than he intended, and I find that he is disappointed with the Expedition. Thought everybody was a greater specialist in their line than they are. He thinks he is practically the only one . . . who is properly fit. He says he has never seen me observe with a theodolite and doubts my accuracy. States

that there was nobody on Shackleton's expedition capable of instrument work; at any rate it appears to have been so and he was told by certain people in New Zealand (evidently Farr and Skey).[45]

Luckily for Mawson's peace of mind he could not know at this time that Clinton Coleridge Farr, of Canterbury College, Christchurch, like his colleague Henry F. Skey an expert on terrestrial magnetism, had earlier that year written to Edgeworth David to say that close analysis of Mawson's instrument readings on the BAE showed their insufficiency, that there must surely have been more records taken than David had sent him (there were not), and that the David–Mawson–Mackay party had clearly *not* reached the Magnetic Pole Area (of oscillation). From Mawson's diary entry here it seems certain that Webb had been confidentially informed on this matter by Farr and Skey. Thus he had something over Mawson, though he merely hinted it. On 18 February 1912 David, unable of course to consult Mawson, had written Farr a long and distressed letter, doing his best to excuse Mawson's work as magnetician, but surrendering to Farr's superior judgement. David would mercifully keep this depressing information from Mawson until 1925, but his scientist's conscience would compel him to write a note to *Nature* on 'the uncertainty of our rough determination'.[46] For his entry in *Who's Who in Australia* Mawson would change his sentence on the Magnetic Pole journey so that from the early 1930s it no longer read 'one of the discoverers of the South Magnetic Pole' but simply 'magnetic pole journey 1908'.

He had wanted all parties but the Western to leave on 6 and 7 November but blizzards descended again. Just before his own party finally set out on the 10th he wrote a brief note to his fiancée: '10 November 1912: The weather is fine this morning though the wind still blows. We shall get away in an hour's time. I have two good companions, Dr Mertz and Lieut. Ninnis. It is unlikely that any harm will happen to us, but should I not return to you in Australia, please know that I truly loved you. I must be closing now as the others are waiting.'[47] Mertz read the glorious weather as 'definitely a good omen'.[48]

6 Death and Deliverance

For the far-eastern journey the most immediate sources are diaries by Mawson and Mertz (Mertz's unpublished), and Mawson's unpublished meteorological notes. *Home of the Blizzard* was written later, with stylistic input from Dr Archie McLean who heavily worked over Mawson's drafts (see Chapter 8). The diaries are preferred here, as they were composed on the spot.

Initially slowed by bad weather, the party had its last contact with Madigan's and Stillwell's groups (also pushing east) on 17 November. Thereafter their paths diverged, Mawson's heading south-east under the power of sixteen dogs. He intended to explore the coast hundreds of miles to the east, far beyond what he would name the Mertz and Ninnis Glaciers. This was why he had reserved the dogs for his own party. Mertz went ahead on skis, except on occasional days when Ninnis led, as sledge-dogs need someone to follow or they track aimlessly. There were three sledges, the front ones roped in tandem.

Progress was relatively rapid, up to 15 miles per day. The Mertz Glacier, 30 miles wide, was reached on 20 November and crossed in just two days, and after another 50 miles the wider Ninnis Glacier was crossed in four. Thereafter, with the coast in view, they continued south-east for three days, then directly east for over a week, across endless sastrugi, to the longitude of Cape Freshfield, then south-south-east, leaving Cook Bay on their left, mapping the coastal features when weather permitted. By then they were just over a month out, 300 miles from Winter Quarters.

There had been few incidents beyond the expected, but those few were startling. His father, Mawson later revealed to Paquita Delprat, 'came to me in a vivid dream' on this trip—a father just dead, unbeknown to his son.[1] (The mother, already ailing, would not long survive the father). On 19 November the descent towards the Mertz Glacier had suddenly become frighteningly steep. 'I halt', Mertz had recorded, 'because the descent speed is too great for the sledge. I was right, for two sledges almost bolted, and Mawson moans, thinking yet again that the entire expedition is ruined.'[2] The superstitious could find prodigy in the sledge dogs devouring their new-born pups, though this is normal in these conditions. Less normal was the multiple birth of fourteen pups from the one bitch. On 21 November Ninnis had fallen into a crevasse, on the snow-bridged lid of which the party had pitched their tent unawares; the following day he had broken through another with his sledge, and the day after that, yet another. The glistening ice-falls and ramparts on the edges of the glaciers reminded Mertz of Switzerland, 'as if it were the Alps at home'. They seemed to call to him like old friends, 'greeted me repeatedly whenever I looked back'.[3] On 9 December, far inland, out of nowhere, 'a snow-petrel flew into Ninnis's sledge. From where could the creature have come?' Mertz asked, puzzled.[4]

There had also been the odd ailment—Mawson's neuralgia on the left side of his face and in his shoulder, and a most painful whitlow on one of Ninnis's fingers which Mawson had lanced. They pressed on. Then on the evening of 13 December nature herself seemed to speak to them in warning. At 8.00 p.m., Mertz noted, 'there was suddenly a cracking several times deep beneath us. The snow masses must have been collapsing their arches. The sound was like the distant thunder of cannon. My companions were frightened, as they had never before heard this collapsing of snow-shelves.'[5] Mawson simply recorded, 'Booming sound heard today'.[6] Ninnis soon forgot about it, pleased with his healing finger. 'Happy and cheerful', he slept the sleep of the just—his first in three nights.[7]

The catastrophe occurred the next day, 311 miles from Winter Quarters, soon after Mawson had taken the noon latitude (68° 53'

53" S) and longitude (151° 39' 46" E).[8] As he wrote that evening in his journal,

> My sledge crossed a crevasse obliquely & I called back to Ninnis, who had rear sledge, to watch it, then went on, not thinking to look back again as it had no specially dangerous features. After ¼ mile I noted Mertz halt ahead and look enquiringly back. I looked behind & saw no sign of Ninnis & his team. I stopped & wondered, then bethought myself of the crevasse and hurried back to find a great gaping hole in the ground. I called down but could get no answer. I signalled Mertz who was on skis ahead & he brought my team up to the scene. We hung over the edge but could see nothing nor get any answer. It was about 11 ft wide where broken through & straight ice-walled. From the other side, by hanging over on an alpine rope, we caught a glimpse of what appeared to be a food bag and one dog partially alive moaning, and part of another dog & dark object, apparently the tent, caught on a ledge. We sounded to the ledge with furlong line—150 ft sheer, ice ledge. No sign of Ninnis—must have struck it & been killed instantly, then gone on down. Our ropes not long enough to go down, or the sledge to span crevasse. Dog ceased to moan shortly. We called and sounded for three hours, then went on a few miles to a hill and took position observations. Came back, called & sounded for an hour.
>
> Read the Burial Service.
>
> Reviewed our position: practically all the food had gone down—spade, pick, tent, Mertz's burberry trousers & helmet, cups, spoons, mast, sail etc. We had our sleeping bags, a week and a half food, the spare tent without poles, & our private bags & cooker & kerosene. The dogs in my team were very poorly and the worst, & no feed for them—the other team comprised the picked dogs, & almost all man food. We considered it a possibility to get through to Winter Quarters by eating dogs, so 9 hours after the accident started back, but terribly handicapped . . . May God help us.[9]

After the burial service, Mertz wrote, 'We found comfort only in the thought that death had been a sudden act at the end of a happy, cheerful life. The ways of God are often inscrutable but everything must apparently work for the best for him.'[10] In the German this reads as though Mertz, unconvinced, is simply echoing his leader's faith in a benevolent deity.

Normally Mawson's forward sledge would be expected to succumb first to any crevasse. This was why he had put the best dogs and most of the provisions with the second sledge, in the rear. The third sledge had been abandoned two days earlier. It should be noted that Mawson was riding on the leading 12-foot sledge, while Ninnis was walking beside his. Mawson points out that 'The whole weight of a man's body bearing on his foot is a formidable load and no doubt was sufficient to smash the arch of the roof'.[11] J. Gordon Hayes, full of praise for the AAE, blames Mawson for the accident. Skis, or at least snowshoes, he points out, should have been mandatory on the expedition, as they distribute one's weight over a much larger area than a pair of feet in finnesko. Fridtjof Nansen, Otto Sverdrup and Roald Amundsen had all demonstrated this truth, which Mawson should have known before setting out. Ninnis's sledge, on its long 12-foot runners, would not have gone down had not Ninnis gone down first. 'Two lives [were] lost for the want of one pair of snowshoes', Hayes concludes. 'These fatalities were pre-ventible, as Scott's disaster was preventible, by knowledge available at the time. These are stern lessons for the future.'[12]

In their present plight there was no thought of sleep, so at 9.00 p.m. they set out on what Mawson termed 'a wild dash of fourteen miles, for the most part over a dangerously crevassed surface',[13] to the camp of the evening of 12 December, reaching it at 2.30 a.m. on 15 December. Here Mertz hastily cut a runner of the abandoned sledge in halves, using the two pieces and a ski as a frame for the spare tent they still had. They now had to decide on the best route back. Outbound, no depots had been laid. They could descend north, down heavily crevassed coastal slopes to the frozen sea, and hazard their luck on the sea ice, but that would lengthen their journey, and by now the sea-ice may have been breaking up. There would be seals to eat, though. Another advantage of that route was that Mawson had left instructions, in the event of his party not returning by 1 February, for Davis to steam east, searching the coast, though not east of the Mertz Glacier tongue.[14] In fact had they taken this course they would almost certainly have met up with the Eastern Coastal Party around Horn Bluff on 20 December. On the other hand they could make a fast return across the plateau, south of their outbound route, avoiding the worst crevassed areas of the glaciers, and by eating the remaining dogs their food supply should last out. This was the course adopted. George, the poorest of the animals, was despatched then and there, part of him fed to the other dogs, part kept for the two of them.

They travelled by night, the sun low down and the crisper surface offering less resistance to the sledge. Pannikins were improvised out of tins, wooden spoons out of bits of the broken sledge. Mertz points out that 'We forgot to hoist the Union Jack at the furthest point, as the disaster preoccupied us, so Mawson hoisted it on the 15th'.[15] Formalities were still important. After a fitful sleep they set out again at 6.45 p.m. on 15 December, a clear, calm evening, just a little alto cumulus out over the sea to the north, though after midnight snow was continuous.[16]

By 5.00 a.m. the following morning they had covered almost 19 additional miles, mainly north-north-west, higher up on the plateau.[17] Camp was pitched, then Mertz treated Mawson's snow-blind eyes with zinc sulphate and cocaine, as he 'could barely sleep for pain'.[18] That evening Mertz recorded

> A 9½ miles run, blind, into snow and fog. The course was extremely hard to keep to because the eyes saw nothing but greyness . . . Johnson fell in harness at 4 miles, exhausted. We put him on sledge and place ourselves in harness once more. Nourishment is hard with little food, how good the lunch of four days ago would taste now (butter, chocolate, tea). We think and dream only food. At 3.00 [am] Mary fell in harness, Pavlova was staggering.[19]

Over the following days, across ice fields ribbed with slippery sastrugi, dog after dog gave out and was shot. Mawson later noted, 'it was worth while spending some time in boiling the dogs' meat thoroughly. Thus a tasty soup was prepared as well as a supply of edible meat in which the muscular tissue and the gristle were reduced to the consistency of a jelly. The paws took longest of all to cook, but, treated to lengthy stewing, they became quite digestible.'[20] On Christmas Day they were skirting the crevassed upper reaches of the Ninnis Glacier. By now Mawson was talking about finnesko soup if worst came to worst.[21] He estimated that they were 158 miles in a direct line from Winter Quarters. The camera, hypsometer and other equipment had been abandoned. There was adequate food, provided they kept up the pace. That night, during a pause in the march, in the cold, hard wind and the drift, Mertz asked Mawson whether, on their return from Antarctica, he would show him something of Australia and New Zealand. Of course he would, he replied, he would go out of his way.[22]

Next day the sun was so warm that 'with cooker heat added tent drips, bags very wet, especially Mertz wet—no burberry'. On the 28th the dog Ginger gave in, on the 29th 'had a great breakfast off Ginger's skull—thyroids and brain'.[23] Mertz recorded for that day a march of only 7 miles, even with the help of the wind and a sail made from skis, tent and glacier rope. Then on the 30th, Mawson observed, 'Xavier off colour . . . He turned in—all his things very wet, chiefly on account of no burberry pants. The continuous drift does not give one a chance to dry things, and our gear is deplorable.'[24] Yet they had managed 15 miles. 'Am really tired', Mertz wrote, 'shall write no more'.[25]

The weather on New Year's Eve allowed them only 7 miles. 'Keeping off dog meat for a day or two as both upset by it', Mawson recorded. Mertz's sledging diary contains nothing beyond 1 January 1913—not even blank pages, for Mawson tore these out, along with the back cover, to save weight after Mertz's death, which occurred on the 8th. During the intervening days they could make little progress as Mertz's state worsened. 'He is generally in a very bad condition', Mawson observed on the 3rd. 'Skin coming off legs, etc.'. For the 4th, 'I doctored him part of the day and rested. Started on new food bag, using on morning of 5th first of it, serving Mertz milk, etc.' On the 5th, 'I tried to get Xavier to start but he practically refused, saying it was suicide and that it much best for him to have the day in bag and dry it and get better, then do more on sunshining day. I strongly advocated doing 2 to 5 miles only for exercise even if we could not see properly. Eventually we decided to rest today but every day after that he would shift.' At 3.30 p.m. they had half a tin of hoosh, followed by cocoa and half a biscuit, 'a rattling good meal'. The sun broke through fitfully ('a good omen'), then brightly. On the 6th he got Mertz up, packed, cooked, and they covered two downhill miles until Mertz 'caved in':

> I did my best with him—offered to put him on the sledge, then to set sail and sail him but he refused both after trial. We camped. I think he has a fever, he does not assimilate his food. Things are in a most serious state for both of us—if he cannot go on 8 or 10 m a day, in a day or two we are doomed. I could pull through myself with the provisions at hand but I cannot leave him. His heart seems to have gone. It is very hard for me—to be within 100 m of the Hut and in such a position is awful . . . both our chances are going now.[26]

It was agreed that the next day they would go on, Mertz in his bag on the sledge, but at 8.00 a.m. he was 'in a terrible state having fouled his pants'.

> He must be very weak now for I do up and undo most of his things . . . and put him into & take him out of the bag. I have a long job cleaning him up, then put him into the bag to warm up . . . At 10 am . . . I find him in a kind of a fit & wrap him up in the bag & leave him . . . it is a good day . . . This is terrible. I don't mind for myself, but it is for Paquita and for all others connected with the expedition that I feel so deeply and sinfully. I pray God to help us.[27]

He later told his friend Richard E. Byrd, the great American explorer of western Antarctica, and others then present, that he carried a small Bible on this journey and occasionally, in camp, read comforting passages from it.[28]

Mertz accepted cocoa and beef tea, but during the afternoon there were more fits, then delirium and refusal of all food and drink.

> At 8 pm he raves & breaks a tent pole . . . Continues to rave & call 'Oh Veh, Oh Veh' [*O weh!*, 'Oh dear!'] for hours. I hold him down,

then he becomes more peaceful & I put him quietly in the bag. He dies peacefully at about 2 am on morning of 8th. Death due to exposure finally bringing on a fever, result of weather exposure & want of food. He had lost all skin of legs & private parts. I am in same condition & sores on finger won't heal.[29]

Lying in a damp sleeping bag for a week with very little food had greatly weakened Mawson, and he now doubted he had the stamina to last the distance, though the food might hold out. He was determined, however, not to give in to the temptation 'to sleep on in the bag'.[30]

First he cut the sledge in two with the 'saw' of his pocket knife, retaining the mast and spars, sewed a better sail and made other improvisations, then had two full serves of hot hoosh. Meanwhile he had dragged Mertz's body, in his bag, outside the tent, and cut blocks of snow, placing these around and over the corpse, finally surmounting the ice-cairn with a makeshift cross. He turned in at 10.00 p.m. On the 9th there was a 50 mph wind— he dared not take the tent down, as he would not be able to re-erect it alone if such winds continued. Instead he had more hoosh. Sores on his skin were not healing, 'the nose and lips break open also. My scrotum, like Xavier's, is also getting in a painfully raw condition due to reduced condition, dampness and friction in walking. It is well nigh impossible to treat.' On the 9th he read the burial service over Mertz.[31]

The question some people insist on asking is, 'Did he eat him?' Dr Phillip Law, director of the Australian National Antarctic Research Expeditions (ANARE) for many years, knew Mawson well and does not believe he could even have contemplated it. 'He was a man of very solid, conservative morals. It would have been impossible for him to have considered it.'[32] In any case the grave was recorded in Mawson's diary as being clearly marked, was just 100 miles from Winter Quarters, and able to be found by any relief party that summer or the next, exhumed and shipped to Switzerland for reburial. This is a factor. Moreover, Mawson had sufficient provisions, barring terrible weather, which could not be foreseen, to last him to Winter Quarters, since food no longer had to be shared. The question should be resolved resoundingly in the negative.

Thick drift and high winds made 10 January unsledgeable, so most of the remaining dog meat was cooked in advance, enabling some of the kerosene to be discarded when Mawson left on the 11th, which broke calm and sunny. After a little over a mile, however, his feet became extremely painful: 'had to take my finnes off. As I had gradually expected it the sight was not such a shock, but the whole skin on almost whole of both feet had large blisters and burst.'[33] He smeared the skin with lanolin and bound the detached soles of his feet back in place with bandages, 'as they were comfortable and soft in contact with the raw surfaces'.[34] Six pairs of socks then covered the bandages, inside fur boots and crampons. Afterwards he removed his clothing and basked in the full, hot sun. 'I felt better and better.'[35] That afternoon he covered over 6 more miles, 'frost-bitten fingertips festering, mucous membrane of nose gone, saliva glands of mouth refusing duty, skin coming off whole body. The sun bath today will set much right however.'[36] Winds and snow enforced a rest on the following day. On the 13th he had two meals—biscuits, pemmican, tea, cocoa, a little dog meat—and covered over 5 miles, then 5 the next day, despite painful feet. 'Am keeping food and mileage list at end of book now as checks on each other.'

On 17 January he was halfway across the southern end of the Mertz Glacier, aware of the unseen dangers. Instantly, without warning, he dropped 14 feet and was snapped to a halt, turning at the end of a taut, thin rope,

> sledge creeping to mouth [of crevasse]. I had time to say to myself 'So this is the end', expecting every moment the sledge to crash on my head and both of us to go to the bottom unseen below. Then I thought of the food left uneaten in the sledge—and, as the sledge stopped without coming down, I thought of Providence again giving me a chance. The chance looked very small as the rope had sawed into the overhanging lid, my finger ends all damaged, myself weak . . . With the feeling that Providence was helping me I made a great struggle, half getting out, then slipping back again several times,

but at last just did it. Then I felt grateful to Providence . . . who has so many times already helped me.[37]

Two years later, in Chicago, he would go into detail on the temptation to suicide he felt in the crevasse: 'I considered slipping out of my harness and dropping to end it, but I couldn't see the bottom of the crevasse and was afraid I'd simply fall on some ledge below me and linger in misery with broken bones. It seemed impossible that I could again muster strength for that climb.' He also told his Chicago audience that the climb upwards was 'a struggle of four and a half hours', and that afterwards 'I cooked and ate dog meat enough to give me a regular orgy'.[38] Because of this harrowing experience he fashioned a rope ladder and kept it attached to himself and the sledge in expectation of similar events.

It is impressive that, in spite of everything, he was still writing up detailed meteorological logs, quite separate from his diary. If he were to die, he wanted his scientific records at least to survive and be found with his corpse. In fact, on the day after this accident he coolly noted that 'it is quite apparent now that the direction of the wind is affected by the glacier valley. Here in the centre of the valley a night wind flows down it and on each side the winds are deflected into it.'[39] These separate meteorological logs were continued throughout the return journey.

Past the Mertz Glacier his mileages increased, excluding the nights of 24–25 and 26–27 January when he was blizzard-bound. Accordingly, he increased his daily rations. 'Grand pem[mican] last night' (22 January), 'then this morning had fine real pem, good half tin dry, a whole biscuit and decent tea and butter. I felt very full after but a most pleasant feeling' (23 January). At the same time his hair was falling out in handfuls and he was shedding patches of beard on one side. These symptoms, and others noted earlier, have been thought by some to result from excessive intake of vitamin A, which is high in the liver of the Greenland dog.[40] This, however, is merely a theory—a pretentious and probably wrong theory, in the view of Phillip Law. 'It's completely unproven . . . The symptoms that were described are exactly the ones you get from cold exposure. You don't have to predicate a theory of this sort to explain the soles coming off your feet.'[41]

On 28 January Madigan Nunatak, a large rock outcrop, became visible to the north. This landmark was just 20 miles from Winter Quarters, and Mawson estimated he had a mere 30 miles to go. He still had 2 lb of food left. Provided he could cheat crevasses and be spared an extended blizzard, he would make it. By now, however, as sometimes happens after extended trials, he had something special coming to him. On 29 January, after forcing his abused feet over another 5 excruciating miles, through the gloom and the low drift whipped by a 45 mph gale, something darkly vague loomed to the right—'300 yds to N of me a cairn with black cloth on it. I went to it and found food and note from McLean, Hurley, Hodgeman—they had left same morning.'[42] The little note, its chances so slim of ever being found, was full of news:

> 29 I. 1913: *Situation* 21 Miles S60E of Aladdins Cave.
>
> Two ice mounds one 14 M S60E of Aladdins Cave the other 5 miles SE of Aladdins—the first has biscuits chocolate etc. Please find biscuits pemmican, ground biscuits tea etc.
>
> Aurora arrived Jan. 13th. Wireless messages received. All parties safe. Amundsen reached Pole December 1911—remained there three days. Supporting party left Scott 150 M from Pole in the same month. Bage reached 300 M SE 1,7" from Magnetic Pole. Bickerton: 160 M West. Aeroplane broke down 10 M out. Madigan went 270 M East.
>
> Good luck from
>> Hodgeman
>> Hurley
>> McLean
>> A L McLean[43]

Three days later, at 7.00 p.m. on 1 February, Mawson reached the comparative comfort of Aladdin's cave with its equipment and store of provisions. It took him that long because high winds on the slippery coastal ice slopes had forced him to spend much time in his tent fashioning crampons, his others having been discarded after crossing the Mertz Glacier. Now, so close to his destination, a week-long blizzard kept him in the cave until 8 February, for he dared not descend the 5 steep miles of slippery ice to the Hut in such weather, without proper crampons and in a severely weakened condition. Would the ship have left? Would a party have stayed behind? The answer was almost certainly 'Yes' to both, though he must have imagined finding Winter Quarters deserted. Descending on the 8th, in clear warm weather, he could see no ship in Commonwealth Bay. Further down, the boat harbour came into view, and after a few more miles, as he wrote that night,

> I saw 3 men working at something on one side of it. I waved for about 30 seconds and then got an answering wave . . . I continued slowly downwards and they ran to meet me. As it was a very steep climb up it took some minutes for the first man to arrive . . . Bickerton it was . . . Very soon 5 had arrived—Bickerton, Bage, Madigan, McLean, Hodgeman—and I learnt that the ship had left finally only a few hours before and they, with a new wireless man, comprised the party left by Capt Davis to search for us.
>
> I briefly recited the disaster and cause of my late arrival from the sledge journey. There were tears in several eyes as the story proceeded.
>
> They took my sledge in tow and we proceeded to the Hut. What a grand relief! To have reached civilization after what appeared utterly impossible. What a feeling of gratitude to Providence for such a deliverance.[44]

How did he look as he was ushered into the Hut? Can one learn at this distance of time? The late Eric Rudd, a student under Mawson and Madigan from 1927 to 1930, told the author that he remembered Madigan talking on this subject around a camp-fire in 1930, during a camel trip from Alice Springs out to Western Australia: 'The gist, as I got it from Madigan, was that Mawson was in a mess, but physically he was much better than any of them expected'.[45] This is not surprising when one looks dispassionately at the diary entries on food intake following the death of Mertz, when Mawson was certainly not on starvation rations. He had also had the period of solitary recuperation in Aladdin's cave.

Inside the Hut he was introduced to the new wireless operator. No introduction was necessary, however, for Mawson had turned this man down a year ago. Now he had turned up again, like a bad penny, with his enthusiasm for wireless and his messianic eyes. He had been appointed by the AAE's Australian manager, Conrad Eitel, with Edgeworth David's agreement, and his name was Sidney N. Jeffryes.

7 MADNESS ALL AROUND

AFTER THE *Aurora* had left the main party at Commonwealth Bay the previous year, she had steamed 1500 miles west before finding a suitable site for Wild's Western base—and then it was not solid land but the Shackleton Ice Shelf. From here she had returned to Hobart, arriving on 12 March. Davis then discovered that the man Mawson had appointed Australian manager of the AAE, Conrad Eitel, had suffered an expensive attack of panic. Although the newspapers had reported some of its side-effects, it was subsequently covered up in the interests of the AAE's image, neither Mawson's *Home of the Blizzard* nor Davis's *With the 'Aurora' in the Antarctic* so much as mentioning it.

Mawson seems to have left no detailed contingency plans with Eitel for action in the event of *Aurora*'s not returning by a specific date, perhaps trusting to wireless communication from Macquarie Island and Adélie Land to keep his manager informed. Eitel had sailed with *Toroa* to Macquarie Island and seen the wireless equipment taken ashore there in mid-December 1911. Then, after returning to Melbourne, he had waited to learn of the expedition's progress. His fretting had set in at the beginning of February 1912. Why on earth had no signals been received from Macquarie Island, or, *via* there, from the Antarctic? Whatever had become of *Aurora*? The more Eitel thought about it, the more it seemed that the fate of the AAE was in his hands.

He rushed about and found a ship, the steamer *Manawatu*, paying £3500 out of the AAE account to charter her for a proposed trip to Macquarie Island and further south. She was no ice-breaker. Then he paid £593 8s 7d for docking expenses, repairs and other necessary work.[1] Meanwhile he was panicking Edgeworth David in Sydney into supporting his heroic venture and dashing off letters to the Australasian Wireless Company, complaining that the Telefunken equipment they had supplied had manifestly failed and that the expenses of his relief expedition would be sheeted home to them.[2] Much later, on learning of this affair, Mawson's attitude would be one of contempt, heightened by his discovery that Eitel had overdrawn his salary and failed to account for several hundred pounds of petty cash and two unexplained cheques drawn on the AAE account. Mawson would be prepared to overlook the petty cash and overdrawn salary but not the cheques. He would finally find himself trying to clear these matters up from London in 1916, by which time Eitel would be off to France with a machine-gun company and his wife Florence, who had helped him with the accounts, would be trying to explain things by letter:

(2) Re the Manawatu—That act of heroism, if you only knew—was a splendid one—He said your whole result depended on it & although he thought he would never return, he was on the point of risking his life. I have a long letter here by my side which you ought to read from the dear old Professor urging him to start at once before too late & saying he would go too if he dared 'wag' it again from the Varsity... Also Prof. Masson approved most strongly.[3]

Fortunately for Eitel, signals from Macquarie Island came through by mid-February stating that all was well. The £3500 was recovered but the accounts were hundreds of pounds to the bad.

Through the winter of 1912 *Aurora* had undertaken a cruise south of Victoria to latitude 52°, then east to Macquarie Island and thence *via* the Auckland Islands to Lyttelton in New Zealand, carrying out soundings to chart the ocean floor, and trawlings for biological specimens using the Prince of Monaco's equipment. The ship returned to Melbourne on 17 August. A spring cruise was planned to the vicinity of Macquarie Island and the Auckland Islands for November and December 1912, under Davis, scientific work to be supervised by Professor T. T. Flynn, biologist, of Hobart. Shortly before the ship was due to set out, Davis and Eitel had a disagreement over their respective spheres of authority, and on 11 November Eitel wrote, 'You are suspended from the command of the *Aurora*'.[4] He had already informed Edgeworth David of the disagreement and David replied on 7 November, warning that nothing must be done before consulting him and Masson. 'I have this of course in writing from Dr Mawson'.[5] This letter reached Eitel just as he was sacking Mawson's second-in-command, and he promptly backed down.[6]

Following this cruise, *Aurora* set out from Hobart on 26 December 1912 for Adélie Land, reaching Commonwealth Bay on 13 January 1913, and waited there for Mawson to return. With nothing to do, the able seamen became bored. One of them was Bertram Clive Lincoln, who resented Davis's having made the men work Sundays during the voyage south. On 29 January he wrote,

> This afternoon when I relieved the man at the wheel . . . he went to the big telescope . . . and was just going to have a look when the mate happened to see him and snarled out, 'Keep your eye out of that, Schroeder' as if the man would defile it by looking through, Schroeder then said 'I am only looking for Dr Mawson', the mate snapped back 'Never mind Dr Mawson, get off '. . . . If the officers only heard us talking in the fore-castle sometimes there [*sic*] ears would burn as they would know then how much we despise them.[7]

Lincoln's diary provides a different view from that normally received of AAE life on board *Aurora*.

Following pencilled instructions left by Mawson, Davis steamed east on 29 January, scanning the coast as far as the Mertz Glacier tongue. Seeing nothing, he returned. Most of the Adélie Land party had consigned Mawson, Ninnis and Mertz to eternity. 'I don't think we will ever see them again', Hannam confided to his diary, Frank Stillwell was concurring, and Laseron was using the past tense: 'The poor old chief—we loved him with all his faults'.[8] Still Davis waited. On 6 February he was pestered by Hannam, who was fretting about the way the gale was making *Aurora* unsteerable. 'How long are we likely to hang on here?' Hannam whinged (his diary preserving the words). Davis turned on him. 'Until the fucking ship sinks! And you'll wish you were in *Dux Ipse*'s place, as, if he's on the plateau his troubles are over, and ours are only commencing!'[9]

Concerned about the increasing risk of not getting through to Wild's base as autumn approached (though February is in fact the *best* month for sailing in Antarctic waters, according to Phillip Law), and having appointed Madigan, McLean, Bickerton, Bage and Hodgeman, with Jeffryes, to stay behind for a second year as a relief expedition, Davis steamed out of Commonwealth Bay on 8 February. Following Mawson's return to the hut that same day, *Aurora* was recalled by wireless, but when she returned the gales, in Davis's view, made it dangerous to put the boat out to collect the men. Knowing they were safe and well provisioned, and their wireless mast re-erected, he felt duty-bound to strike west in relief of Wild's party.[10] This decision was not liked by the crew. C. J. Hackworth, one of their number, confided to his diary,

> He made no attempt to put off in the boat which could very easily have been done as all of us were ready to go in the boat at any time and would have risked anything to get those men aboard. It is a disgrace to the Expedition to turn away like this and leave a man in such bad health in this awful hole.
>
> All hands aboard the ship have turned away from Adele Land [sic] very unwillingly and disappointedly—in fact, very angry at the idea of it all and would be very glad to turn back again as the wind is now dropping.[11]

The following day broke calm. Phillip Law is also strongly critical of Davis's decision to steam west, but concedes that Mawson's recovery was better assured on land than at sea—in fact Mawson told Law that he probably would have died had he gone on the ship.[12]

So the 'relief expedition', with their recuperating commander, faced another year in the Antarctic. Although Mawson had always reserved the option of a second year (in fact Davis must have reckoned on this possibility by virtue of taking Jeffryes south), it was now undesirable. He devotes a few pages to this period in *Home of the Blizzard* but there is something forced in consolatory sentences like 'Every avenue of scientific work was not yet closed'.[13] Only when he writes about the wireless does this section come alive, and Jeffryes was the hero of the hour, for it was he who, as early as February, made two-way contact with Macquarie Island where a small team were also staying on for another year, he who kept the stays of the masts fastened, he who was their link to the world every night. McLean noted on 17 March, 'Jeffries—we call him Jeff— . . . takes spy-glasses out with him to see that everything is ship shape. We chuff him about his conscientious scruples. Of course the real event of the day consists in the wireless intelligence and by 10.30 we are all agog.'[14] His excellent work, 'tedious and nerve-wracking'[15] Mawson calls it, enabled the party to send a large number of messages to Australia and receive replies.

The men nursed and cared for their leader and later told Paquita 'that for the first few weeks he would follow them round, not so much to talk to them as just to be with them'.[16] He missed her, as he told her in numerous letters that had to remain unsent; she was free to change her mind and it was unfair to expect her to wait. He himself was reduced 'to roaming in the empyrean of mind. It is now midnight—and where are you? And where am I? And where might we not have been?'[17] He could receive wireless messages from her in morse code and reply to them. One example: 'Greatly joyed receipt your message gratified you well glad letters parcel love to self and family Dr McLean producing quite good results new hair restorer am very fit now Mawson' (3 April 1913).[18] He could control the formerly loose cannon Eitel, warning him that Davis was second-in-command 'and has precedence of yourself in all matters . . . You have apparently been very foolishly advised in action with the wireless people.' He sent messages to the families of Mertz and Ninnis, and to the press. There were others to and from the King, and later from the Queen—King George V Land,

east of Commonwealth Bay, and Queen Mary Land in the region
of the Western Base, were named for them. From Kathleen Scott
came the words 'Love and sympathy come back safe'. He replied to
this by wireless in early March, having just learned of her tragic
loss: in early 1912 Robert Falcon Scott and four of his men, having
reached the South Pole only to find that Roald Amundsen's team
had beaten them to the goal, had died on their return march, just a
few miles from safety. Mawson also wrote a letter to Kathleen Scott
at this time, though it could not be posted until the following
summer:

> My dear Lady Scott,
>
> Your message touches my heart and presses the key of the most
> tender feelings imaginable. So notwithstanding the lengthy delay
> which will intervene between the writing and receipt of these lines,
> I cannot refrain from addressing myself to you, now, nearest the scene
> which has riveted your mind so long . . .
>
> My own case has enlightened me in the secret feelings of the
> soul, the willingness to pass into oblivion . . .

To Mawson, as to many in his day, and others who admire him now,
the highest and purest virtue was valour. He eulogised Scott's
heroism, and ended, 'Please accept my love. / Douglas Mawson'.[19]

For all his good wireless work, Sidney Jeffryes' photograph
nowhere appears in *Home of the Blizzard*, nor does his signature
stand among those of the land parties in Volume II. Mawson's diary
reveals the development of the 'case'.

Towards the end of May he observed that 'Hodg, Madi & Bage
are doing the best work for expedition at present time. McLean is
good, but cannot find any research to do—not too ready to skin
animals. Works hard at *Blizzard* [*Adélie Blizzard*, a periodical
produced through this winter]. Jeffryes good so far. Bickerton likes
doing things he likes to do.'[20] Five weeks later, deep into the winter
blackness, all appeared serene. 'Everyone seems quiet tonight',
McLean noted on 4 July. 'The Doc writing, Hodge sewing, Madi
working at the Meteorological Book, Bob sleeping, Jeff reading.
Bick—I think sleeping—no! fitting a new cap for the mast.'[21]

Then, on 10 July, Jeffryes confided to Mawson that venereal disease from years back was bringing on 'seminal emissions'—would Mawson please ask McLean to give him some poison?

In fact there was no trace of venereal disease in Jeffryes. The next day he 'wished we would state clearly all the accusations against him'. There was nothing but good feeling, Mawson replied. On 17 July Jeffryes, 'though curiously logical at times', was warning that the others 'will all be put in gaol on arrival in Australia for contemplating murdering him'. Mawson worried that he might become violent, 'so always have someone watching him. Last night I felt almost at the limit, my brain . . . on the point of bursting. All the worries and the indoor life, want of exercise and Jeffryes' trouble on top.' On 21 July 'He made a speech in which he spoke clearly and well, but the matter foolish cant'. On 27 July Jeffryes, believing his life in peril, tendered his 'resignation'.[22]

A particularly worrying aspect of all this was Jeffryes' continuing threat to 'expose' the others on return to Australia. It therefore became imperative that he acknowledge he was unwell. Following the 'resignation', Mawson assembled the men including Jeffryes around the long table and read out a prepared speech, jotted down in pencil and still preserved, though (like so much in Mawson's vast store of papers) never before printed and never before studied, if ever read. The speech merits quoting at length, for in watching how Mawson handles this crisis one sees his leadership under stress. He had read, just months earlier, F. A. Cook's horrifying account of Adrien de Gerlache's *Belgica* expedition, the first to winter in the Antarctic. He therefore knew that in the long Antarctic night, melancholia and madness can be contagious, and that madness in particular must be ruthlessly contained—isolated. In Jeffryes' case it had to be 'him' and 'us', and if this intensified his paranoia, so be it. Spirits might even be *lifted* at Jeffryes' expense if one chose the words with cold and steady calculation, refusing to give in to a decadent compassion, and this was why Mawson wrote the speech out rather than trusting himself to two or three points. 'Have I not to thank Jeff', he began,

> for the steady and constant manner in which he has selflessly laboured during the past month, culminating in his efforts of today

to help on the work of the expedition? I might add that in this modest member... we have one who in return for his giant efforts is seeking, to use his own words, for no more credit than falls to the share of any ordinary member of the expedition. This sacrifice is touching.

To leave such pleasant topics as this chivalrous devotion and descend to more mundane matters, I wish to make a public statement... This is the outcome of an intimation received in lead pencil characters on the back of a torn astronomical form and thrown before me yesterday to the effect that he (Jeffryes) therewith resigned from his position as a member of the expedition.

This news will be received by all with the utmost concern because of the meritable sacrifice which it entails to our comrade. The accommodation houses are few and far between in the Antarctic and I am quite concerned that our tariff is too high to enable Jeffryes to remain at this admirable hostel. We are certainly prepared to let out an ice cave for his use on comparatively moderate terms. But then the acquisition of food and raiment is to be considered, and even the uniform which he stands up in is the property of the expedition, to be returned if required on the termination of relations... Furthermore, having withdrawn from the expedition I fail to see how he can ever get back to civilisation, for a passage on the *Aurora* necessitates the signing of an affidavit as a member of the expedition.

What a dilemma! Fortunately it is all a vapour of the mind for as every thinking person knows, there is no such thing as 'resignation' on an enterprise of this kind. You might as well assume that the luckless passenger on a sinking liner could resign and be wafted back by fairy wings to *terra firma*. No—every member of the expedition signed articles just as binding and onerous as in the case of military or marine service. Those articles give me supreme command for good or bad, during the term of the expedition, after which any complaints can be referred to the civil courts of the home land. Jeff, as you all know, has been unwell... Unfortunately he is not yet sufficiently recovered to understand that he was ill. In view of this, possibilities in the future are suggested, especially as he believing that we have been doing him an injustice instead of the boot being on the other foot, has repeatedly stated . . . that he intends seeking retribution at . . . the civil courts . . .

For his own sake, if for no other, we do not wish this to take place, for it can only have one end—a revertion onto his own head, and a blighting of his life . . . However much liking some people may have for dirty linen, we have none. If Jeffryes takes this action it is the clearest possible evidence that he is still ill. What I desire is that he shall recognise that he was ill for a time and to continue a full member of the expedition, then the matter will be forgotten.

I believe that the handing in of what he pleases to call his 'resignation' was the outcome of overhearing a conversation between myself and Dr McLean . . . when McLean . . . stayed my hand from forwarding to Jeffryes an edict . . . that before landing in Australia Jeff would either have to own up to his illness or consider himself dismissed from the expedition . . . On account of his recent actions I now reiterate this statement . . . In the event of Jeff convincing people by some subtlety that he was not ill then the excommunication comes into force . . .

You can see, gentlemen, the necessity for this provision, it is his illness that maintains him as a member of the expedition now. Any normal member acting as he has done would have been court-martialled and dismissed long ago.

In the case of knavery my jurisdiction under the present circumstances can go no further than placing mutineers in irons.

I hope this explanation will clear the atmosphere a little.[23]

The scene speaks for itself. Mawson consolidates and stimulates the *camaraderie*, isolates the infection, prescribes a 'cure', and guarantees the survival of the team. Harsh measures, harsh world.[24]

Jeffryes' fluctuating moods and mania had to be tolerated to some extent, since he was the only one who could operate the wireless. He worsened again in early September, Mawson noting in his diary, 'Jeffryes is quite off. Tells me that he and I are the only two not mad . . . He starts to put spikes in his boots, says that he is going sledging.'[25] The following day he was found transmitting in Mawson's name: 'Five men not well probably Jeffryes and I may have to leave the hut'.[26] Mawson immediately ordered Bickerton, who was extremely slow with morse, to transmit the following to Ainsworth at Macquarie Island: 'Censure all messages Jeffryes insane Mawson'.[27] From now on Bickerton or Mawson normally ran the wireless, though Jeffryes on his better days would operate it— 22 September was one of those better days:

> He speaks moderately rationally at dinner. Plays gramophone after dinner. Mclean says to him when playing (gramophone) a weird thing: 'I never can understand that piece.' Jeffryes immediately packs his things, turns the sennegrass out of its bag in next room, puts his clothes in, tells Dad [McLean] that he is moving.
>
> 8 pm: I am now waiting for him to come and say goodby to me.
>
> 10 pm: After standing at the verandah door for some time he returned and later went on with the wireless.[28]

As summer approached he improved, and by the time *Aurora* anchored in Commonwealth Bay on 13 December he seemed almost normal.

By then Mawson, with Madigan and Hodgeman, had made a short sledging journey to recover instruments left by the Eastern Coastal Party at Mt Murchison, 50-odd miles out by the western edge of the Mertz Glacier. Not finding them for the massive winter snowfalls, and unable for blizzards to reach others cached by the Southern Party, they returned just as *Aurora* was entering the Bay. On this trip Mawson carried a copy of *Hamlet*, and as he lay in the tent he jotted down in his diary lines he found profound or memorable:

> When sorrows come they come not single spies, /
> But in battalions   (IV.v.74)
> There is a divinity that shapes our ends /
> Rough-hew them how we will   (V.II.10)
> The undiscovered country, from whose bourn /
> No traveller returns   (III.I.79)
> What a noble mind is here o'erthrown   (III.I.149)

Then directly below he wrote:

In blizzard bound.
The dreary outlook, the indefinite surroundings, the neverending seethe, rattle and ping of the drift. The flap of the tent; the uncertainty of clearance, the certainty of protracted abomination. The dwindling of food, the deterioration of tent, dogs, etc. The irksomeness, bone-wearying cramped quarters, the damp or the cold. The anxiety for the future, the disappointment for prospects.[29]

The blizzard had become his metaphor for the blindness, frustration and disappointments which mark one's progress to an unknown, pre-shaped end. And Ninnis and Mertz, further east, across whose graves this blizzard blew—how were their deaths to be viewed, philosophically, in retrospect? Mawson put it eloquently in a letter he had recently written to William Bragg: 'the fortunes of war', 'part of the game'.[30]

After long days of packing and stowing, *Aurora* left Adélie Land, but not for Australia in the first instance. This voyage was to be used for further marine work. After skirting the pack as far to the west as the newly-named Queen Mary Land, the ice coasts to the west of Wild's base, abandoned the previous summer, were explored, oceanographical work continued, dredgings and tow-nettings carried out.[31] Not until early February 1914 were they homeward-bound for Adelaide.

Their first sight of civilization came on 21 February 1914, still five days from home—one of the great sailing ships, the *Archibald Russell*, full-rigged in brilliant white, fifty-four days out from Buenos Aires and bound for South Australia. Like *Aurora* she was a relic of the past in a world of steamers, submarines and dreadnoughts.

On *Aurora*'s deck, watching her pass, stood Sidney N. Jeffryes. He stood apart, hunched in his overcoat, the bleak south wind against his face. Soon he would be in Adelaide, ushered onto the Melbourne Express, destination Toowoomba—destination unreached. There his sister Norma waited. She learned with horror of her brother's story from his own letter and from Mawson, who telegrammed her from Adelaide and wrote a brutally frank letter.[32] She telegrammed back: 'Very worried . . . send here with warder all expenses journey defrayed this end failing that I will go to Adelaide'. There was no warder. She felt let down, and said so in a long and eloquent letter.[33] But to Mawson Jeffryes appeared normal in Adelaide.

On the train, it must be said, he was not normal, and was escorted off at Ararat, directly into the local asylum. Soon he was the guest of various Melbourne asylums, writing to Mawson through 1915. The style was King James Version. 'We seven were chosen that scripture might be fulfilled', he revealed. 'I am come as Christ in the Spirit of Prophecy, & the Wrath of God in the Flesh.' The asylums were nests of Freemasonry, his enemies compassed him about, but he knew his Antarctic commander for one of the redeemed, blessed on the path 'where Ninnis was lost, & you stood by Mertz on the plateau'. There were trials ahead, but God would see Mawson through. 'The war', he wrote on 20 August 1915, 'shall continue 1260 days in all'.[34] In this, at least, he was a false prophet.

Had Jeffryes known he was of unsound mind when he sailed south, then (as Mawson told the sister) it was criminal to have come and he deserves no sympathy. Mawson found it impossible to believe he did not know, but the sister had never before detected the slightest sign of insanity.[35] It comes down to choice and fate. Jeffryes chose to sail south, letting the Furies loose, on himself.

The major geographical achievements of the AAE were well known in Australia a year before Mawson returned. Scott's disaster, however, overshadowed them, and their full significance was not widely appreciated at the time. It was an Englishman, J. Gordon Hayes, who in 1928 first put them into proper perspective. 'Sir Douglas Mawson's Expedition', he wrote, 'judged by the magnitude both of its scale and of its achievements, was the greatest and most consummate expedition that ever sailed for Antarctica'.[36] From the Main Base a total of '2600 miles [out and back] were sledged entirely over countries previously unknown'. This included, aside from Mawson's journey and marches by support parties, one journey of 160 miles west, one of 300 miles to the south-south-east to within 50-odd miles of the South Magnetic Pole Area, and another of 270 miles to the east, much of it over sea ice. From the Western Base 800 miles were traversed including a journey of over 200 miles west to Gaussberg, and another of around 100 miles east to the Denman Glacier. All of this was in the face of often appalling weather. During the ninety-one days of Mawson's own journey, for instance, there were forty-three days with winds of force 8 or stronger, seventeen days with winds of force 10 and over, and seven days with winds of force 12 (80 mph).

In addition to the exploratory activity there was the pioneering wireless work (including the use of wirelessed time signals to establish the fundamental longitude for Cape Denison), the exploratory and oceanographical work of the *Aurora*, and the diverse scientific work at each of the three bases. But Hayes's most telling point is his distinguishing between territory *discovered* and territory *explored*—that is, charted. By this test Amundsen discovered 1300 miles of land and 450 miles of shelf ice but explored very little of it. Scott's first (*Discovery*) expedition discovered 1050 miles but explored only about 200; his second (*Terra Nova*) expedition discovered about 285 miles of new ground but explored only 100. Shackleton's BAE discovered 1035 miles of new land and explored 'most of this'. Hayes tabulates the results in very clear form.

As [Mawson] discovered and explored so much, care has been taken not to over-estimate his results. Amundsen, owing to his skill in the use of dogs, comes next in geographical discovery alone; but his maps make accuracy very difficult, and his work was not on the same level as that of the other explorers. Mawson's result, for one expedition, is magnificent, when his scientific work is included also.[37]

Dr Phillip Law, former director of ANARE, reiterates Hayes's distinction between discovery and exploration, on both of which counts Mawson's AAE is so impressive.[38]

Even at the time, as the AAE was returning to Australia in February 1914, there was one man qualified to judge who summed things up correctly—W. S. Bruce, leader of the fine *Scotia* expedition of 1902–4 to Graham Land: 'It is not too much to say', Bruce wrote to Mawson, 'without any intent to flatter, that your expedition has been the most successful of any recent Antarctic expedition. As a scientific man you have trusted your own powers to conduct the expedition entirely on scientific lines without seeking to secure popular éclat by proposing a sensational advance of an athletic kind'.[39]

The final word on the scientific work should come from the commander himself, as expressed in a letter to Edgeworth David years later (he would never say this publicly):

> The men were nearly all very young and without previous extended field experience and that meant the utmost drain upon my abilities in order to secure the measure of results that accrued. Even with dear old J. K. Davis . . . the oceanographical work apart from the sounding was quite unsatisfactory until I was on board during the last summer . . . Having had a broad scientific training I spent myself in all branches of the observations wherever most needed.[40]

The great value of the AAE, then, derived from the quality of its scientific leadership. Unlike the Shackleton and Scott expeditions, it always put science first, with the scientific ideal embodied in the commander himself.

8 FAME WITHOUT FORTUNE

AFTER DISEMBARKING, Mawson's destination was the South Australian Hotel on North Terrace, opposite Parliament House. Here Paquita Delprat and her mother had taken a balcony room just to receive him. As the former recalled it,

> There was a message . . . that I was to wait for Douglas there . . . It is hard to describe the feelings one has when meeting someone whose image has lived only in one's thoughts for so long. When he entered the room, I just had time to think: 'Yes, of course, that's what he is like!' Douglas said: 'You have had a long time to wait', and then everything was all right. We stayed together for the rest of the day.[1]

They dined in the room, a foursome, for the man now closest to Mawson, John King Davis, had been invited to join them. Mme Delprat had come over from Melbourne, where she and her husband were now living.

There were two public receptions, one at the Adelaide Town Hall, the other in the Elder Hall at the University, attended by the Governor-General, Lord Denman. The Chancellor, Sir Samuel Way, 'waxed most eloquent', Mawson later recalled in a letter to Way's biographer:

> During the speech Way referred to my impending marriage to Paquita. At the conclusion of proceedings he brought his Excellency

down from the dais to the front row of the audience and, saying 'and this is the happy lady', he pushed Miss Murray (Sir George Murray's sister) forward to meet Lord Denman. The latter blinked in surprise (he had seen a picture of Paquita in the daily Press) until Miss Murray saved the situation by pushing Paquita (who stood beside her) forward, bringing the event to a happy and hilarious conclusion.[2]

Amid the celebration, Mawson was worried. Following the second year in the Antarctic the AAE's costs had risen to £57 000, and while there had been supplementary contributions including an additional £5000 from the Commonwealth Government, the debt in early March 1914 stood at over £8000. This was reduced by £3700 almost immediately with the sale of the ship and materials—*Aurora* went to Shackleton for a low £3200, which was fair, given the thousands Sir Ernest's appeal had raised.[3] Mawson had tried and failed to sell her with her scientific equipment to the Australian Government as an oceanographical and coastal survey ship—for £15 000! This would have cleared the debt and paid for the publication of the scientific results to boot.[4]

The wedding, a large affair, took place on 31 March 1914 in Melbourne, at Holy Trinity Church of England, Balaclava, and was followed by a wedding tea in the gardens of the Delprat home, Linden, in Williams Road, Toorak. Edgeworth David came down from Sydney, and University Registrar Charles Hodge from Adelaide. Davis was best man. Other members of the AAE acted as ushers. The bride's necklace of black opals was a gift of the bridegroom, as were the diamond-and-emerald necklets worn by the bridesmaids. Inside the marquee at Linden an 'Aurora Australis' trailed overhead, while on every table sat a flower-decked model of the *Aurora*, coated in white sugar, around which, in their black-and-white icing, Adélie penguins stood guard. An 'iceberg' surmounted the wedding cake, on each tier of which sat groups of miniature sledge dogs and snow petrels.[5] The bride and groom spent the night at the Oriental Hotel in Collins Street. Next morning they took a taxi back to Linden, then went directly to Port Melbourne where they boarded the *Orama* for Marseilles, along with Davis, Dr Archie McLean and other friends.

While the ship was at Suez they visited Cairo, in Naples they were guests of honour at a luncheon given by Admiral Leonardo Cattolica, President of the Royal Geographical Society of Italy, and at Marseilles they were met by William Heinemann and entertained at the local Geographical Society before travelling by train to Paris, where Mawson met French scientists. On 3 May they arrived at London's Victoria Station where they were welcomed by Sir Ernest and Lady Shackleton, Frank Wild, John Scott Keltie (RGS Secretary) and others.[6] They had booked into the Grosvenor— Mawson and Paquita were in adjoining rooms, 115 and 116, Davis next door in 117, McLean around the other side in 162— commander, wife, second-in-command, and amanuensis.[7] McLean was crucial, for first priority was to complete *Home of the Blizzard* and reap the royalties.

Mawson and McLean worked assiduously, McLean substantially re-writing and compressing Mawson's drafts, ensuring grammatical correctness, and giving the book its sense of style. According to Mawson, in a letter in which he purposely downplays McLean's role, McLean wrote Chapters IX and XXVIII from skeletons supplied by Mawson, substantially added to Chapters XXIII and XXIV, and supplied Appendix V.[8] There is no doubt, however, that McLean went over all the other chapters and heavily edited and improved them, as is clear from his letter of 13 December 1916 to Mawson, cited below. For this considerable labour he was paid £300. Two years later Mawson would be contemplating a shorter, more popular version, in one volume, and McLean would write to him on the subject. This important letter is instructive on the genesis of the first edition:

> If I had not had so much to do with the editing of the Book—it was mostly much more than editing—it would be impertinent for me to make these remarks, but I do think this 'cutting down' of the Book is very much my affair. In this way: you have held me responsible in the Preface for any literary style which the Book may possess and if the amended or reduced Book is to go forth with any gram-

matical slips, inartistic arrangement of chapters or abrupt transitions
I will not have my name in the Preface. . . . It was 6 months of very
hard work . . . You could hardly expect me to be human unless I
regarded the work almost with a jealous affection. Not altogether
jealous because I was ready to submit to others' better judgment.
Dr [H. R.] Mill [whose eyesight was bad] listened to every word of
it. You can hardly expect me, for you gave me almost complete
freedom, not to be sensitive about it . . . The 'Morning Post' said 'It
is literature all the way through'.[9]

The contemplated popular edition to which McLean refers was
turned down because the expensive first edition in two volumes,
which appeared after the outbreak of war, early in 1915, made very
little money. Mawson received a £500 advance in September 1914
and another £500 on publication the following January. His
royalties were agreed at 20 per cent.[10] Because of the war,
Heinemann rightly limited production to around 3500 sets,
including those sold in the United States. Their London works,
with all set-up type and blocks, was burnt down during the war,
but there was no call for a further printing in any case. In the
United States and the United Kingdom, by war's end, only some
2200 sets had sold, and the British sales included Australia. (The
American edition was substantially the British, with minor changes,
for instance to the imprint page.) A hundred or so went to
reviewers, perhaps another hundred were given away (including
twenty-five 'private copies' and thirty-seven 'official copies',
stamped on the fly-leaf 'With the Author's Compliments'). Quite a
few exist with personal inscriptions by Mawson. Heinemann sold
the sets for 36/- in Britain, two guineas (42/-) in Australia. Prices
on the remaining 1100 sets were savagely reduced to 12/- after the
war. Unlike Shackleton's *Heart of the Antarctic*, none were made
available in an autographed 'edition de luxe' bound in vellum and
lettered in gold. From the two-volume *Home of the Blizzard*
Mawson made £673 3s 5d to 20 April 1918, in addition to the
£1000 advance, less McLean's £300.[11]

The summer of 1914 saw the last London Season before the
Great War, and everyone half-sensed the coming storm. Money and

power and their flagrant display seemed to be all that counted. The *Graphic* and the *Illustrated London News* were full of photographs of grand balls, lavish dinners, of military and naval exercises, the latest dreadnoughts, fold-out panoramas of the entire frustrated fleet—which must surely *soon* be used?

In the social London of that summer the Mawsons were relatively small fry—he was not as thoroughly 'lionised' as has sometimes been made out, but his presence was noticed at Court and in the newspapers and weeklies. Scott, even in death, largely eclipsed him, for the spectacular goal, the glory of epic failure, were strongly to the taste of a nation spiritually spent.

On Wednesday, 13 May, Mawson was received at Buckingham Palace by the King, who showed much interest in the expedition.[12] Then on Saturday, 30 May, he had an audience with Queen Alexandra and the Dowager Empress of Russia at Marlborough House.[13] And around midday on Monday, 29 June, the day after the assassination of Archduke Franz Ferdinand of Austria-Hungary, he was knighted by the King in the Throne Room at St James's Palace, along with many others. Over a month earlier, on Friday, 22 May, Sir George Reid, Australian High Commissioner (like Mawson aware of the knighthood well in advance), held a luncheon for him at the British Empire Club—Earl Curzon, Lord Sydenham, Lord Tennyson, Lord Chelmsford, Lord Lamington and other notables were present.[14]

There were good musical offerings. At Covent Garden the Mawsons saw Caruso and Emmy Destinn in *Tosca*; at Drury Lane, Chaliapin in *Boris Godunov*, one of his great roles; at Queen's Hall, Frieda Hempel, the outstanding fioritura soprano of the time, in her first concert appearance in England. They attended the theatre too, seeing Mrs Patrick Campbell, the original Eliza, in Shaw's *Pygmalion* at His Majesty's Theatre, and Lilian Braithwaite, foremost actress of her age, in *Mr Wu* at the Strand. At Olympia they watched the Royal Naval and Military Tournament, and on Wednesday evening, 10 June, they attended the Anglo-American Centenary Peace Ball, an extravaganza in costume at the Albert Hall. It featured a procession of the nations, and the Australian contingent, arranged by Lady Reid, included Mawson.[15]

AAE Main Base locality, Cape Denison, Adélie Land, January 1912. Mawson rests on the edge of the launch at the boat harbour. The penguin is the star.

Late January 1912, and the main hut nears completion.

Geologist in the field. Mawson at Cape Denison, 1912

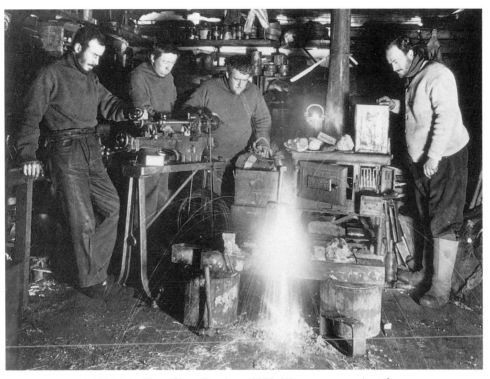

AAE Main Base, Cape Denison, 1912. Mawson supervises the
thermiting of a broken vice.

AAE Main Base, Cape Denison, 1912: Midwinter dinner

AAE Main Base, Cape Denison, 1912: W. H. Hannam at the wireless

Mawson kitted for sledging, on the way to Aladdin's Cave, November 1912

Fate rules here. Mertz and Ninnis arrive at Aladdin's Cave with dogs,
impatient to set out with Mawson on the far-eastern sledging journey,
10 November 1912. Neither would return.

Survivor by existential force of will, and special favour, perhaps: Mawson in recuperation at Cape Denison, 1913

BELOW AAE, January 1914. Members of the Main Base party who wintered a second year, and the Macquarie Island party, returning on *Aurora*. From left, back row, standing: Blake, McLean; main row, standing: Bickerton, Hunter, Ainsworth, Madigan, Bage, Mawson, Sandell, Correll; front row, seated: Hodgeman, Hurley, Hamilton. Jeffryes is somewhere out of sight.

Three transposed stereoscopic pairs, for readers who have the knack of free-viewing in 3-D, or a suitable hand-held viewer. *Aurora* pushes through loose pack-ice.

Captain J. K. Davis (left) and Captain James Davis, an expert on whaling invited on *Aurora*'s cruise south in early 1913, pace the decks.

Western Base party after being picked up by *Aurora*, February 1913

They also serve who only wait: a young Francisca (Paquita)
Adriana Delprat, probably south of Adelaide

Mawson (centre) with (from left) Griffith Taylor, Frank Stillwell,
Edgeworth David and J. K. Davis, *c.* 1914

As an officer with the Ministry of Munitions in England during World War I

October 1916, at sea in the Pacific. Paquita Mawson with baby Patricia sails to San Francisco *en route* to join her husband in England. The baby will be left with family in America for the remainder of the war.

Mawson with Canadian Arctic explorer Vilhjalmur Stefansson at
Rembrandt Studios, Adelaide, August 1924

The Duke and Duchess of York's visit to Adelaide, 1927, Mawson on the left

Wellington, November 1928. Commander Richard E. Byrd, greatest of American Antarctic explorers, with pet dog Igloo, Mawson, and A. Leigh Hunt, founder of the New Zealand Antarctic Society and prime mover in the Sounds hydro-electric scheme which Mawson supported. Byrd was south-bound on his first Antarctic expedition.

Early June 1929. Sir David Orme Masson (left) visits chocolate millionaire Macpherson Robertson in his Melbourne office to accept a donation of £10 000 towards the costs of the BANZARE.

The Duke and Duchess of York, with Prince George, are shown over the *Discovery* by Mawson (right, in customary Homburg), West India Docks, London, mid-1929.

Mawson assists the Duchess, who is trying on a pair of wolfskin mitts.

Just the night before, he had addressed the RGS at Queen's Hall.[16] He used striking lantern slides prepared by Hurley, concluding with a summary of the scientific work—terrestrial magnetism, biology, glaciology, meteorology, bacteriology, tides, auroral observations, and of course geography. In the audience were Belgrave Ninnis's father (of the same name), Shackleton, and members of the AAE—Davis, Wild, McLean, Hodgeman, Bickerton, Madigan, and two of Davis's officers, J. H. Blair and Percy Gray. The following year the RGS would honour Mawson with its Founder's Medal for the AAE's 'highly important scientific results'.

Nothing could distract his mind from the debt, though. He mentioned it to Kathleen Scott over dinner on 21 May. On the spot she offered Mawson £1000, with the understanding that it would remain their secret. Next morning she wrote,

> Dear Dr Mawson
>
> This is just to confirm what I said last night. . . . As I told you, I do not like using the sum derived from the book [*Scott's Last Expedition* (London, 1913)] for private purposes . . . Up till now not a single individual, save those concerned, know the use to which I am putting this money, and unless you, yourself, choose to tell people (as a lever to further subscriptions) . . . you may be quite confident that no one *at all* will hear of this.
>
> It is not only that I have an uncomfortable feeling about this money, but also the amazing fact that I have very little use for it, moreover I feel it a better investment than 4%, and I shall be very grateful to you for helping me out of a difficulty. Very sincerely, Kathleen Scott.[17]

The money went into the AAE account. The following 8 March Lady Scott, now working in a field hospital in France, would write again, asking not to be acknowledged in *Home of the Blizzard*:

> Can't you ever make yourself believe that there still remain in this wicked world people who care more about helping than 'Kudos'! besides it appears merely stupid in the eyes of most people for a woman who is *known* (alas!) to have an income of £700 a year to

keep giving £1000s away—so please, dear person, say no more about it than you can help.[18]

Nothing was ever said on the subject by Mawson, or for that matter Paquita Mawson (who did not like Kathleen Scott), and it has remained an unknown kindness.

Before leaving London one of Mawson's tasks was to assemble the photographs for his book. Hurley sent the required negatives but neglected to send the autochromes. 'Altogether', Mawson wrote him on 18 June 1914,

> the book will suffer considerably by your rushing away into the interior of Australia before the work was adequately arranged for . . . It has annoyed me extremely . . . I gave you my advice as to . . . Shackleton's [incipient Imperial Transantarctic] Expedition and you decided otherwise . . . I would certainly never have advised you, man to man, to go with Shackleton, as you know. However, it is your business, not mine.[19]

His paternal concern for Hurley was fast eroding—the man was impulsive and undependable. He was indisputably a superb photographer, and a very competent technician in the way he superimposed different photographs for effect, but now, just when he was needed to prepare the AAE cine film, he was off on the *Endurance*.

The Mawsons left England for Holland on 20 July, paying a fleeting visit to Paquita's relatives,[20] then went straight to Basel where they spent several hours on 22 July with the Mertz family before catching the evening train to Geneva, thence to Toulon and the ship home. Xavier Mertz had been the family's delight, representing the future of the large Machinen-Fabrik Mertz, and even now they were inconsolable.[21]

On his return to the University of Adelaide, from which he had now been absent for over two and a half years (paying a stand-in out of his own salary), Mawson put in a full term's teaching. In addition he was raising money through public lectures, beginning with one in Sydney on 26 August, illustrated with the cine film he had himself edited on the voyage home.[22] At this time, too, he attended the Sydney meeting of the British Association for the Advancement of Science, speaking on the expedition.

Then at the end of October, as soon as the term's teaching was finished, he and Paquita left the country again, an American lecture tour having been arranged for him through the Lee Keedick Agency in New York City. After giving a series of lectures in New Zealand, and with Paquita now four months pregnant, they sailed eastward for England on the *Ruahine* by way of Cape Horn, Montevideo and Teneriffe.[23] The cold grey waters around southern Chile and Argentina through which their ship ploughed were being contested at that very time, at Cape Coronel on 1 November when Admiral Count Maximilian von Spee sank the British squadron under Admiral Sir Christopher Cradock, and at the Falkland Islands not long after, when von Spee's fortunes were less good. Naval commanders were still noble knights and there was no danger to commercial shipping, yet. The point of travelling first to England was that Mawson had to wind up arrangements previously made to lecture on a Continent now at war. Berlin had been foremost on his agenda—Erich von Drygalski was to have been his host there in January 1915, the Geographical Society of Berlin his audience.[24] He had wanted Cecil Madigan to accompany him and lecture to the AAE film at venues throughout Germany.[25]

From London Paquita returned to Australia almost at once on the same ship by way of Cape Town, while on 2 January 1915 Mawson sailed for New York. His lectures were to commence on 15 January in Washington, DC, where he had an appointment to lunch with the lean, bespectacled, shovel-bearded General Adolphus W. Greely, Civil War veteran, leader and survivor of the horrendous Greely expedition to the Arctic—eighteen dead. Greely had eclipsed Albert Markham's 'furthest north' on Ellesmere Island in 1882, but the promised ship failed to arrive, so Greely led his men south to Cape Sabine, where he had to execute one for stealing another's food. Their plight lasted two years. When the half dozen survivors were found, one of them was blind, with his jaw hanging free, another had lost his hands and feet (presumably removed because of gangrene), and had a spoon affixed to the stump of his right arm. Greely was as skeletal as the others, with his hair in pigtails, his joints bulbous. The graves of some of the dead were uncovered, revealing that their flesh had been carefully (and respect-fully) cut away.[26]

What the Australian and the elegantly precise general discussed is not recorded. Mawson had sought Greely out.[27]. One would have liked to have been present. Greely was highly intelligent, and inter-ested in the physics of glacial ice. He believed that ice should increase in temperature with depth, like rock. Thus at the South Pole the surface temperature might be many degrees below zero, but 2 miles down where the ice meets the basement rock its temperature should be much higher, perhaps zero or above, so that the ice cap, forever pushing out towards the rim of Antarctica, perhaps rides on water, at least where the ice cap is very deep. This is an interesting theory, recently confirmed below the Russian station, Vostok.[28] That evening Mawson dined less interestingly with Alexander Graham Bell, whom he had previously met on his 1910 trip from Vancouver to Sydney. Perhaps they discussed wireless.

It had been one thing to live through the six weeks following Ninnis's death. To have to relate the experience, for hire, night after night, town after town, to inquisitive strangers paying their nickels and dimes for exotic tales was poison to the soul. From 15 January to the end of February he slept in pullman cars. 'These pullman cars are bad', he wrote home. 'It is usual for me to travel each night after the lecture arriving about 7 a.m. at next place.'[29] After two nights' lectures in Washington he caught the train to New York (three nights speaking at the Aeolian Hall), then two nights in Philadelphia, up to Toronto, on to Montreal for three nights, to Ottawa, back to New York (the Engineers' Club), over the East River to Brooklyn, up to Boston for four nights, across to Cleveland, to Detroit, down to Baltimore, over to Harrisburg, thence to Buffalo, around the lake on the Twentieth Century Limited to Toledo, change for Ann Arbor (*via* Detroit), three nights in Chicago (where he was awarded the Helen Culver Gold Medal of the Chicago Geographical Society), then off to Kansas City, St Louis, Davenport, Madison, Crawfordsville, Pittsburgh, and back to New York again, speaking in Brooklyn and Manhattan. Ninnis and Mertz died every night.

After midnight on 4 February, on a train bound for Cleveland, with the moonlit snowfields racing by outside, he wrote his wife one of his regular letters, using a variant of his pet name for her, 'Munk', the significance of which eluded even her:

> The 8 millions of Germans here are storming because America won't side with Germany. They are trying to get the discontented Irish on their side and work points . . .
>
> At Ottawa I struck Lord Richard Neville (formerly a.d.c. Melbourne) and lunched with the Governor, the Duke of Connaught—sat between the Duchess and Princess Patricia. The old girl seems of a German type—the Princess is taking but not as remarkably pretty as made out . . .
>
> The manager at Boston made a mess of it—nobody knew anything of my being there. However had a good look over Harvard University and cemented a former letter aquaintanceship with a prominent Geologist . . .
>
> All this north country is under snow . . . [30]

The total profits to 12 February were $1578.52 after Mawson's expenses; from then to 27 February, $1539.18. The arrangement was that he took half the profits. Now it was New York, at the Webber Theater, matinée *and* evening, every day of March from the 1st to the 28th—total box office, $10 126.05; theatrical and other expenses, $10 986.17; net loss, $860.12.

There were redeeming features of the period aside from the January and February profits, and particularly meetings with friends, colleagues and fellow explorers—lunch with Admiral Robert Peary (first claimant to the North Pole, 1909) at the Peary Arctic Club in New York; honorary membership of the Union Club, the Century Club, and a key to the Explorers' Club, all thanks to generous American friends. At a grand luncheon in March attended by other explorers, he was welcomed by Theodore Roosevelt.[31] Lunching with Captain Robert A. Bartlett, commander of the *Roosevelt* on Peary's polar expedition, and of the ill-starred *Karluk* on the recent, disastrous expedition led by Vilhjalmur Stefansson to the Beaufort Sea (eleven dead), Bartlett confided the reason why Mawson's BAE sledging partner, Alistair Forbes Mackay, and James Murray, the BAE's biologist, had perished there. 'They practically mutinied', Mawson wrote to Paquita, 'and went off on their own to sure death, unfortunately taking a good many others with them'.[32]

It was on this trip that he met William Herbert Hobbs, whose friendship would develop and stale over the years. Hobbs was professor of geology at the University of Michigan at Ann Arbor. In 1914, perhaps angling for a position at Ann Arbor, Mawson had sent him copies of his long articles on the Precambrian stratigraphy and glaciology of the Broken Hill region, one of them essentially his D.Sc. thesis.[33] Hobbs was a pioneer in glaciology and Arctic meteorology and would lead the University of Michigan's three Greenland expeditions of 1926–29. He invited the Australian to speak at Ann Arbor on 12 February. When Mawson arrived from Buffalo that morning, Hobbs drove him to his stately house, in its treed park, so that he could freshen up, then to the university for lunch with the geology faculty. Hobbs had heard glowing accounts of the Washington lectures, and there was a good audience at the university that night. Professor Alenby, a Scot on the faculty, did the introduction, winding up with 'I now have great pleasure in presenting the speaker, Sir Muglas Dawson!'[34] A few days later Hobbs wrote,

> I continue to hear the most enthusiastic comments upon your lecture, and it is quite evident that you took your audience captive from the start. You seem also to have cast a spell over those who met you socially. Speaking of myself I can say that I have never been so drawn to anyone whom I have met for so short a time.[35]

Hobbs hoped another visit would be possible that month, but the itinerary was too tight. Mawson later claimed that he had had verbal proposals of appointment at two American universities on this trip, and Michigan was no doubt one of these. The other was Harvard, according to Sir William Mitchell.[36]

In addition to his paying lectures and the odd guest lecture, he spoke to the American Geographical Society in New York, the National Geographic Society in Washington, and the Chicago Geographical Society. This tour enhanced Mawson's admiration for America, her scientists and explorers, with whom his relations would henceforth be generally warmer than with his British colleagues.

Home in Australia he was presented with a daughter, Patricia, born at the Delprats' in Melbourne on 13 April. In Adelaide he found a flat and settled back into his University work, but these years were obviously not a period of steady geological research—not until 1922 would he again be publishing much in this field. At the end of the year he attended, as his university's representative, Prime Minister Billy Hughes's conference to consider the inauguration of a Bureau (later Institute) of Science and Industry which would evolve into the prestigious Council for Scientific and Industrial Research (CSIR), which later still would become the Commonwealth Scientific and Industrial Research Organisation (CSIRO). Mawson was on the first executive committee charged with devising a scheme to manage and operate the Bureau, and attended a series of meetings in Melbourne in early 1916.

His American tour had stimulated sales of the book, and the debt was reducing. Courtesy of Lloyds Film Agency, the AAE film was screening at the Alhambra Theatre in London from 20 April to 5 May 1915, and later at the Pavilion, Marble Arch, but there had been problems. Gaumont, Mawson's first agents, had seen no margin in it, and he had initiated suit for breach of contract in mid-1914.[37] He had then entered into an arrangement with Lloyds, but by September 1915 they were in voluntary liquidation. War was bad for business. From June 1915 the film was shown in the United States by Keedick, who always supplied an accompanying speaker with a script written by Mawson.[38] Keedick's statement for June–September 1915 recorded a massive deficit of $2071.53 for New York alone (Lyric Theater). Interestingly, the Scott picture also flopped in America. Through 1916 the film ran in smaller towns, the returns still disappointing. (In Australia it would run after the war, but screenings would be spasmodic and not helped by Hurley, who was showing his new *Endurance* film.[39]) Lee Keedick's final statement for the long period from July 1918 to April 1920 would give Mawson a net $1233.37.[40] By then, though, the debt would have disappeared, along with the war and millions of Mawson's contemporaries.

9 THE MILLS OF WAR

THE SINKING OF the *Lusitania* on 7 May 1915 by a German submarine, and the use by Germany of poison gas at this time, hardened Mawson's patriotic attitude to the war. This enemy seemed bound by none of the traditional laws of honour or conscience. 'We have a criminal on a large scale run amok', he wrote to Hobbs in August, 'and it is the sad lot of our generation to cage the wild beast. Great energy, great forethought, great patriotism draining away in this perverted channel, and, worst of all, dragging down with them the other leading nations of Europe.'[1]

Ties of kinship and loyalty to the Empire bound Australia to Britain—many Irish Australians did not share such sentiments, but they were quiet, at least until the idea of conscription began to be pushed by various patriotic groups through 1915. In South Australia it was Mawson who, through the winter and spring of that year, at Edgeworth David's urging, organised the pro-conscription campaign, functioning as its secretary. The climax came with a big rally at the Adelaide Town Hall, where the leaders of the State Government and Opposition pledged themselves to welcome conscription whenever the Federal Government might choose to introduce it.[2]

Meanwhile he was seeking war work, writing on 9 September to the Department of Defence in Melbourne offering his services in any capacity.[3] On 10 November T. Trumble, the Department's assistant secretary, wrote that 'enquiries are being made of the Administrator at Rabaul as to the manner in which your services might be utilized in connection with Australian Forces at Rabaul'.[4] This was patently absurd—the Germans had already been pushed out of the islands. What good could he do there? He would obviously have to go to England where his talents could be useful. By early March 1916 he had persuaded Brig. Gen. Hubert J. Foster, Chief of the Australian General Staff, to write to Chancellor George Murray (Way had just died) asking that the necessary leave be granted:

> The University may demur to granting leave to Sir Douglas on the ground that he has not received any appointment, but it is not possible for the War Office to give him suitable work until he has personally discussed the matter, so that his journey to England is a necessary preliminary to his employment.[5]

Leave was granted, Paquita and the baby moving to the Delprats' in Melbourne, and Mawson soon afterwards sailing east, to see more of America on his way.

After landing at San Francisco he bought a ticket on the spectacularly scenic Denver and Rio Grande Railroad. This ride would appeal to any geologist, the train first winding its tortuous way across the Sierra Nevada, then the even more impressive Rocky Mountains. He visited the Great Salt Lake, Pike's Peak and the mining field at Cripple Creek, and along the way he purchased a .32-calibre Colt automatic pocket pistol (serial no. 19862), which would later be kept loaded in a drawer at his home in Brighton.[6] Then in New York he took the *Orduna* for England, arriving on 10 May 1916.[7]

Literally at once he found himself 'conscripted' as an executive member of the Admiralty Committee for the Shackleton Relief, chaired by Admiral Sir Lewis Beaumont and including Dr W. S. Bruce.[8] Sir Ernest's grandly conceived Imperial Transantarctic Expedition, which had sailed at the outbreak of war, never reached Antarctica. Trapped in the ice of the Weddell Sea in 1915, *Endurance* had finally been crushed to pieces, its human cargo (including

Hurley and Wild) reduced to living for months on the floating ice until it melted and they rowed to uninhabited Elephant Island. From there, in late April 1916, Shackleton and a small group made a 700-mile journey through the turbulent South Atlantic to South Georgia in a small, open rowing boat rigged with a makeshift sail, an unsurpassed feat of genuinely epic proportions recounted in the most thrilling of Antarctic narratives, Shackleton's *South*. In May 1916 the Relief Committee knew nothing of all this—Sir Ernest's expedition had not been heard from for almost two years, and despite the exigencies of war something must be done for them. Mawson even toyed with going on the relief expedition himself.[9] A vessel was prepared, J. K. Davis appointed to command it, and equipment purchased for a voyage to the Weddell Sea. Then, late on the evening of 31 May, the Admiralty, preoccupied with alarming reports being coded in of the Battle of Jutland, received a cable from the Falkland Islands. Shackleton had arrived there from South Georgia and was now setting about rescuing the men left on Elephant Island. Davis would subsequently captain *Aurora* to the Ross Sea to rescue members of the expedition at McMurdo Sound on the other side of Antarctica, where they had been sent by Shackleton as a support party to lay depots towards the Pole for the main party, supposedly advancing across from the other side.

All this, however, was a distraction from Mawson's real purpose for being in London. There was little sympathy for Shackleton who, though undeniably heroic, had emerged from his cold and pristine time-lock into a world glutted with heroes, most of them dutifully dead. Mawson, it has to be said, had been trying to keep expenditure on the relief of his old commander and AAE supporter as low as possible. On the evening of 20 May he had written to Kathleen Scott from the Euston Hotel,

> I calculated the programme would cost £45,000, but the remainder of the Committee were unanimous in asking for £65,000—so it has gone in as such.
>
> I am suffering from a bad cold—when that is gone I will call on you again for it is really a great pleasure for me to see you and to talk over these things with you. Believe me, yours, Douglas Mawson.[10]

When she heard the saga of Shackleton's reappearance on 2 June Kathleen Scott thought it 'magnificent'. '[Admiral] Sir Lewis Beaumont and Douglas Mawson both came', she recorded in her diary. 'They were both full of Shackleton's journey.'[11] Mawson wrote to Paquita that evening, 'lunched with Lady Scott . . . bad news of serious sea fight . . . it does not seem to have gone well with us'.[12] This was correct. Outnumbered two-to-one, the German fleet had fought better, lost a lot less tonnage and suffered fewer than half the casualties borne by the British. Neither fleet did much fighting after this—in fact it was the last fleet battle ever fought by the Royal Navy. A few days later, to cap a bad week, Lord Kitchener went down with the *Hampshire* off the Orkneys.

By mid-June Mawson was still without satisfactory employment, though he had been in contact with the Ministry of Munitions. On the 14th there was a letter from Lieutenant-Colonel J. C. Matheson, adjutant of the Trench Warfare Department of that Ministry, offering him a commission as second lieutenant in the Special Brigade, Royal Engineers (Chemists).[13] This was absolutely unacceptable—he had not come half-way round the world for that! There was only one thing to do in the circumstances, and he should have done it at once—write directly to the Minister of Munitions, David Lloyd George. This he did on 17 June, and got his reply on Tuesday the 20th, by way of someone in the Ministry with an illegible signature:

> I am desired by Mr Lloyd George to acknowledge the receipt of your letter of the 17 instant, and to thank you for your kind offer of services which he much appreciates.
>
> The difficulty is that this Department has been fully staffed for some considerable time past, and very few vacancies occur, particularly in the better posts where your attainments would be most useful.
>
> At the same time, in view of the patriotic manner in which you have come over here and the trouble to which you have been put, Mr Lloyd George suggests that you should call here and see me or one of his private secretaries, when I will see whether it is possible to place you anywhere in the Department.[14]

Mawson promptly followed this suggestion, probably the next day, Wednesday, and was directed to Lord Moulton (John Fletcher Moulton), director general of the Explosives Supply Department of the Ministry of Munitions.[15] Moulton took a liking to Mawson. Both knew Kathleen Scott. There was a position available as representative of the Commission Internationale de Ravitaillement (CIR, co-ordinating allied supplies) at Liverpool, effectively as Moulton's liaison officer with the Russian Government Committee, to look after the safe embarkation of high explosives and poison gas bound for northern Russia. Mawson could have £400 a year and the rank of temporary Captain, but he would have to live in Liverpool. This offer was probably made on Thursday 22 June. When would he be able to start, Moulton asked. Mawson replied that he had to go to the country for the weekend to correct the second volume of the BAE's Scientific Reports on Geology, for Heinemann. He could start after the weekend.[16] Altogether this was turning out to be a pleasant week. He had written to Paquita that very morning that

I dined with Sir George Beilby [a distinguished industrialist interested in chemical warfare] at the Atheneum Club last night and went on with he and Sir Charles Parsons (the turbine man) to an At Home by the President of the Royal Society (Sir J. J. Thompson [Thomson]). There I met lots of people I knew. Today... Lunch at the British Empire Club with Sir Napier Shaw [foremost meteorologist of his day] and call on Lord Moulton in afternoon to try for an appointment... All sorts of love, Douglas.[17]

And just the previous day, Wednesday 21 June, as he told Paquita in a supplementary letter of Friday 23 June, he had gone with Kathleen Scott and her son Peter to the Naval Air Section at Hendon:

They gave us afternoon tea at the officers' quarters—we saw a fine lot of machines... The latest, a warplane, is huge—carries 4 guns and 6 gunners—two engines—wireless telegraphy—and bomb chutes in which the bomb is automatically ignited as it leaves... Their crack flier, only 18 years of age, did some wonderful things for our edification. One of his stunts was to go up to 1500 ft then let his machine tumble, anyhow, over and over—suddenly righting it when 150 ft from the ground.[18]

At this time he had another iron in the fire, at the Admiralty, to which he had written on 16 June, but they turned him down.[19] By then he had accepted Moulton's offer.

The weekend for which Mawson had requested freedom before beginning his work was in fact spent on the Kentish coast at Sandwich with Kathleen Scott, though he did take the geology manuscript along with him. His close friendship with this woman, which he never hid from his wife or from Lord Moulton, seems to have been important to him. Her husband had died in Antarctica while Mawson had been down there, her heart was there, and in little Peter Scott the father still lived. Add to this that she was of a generous nature, had powerful friends, did not care a damn about formality or common opinion, and was someone with whom he could relax and be himself, and one understands why, on the following Tuesday, 22 June, he wrote

> My dear Kathleen,
>   Just a line to let you know that I am still enjoying my trip to Sandwich—I will always be able to enjoy it—certainly when you have forgotten all about it, it will be fresh with me. The pity was that it ended so soon in actuality, but fortunately the aftermath of contemplation lingers on.

He boasted that that day he had lunched with William H. Bragg (who with his son William Lawrence Bragg had received the Nobel prize for physics the previous year) and Sir Ernest Rutherford (author of *Radio-Activity* and other pioneering works), 'two out of three of the leading physicists in the Empire', the other in his opinion being J. J. Thomson at whose house he had dined the previous week. More interesting is his comment about how

> Lord Moulton asked me straight out 'where did you go' referring to weekend—seemed very inquisitive—I thought perhaps you had

written him mentioning that I had been with you, so told him had been down to your house at Sandwich for week end—correcting Shackleton manuscript.[20]

Thus Mawson's relationship with Moulton was cosy from the start. Unfortunately his new job, which it was now decided would officially date from 15 July, did not turn out to be very interesting, and he would quickly tire of it.[21]

On arrival at Liverpool he took a permanent room at the North Western Hotel, telling Paquita that he was 'attached to Colonel Essel who is the head British shipping man here—has his headquarters in this Hotel. Liverpool is a real business town and only to be tolerated for work—It is a very busy port in wartime—most supplies enter here.' He told her that he was very upset to hear that the Delprats, with whom Paquita was living, were not using the given name of the Mawsons' pet dog D'Urville, the Antarctica-born offspring of one of the finest dogs on the AAE. Mawson reminded Paquita of 'D'Urville's pedigree—a pure Greenland dog—son of Ginger—D'Urville is the finest Greenland dog I have ever seen. They must not change his name. If they don't keep his name they can send him to my Brother.'[22] He must have been feeling lonely, for less than a week later he was writing home, 'I don't know how you feel about it my Darling—I am sure you long to be here—and you would be a delight—a help—and a grand companion for me . . . If you can arrange to leave the child, then we can go into the matter.'[23]

The trouble with the work was that it did not require brains or specialised scientific knowledge. All he had to do was follow a memorandum already issued by the Russian Committee at India House, Kingsway. This told him in or on what parts of a ship to store the fulminate of mercury, the picric acid, the white phosphorus, the Red Star gas (chlorine) and so on. For instance, he would note that the White Star gas (chlorine/phosgene mixture) 'is exceedingly poisonous and to be carried on the open deck in such a position that it may be readily jettisoned in case of serious leakage', and he would have it so placed.[24] He was also responsible for overseeing the safe railing of these materials to Liverpool from the plants which produced them, so he was not always bottled up in one place.

This work continued unabated from late July until the second week of October, when the last ship for Archangel left Liverpool, Archangel being frozen-in during winter.[25] In early September he was in London and went around to 174 Buckingham Palace Road to pick up some of the slides he kept there, and to see Kathleen Scott. The maid let him in—Lady Scott was in Ireland. That was the night of the great Zeppelin raid on London, 3 September, and afterwards he wrote,

> My dear Kathleen,
>
> You just missed the air raid—and I happened to arrive in good time for it. But I suppose air raids are commonplace with you—it is different when it is your first, as with me. Well—I . . . got my slides—that is to say I got those I wanted of them—
>
> It did not seem the same place without you—I hope you will be in town the next time I visit.
>
> I don't know what to do—the Russians tell me there is lots [for] me to do all winter, and I don't want to go off to Russia . . . 'If I want a trip to Russia they will arrange for me to go over any time' and so on—
>
> If I knew that I was to be settled in a job I would get Paquita over as I know she would like it—but I don't feel at all settled . . . [26]

Soon there were Zeppelins over Liverpool. On 6 October he was writing to Kathleen, 'Zepps came quite close . . . Bombs dropped on Bolton and Preston. I heard that they dropped a bomb on a furnace at Sheffield'.[27]

In early October he learned the result of the conscription referendum at home. 'I am disappointed', he told Kathleen. 'It must be largely the Irish vote . . . I only wish you knew [Prime Minister Billy] Hughes I think you would like him.'[28]

With the last ship to Archangel gone, there was nothing to do apart from taking stock of what cargo remained and seeing to its safe storage. He cabled Paquita in the second week of October to join him and she left with baby Patricia soon after, *via* the United

States where the baby was left with family for the remainder of the war. In San Francisco she saw Shackleton—he was now *en route* to New Zealand to relieve his McMurdo Sound party (three of whom, it would turn out, had perished).[29] Yet even as Paquita was on her way, Mawson was booking their return to Australia, so idle had he become by early November 1916. Already on 17 October he had written to Charles Hodge at the University of Adelaide that he was planning to return because of the 'adequate supply of men of...high scientific attainments' in Britain, the over-supply of officers, the importance of research in Australia, and the need to get the AAE's scientific reports out.[30] Besides, this war might last for a decade, and had already lasted long enough to try anyone's enthusiasm.

So at the end of October he asked Thomas Cook & Son to quote for first-class travel, Liverpool–Bergen–Christiania–Stockholm–St Petersburg, thence by the Trans-Siberian Railway to Yokohama or Shanghai *via* Tientsin or to Hankow *via* Peking, and on to Sydney. This was the only safe way home, and while certainly constituting an exotic holiday, it hardly promised to be luxurious. The quotes were in his hands by 5 November 1916 and totalled just under £160 each.[31]

Paquita's arrival was a tonic. Just as at the South Australian Hotel, there was a special room he had booked at the North Western where they could take their gloves off, sit by the fire, have tea using a tea-set he had bought for the occasion, and just talk for a while.[32] He told her the news about Edgeworth David, who was the Consultant Geologist to the Australian Tunnelling Battalion in France. Poor old David, now fifty-eight, had fallen 70 feet down a shaft, been badly hurt, and was recovering in England. He must also have told her how the AAE's debt had just been reduced by £955 as a result of the kindness of Sir Trevor Dawson, director of Vickers Ltd., who were awash with lucrative war contracts. Mawson had forgotten to pay for the REP monoplane and been reminded by Vickers in 1914. Finally, in November 1916, he had asked Sir Trevor to write it off as a donation, which Sir Trevor had obligingly done.[33] The Thomas Cook itinerary would also have been discussed, and Mawson's feeling of utter uselessness in England.

As he put it in his letter of 8 December 1916 to Lieutenant-General Sir John Cowans, Quarter-Master General of the British Army, 'I am wasted here'. Could Cowans, he asked, find him something more suited to his talents?[34] Nothing came of this. He made one last attempt, through Walter (later Lord) Runciman, President of the Board of Trade to which the CIR was attached, and in early February 1917 Runciman promised to find him something more congenial.[35] A considerate and decent man, unfairly denigrated since Munich, Runciman was as good as his word. He immediately went out of his way on Mawson's behalf and managed to find him ideal work, writing again just three days later,

> I have heard from Sir Edmund Wyldbore Smith [Director, CIR] that he is making arrangements for you to undertake with Lord Moulton's consent, the drawing up of a report which the Russian Government requires, relating to the manufacture of certain explosives in this country.
>
> I gather that the Russians would like you to undertake this work, and, as it would appear to be congenial, I trust that you will find it a useful change from the drudgery of your present tasks.[36]

The Russians wished to manufacture more of their own high explosives and chemical weapons, and Mawson's report would help them do it. At this stage their munition factories were producing liquid chlorine, chloropicrin and phosgene, but in very small quantities,[37] and their output of high explosives was inadequate to demand. Runciman had found him work fully appropriate to his qualifications, which were strong in chemistry, his first university post having been in that discipline. He therefore accepted this gift at once. It also meant that they could live in London, or near it, at May Meadow, Bell Weir, Egham-on-Thames (in September 1917 they would move into London proper).

He was still just a temporary Captain, but now he had entry into the vast munition factories of the North, with authority to analyse and report on their guarded processes and their efficiency. Among them were the new 'National Factories', which he found awe-inspiring, particularly HM Factory Gretna, the largest of all these dark, remorseless mills. It occupied no less than 25 square miles, had been entirely constructed within a year after October 1915, and required 13 000 young women and 7000 men to operate it.[38]

The report he was to prepare was really a whole volume of reports, which were to be published in Russia on completion and made available to munition enterprises there.[39] One of them detailed the preparation of phosgene gas, another described picric acid production at Graesser's Plant, Ruabon, yet others analysed the refining of crude phenol from tar oil, and compared tar distillery in five different private plants. It was precisely the comparative nature of many of these reports which made them valuable. For instance, Mawson drew up a report comparing the efficiency and quality of oleum manufacture by the Grillo method and by the Mannheim process, both used at Gretna, then further comparing these with oleum manufacture at HM Factory Queensferry and at the South Metro Gas Co., Greenwich. Manufacture of nitroglycerine at Gretna was compared with that at Queensferry, another report doing the same for nitrocellulose. Techniques used to make TNT at Queensferry were compared on a cost-and-efficiency basis with the four-stage process used by the Lothian Chemical Co. at Edinburgh. Sulphuric acid concentration by Gaillard Towers at Queensferry was compared with the Gilchrist method used at Gretna, and with that employed by South Metro. The same comparative analysis was done for nitric acid, synthetic phenol and ammonium nitrate. The Cotterell acid-fog entractors [*sic*] at Queensferry were precisely described. And so it went. This work justified a new status for Mawson, who from May 1917 was the Ministry of Munition's liaison officer with the Russian Military Commission, under the title of Special Intelligence Officer. As he told Orme Masson, he was now the direct link between the Russian and British Explosives Departments.[40]

By the end of November 1917, following the Bolshevik coup in St Petersburg, Russia was effectively out of the war. Mawson's official position at this time, as he told T. H. Laby, was Research Officer for the CIR attached to the Russians, but

Now that Russia is in a pickle all the work will go for nothing—
except that, of course, I am much the wiser and may be able to apply
some of the knowledge in Australia . . .

The great blot on the Empire just now is the Sinn Fein trouble
in Ireland. The Irish have never been so well off—they are better off
than any other part of the Empire just now—and yet they are not
satisfied but trump up imaginary wrongs.[41]

As he would point out to Essington Lewis, 'I was about to
follow my reports to Russia when the [October] revolution broke
out'; indeed, he never went to Archangel.[42] Such trips were dangerous in any case (as Kitchener's death showed), and Mawson now
had a new responsibility, baby Jessica, born 28 October 1917.

On New Year's Day, 1918, he was made commanding officer
of the High Explosives, Chemical Warfare and Petroleum Section
of the CIR, headquarters in Empire House, in place of Major
Stomm.[43] He was also appointed ex-officio member of the
Petroleum Executive which oversaw the supply of petroleum to
the allied nations, with monthly sittings alternately in London and
Paris, and in early 1918 was a member of Major General Sir Charles
Callwell's staff on the British Commission to Rome to confer on
supplies of munitions following the Italians' big retreat along their
north-eastern front. For two months he remained honorary
temporary Captain, then on 16 March wrote to Sir Edmund
Wyldbore Smith, asking for promotion to honorary temporary
Major, receiving it within two or three days.[44] In this position and
with this rank he served out the remainder of the war.

In March 1919, a few months after the Armistice, the Mawsons
sailed back to Australia on the troopship *Euripides*, in company with
Edgeworth David, who had been mentioned in General Sir
Douglas Haig's dispatches, won the Distinguished Service Order,
and ended the war as a Lieutenant-Colonel. After J. K. Davis,
Edgeworth David was the Mawsons' dearest friend. Now, with the
conflict behind them (for between them what cause of conflict
could there possibly be?), they had nothing to do but recline in
their deck chairs alongside Paquita, enjoy the sun, watch little Jessica
toddling to and fro, and contemplate serene tomorrows.

10 THE SYDNEY CHAIR

OF MOST IMMEDIATE concern on his return to Australia were mundane imperatives—a house to find, furniture to buy, work to catch up on—but no sooner was Mawson off the ship than reporters were pressing him on Antarctica. The Versailles Conference, he told the Melbourne *Argus*, should deal with the allocation of Antarctic spheres because they would be of economic value; and Australia should claim everything between 90° and 180° East (Gaussberg to the Ross Sea). 'Once whaling and sealing begin in earnest', he added, introducing a conservationist theme he would develop, 'there will have to be some authority to control the killing of the animals, or what happened to the old-time sealing grounds of Bass Strait, New Zealand and Macquarie Island will be repeated'.[1] To these reporters, five years after the AAE, his name meant only Antarctica, and it remained his personal obsession. Even during the war the white continent had never been further from him than 174 Buckingham Palace Road, where as recently as 1 March 1919 he had lunched with Nansen and other friends of Kathleen Scott's including the novelist and dramatist J. M. Barrie.[2] Throughout the war he had been frustratedly aware of the urgent need to organise the writing and publication of the AAE's scientific reports.

Paquita stayed with the children at her parents' in Melbourne while he put up at the South Australian Hotel and searched for a suitable house. He looked at many, for sale and rent, but he looked longest at his father-in-law's block of land by the sea in Brighton,

7 miles from the centre of Adelaide—'about the best piece of land unbuilt on in Brighton as a home site'.[3] He kept going back to it. 'A University man', he pointed out to Paquita,

> is particularly well suited to live at Brighton for the hours in town are easy—and vaccations [*sic*] numerous. Further the long vac. when one might wish to travel . . . is in the hot period when there is a scramble to the Beaches ensuring easy letting . . . A nice 8 or 9 roomed Bungalow could be put up on it within 6 months— embodying the best American principles . . . with tennis court and brick motor garage . . . it should be very nice for £1500. This is without the ground. I don't know what the value of the ground is.[4]

Nor did he need to know—a month later Delprat made him a gift of it.[5] Within a year they would be living in the house he envisaged, named 'Jerbii', in King Street, Brighton (no. 36, tel. Brighton 155), a house for which he had sketched preliminary plans in Antarctica. There were trees on the 1¼-acre block and Mawson would plant more, including fruit trees. Soon they would buy the first of several contiguous farming blocks at The Meadows, south of Adelaide— 187 acres initially, unimproved value £498. Here, on the edge of the Kuitpo Forest, Mawson would run the gradually expanding property as a mixed farm (sheep, pigs, cattle) after clearing it, though leaving some of it timbered. They would call it Harewood after the estates on which the Mawsons had farmed in Yorkshire, clean up its ruined cottage and install a manager, and Mawson would plant the sides of the drive with alternating redgums and wattles. He would also plant numerous European and American trees on the property for love of them and their rich autumn tints. Here he would develop an interest in hardwoods and, using a timber mill constructed nearby, form with neighbours a private company, South Australian Hardwoods, of which he would be chairman—all this lay in the near future.

At the University he found that his 74-year-old colleague, Walter Howchin, who did not even have a university degree, had just been designated honorary professor. Howchin, an ordained Methodist minister, had come to Australia from England in 1881

because of lung disease and thrived in the dry climate. His geological interests, already strong at home, were further developed in
South Australia. As lecturer in geology and palaeontology from
1902, he had done the pioneering work in South Australian
Cambrian and Precambrian stratigraphy—that is, the working out
of the order and relative position of the elements of the earth's
crust as they were sequentially laid down across geological time,
in this case with particular focus on a period now dated to over
500 million years before the present. This was to be Mawson's great
field too. Not only had Howchin defined the stratigraphic sequence
in the Adelaide region, he had established in the Mt Lofty Ranges
the fact of a great 'Cambrian' glaciation (actually Precambrian—
570 million years or more before the present)—an astonishing
and initially controversial find of high international importance—
as well as another ice-age in the Permo-Carboniferous (280–300
million years before the present). Howchin's geological achievements were far greater at this stage than Mawson's, and he had just
published *The Geology of South Australia* (Adelaide, 1918), which
would be used as a university text book into the 1950s. His most
important work was carried out in the Mt Lofty Ranges and between Hallett's Cove, near Adelaide, and Kangaroo Island, embracing
the interlying Fleurieu Peninsula—that was why Mawson, by
'etiquette', had been concentrating on the Flinders Ranges, which
is in turn why Cecil Madigan would concentrate on the Fleurieu
Peninsula following Howchin's retirement, and on Central Australia.[6]
One reason why Mawson never published a book on the geology
of South Australia is because Howchin had already done this and it
was too early to do better. In 1997 the late Eric Rudd, a student of
Mawson's in the 1920s who in 1949 was appointed foundation
professor of the University's new chair of Economic Geology,
remembered Howchin in the 1920s after his retirement:

> I used to meet him up in the town and we would walk the length
> of King William Street, much to my embarrassment in those days,
> because he had a sort of frock coat on, and sticking out the back was
> a geologist's hammer in a belt, and that thing used to flap up and
> down as he walked, and I wondered what people thought of us.[7]

There had been some bad feeling between Mawson and Howchin from at least 1915–16. In December 1915 Mawson had submitted a report to the University Council on accommodation, in which he had argued that his section of the geological studies needed the larger share of laboratory space because of his strong interest in mineralogy and geo-chemistry, and he had explained why he and not Howchin had been pressing so hard for additional accommodation. The report sat around for many months, and before it ever got to Council it was shown to Howchin because of some expressions it contained. In December 1916 Howchin had sent off a letter to Mawson in Liverpool. 'Who constituted you', he asked,

> a censor over a Department in which you have neither control or responsibility? . . . I do not admit that you are capable of appraising the value of my work . . . How is it, Mawson, that I have received less sympathy and less appreciation of my work from you than from any other of my colleagues? And, when making sundry requisitions from Council, how was it that you went out of your way to inform the Council of my 'advanced age', and that I have not passed through a regular University course (both of which facts were well known to the Council) and that in your opinion your colleague was 'somewhat crimped'? The personal interest that you might have in such innuendos is too transparent not to be recognised at once and detracts from the value of your statement as a disinterested judgment. I did not think, Mawson, that you could have been capable of such an act![8]

Howchin demanded that the report be rewritten before submission to Council or he would insist on the right of reply. Mawson sent an apology, expressing admiration for Howchin's geological work.[9] The hurtful words could not be erased from Howchin's mind, but he replied that he was 'willing to take your letter as the *amende honorable* and will dismiss the matter for the future'.[10]

After learning of Howchin's honorary professorship Mawson arranged a meeting with the Vice-Chancellor, Professor (later Sir) William Mitchell—there was something Mitchell should know. Earlier that year Mawson had turned down the geology chair at

Manchester. He may also have mentioned an informal offer from
Liverpool.[11] The Vice-Chancellor at Manchester, Sir Henry Miess
FRS, had written to him on 29 January 1919 to say that Sir Thomas
Holland had vacated the chair, and to ask 'whether you would
yourself consider the post if it were offered to you'. The salary
would be £900.[12] Mawson had declined because of a sense of obligation to the University of Adelaide for the generous leave it had
extended to him, and more especially because of the urgency of
getting out the AAE's scientific reports. Now, he told Mitchell, he
no sooner arrives home than he finds the degree-less Howchin
ensconced in a chair. 'They appear greatly surprised that I think
anything of it', he wrote to Paquita,

> they say that I am entirely independent and therefore why worry
> about Howchin. They are obviously sorry to have so upset me and
> there is no doubt whatever would be greatly sorry to have me
> go . . . [Mitchell] said that he felt Howchin should receive some
> reward & honour for his long service.
>
> Truly they have no leg to stand on but of course they can't go
> back on what they have done. It is open to them to give me the
> same title; they have not suggested it, and in any case it would set up
> a precedent not altogether desirable.

He went on to point out that 'The climate is splendid, the work is
easy; attractions that would make a two years' stay whilst working
up the Antarctic things, very desirable'. He could meanwhile 'look
out for a post elsewhere'. Probably Manchester was now gone—

> and in any case it is a bad climate. Sydney should be coming on,
> and, if the worst came to the worst Adelaide should be free of
> Howchin soon . . . I believe that other good posts will be offering in
> England, and I don't think I could ever be left without a good post
> after I have the Antarctic work out.
>
> So things rather point to staying here.[13]

A few days later he saw the Chancellor, Sir George Murray,
and was assured that 'as soon as I publish something on the

Scientific work of my Expedition they will seize the opportunity to elect me also an (honorary) Professor'.[14] The scientific reports, written by a range of scientists, had been appearing since 1916 but Mawson had not yet authored any. He was in fact appointed Professor of Geology and Mineralogy in 1921 following Howchin's retirement in 1920. As the reports were based on evidence supplied by his expedition, they were all in that sense his achievements. This was particularly so as he edited them and oversaw their publication, the strange saga of which merits a separate chapter.

It is easy to understand Mawson's impatience for promotion. Geography and geology are inextricable, and for his geographical achievements he had received a knighthood and the RGS's Founder's Medal, its highest honour. He moved in circles unknown to the average academic, though he was personally indifferent to class distinctions. In the week following his interview with Mitchell, just for instance, he accompanied the State Governor, Sir Henry Galway, to the new Tivoli Theatre, along with Mrs Smeaton (wife of prominent surgeon Bronte Smeaton), Major James Deane (Galway's ADC) and his wife Phyllis (a friend of Paquita's). Like most of Adelaide society, Mawson found Galway's careless outspokenness entertaining—striking ironworkers in 1915 should be 'put in khaki' and 'shipped to the front', the defeat of a conscription referendum was 'a joyful day for Germany', gambling and drinking were inalienable rights, and starchy temperance-union types should focus on their teapots, not threaten other people's freedoms. 'I'll say what I like and damn the consequences' was his attitude, which amused his charming wife and their friends but scandalised the left and the middle-class prohibitionists. In 1920 the entire State Labor Party boycotted his farewell, which was crowded out.

Through the remainder of 1919 Mawson was busy in and out of the University, as a member of the Advisory Board of the South Australian Bureau of Science and Industry, and in reorganising the mineral collections of the South Australian Museum on a comprehensive scale, including their proper exhibition, which would require years of patient, voluntary labour. More significantly, he was appointed an Executive Member of the Australian National Research Council (ANRC), an offshoot of the AAAS.

From 1922 he had his Antarctic companion, Dr Cecil Madigan, with him in the Department as Lecturer, and between them they carried out most of the teaching through the 1920s and 1930s. In his field work he returned to the Precambrian areas of the Mt Painter and Olary regions in the north, investigated prior to the AAE and already discussed in a short paper for the AAAS.[15] This work issued in a longer paper in 1923 focussing on the core of igneous and metamorphic rocks beneath an overlying sedimentary series similar to the series overlying the basement of the Adelaide region, and he used the term *Adelaidean,* which Edgeworth David had applied to the Adelaide Series, to classify them.[16] Thus Mawson, as David had done, was pushing Howchin's Cambrian dating of the Adelaide Series even further back. He continued his work in the region through the mid-1920s. Additionally, he discovered, in 1924, near the Italowie Gorge in the Flinders Ranges, what he described as 'an algal limestone composed almost entirely of Cryptozoön in which the structure is beautifully preserved'. Then-recent work in the United States by C. D. Walcott had demonstrated algal remains in Precambrian rocks in Montana. Now Mawson was doing the same for South Australia at a time when Precambrian life-forms were a *terra incognita.* His 'cryptozoöns' were algal stromatolites and would be found abundantly in particular Precambrian formations in the Flinders Ranges.[17]

The early 1920s added to Mawson's list of significant honours. For his war service he was awarded the OBE (1920), the Italian Order of St Maurice and St Lazarus (1920), and made Commander of the Order of the Crown of Italy (1923). For his Antarctic work he now had, besides the Antarctic Medal (1908) and Founder's Medal (1915) from the RGS, and the Helen Culver Gold Medal from the Chicago Geographical Society (1915), the King's Polar Medal, two bars (following the AAE), the David Livingstone Centenary Gold Medal of the American Geographical Society (1915), and the Bigsby Gold Medal of the Geological Society of London (1919). The most significant of his scientific honours, however, came in 1923 with his election as a Fellow of the Royal Society, whereupon he immediately took out a life subscription for £75.[18]

In the meetings of the AAAS he was a prominent participant. At the fifteenth meeting, in January 1921, scheduled for Hobart but strike-bound in Melbourne, he was President of the Geography-and-History section, and in an interesting address reviewed developments since the last meeting, eight long years before, paying special regard to political geography. He considered the consequences of the break-up of the great pre-war continental empires—in Russia, for example, there was presently 'a dictatorship of the uneducated replacing a dictatorship of those educated and trained to govern; a change which has cost millions of lives'. He reiterated his view that the resources of the Antarctic seas required controlled exploitation—to this end the 'Australian quadrant' should be made the subject of a British claim ('British' including Australia in contemporary usage), for otherwise 'no regulations can be enforced to control whaling and sealing, the chief natural industries'. He also pointed out that of the Australian coastline, 'more than one-third . . . is uncharted in the modern sense of the term'—information from J. K. Davis, now Director of Commonwealth Navigation.[19] Outside, he complained to the *Argus* reporter that the Australian Government seemed totally uninterested in pressing Antarctic claims.[20]

Two years later the AAAS met in Wellington, and Mawson sailed across with Davis, giving one of the less specialised evening addresses at the Town Hall, on Antarctica. Davis gave two papers, one on the meteorological station he had just installed on Willis Island, intended to give Queensland advance warning of hurricanes, the other paper on the almost wholly unknown African quadrant of Antarctica (from the meridian of Greenwich to 90°E). Davis advocated landing a party at Cape Ann (halfway around at 45°E, discovered by Captain John Biscoe in 1831); equipped with an aircraft for reconnaissance, they would sledge east and west. This was a more imaginative and bolder project than Mawson's own later BANZARE cruises but nothing came of it.[21] During his stay in New Zealand Mawson also found time to visit Mt Cook in the South Island and briefly inquire into the country's timber industry,[22] which he would investigate extensively in 1926 (see Chapter 12).

From 13 August to 3 September of that same year, 1923, in Melbourne and Sydney, Australia hosted the Pan-Pacific Science Congress under the auspices of the ANRC. Mawson gave two brief, ten-minute papers, one in Melbourne on Antarctica, the other in Sydney on the Solomon Islands. He represented the RGS at this Congress. Delegates were honoured at receptions hosted by the Governor-General, Sir Henry Forster, the Parliament of Victoria, and Sir Walter Davidson, Governor of New South Wales.[23] W. H. Hobbs came from Ann Arbor a few weeks earlier and stayed with the Mawsons at Brighton, and in Melbourne Mawson introduced him to Billy Hughes who subsequently stayed with Hobbs at Ann Arbor.[24]

A far closer friendship, however, was drifting daily closer to shipwreck in the treacherous shoals of ambition and hard feelings. Mawson knew that Edgeworth David would be retiring at the end of 1924, and, as already seen, had contemplated filling his chair since at least 1919. The second half of 1924 saw tensions build and the relationship practically founder. Although there were rumours abroad in regard to David's approaching retirement, Mawson did nothing until this was announced publicly in the press, in early July. On the 10th he sent off a letter to the Registrar at the University of Sydney, Walter A. Selle: would the position be advertised, or was it already decided? He told Selle that he had not written to David 'as I assume that he does not wish to be implicated in the selection of a successor'.[25]

This was disingenuous in the extreme, for Mawson had almost certainly heard by now that David's choice was his Acting Professor, Leo Cotton (the BAE's *Nimrod* passenger, down to Antarctica and straight back in early 1908), who had run the Department through the war years and on occasional years since, for a total of six years. Even Hobbs had heard that 'it was as good as settled' on his visit in 1923.[26] Cotton's beautifully printed application had already gone in during June.[27] Selle showed Mawson's letter to David, who wrote to Mawson on 15 July, enclosing copies of Cotton's application, pointing out how well Cotton had run the Department, and praising his recent research papers on geotectonics in the *American Journal of Science* and elsewhere. It was David's sense of obligation to

Cotton that clearly weighed most. The University Senate, he wrote, had asked the former Professor of Anatomy now at Cambridge, J. T. Wilson, to act with Professors J. E. Marr, W. W. Watts and J. W. Gregory (all eminent geologists) as a 'Home Committee' in England to decide whether, should the position be advertised, there would be anyone likely to apply with qualifications superior to Cotton's. Wilson's reply was not expected until late August or September.[28]

What David neglected to mention was that he and Cotton had written to Hobbs at Ann Arbor seeking his endorsement of Cotton and asking him to send it to Wilson in Cambridge.[29] Hobbs had done this, but then considered that Mawson just might apply should the position be advertised, and so had written again to Wilson, with some embarrassment, stating that if the field were to be open, Mawson would be his first choice. He then wrote to David to point out that he had done this.

It is no exaggeration to say that in Mawson's view the entire affair was scandalous on several counts. For a start, as his application showed, Cotton was insular in the extreme. He had studied and taught (and, as it turned out, would teach for the rest of his career) nowhere but at the University of Sydney, and although he had visited Hawaii and New Zealand, he had never been to the United States or Europe. His international connections were almost non-existent. Predictably, he would never become an FRS. Secondly, he was being ushered in through the back door—the Home Committee were in effect being invited to cable the Senate, 'No need to advertise. Nobody better qualified likely to apply this side.' Thirdly, Cotton had built his administrative experience during the war when other men had been sacrificing career (and often life) to country—Cotton was a pacifist, and this was the worst of it to Mawson. In fact, as he would later learn, it was only because of a number of questions having been raised about the war issue in June that it had been decided to set up a Home Committee at all—otherwise Cotton would have been appointed straight away.[30] Mawson decided to hang fire, at least until the AAAS meeting in Adelaide in the last week of August, when David had said they would discuss the matter. Meanwhile it was some satisfaction to know that the Home Committee had Hobbs's view—a stainless steel spanner in David's works.

At the Adelaide meeting Mawson's nerves were bad. During the second AAAS Council meeting on the afternoon of Wednesday, 27 August, the permanent honorary general secretary, E. C. Andrews, of the Mines Department in Sydney, sought Council's authority to spend £200 a year on permanent clerical assistance for his administrative work. Andrews was a man of strict integrity, imbued with the scientific ideal, and gave voluntarily of his services. The AAAS was his chief interest, and to it he was totally devoted. At this time he was also under nervous strain, organising the Adelaide meeting. Mawson, who may not have been listening to Andrews very closely, then asked bluntly whether Andrews wanted the £200 for himself. Perhaps Alf Reid had momentarily popped into his mind, or Conrad Eitel. Andrews was extremely upset by this question, which struck everyone there as rude, and subsequently tendered his resignation to the President, Lieutenant-General Sir John Monash (with whom Mawson had good relations, having dined with him in London during the war[31]). Monash refused to accept it. Edgeworth David, who had not been present at this Council meeting, later wrote to Mawson pointing out the injustice of his query and asking him to write to Andrews, apologising and explaining that he had mistaken what Andrews had been saying.[32] This incident possibly reveals something of Mawson's state of tension over the Sydney chair.

Whether or not he discussed the chair with David during the AAAS meeting is unclear, but he now decided it was time to act. On 11 September he wrote to Selle, pointing out that as the AAE Reports were now being published in Sydney (see following chapter), and it would be convenient to live there, he would be a candidate should the position be advertised, and provided he were satisfied on salary, tenure of office, superannuation, commencement date, leave of absence and so on. Selle forwarded the letter to the Chancellor, Sir William Cullen.[33] Mawson also let it be known among friends at Sydney that he was thinking of the chair, and these people then informed him of any relevant developments. Sir Henry Barraclough, Russell Professor of Mechanical Engineering, was one of these friends. During the war he had been officer-in-charge of Australian munition workers in Britain, with the rank of Colonel, and his attitude to Cotton was identical to Mawson's.[34] He told Mawson that the Senate were to be informed of Hobbs's letter, and he passed on other encouraging news, though he gave what would turn out to be an exaggerated estimate of the support Mawson would have on the Senate.

David, it must be said, also kept him informed of developments. On 25 September he reported that a cable had gone off to Wilson in Cambridge alerting him to Mawson's willingness to be a candidate, and that William Noel Benson of Otago also desired to be considered. The Home Committee had been asked 'to consider you both as willing to accept the Chair if it were offered to you, and we asked [them] to include this aspect of the case in their report'.[35] In the event, the Home Committee decided (though not unanimously) for Mawson, putting Benson second and Cotton last.[36] On 6 November, just before this became known, Mawson cabled Selle to withdraw his name, feeling that the game was rigged.[37] David was magnanimous enough to write on 16 November asking whether, in the light of the Home Committee's recommendation, Mawson would like to reconsider his withdrawal. 'I state frankly that I like you much better than I like Cotton', he pointed out, while reaffirming his belief that Cotton should get the Chair because of having effectively run the Department so well for so long.[38]

The Senate was due to meet on 22 December. Mawson's position at this stage changed. It changed because the Registrar, Selle, wrote on 5 December asking whether he was correct in interpreting Mawson's withdrawal of 6 November to imply that if the Chair were offered to him he would accept it. Selle went on to say that with (Sir) Mungo MacCallum, the University's Warden and prospective Vice-Chancellor, leaving for London for several months, Selle was effectively running the University and would have to advise the Chancellor before 22 December in regard to the Chair of Geology. 'I may say', he went on, 'that there is a strong feeling here that the successor should not be Cotton, but Mawson. The former's "stocks" are by no means high. . . . I do hope, for the sake of the old Varsity, that we'll have you with us in 1925.'[39]

After reading this remarkable letter, Mawson decided that if the chair were offered to him he would probably accept it, but with the proviso that he could not take up the position until the end of 1925. At no stage did he put in a formal application, and this is an important point. He had learned that when one has attained to a certain level in the professional world one generally does not 'apply' for things, especially if the dice appear to be loaded. One lets it be known, among a number of people concerned (who will deliberately let it out) that a certain position would probably be accepted if offered. A *curriculum vitae* might be sent (preferably indirectly), but never an 'application'. The point of this approach is that one can gain but not lose by it, for one can never be said to have *failed* to get the position. It is therefore a sound strategy, in fact the best approach in such matters, particularly if one is objectively the best person for the job, for then not being offered it will only be embarrassing to those rigging the game. He had certainly never 'applied for' the positions he held in London during the war, at the Ministry of Munitions and the CIR. He was also used to chairs being offered to him, in the United States and at Manchester. In addition, by letting it be known that he could not take up the position until the end of 1925, which *he* knew the *Senate* knew would put Cotton in the impossible position of having to run a department while awaiting his new boss, he was setting the ground rules and, if unsuccessful, might be said to have half-rejected *himself*.

The University's administration appear to have been wrong-footed by this approach. They sent urgent telegrams during the seventy-two hours leading up to the 22 December Senate meeting. On 19 December, 'Chancellor asks whether you are definitely candidate for Geology Chair. Selle'. Mawson did not reply 'yes' or 'no', merely stipulating his inability to come until the end of 1925. Not comprehending, they sent another urgent telegram on the 20th: 'In view of misunderstanding [about whether he was a 'candidate', not a term Mawson liked to apply to himself] it seems most expedient that you telegraph Registrar that you will accept Chair if appointed'. His reply is stunningly indifferent: 'Lateness of appointment would prevent me finally transferring to Sydney before end of coming year but if chair offered will proceed Sydney in weeks time or at time to suit Senate to fully investigate and finalise. Am candidate under these conditions.'[40]

When the Senate met on the 22nd, David had the acutely embarrassing task of again pressing the claims of Cotton, now openly revealed as the Home Committee's bottom-ranked candidate. Such was David's authority, however, that his advice, based merely on a sense of obligation, won the day.[41] Mawson left Adelaide for Harewood over the Christmas–New Year period. He needed to help in the reorganisation of the Kuitpo Forest timber mill, in which he had the principal interest—it had now grown to employ fifty men full-time. While up there, on 26 December, he read in the newspaper that Cotton had been appointed to the Sydney chair. On returning to Adelaide he found a telegram from Selle with the same news, and not of course using any words to the effect that Mawson had been unsuccessful. He answered this, reminding Selle that in any case he had only been prepared to *consider* the chair if offered—'to investigate and if satisfied to place my Record before the Senate'—regretting that his 'offer was not entertained'.[42] He later told David that 'under the peculiar circumstances of the method of appointment I was much too proud to push myself until a majority of the Senate should express a desire to hear my case'.[43]

He knew that he was the choice of the Home Committee, that David and Cotton knew it, along with everyone else at Sydney, and that posterity, if it ever cared to interest itself in his files, would know it too. There was satisfaction in that.

Mungo MacCallum, Vice-Chancellor in 1925, was so impressed by the way Mawson had handled himself in this whole affair that five months later he wrote to say that he would be recommending him as his successor:

As I gathered from a remark of yours, you would find it easier to come in the beginning of 1927 than in the beginning of 1926.

Meanwhile, if you favour the proposal, I wish you would let me have a summary of your career, including your success in your lecturing tour in the States. *Of course I understand that the offer must be made to you, and that you will not be a candidate.*[44]

MacCallum was no fool—he knew how the game was to be played, that the best people would never 'apply'. One notes that whereas in 1924 Mawson had been a 'candidate' of sorts though not an *applicant*, now he was not even to be considered a candidate. MacCallum tried to get his Appointments Committee to make the offer, and although they finally accepted that the position should be offered, they insisted on consultation with a Council of Vice-Chancellors in the United Kingdom.[45] On 14 February 1926 Mawson was informed by Edgeworth David, writing from England, that the Imperial Inter-Universities Board were sending a list of possible men, with Mawson's name on top.[46]

He backed out, however, perhaps feeling that while his position in Adelaide was compatible with another Antarctic expedition (which he and the ANRC were then pressing on the Commonwealth Government), this would not be so with the Sydney Vice-Chancellorship. Still, he let it be known among his friends that he had been offered the position, and Sir William Mitchell later referred to the fact publicly. The letters quoted above, from MacCallum and David, are the proof.[47]

Meanwhile Mawson's friendship with David was at breaking point and David was aware of the strength of feeling at Sydney. On 23 December, the day after the Senate had endorsed Cotton, the Professor of Pure and Applied Mathematics, Horatio Scott Carslaw, who had earlier lobbied members of the Senate on Mawson's behalf, happened to see David walking past after lunch. As Carslaw represented it to Mawson,

> He was going about the refectory looking as pleased as if he had inherited a fortune, or carried off some piece of business on which his heart had been set. . . . I said 'David, I want a word with you', and we went into the adjacent room, then empty.

Carslaw then told David how deeply disturbed he was at what had happened the previous day. David demanded to know what he

meant. 'The election to the Chair of Geology', Carslaw replied.
David asked whether Carslaw was making a private protest, and
Carslaw answered that he was simply unhappy for the University—
if MacCallum had been there the decision would have been
different.

David lost his temper and 'flounced away', according to
Carslaw, and next day wrote him an angry note saying 'that only
once in his life before had he been so affronted by anyone! (I fear
the culprit was [Physiology professor] Anderson Stuart.)'[48]

Although David had many friends, he valued none more than
Mawson, towards whom he felt paternally and deeply affectionate.
Now he correctly sensed that this friendship was lost to him. He
sent long letters, explaining his point of view, the first one sixteen
pages long, written on Christmas Day. Mawson replied on his
return to Adelaide in mid-January 1925, beginning charmingly,
then going on for a number of paragraphs about conscientious
objectors. As for himself, he wrote,

> When the war broke out, having just returned from the Antarctic
> with a great bulk of scientific data to prepare for publication, I might
> have been excused more than most for staying in Adelaide and
> addressing myself to scientific productions thereby enhancing my
> reputation . . . but I turned to where duty seemed to lie and having
> spent some months (at your bidding) whipping up the national con-
> sciousness in S.A. towards conscription, I then spent some 3½ years
> in war duties thus throwing my clock back correspondingly.

Cotton's record should have been 'docked in proportion', for those
three-and-a-half years had been spent by him in serving his own
career. The real sting of the letter, though, was in the tail:

> Finally, the more I think of it, the more do I long to have been
> present when the learned judge at the Senate Meeting discoursed
> philosophically upon the merits of Cotton and myself in his endeav-
> ours to secure a balance with one foot on terra firma and the other
> in the clouds, for his information concerning my record must have
> been rather nebulous.[49]

He signed it 'ever yours sincerely', and David seized on this as a life-belt: 'Only a man of noble and generous nature could under the circumstances have done that'.[50] But David heard nothing from Mawson over the following weeks, and he became extremely worried, writing desperately on 19 March:

> You have befriended me many times and oft, and I look to you still with confidence to befriend me again.
>
> I realise that I am getting an old man now, and in the eventide of life one clings more than ever to early friends. It would be a bitter disappointment to me to lose your friendship now.
>
> I feel that you will have the greatness and goodness to brush aside all feelings of resentment through disappointment . . . and will help me with my research in my old age . . . Your friendship is very dear to my heart.[51]

On receipt of this, Mawson wrote his old friend a kindly letter, and then for good measure another. To David these were 'an immense relief to my mind':

> I never perhaps fully realised what your friendship means to me until my experiences of the last few weeks. The first thing in the morning and the last thing at night you were in my thoughts, and every mail I was eagerly looking for a letter from you. It was a great joy to me when it came at last.[52]

David's humility had revived a friendship that had died through pride. His letters were like the cries of a drowning man, and it was impossible to deny him the rescue he sought.

11 'A Contract
is a Contract'

~

THE MOST INFURIATING project in Mawson's life was organising, editing and publishing the long series of scientific reports flowing from the AAE. The majority were farmed out to other scientists, some dependable, others exhibiting human nature at its slack, comedic worst.

There were ninety-six individual reports for the AAE in twenty-two volumes, and for the later BANZARE expedition there would be over sixty more in nine volumes.[1] AAE reports were issued between 1916 and 1947, BANZARE reports between 1937 and 1975. A descriptive analysis is out of place here, but Mawson's problems with the AAE reports throw interesting lights on his character and have the ingredients of narrative, sometimes of farce.

Scientific reports are relatively unsaleable and unglamorous, but for the AAE they were meant to justify the costs of the expedition itself. They would verify Mawson's claim, made to his university colleagues in his speech of thanks for their wedding present, that 'I have been an active member of the Adelaide University all along . . . One can work for the University just as well in the Antarctic and elsewhere as in the building itself. I trust that all that has been accomplished by this expedition will benefit the University as I feel sure it will.'[2] To this end it would not suffice to publish a popular work such as *Home of the Blizzard*. The responsibility for hard scientific results weighed more heavily on Mawson than it could have on Scott or Shackleton because they were not themselves scientists.

In October 1914 he had written to the Prime Ministers of Australia and New Zealand, Andrew Fisher and W. F. Massey, requesting £5000 from the first and £500 from the second towards publication of scientific results, to no avail. There was a war on, and the Australian Government had already given the AAE £10 000.[3] Mawson then approached the South Australian Government, who in November 1915 agreed to his request.[4] The first reports were produced by the Government Printer on North Terrace in 1916— the important *Fishes* by Edgar Waite, and the *Mollusca* by C. Hedley. By the end of 1919 seventeen reports had appeared, all on zoology or botany. At this point the South Australian Government pulled out. The Premier's Office informed Mawson on 25 July 1919 that it had reluctantly been 'decided to discontinue printing the reports, owing to the cost involved, unless the other states were prepared to contribute a share of the cost'. Enquiries had been sent to them, but 'the Governments are not disposed'.[5]

Mawson knew this was coming, and two months earlier, in May 1919, he had already put a proposal to the New South Wales Government for taking over the printing. This approach bore fruit at the end of May when E. H. Stoney wrote on behalf of Nationalist Premier W. A. Holman to say that Mawson's ideas were being considered by the Government Printer. These ideas amounted to a *quid pro quo*: the Government would print the reports, and in return receive valuable AAE artifacts and documents, details to be negotiated. Stoney went on to say that

> The Premier has directed me to enclose a card, for lunch with French Governor from Noumea and guests. [State Governor] Sir Walter Davidson, Ministers, Mr. A. C. Eliot (now at Government House) and others also may come whom you might presently meet with advantage to your plans, and to mutual pleasure.
>
> A phone ring (City 516) to me, accepting or regrettedly otherwise, would quite suffice.[6]

This luncheon, on a day when rain fell in sheets, effectively sealed the deal while leaving the fine print to be worked out later. Mawson found himself seated next to Davidson on his right and Treasurer J. C. L. Fitzpatrick on his left. The Treasurer was the key minister in the matter and Mawson made the most of the opportunity. Fitzpatrick, a dapper, mercurial man who wore a flower in his buttonhole, was very different from Mawson, yet they got along well. He seemed 'very careful with the money', Mawson told Paquita, 'but before I left him had promised to see the printing done'.[7]

Holman had also been supportive, and in June he appointed a small committee to report on detailed recommendations. This consisted of the Government Printer as Chairman, the Principal Librarian W. H. Ifould, and Charles Hedley of the Australian Museum. An agreement was drawn up by 22 August 1919 and signed in 1920.[8] This was absolutely clear. Practically everything was to go to Sydney, including all photographic negatives (to be handed over 'at once'), prints and enlargements, all the sledges and gear ('at once'), the official diaries, all the meteorological logs and documents, magnetic and tidal records, geographical logs and papers, reports of sledging parties, the sounding logs from *Aurora*, the managerial and financial papers, and the biological, geological and mineralogical trophies. Private diaries, of course, could not be insisted on (though most of these found their way into the Mitchell Library in Sydney), but all AAE-related correspondence obviously came under 'managerial . . . papers'. A sum of £5000 was set aside by the New South Wales Government to cover costs of printing, which was to be completed by March 1925.

The Government appears to have observed its side of this agreement quite scrupulously throughout, and as will be seen, when in 1931 it temporarily ceased to print the reports it did so on good grounds—a sum in excess of the agreed £5000 had been spent and the Printing Office was frustrated by not receiving certain long-promised manuscript reports. The only problems with the agreement through the 1920s seem to have been caused by non-compliance on Mawson's part. Already in November 1920 the Committee had threatened to suspend printing, after just one report had been produced, unless he answered previous queries regarding relics promised to the Australian Museum and the Mitchell Library. Again and again they made the threat, and each time he gave them just enough by way of artefacts or (mainly) excuses to keep them temporarily quiet. His chief excuse, a valid one, was that he needed unforwarded material for the preparation and editing of the individual reports, and that as soon as material was no longer required for this purpose it would be sent. Thus in March 1923 he wrote to the Committee,

> I am taking steps to have forwarded to you all material listed in the agreement that can possibly be handed over at this stage.
>
> As explained and agreed when the agreement was drawn up the log books, diaries, photos and specimens can only be handed over as such are finished with in the preparation of the manuscripts for printing.
>
> I will now go over the various items and arrange to have forwarded everything possible.[9]

The relevant department overseeing the matter was the Ministry of Education, who were pressuring the Chairman, now A. J. Kent. Towards the end of 1924 the same trouble arose again, with other worrying matters. Kent wrote,

> The expenditure on publications to date amounts to £3,996, and the time for the issue of the complete work will expire in March 1925.
>
> Although a large number of Parts of Series 'C' [zoology and botany] have been issued, the state of Series 'A' [geology and geography] and 'B' [terrestrial magnetism and meteorology] leaves a lot to be desired . . . Subscribers will expect something regularly . . .
>
> I am instructed to express [the Committee's] regret that you have not acknowledged their letter of the 18th September and 11th November, requesting some information as to when you propose to hand over the Logs, Diaries, Photos and Mineral specimens which have been the subject of so much correspondence.[10]

The reason why Series C reports were appearing at a good rate was that in them many new species were described, and if publication were delayed many of the findings would be anticipated by scientists in other countries.

In Mawson's defence he had now handed over a large collection of equipment and relics illustrative of a range of AAE activities, and many negatives and prints. The vast majority of materials, however, remained and would always remain in Adelaide, even after the late 1940s when all AAE reports had been published. No doubt he felt bad about having been forced to trade so much of what was dear to his heart for the 'privilege' of seeing the scientific fruits of his expedition made public, and after 1924 and the fiasco over the Sydney Chair of Geology this feeling was probably exacerbated. It was not even as though all financial worries over the reports had been lifted from him, for through the 1920s, as he later told William Davies, New South Wales Minister for Education in the Lang Labor Government, he 'had to find a good deal of money to pay for computations and other incidentals in the preparation of same. This has amounted in all to about £1,900.'[11]

He was probably betting that he could string the Printing Committee along, as he in fact did for ten years. It is always easier to handle governments on such matters than private enterprises, for the governments are spending other people's taxes and are therefore more likely to prove flexible than a company spending its own money. The Committee would warn and warn again until it tired of its own warnings. These were roughly annual affairs until November 1925, when Kent wrote to reiterate 'my repeated requests that you forward all logs, Diaries, Negatives and Geological specimens . . . Send them without further delay. The continual correspondence . . . over this matter is a source of embarrassment to the Committee.'[12] Thereafter the Committee's embarrassment seems to have prevented them from corresponding on the question for three and a half years, until in March 1929 Kent sent yet another letter of the same kind, also fretting over Mawson's imminent departure on the first BANZARE cruise. Mawson replied that he would only be gone five or six months and advised Kent 'not to get rattled'.[13]

The Government of T. R. Bavin generously agreed in 1930 to spend more than the £5000 originally stipulated, although Mawson was told that all outstanding reports would have to be in to the Printer in 1931 or the deal would be off. In October 1930 a Labor government came to power in New South Wales, headed by Jack Lang, perhaps the most interesting Labor leader in Australia's history, a populist who blamed the Great Depression on the secret power of the 'Money Ring', while also being anti-communist. With unemployment climbing towards 30 per cent through 1931 the Lang Government looked to cut unnecessary expenditure, and in the second half of that year the Department of Education signalled that printing of the AAE reports would be terminated.[14] This decision, in accord with the previous Bavin Government's agreement to continue printing only until late 1931, was announced in the press early in October. It certainly could not be represented as a reneging on the original Agreement, and in any case all outstanding reports had not been submitted. In the event it proved merely a temporary freeze, printing by the New South Wales Government Printer resuming in 1937 and continuing until 1947. (By 1937 the Federal Government under Joseph Lyons had so successfully battled the Depression that unemployment was back below 10 per cent—below 9 per cent in 1938—and the Federal Treasury was funding publication of the BANZARE Reports.)

Mawson had made some unfortunate choices in his authors. The report most eagerly awaited by the New South Wales Government Printer, because it promised to be the most attractive to subscribers, was the *Birds*. A great number of specimens had been taken on Macquarie Island and in Antarctica, and Mawson had pointed out in Appendix II of *Home of the Blizzard* that 'The eggs of practically all the flying birds known along Antarctic shores were obtained, including those of the silver-grey petrel and the Antarctic petrel, which were not previously known; also a variety of prion, of an unrecorded species, together with its eggs'.[15] A large rookery of Emperor penguins, only the second on record, was located and studied. An impressive collection of parasites, internal and external, was secured from a wide range of Antarctic birds. Striking photographs of birds had appeared in *Home of the Blizzard*, whetting the appetites of subscribers to the zoological reports. For the writing of this report (and others) Mawson turned to Harold Hamilton, who had been the biologist at the AAE's Macquarie Island base. Hamilton worked in the Dominion Museum in Wellington, and Mawson, after waiting patiently for several years, had finally secured his firm agreement to submit the *Birds* by the end of June 1923. Hamilton also faithfully undertook to supply the report on *Penguins* by the end of 1923, the *Seals and Whales* by June 1924, and the *Sea Elephants* by the end of 1924. Naturally all specimens needed for this work were with him in Wellington. These reports should have been the cream of the zoological series, certainly to the average subscriber, who could not be expected to take quite as much interest in the *Parasitic Infusoria*, the *Mallophaga and Siphunculata*, the *Cirripedia*, the *Ticks*, or any of the other fifty-odd reports scheduled for Series C.

By mid-February 1924 neither the *Birds* nor the *Penguins* had emerged from their long incubation, so Mawson appealed to Hamilton's sense of honour: 'Now, Hamilton, a contract is a contract . . . You took a post on the staff of the Expedition and signed a contract at a stated salary—the contract I have here now;—up to the present moment you have done nothing for that salary.' The least Hamilton could do was to send his rough working papers to the Printing Committee in Sydney. 'If you can send over the complete notes or MS. on the Bird section forthwith it will, I believe, give you some breathing room for the mammalian notes or MS.'[16] A month later Hamilton replied with a letter that must have given Mawson immense relief: 'I hope to post the bird MSS. and notes by the next mail direct to the Government Printer Sydney. As soon as I do so I will write you further.'[17] By not fulfilling the first part of this promise he absolved himself in regard to the second. Mawson finally had to go to New Zealand to take possession of Hamilton's rough notes on the spot.[18]

Having given up on Hamilton, he turned to the noted ornithologist Thomas Iredale at the Australian Museum in Sydney. All the bird skins, eggs, photographs and so forth came back across the Tasman Sea. Mawson allowed him a reasonable time to get the work done. On 12 August 1930, after the Bavin Government had extended printing for another year on the understanding that all reports would now come in, he informed Iredale that the situation was urgent but received no reply. He wrote again on 15 July 1931, reiterating 'the extreme urgency in completing the report'—it was 'a case of necessity'.[19] Still no reply. By 8 October the Agreement had been terminated, and Mawson wrote once more to berate Iredale for his laziness, deception and lack of common courtesy. 'On various occasions you have told me that completion would be a matter of only a few weeks, and so it has drifted on. I am at a loss to know why you should so injure myself and the Expedition Reports.'[20] Yet even as he lashed out he was forced to maintain a reserve, for surely Iredale had done *something*? He ended by demanding a definite answer one way or another.

To this third letter there was again no reply, so in December he sent two letters, one to Iredale, the other to Dr C. A. Anderson, Director of the Australian Museum, asking him to investigate the situation.[21] This produced results. Iredale replied that he now wished to work with R. A. Falla, the BANZARE ornithologist, on a *combined* report on birds. This idea was no good at all—Mawson had advertised for years that the AAE report on *Birds* was imminent, and in any case he no longer trusted Iredale. Accordingly at the end of November 1932 he wrote to Iredale to say he was asking Anderson 'to collect the whole of the material that has been placed in your hands . . . we have already had some great disappointments where collaborators have died before handing their materials back to the New South Wales Government with resultant loss of specimens and notes'.[22]

The AAE *Birds*, like the *Penguins*, *Sea Elephants* and *Seals and Whales*, would never eventuate. All should have appeared in the early 1920s. Repeatedly throughout his life Mawson would feel let down by trusted associates because his expectations of human nature were in general too high. In this instance R. A. Falla would retrieve the situation somewhat by producing the BANZARE report on *Birds* right on schedule, in 1937. Moreover, it would include in its analyses and findings all the ornithological evidence brought back by the AAE. And on its title page no credit would be given to the two temporizing individuals who had produced nothing towards it for so long.

A more pathetic instance of the same human problem was the proposed AAE report on *Pycnogoniga* (sea-spiders). This work was entrusted to Theodore Thomson Flynn, Ralston Professor of Biology at Hobart. Flynn had directed the marine biological work on *Aurora* during its cruise of November–December 1912. However, for twenty years he produced nothing on the pycnogons whatsoever, not even working papers. Maybe he was too busy with his amateur theatricals and debating. His rebellious son Errol Flynn, the future film star, never took up much of his father's time, growing up wild, expelled from a string of schools and embarked on the 'wicked, wicked ways' described so lovingly in his 1959 autobiography. Mawson waited until March 1931, having received no replies to his numerous letters, and now having learned from someone else that Flynn had left the previous September for London. He had to ask the Registrar to collect all the dusty, faded, forlorn and abandoned sea-spiders from whatever benchtop, store-room or cabinet they had been languishing in or on, pack them up and send them to the Australian Museum in Sydney, where Isabella Gordon would work on them, producing the report under her name exclusively in 1938.

The AAE reports, like the BANZARE reports later, were farmed out to specialists all over the world and it was a major task to ensure that work on each of them was progressing. Mawson had to proof-read the reports as they went through the press, first editing them if necessary, sometimes re-writing them, while re-directing unfinished papers and specimens from one contributor to another as people died or defaulted on their obligations. His own reports were long delayed by exigencies of war, by the BANZARE cruises and by his tendency to take on more work than he could comfortably handle. They included the *Records of the Aurora Polaris* (1925), the *Hydrological Observations* (1940), the *Marine Biological Programme and Other Zoological and Botanical Activities* (1940), the *Sedimentary Rocks* (1940), the *Records of Minerals of King George V Land, Adélie Land and Queen Mary Land* (1940), the *Catalogue of Rocks and Minerals* (1940), the *Geographical Narrative and Cartography* (1942), and *Macquarie Island—its Geography and Geology* (1943). These titles represent a major contribution to the science of Antarctica.

The later BANZARE reports (1937–75) were financed by a trust fund established by the Commonwealth Treasury and overseen by a committee, and later by the Mawson Institute for Antarctic Research. There was also a contribution from the Antarctic Division of External Affairs, arranged by Phillip Law. Mawson reserved the most important of these reports, the Geographical Report, for himself, but would never complete it. After his death it would be written up from his papers by Archie Grenfell Price and published in book form in 1962.[23] Mawson's input into the BANZARE reports was less considerable than his contribution to the AAE reports. He was older, his contributors on the whole were more reliable, and his daughter Pat had the necessary energy to help him edit them. Interestingly, the book he intended to write about the BANZARE, *Frozen Frontiers*, would never eventuate. Altogether he seems to have lost some of his interest in the BANZARE once its geopolitical goals had been attained. Moreover, as will be seen, there were souring qualities in the aftertaste.

12 POLITICS AND POWER

ANTARCTIC POLITICS CAME of age on 21 July 1908, when Britain established the Falkland Islands Dependencies, administered from Port Stanley and covering a swathe of ocean, islands and unexplored Antarctica across 60 degrees of longitude, and south to the Pole. Subsequently this action enabled Britain to regulate and license the whaling industry within this vast region, levy royalties on catches, and prohibit the killing of females and calves.[1] In 1923 the British set up the Ross Sea Dependency which achieved a similar effect to the south of New Zealand, the whaling revenues after 1923 going to the New Zealand Government. Then on 29 March 1924 the French claimed Adélie Land. Mawson publicly opposed this, but in the interests of Franco-British relations it was soon recognised by Britain, and was in any case justifiable—Dumont D'Urville had discovered that piece of coast as long ago as 1840 even if he had not actually landed on it, just as Mawson would soon be claiming Enderby Land, Kemp Land and Princess Elizabeth Land all the way to the Pole without landing on any of them.

In Mawson's view it made sense for Australia to claim the Antarctic quadrant to its south. He had been quoted by the Melbourne *Argus* as early as January 1921 as saying that

It has become an axiom accepted by the whole world that the un-inhabited polar regions should be controlled by the nearest civilized nation. Our government will not recognize this fact. But when a place is 'No Man's Land', the animals which inhabit it are bound to suffer. That is why I am so anxious to see Macquarie Island protected. Our claim to control in the Antarctic is based partly on our work of exploration and partly [on] the international axiom I have mentioned. The government should not neglect its duty.[2]

Through the mid-1920s he continued to hammer the point, notably through the ANRC which discussed the question on 6 March 1925. In response, Prime Minister Stanley Melbourne Bruce told the press that the matter had been discussed with the British Government over the previous eighteen months.[3]

Nevertheless the ANRC formed a delegation to see him, headed by Professor Sir David Orme Masson, but found it hard to arrange a meeting. 'If the P.M. fails us in the end', Masson told Mawson in May, 'we must go for publicity'.[4] In the event, Bruce saw them on 3 July when they urged that Australia challenge the French claim and act in concert with Britain to secure for Australia the administration of the Antarctic continent between 90°E. and 160°E., using the AAE's exploration in the region as a justification. Bruce indicated that the Government would pursue these claims 'through the proper channels'.[5] The following year the Imperial Conference of Commonwealth countries, meeting in London, considered the question and listed areas of Antarctica within the Australian quadrant which might justifiably be annexed by the British Government on the basis of British sightings in the nineteenth century or exploration by expeditions under Mawson and Scott, including Enderby Land between 45°E. and 53°E., Kemp Land between 58½°E. and 60°E., Queen Mary Land between 86°E. and 101°E., Wilkes Land between 131°E. and 135½°E., King George V Land between 142°E. and 153°E., and Oates Land between 157°E. and 159°E. Although the Conference advocated further exploration and research in these regions, no concrete schemes to plant the flag and read proclamations were mooted at this stage.

In the meantime Mawson had other things on his mind, among them timber. As noted earlier, the farm on the edge of the

Kuitpo Forest at The Meadows was rich in redgum trees, and he had joined with others in the area in developing a mill and exploiting the local hardwood resources by selling paving blocks and railway sleepers to the South Australian Government, and larger cuts to BHP for use in their mines. This business went under the name of South Australian Hardwoods. Later they acquired the Commercial Case Company in suburban St Peters and concentrated on pine. Keen to see the development of a strong forestry school at the University, Mawson wrote to Prime Minister Bruce in June 1925, protesting against a Government proposal to establish a forestry school at Canberra—'a cruel injustice to and in defiance of Adelaide University', and something that was 'reflecting very badly against your [Nationalist] party over here'.[6]

In the following January, during the university vacation, he was in the northern island of New Zealand, studying the forestry industry at first hand, having earlier (and more briefly) looked into the economics of commercial pine plantations there during his visit of early 1923, when he had attended the AAAS meeting in Wellington.[7] This time he began with the big government forests around Putaruru, then toured extensively the other forests of the island. The country through which he was driven was mountainous, the roads narrow and dangerous, cutting round the precipitous sides of the ranges, with no fences on the outside to prevent careering down almost vertical falls of hundreds of feet. The car wound its way round the spurs in a seemingly endless series of bends, as he reported to Paquita, 'of sharp curvature, rising as they go steeply to the summit then plunging into the next valley beyond—Rises of 2000–3000 ft.'. They covered up to 250 tiring, nerve-wracking miles per day.[8] At this time he was looking to expand his property at The Meadows by purchasing adjacent land, and South Australian Hardwoods were interested in buying elsewhere in the Adelaide Hills—in the early 1930s they would buy properties at Lenswood ('Coralinga') and Myponga ('Spring Mount'), clearing them and planting pines. The New Zealand trip reflected Mawson's general interest in the timber industry and his concern to see it more widely developed in South Australia.

In October 1926 the Mawsons travelled to England via South Africa, leaving the children with Dr Will Mawson and his wife at Campbelltown in New South Wales. In South Africa they visited gold and diamond mines, and stayed in Cape Town with Paquita's sister Mary and her husband, the Dutch Consul-General. The ship also called at St Helena, the home-in-exile of Napoleon, and at Ascension. From London Paquita went to Holland while Mawson visited British academic colleagues and friends, and scientists who were contributing AAE reports. He based himself for some of the time at Ford's Hotel in London, and dropped Kathleen Scott a note soon after putting up there, in early November.

This friendship had been on ice for six years. After he had left England at the end of the war she had written just once, in 1920, a nostalgic letter which took a while getting to the point:

> My dear Douglas,
>
> I'm down at Sandwich which never fails to remind me of you. Do you remember your potato patch, and the little tent on the beach which when the wind blew its canvas used to send you to sleep? No, of course, you don't remember any of these trivialities—but I do . . .
>
> I've been seeing a good deal of Stefansson, he is a *most* interesting, highly cultivated and intelligent person. I wonder why people have not made more fuss about his exploits. Is there anything wrong with him? . . .
>
> Goodbye my dear. I wish you were here. Don't get completely lost.
>
> Ever K. S.[9]

Now it was six years later and he was curious to see her again. She answered his note at once:

> Hurray! Hurry up and come to see me—Come before Saturday because I go away for the week end—I am very free until then— My cook is away but I could give you some sort of meal and anyway I must see you quickly—Ring up before though for I am so much out—Don't forget it is about 10 years since you saw me and I am an

old grim grey decrepid [*sic*] hag—& Peter is 3 inches taller than me and broad in proportion and goes to Cambridge in a year's time. Come soon. Ever Kathleen (Mrs Hilton Young—he is away—is my new name.)[10]

If he saw her that month there is no record of the visit. He certainly saw her on 8 December, for he told Paquita. He had gone along to Nellie Melba's farewell concert in the afternoon, and called on Kathleen for drinks at 6.00 p.m., not staying for dinner. 'Walking home I note in Swan & Edgar a catch line of perfectly splendid leather attache cases (small) for 6/9 each. We should have one each for the children.'[11] There are no records of the two ever meeting again after this, though they may have seen each other on his subsequent visits to London. It was a significant friendship, particularly during 1916, and earlier too, when Kathleen's generosity had slashed the AAE's debt by 25 per cent. Such friends are scarce.

After spending a few days in Paris, the Mawsons travelled on the *Aquitania* for New York in early January 1927. Lee Keedick had organised a lecture tour like that of 1915, but less hectic, and Mawson had to prepare an article for the American Geographical Society on 'Unsolved Problems of Antarctic Exploration and Research', a key paper which put at the top of its list of 'problems' the continentality or otherwise of the Antarctic land beneath the polar ice cap (some thought a group of islands underlay the ice), and possible ways to an answer. The paper appeared in *Problems of Polar Research* (New York, 1928)—the most advanced body of scientific thought on the field at the time, with a Foreword by Isaiah Bowman, Director of the American Geographical Society, soon to be one Mawson's most important allies in the funding of the BANZARE.

In New York they checked in at the Old Waldorf, one of the great hotels of its era—room 394, for two weeks from 13 January.[12] They saw Stefansson, whom they had known for several years (he had lectured in Australia in 1924 and stayed more than once with the Mawsons at Brighton).[13] They also dined with the President of the American Museum of Natural History, Dr Fairfield Osborn, and his wife.

One morning that fortnight Roald Amundsen was breakfasting at the Old Waldorf with Lincoln Ellsworth, an American millionaire with a passion for Arctic aviation. The two had flown together over the Arctic twice, in 1925 and with General Umberto Nobile in 1926 when (given the recent suggestion that Richard E. Byrd faked his logs) they probably became the first to fly over the North Pole.[14] It was quiet in the elegant dining room, just subdued conversation, cutlery clinking on china, the turning of newspaper pages. Amundsen noticed Mawson breakfasting at the other end of the room and pointed him out, though he chose not to disturb him. In the mid-1930s Ellsworth and Mawson would become good friends.[15] There was nothing extraordinary in this 'sighting'. All the great explorers of the day moved in an international world of hotels and liners, seeking money for the next expedition or making it by talking about the last. Like the diner at the other end of the room, Ellsworth was preparing his own article for *Problems of Polar Research*—in fact almost all the contemporary or recent polar explorers would be represented in this magnificent American collection.[16]

At Hobbs's invitation Mawson took the train to Ann Arbor to try out his lecture at the University of Michigan on 22 January. The advertising leaflet indicates his typical presentation—headlines run 'Racing with Death in Antarctic Blizzards. Thrilling Story and Moving Pictures', and there are testimonials such as 'Unforgettably impressive'. Seats were 50¢ and $1.00. It was all frankly commercial.[17] He was concerned that the money for printing the AAE reports was running out, with many reports unpublished and their preparation often involving incidental expenses he had to meet.

The lecture tour, intended to solve these financial problems, began on 1 February at the American Museum of Natural History in New York, and took in the University of Pennsylvania, the University of Rochester, Ohio State University and Iowa State University. The addresses were all titled 'Racing with Death' as at Ann Arbor, except in New York where Mawson cannibalised his article for *Problems of Polar Research* and added autobiographical elements.[18] What the returns were is unclear, but speaking at universities meant minimal overheads (though Keedick took a fee, of course). While Mawson was touring the lecture, Paquita travelled to San Francisco to stay with one of her sisters and her brother, visiting child welfare centres on the way across. (In South Australia she was involving herself more and more in this area through the Mothers and Babies Health Association.) As soon as the tour was over Mawson joined her and they sailed home on the *Wanganui*. This turned out to be the last overseas trip they ever took together.

In March 1927 the Australian Government finally moved on the matter of an Antarctic expedition to assert British claims and show the flag in the Australian quadrant. On 21 March Percival Deane, Secretary to the Prime Minister, wrote to Orme Masson, citing recommendations of the recent Imperial Conference, including 'the taking possession by an officer authorised for the purpose of such . . . areas as are not known to have been so taken possession of at the time of discovery'. What were the ANRC's views on how to give effect to this recommendation, the Prime Minister wondered.[19] Masson replied, enclosing a map supplied by J. K. Davis, and recommending that the ANRC set up an Antarctic Committee with power to act and advise—it should include Masson, Mawson, Davis, Richard H. Cambage, President of the ANRC, and Masson's protégé David Rivett (on the executive committee of the newly formed Council for Scientific and Industrial Research, or CSIR, intended to facilitate the application of science to industry). At the same time Masson sought Mawson's views on recommendations hammered out by Masson and Davis— use of Scott's old ship, the *Discovery*, to be loaned, they hoped, by Britain, landings and flag-raisings along indicated parts of the Australian quadrant on the assumption that these would subsequently be placed under Australian control, a second season in the Antarctic if necessary, a scientific programme compatible with the territorial objectives, and use of an aeroplane.[20]

Mawson was delighted: 'I can come to Melbourne when required as all else with me takes a second place'. He agreed with Masson and Davis on territories to be annexed, with the exception of the area around Gaussberg: 'the Germans landed upon Gauss Berg and raised their flag long before we did. Their claim for Gauss Berg is ever so much stronger than France's claim for Adélie Land.'

He also queried Masson's sentence, 'We presume that these [terri-
tories] will subsequently be placed under Australian control'.
'Should they not now be under Australian control?' he asked.
'Canada does not ask Great Britain for permission to explore and
take possession of unknown lands to the north of Canada.' A good
point.[21]

There followed seventeen months during which the
Government digested the recommendations. Masson continued to
consolidate the ANRC's Antarctic Committee and garner influential support in Canberra. For instance on 5 July 1927 there was a
luncheon, to which the Mawsons were invited, at the Lyceum Club
in Melbourne, given by Lady Masson, the twenty-four guests
including Commonwealth Attorney-General J. G. Latham, Major
R. G. Casey (the Australian Government's political liaison officer in
London, a man with a strong interest in Antarctic matters), Rear
Admiral W. R. Napier, First Member of the Naval Board and an
addition to the Antarctic Committee, and others including Sir John
Monash, Vice-Chancellor of the University of Melbourne.[22] By
January 1928, however, Mawson felt that the Government had lost
interest, and suggested as much to the press, which drew a denial
from the Prime Minister.

With momentum on the Antarctic front stalled, Mawson left
Australia at the end of March 1928 heading east on a radically new
venture, this one, he sensed, a money-spinner. As an eminent
geologist he had been approached by a group of New Zealand
businessmen to assist in the promotion of a gigantic hydro-electric
proposition, for which they held the concession, to harness the
waters of Lake Manapouri at Deep Cove in the south-west of the
south island, in the heart of the New Zealand Sounds. The leading
figure in the group was A. Leigh Hunt of Wellington, and the
'Sounds' scheme, which went under the titles of the Pacific Power
Production Ltd. and (later) the New Zealand Hydro-Electric
Concessions Ltd., envisaged the production of electricity for a
number of new industries that could be developed alongside the
hydro venture—industries involving the fixing of atmospheric nitrogen, production of metallic aluminium and magnesium, manufacture
of phosphorus and concentrated fertilisers, and of pure, soft iron

and electrolytic zinc.[23] This would open up the isolated region, though Mawson apparently hoped it could all be done without spoiling the intense beauty of the natural environment.[24] 'A cable assured us he was interested', Leigh Hunt later wrote, 'and stated he would journey to Melbourne to meet our representatives . . . We were not long in this great man's company before we agreed he had all the qualifications necessary and that geology would play a prominent part in the negotiations overseas.'[25]

In New Zealand Mawson was shown around the site of the projected scheme and thoroughly briefed, and a few days later sailed on the *Rotorua* for England by way of the Panama Canal. At meals he was on the Captain's left, with Sir Joseph Ward, former New Zealand Premier, on the Captain's right. Ironically, while the then-current New Zealand Government under Gordon Coates was interested in the Manapouri scheme, Ward would refuse to endorse it on returning to power at the next election. This speaks less than volumes for Mawson's convivial influence, at least on that voyage, though he did manage to persuade the Captain to have rocks brought aboard at Pitcairn Island—the first rocks ever collected there for study.[26]

It was a slow trip, with a stop in Panama. The agent for the shipping company took Ward and Mawson to see the sights, including the exclusive Spanish American Club with its open-air dining room and ballroom jutting out over the waters of the Pacific. They toured Balboa, driving along avenues lined with Royal Palms and streets overarched with poinsettias meeting in a continuous flow of scarlet flowers. Along the sides of the streets red hibiscus bushes gave relief to wide green lawns and carried the floral display all the way up to the brilliant purple of the bougainvillea-draped walls of the houses.[27]

On his arrival in London on 9 May, Mawson established himself at the Royal Societies Club and set about promoting the hydro scheme and finding the massive sums required to fund it. One of the first things he did was to re-draft the material with which he had been briefed in New Zealand, producing an attractive brochure to use in approaching European capitalists. He was advised that a Dr Adler of the German General Electric Company in Berlin would be interested, and that Dr Theo Haege of Heidelberg would prove a good source of technical information. Accordingly he travelled to Berlin in late May to see Adler, who promised to use General Electric's connections with electro-chemical concerns in the United States, Sweden and Belgium. While in Berlin he attended the centenary celebrations of the Geographical Society there, and in Frankfurt he discussed the scheme with Haege.

Back in London in early June he approached Imperial Chemical Industries Ltd. who turned the proposal down flat, partly because it would compete with their own synthetic nitrogen plant at Billingham-on-Tees, partly because they were already involved in promising negotiations with the Australian Government to produce fertilisers. By late June Mawson could see that to persuade any financial house to float the project he would have to provide full details of how the power would be employed, of the programme of production, of markets, statements of costs and real-isation prices, assurance of the supply of raw materials and their costs, a close estimate of total capital required, and the incidence of its projected expenditure. To this end it would be necessary to prepare details of plant and manufacturing costs for each of the proposed industries—technical information which had to be sought out and carefully checked. All of this involved him in a great deal of work, day and night, and consultation with Dr Haege and other authorities, as well as with firms manufacturing plant for the various productions contemplated. Eight weeks were consumed in collecting and elaborating all these data, and, on the side, in numerous interviews with representatives of companies likely to be of help in floating the venture. In all, he had meetings with London representatives of six large British concerns and four American, as well as with two large Continental industrial companies, I. G. Farben of Germany and ASEA Electric of Sweden. These were exhausting and depressing weeks for him as one avenue after another was closed off.[28] To make matters even worse, he heard at this time that (in his own words) 'The Australian Govt. is rather backing down over the Antarctic business though the ship "Discovery" is available'.[29]

By the middle of August he had submitted the scheme in all its detail to a City finance firm, Medley, Hartmann & Co. Ltd., and they and their associates offered to underwrite it to the sum of £6 500 000 on certain conditions, including payment of 5 per cent interest by the New Zealand Government on expended moneys during the anticipated five-year period of construction. According to Mawson the Coates Government felt unable to accede to these terms and the offer lapsed.[30] In November Sir Joseph Ward came to power and refused to reopen the issue. Mawson remained hopeful, though, of being able to interest other potential backers.

He was back in Australia by the end of September and within days had a letter from Dr W. Henderson, Director of the Department of External Affairs, to say that 'The Prime Minister has asked me to see you on your return ... with respect to the Antarctic'. Mawson saw Henderson at the University of Adelaide at 3.00 p.m. on Thursday 11 October. This was the go-ahead for which he had been waiting.[31] However, the Prime Minister took no formal action until after the elections, held later that year. The Government were already anticipating tangible profits from the creation of an Australian Antarctic Dependency in the licensing and control of whaling. Mawson told Davis in early November,

> When in England I had many talks concerning whaling with the authorities—I went so far as to advise the Commonwealth Government that a whaling Coy. was in preparation in Australia–New Zealand and would wish to operate after the zone had been taken possession of by Australia—on formal permit. Accordingly the Australian Government has *reserved a permit*—but the only other permit they may offer has been given under cloak of British permit. This is a secret and they asked me to tell nobody just yet. I can tell more on reaching Melbourne.[32]

The letter also reveals that at this stage Mawson was planning to take two Moth aircraft on the expedition rather than the one he finally settled on.

During November he visited New Zealand again in connection with the Sounds scheme. By now he and others had taken out

leases over alunite deposits in Western Australia. Workable consign-
ments were sent to Britain and the United States for reports on
appropriate processes for treatment, and Mawson himself patented
a process.[33] He doubtless intended to sell the alunite to his New
Zealand friends once they got their scheme going, for he told Sir
Robert Horne in 1933 that the Sounds project envisaged 'Fixation
of nitrogen . . . and . . . production of . . . fertilizers utilising perhaps
Australian alunite and Nauru phosphate', and 'Production of
Aluminium . . . from Australian alunite'.[34] It was yet another
'bonanza' that never paid out, like Shackleton's Hungarian gold
mines and Mawson's radium mines. He wrote Paquita from New
Zealand, 'My time is being fully occupied in interviewing
Government officials and others relative to the Sounds proposition . . . The Sounds scheme looks definitely brighter now.' That
was before the new Government dissociated itself from the idea.
He also mentioned bad news he had received from home on the
timber front—the Broken Hill South Mine had decided not to buy
any more timber from South Australian Hardwoods.[35]

Mawson was home for Christmas but off again in the New
Year, once more for England, on the *Orama*. At Port Said he
received a cable confirming that the Government were definitely
backing the expedition (though not bankrolling it), and learned
that the British had agreed to lend *Discovery* for two seasons.[36] In
London he set about ordering equipment and provisions. 'I am
filling every moment', he wrote home, 'in sending out begging
letters to firms for foods and goods. They are responding well. It
would have been nice if you had been here. I have two offices and
nobody to help. One office is in the Dominions Office and also
one at Australia House. I am getting lots of applications to join the
expedition from people on this side.'[37] The first meeting of his
London (or Discovery) Committee was held at the Colonial Office
on 20 February 1929—himself as chairman, with Rear Admiral
H. P. Douglas (hydrographer, RN), Major R. G. Casey, J. B. Borley
and a secretary. Preparations seem to have gone smoothly. Before
leaving for Australia on 9 May on the *Maloja* he showed the Duke
and Duchess of York over the *Discovery*, the Duchess trying on
wolfskin mitts and sampling pemmican. Stefansson was there too.

During his time in London he lectured on the Sounds project to the RGS. He was still trying to find a backer, and turned to the American Cyanamide Company which was aiming at a world trade in nitrogen fertilisers. They commissioned a hydro-electrical engineer, H. P. Gibbs, to supply a report, completed in May 1930. This was satisfactory, but by then the Depression was deepening fast. American Cyanamide backed off, while in New Zealand the shutters at the Treasury were closing against the bleak, hard winds of fate. All of Mawson's work on this grand scheme would finally come to nothing.

13 Divided Command

THE NEW EXPEDITION laboured under two impediments from the start, the *Discovery* and a divided command. Nothing could be done about the first. The ship was provided by the British Government, with nothing to pay but insurance. She was a barque with auxiliary, triple-expansion steam engine, purpose-built for Scott's first expedition, of wood, which is flexible in the ice—in fact so thick was her hull that internal space was limited, particularly in the coal bunkers. On the principle that what looks good goes well, any fool could see that *Discovery* would sail poorly. Compared to *Aurora* she looked unbalanced, and as Shackleton had observed, she 'steered badly, there being too much sail aft and not enough forward'.[1] Everyone knew, as BANZARE's biologist/zoologist Harold Fletcher noted, that Scott 'did not take her on his second ill-fated expedition because of her extreme rolling propensities'.[2] To give her minimal stability she required, on top of the weight of complement, stores and gear, at least 50 tons of coal reserved as ballast. This was well known, and Davis emphasised the point to Mawson months before they sailed: '*Ballast*: At least 50 tons of ballast would be required in the bottom of the vessel when returning from Enderby Land'.[3]

The second impediment was the command structure: Mawson in command, Davis second-in-command and master of the ship, but only when Mawson was not on board. This may seem strange, but it was the case. 'The expedition', Mawson later told J. S. Cumpston, 'was purely a ship expedition. Therefore Captain Davis was not in command of the ship when I was on board. He was the ship's captain but when I was not on board Davis could be said to be in command. I would not have sailed if things had been otherwise.'[4] So in Mawson's own words, Davis was 'the ship's captain' yet 'not in command of the ship'! This paradox is apparently not exceptional in modern times.[5] There was a reservation built-in to complicate matters still further:

> The [Australian] Committee . . . did give Davis the right to veto my instructions if he as Ship's Captain was of the opinion that the safety of the ship was too gravely endangered thereby.
>
> That power of veto seemed reasonable to the Committee and in most respects it was. However, it was just that which halved the geographical results we could have obtained on the 1929/30 cruise and robbed us of a crowning feature on the 1930/31 cruise.[6]

It used to be regarded as a good general rule that a marine exploring expedition should sail under a naval officer, as most of the great ones historically have—James Cook and Matthew Flinders are obvious examples. He then has every incentive to push himself and his ship to the limit, for the achievements and honours will be his. Lieutenant-Commander Davis was the most experienced Antarctic navigator of his generation and he was being required to sail south not even in command of his ship. Of course Sir Douglas Mawson, supreme commander of the AAE, could hardly be appointed Davis's second-in-command. So traditional principle was sacrificed to a command structure custom-made for conflict.

Even so, steps might have been taken to forestall possible problems. Davis was an intensely proud man. He had won his extra-master's certificate at an early age, with experience in full-rigged sailing ships like the *Celtic Chief*, and in Antarctic waters he had been chief officer and later master on *Nimrod*, master of *Aurora* on its cruises of 1911–14, and commander of the Ross Sea Relief Expedition which rescued survivors of Shackleton's Imperial Trans-Antarctic Expedition marooned at Cape Evans in 1916. During World War I he had commanded Australian transport ships, and in 1920, at thirty-six, had been appointed Director of Commonwealth

Navigation, based in Melbourne. Yet no honours had come his way apart from the FRGS he always put at the top of his entry in *Who's Who*. A Companionship bestowed at the level of CVO or CBE would have been appropriate. Mawson saw the advisability of this during the voyage and mentioned it, but tensions had built and Davis angrily rejected the idea. After the first BANZARE cruise Mawson drafted an unaddressed letter (probably to R. G. Casey) on the Melbourne Express, pointing out that while Davis had emphatically rejected the suggestion, 'I have much reason to believe that recognition by the King is the very thing which he has subconsciously desired.' Admiral Evans (Lord Mountevans), he thought, would support it.[7] This was one of the sharpest insights into Davis Mawson ever had. Nothing eventuated, perhaps because Davis got wind of it. The matter was delicate.

In addition to this sin of omission, there were sins of commission. Mawson should have strenuously avoided provoking or slighting Davis, an irascible man who knew how to bear a grudge, yet provoked and slighted he was. Through the early months of 1929 Mawson was in London, Davis in Melbourne. After June the position was reversed. Misunderstandings were inevitable. In February Davis was approached by the Melbourne press for details of the expedition and gave them some basic information. An angry letter came from Mawson in London:

> In the middle of one of our Committee meetings [at the Colonial Office] yesterday a furore arose when a special messenger brought in an urgent cable from [Australian Prime Minister] Mr. Bruce stating that the press in Melbourne had got hold of our proposals from yourself. The Government is tremendously upset about this and wonder what on earth caused you to give them away. They have decided that the only possible thing to do now is to make a simultaneous public statement in Australia and London.[8]

The style and tone are very Mawsonian.

The men differed on how to tackle the Australian quadrant of Antarctica (45°E. to 160° E.), letters literally and symbolically crossing each other's paths. One from Davis, sent on 12 March, urged a start from Hobart, thence south and westward along the sector, taking on 200 tons of coal from a whaler by pre-arrangement in the shelter of the Shackleton Ice Shelf in order to probe the coasts of Enderby Land, likely to be explored also by the Norwegians, in late summer when they would be more approach-able. They would finish at Cape Town. Davis put this plan to the first meeting of the organising committee set up by Bruce, where the expedition's priorities were defined as 'firstly, political; secondly, economic and commercial; thirdly, scientific', the flag to be 'hoisted and British title asserted at all places practicable between King George 5th Land (160° E) and Enderby Land (45° E.)'.[9]

Contrary to Davis's view, Mawson thought Enderby Land should be first priority as there was 'a real danger that the Norwegians would get in first'. He therefore wished to start from Cape Town.[10] His plan would seem to get them to these western coasts earlier, but as he would want to stop at the Crozet Islands, then at Kerguelen Island to coal, and also at Heard Island, the differ-ence is insignificant. Clearly neither Mawson nor Davis was taking seriously Norway's agreement of late 1928, in return for Britain's recognition of Norway's claim to Bouvet Island, not to claim terri-tories stipulated as British interests at the Imperial Conference of 1926. This had mentioned Enderby and Kemp Lands at the western end of the Australian quadrant but not undiscovered lands to their immediate east—the future Mac-Robertson and Princess Elizabeth Lands which Mawson would soon name. In any case Norway had not waived any right to *explore* the largely unknown coasts of Enderby and Kemp Lands, and discovery and exploration are the preconditions of claims.

By June Davis was in London operating out of Australia House and frantically busy ordering everything on Mawson's endless lists of requirements. Davis's biggest worry was *Discovery*'s lack of space. Her *prima facie* coal-carrying capacity he found to be fully 200 tons less than *Aurora*'s, partly because of changes made to turn her into a 'Royal Research Ship' over the past three years.[11] He wrote in June,

We are already in process of assembling in London more stores and equipment than we can possibly get into the ship without excluding coal which has already... been reduced to such a small amount that it is going seriously to jeopardise our chance of carrying out an extensive programme. I would ask you to give consideration to this problem when ordering stuff in Australia.

A week later he wrote that on his own initiative he was reducing Mawson's lists of clothing to be purchased to a minimum, as it was crucial 'not to load the ship up with boxes of impedimenta which we may never use'.[12] This involved altering the numbers assigned to the various packing cases, something Mawson subsequently told Davis he 'deplored'.[13]

Then there was the matter of the writing paper Davis had had printed in London and was now using, headed 'The British, Australian, New Zealand Antarctic Research Expedition of 1929–30'. It went out to all suppliers and correspondents including Mawson, whose reaction was not favourable:

I was very upset... [The heading] has never been agreed to either by myself or the Committee. Accordingly I have asked Dr. Henderson to cable me to scrap all printed paper with that heading, and to have the new paper printed with the heading that was formally adopted at our last Committee meeting in Melbourne, 'British Australasian Antarctic Expedition'—leaving out the word 'Research' and leaving out any date. As this Expedition is to [run] for two summers the date you have put on the paper is not correct. The long winded title on your paper is, in my opinion, absolutely ridiculous.[14]

It was too late—Davis's stationery, already sent to all and sundry, ensured that this expedition would forever bear the 'absolutely ridiculous' title Davis had given it. All Mawson could do to 'shorten' the title was to have new reams printed with the top line reading 'BANZ', the second line 'Antarctic Research Expedition', which was still ridiculous of course, and for many recipients probably indecipherable to boot.

Davis also made the mistake of arranging the purchase of the ship's launch in Australia after cabling *via* Casey to the Australian

Antarctic Committee, 'impossible to obtain suitable launch in London in time'.[15] Mawson told him that it was 'like carrying coals to Newcastle. A motor will have to pay duty to come into Australia and there will be the cost of transport to South Africa.'[16] Thus *Discovery* reached Cape Town on 7 October under a captain who had 'tremendously upset' the Australian Government, 'deplorably' altered Mawson's packing arrangements, foisted an 'absolutely ridiculous' title on the expedition, and foolishly 'carried coals to Newcastle' over the motor launch.

Still, Davis was treated with great respect by a talented Cape Town correspondent, who came away impressed:

> He knows his mind and has no awkward habit of speaking it; he has an unerring eye for mountebanks, rustlers and charlatans. Adventurers and get-rich-quick sham explorers, would-be Shackletons or Wilkins, have been known to dissolve quickly when he has put the acid test on them. He does not suffer fools gladly. But in spite of or because of his journeyings he manages to retain a lively interest in life.

The correspondent then modulated into a Conradesque key, accurately catching the very soul of John King Davis:

> It seemed as if he was supremely conscious of the traditions of exploration and had not so much interest in personal achievement as in the maintenance and progress of that tradition. He reads widely and is a dreamer, and probably an incurable romantic, and yet his dreams and sense of the romantic have never succeeded in mastering his great good sense and intuition of what is practical.

This tight, acute analysis was read by the very unromantic Mawson on arrival in South Africa and transcribed onto notepaper, probably as further evidence of Davis's foolishness. In any case it was filed with a list of Davis's most recent sins.[17]

Meanwhile Mawson had been highly successful in raising funds for the expedition, and some donors would increase their gifts during the following two years. Like the AAE, this was essentially a private enterprise expedition supported and partly funded by the Government, with Government input on its organizing committee, now consisting of Sir George Pearce (Vice-President of the Executive Council) as Chairman, Mawson, Davis, Rear Admiral W. R. Napier (First Member of the Naval Board), Masson (Vice-President, ANRC), David Rivett (Chief Executive Officer, CSIR), and Dr W. Henderson (Director, Department of External Affairs); later, others were added including Sir Edgeworth David, H. J. Sheehan (Assistant Secretary to the Treasury), and Macpherson Robertson, or Mac-Robertson as he is usually called, confectioner, maker of 'Old Gold' chocolate, 'Cherry Ripe' and a host of other lines—the expedition's biggest donor. Up to 20 November 1931 Mac-Robertson donated £14 000 to the BANZARE (and in later *Who's Who*s he would give the final figure as £20 000).[18] The Commonwealth Government to the same date had contributed a matching £14 000. New Zealand gave £2500. The first £10 000 of the Mac-Robertson money came in during June 1929 after approaches by Mawson and Masson, who saw Mac-Robertson personally to finalise the deal.[19] The other great coup was the American press rights which Mawson sold to Randolph Hearst for $40 000 (£8200), far beyond any other offer. The *Times* bought the British rights for £1070, Australian United Press the local rights for £556, both chicken feed in Mawson's view.[20]

Discovery to one side, the BANZARE received more support from the United States than from Britain and might even have been titled (even more ridiculously) the BAANZARE, the second 'A' for 'American'. The Rev. J. Gordon Hayes, who had so praised the AAE in his book *Antarctica: A Treatise of the Southern Continent*, and actually applied to join the BANZARE ('I shall work only for love, and can do something towards my own expenses', he fondly pleaded[21]), wrote after the expedition asking why Mawson had published his first serious account of it in the American *Geographical Review* rather than the British *Geographical Journal*. Mawson answered the strange question in this way:

> There were two reasons for this—one was that the Director of the American Geographical Society's publication [the *Geographical*

Review], Dr. Bowman, is himself a fine geographer and an ardent enthusiast of geography. Also the American Geographical Society have set themselves out to help on Antarctic exploration as far as they possibly can. Bowman, therefore, was very ready to help me in everything connected with the realisation of the Expedition. He was actually mainly instrumental in our securing £8500 from the Hearst Press for the first voyage . . . On the other hand, the RGS in London took very little interest in our proposition and did not help us any more than lending us £15 worth of equipment which we returned . . . We were, therefore, much more encouraged in our work from America than from Great Britain.[22]

He would name an Antarctic promontory Cape Hearst, later changed to Cape Wilkins after Sir Hubert Wilkins. W. H. Hobbs chided Mawson for his association with Hearst.[23] However, Mawson's letter to Hayes shows how delighted he really was with the deal Isaiah Bowman had negotiated, and Grenfell Price is quite wrong to say that 'Mawson accepted this arrangement sadly'.[24] He was so 'sad' about taking Hearst's money, which folded as well as anyone else's, that he tried to get more of it for the second cruise of 1930–31, but it was 'no deal'—Hearst was disappointed in the 1929–30 cruise, which was not very newsworthy, and Mawson had to make do with a low offer from the *New York Times*.

The Australian Government helped with insurance, offering cover of £750 per expedition member. At this time Mawson wrote out a statement titled 'Realization Value of Estate', perhaps intended for Government eyes, as they had promised 'that if I was lost on the expedition the Government would pay a lump sum . . . not less than 5000'.[25] The 'Realization Value' has biographical importance, revealing Mawson's total material assets in 1929. He estimated the knock-down value of his Brighton home and land at £6000, his furniture and other effects at £930, his library and photographic collection at £200, his scientific instruments at £160, the Harewood estate (with the timber and mill interests, presumably) at £5370, his shares at £1400 and his life insurance at £1500. Other small categories took the total to just £16 150. This was a modest figure for a man of Mawson's national stature, and certainly insufficient to relieve him of worries about his family's future in the event of his death, as will be seen.[26]

He travelled to South Africa with other members of the expedition on the *Nestor*, arriving in Durban on 8 October. The press were inquisitive. What did he know about rumours that Hjalmar Riiser-Larsen's new *Norvegia* expedition was about to annex Antarctic lands for Norway ahead of *Discovery*? Mawson disclaimed any intent to race, and on 9 October sent the London *Daily News* a cable in reply to their cabled queries, stating that he was confining himself to an arc of lands in which Britain had long shown interest—Norway should focus its activities elsewhere, and practise scientific co-operation, not geographical contestation. This storm in a teacup, which has been analysed by Grenfell Price, was quickly smoothed over by Britain and Norway, and the Australian Committee's Dr Henderson of External Affairs cabled Mawson asking him to avoid saying anything controversial.[27]

On 13 October Mawson met up with Davis in Cape Town and at once they were in conflict. On board *Discovery*, the sails of which were being converted to barquentine configuration, was a DeHavilland DH60 Gipsy Moth, VH-ULD, bought new in England. Mawson had cabled Davis from Australia, 'erect anything and everything possible to adequately house the aeroplane', but because of the physical constraints of the ship, Davis had merely secured the cased fuselage and parts on board, not 'housed' everything. Mawson was furious. Davis countered by complaining about the 'immense job' Mawson had left him to do in England. Neither showed restraint and Davis threatened to resign then and there. This forced Mawson to back off and mend fences, for the chief officer, K. N. MacKenzie, had insufficient Antarctic experience to take over at this stage. Davis agreed to carry on, but warned that at this rate 'everybody on board would within a couple of months be sick of every other body'.[28] The BANZARE was off to a rough start.

14 THE FRUITS OF DIVISION

DISCOVERY SAILED FROM Cape Town on 19 October, to loud cheers and sirens,[1] heading south-east, heavy laden at a reluctant 4 knots, rolling her way through the swell (see maps, between pages 173 and 174, for the routes of the BANZARE cruises).

It took fourteen days just to reach the Crozets, where they found sealers butchering every last sea-elephant for its blubber on the shores of Possession Island, including mothers and their suckling young. 'The beach was soaked in blood', Professor Harvey Johnston, the expedition's chief biologist, observed. It was 'disgraceful since it means practically wiping out the entire herds that congregate there to breed'.[2] There were no controls on these sealers, who took their ship from island to island, ruthlessly harvesting the seal and penguin populations.

After securing large botanical and geological collections, the expedition sailed for Kerguelen Island, which was reached on 12 November. Here they re-coaled from stocks left by a South African whaling company by pre-arrangement at Port Jeanne d'Arc, in Royal Sound, on the south-east of the lonely, windswept island. Scientific observations and collections were made for twelve days while the long job of coaling proceeded. The island, or more properly archipelago, rises from peaty lowland bogs to the glacial peak of Mount Ross, an extinct volcano 6120 feet above sea level. Deep glacial valleys run down the mountains in all directions to the many deep fiords which knife the coasts. Much of the rock here is built up of an immense volcanic series.[3] Everywhere Mawson found evidence, as he wrote in the American *Geographical Review*, 'that formerly the ice flood extended over the whole of the island—everywhere are ice-worn surfaces, moraine débris, and deeply entrenched fiord grooves. The past glaciation has been on an overwhelming scale, evidently chronologically concurrent with the Pleistocene glaciation so well recorded in the northern hemisphere.'[4]

They sailed again on 24 November, Mawson dissatisfied at their failure to conduct a full oceanographic programme in Kerguelen waters. Yet had he not stopped at the Crozets they could have achieved more here. Again and again one finds his ambitions exceeding his time and resources. The expedition's goals, as set out for him in Bruce's signed and secret instructions of 12 September 1929, were primarily political: 'You will plant the British flag wherever you find it practicable to do so . . . read the proclamation of annexation', and so on.[5] And as we have seen, as early as the first meeting of the Australian Antarctic Committee on 12 March 1929 the expedition's purposes had been clearly spelt out as 'firstly, political; secondly, economic and commercial; thirdly, scientific'.[6] Yet Mawson would not sacrifice any of the time-consuming scientific work to get to the Antarctic as soon as possible. Kerguelen was a necessary coaling stop; the Crozets were dispensable. Even now they were not making for Antarctica but for Heard Island. Here, with a shore party, Mawson spent nine days inspecting the flora and fauna, carrying out survey work, dredging in Atlas Cove, and collecting and labelling geological specimens while *Discovery* rolled about in the turbulent waters of Corinthian Bay, burning up coal.

Davis developed a bad cold and was soon worn down by lack of sleep and anxiety for the ship's safety. The shore party, stationed in Atlas Cove, depended on the ship's launch to get them back around the intervening point to Corinthian Bay and the ship, Davis being reluctant to take *Discovery* into the Cove, given the heavy seas running on the point. When he still declined to come for them on 2 December, Mawson with three of the shore party set out for the ship in the launch. Harold Fletcher, one of the biologists, described this hazardous venture in his diary that night:

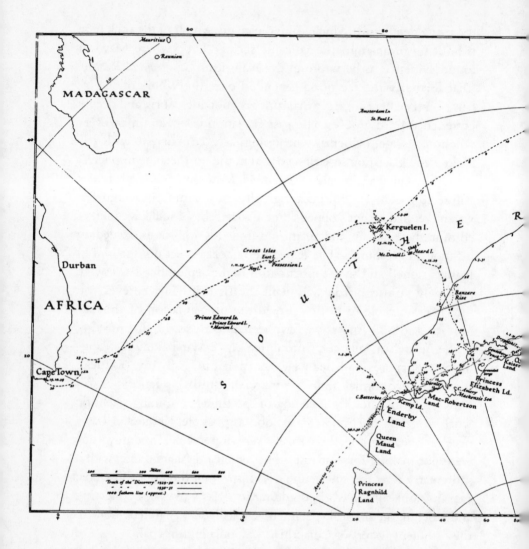

The route of the *Discovery* on the two voyages of the BANZARE.
Original map prepared under Mawson's supervision

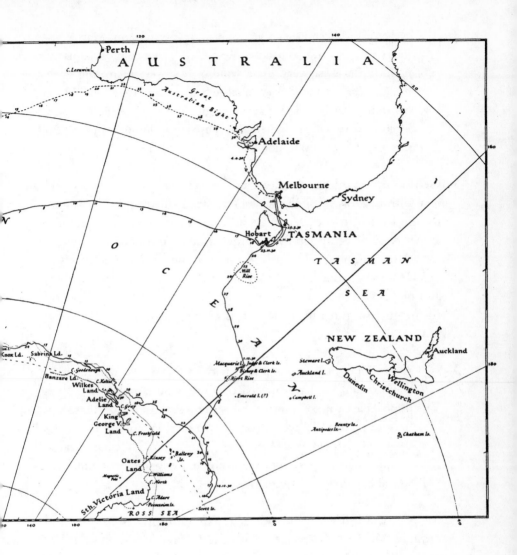

Never have I been in such seas before. . . . It was still snowing & visibility was very bad, so bad that we had to steer a compass course to pick up the 'Discovery'. The wind & seas were increasing every minute & we doubted very much whether Capt. Davis could keep his ship at anchor, and that we might find it gone. Things were looking very serious when the 'Discovery' loomed out of the snow—pitching and tossing like it never had before.

Getting on board was perilous, as 'she was ranging a good 12–15 feet with convulsive pitching. . . Gear was hauled up by. . . waiting for the launch to rise . . . and as the launch rose we had to grab the ladder & clamber up rapidly to prevent being crushed.'[7]

After climbing on board, Mawson immediately asked Davis to take *Discovery* round to the Cove to pick up the rest of the party, and he refused—'I don't see any urgent necessity to get them off till tomorrow morning.' Finally, as Davis put it in his 'Personal Journal',

> After a lot of messing about my advice to wait till morning has been adopted and we have hoisted the motor boat on board . . . It is impossible to make a man who is not a seaman realize that ships have to be handled with prudence, to take 'Discovery' into Atlas Cove today would have been quite possible to save life but to do so in order to pick up some people who can easily wait until tomorrow would have been the act of a fool.[8]

On the following morning, at 7.30 a.m., the ship's steward brought Mawson a message: 'With the Captain's compliments', it began, 'he says the men can come off now and if you are not taking the launch ashore he proposes send an officer with it'.[9] Mawson was incensed—Davis was in effect saying, 'I'm not risking my ship in these conditions, and if you don't have the guts to take the launch, then one of my officers will do the job'. Mawson then sat down at his desk, took an envelope and wrote on it 'Please post this letter / Dr. W. Henderson / External Affairs Dept. / *Canberra* / Australia.' Then he took a sheet of BANZARE notepaper and wrote out:

Heard Island
3. 12. 29

Dear Dr Henderson,

Just a line to say that am about to undertake risky job of taking launch around to Atlas Cove to bring off remainder of men ashore. It is important that these men should come off without further delay or expedition programme will be crippled. They would have come off some days ago but that Davis will not take ship to Atlas Cove for an hour to do job in safer water.

Should I not return please inform the government that my wife and family have only very slender means, and I hope that it will be found possible to provide a suitable sum for their sustenance.

With best regards

Yours sincerely,

Douglas Mawson.[10]

He folded the letter, sealed it in the envelope, handed it to somebody he trusted to send it, then asked Eric Douglas, the second aviator, whether he was willing to accompany him in the launch. 'I'll give it a go', Douglas replied. So at 8.10 a.m., in a rising wind, the launch was lowered and the two men set off.

The seas were wild around the point so they gave it a wide berth. Their approach to the shore took them past basalt cliffs, towards which the seas tended to drift the launch, so they steered well away from them. Then the engine struggled, coughed and stopped. Douglas assumed the problem was in the fuel feed, disconnected the lead from the tank, and accidentally let the retaining nut slip from his freezing fingers. It fell under the floor planking. They cast out the anchor but it took all the rope without bottoming, so they attached a dredging line and the anchor now reached the sea-floor and held. With the launch pitching viciously, Douglas pulled up the floor-boards and managed to find the nut, clear the fuel line and start the engine. Then the two of them hauled up the anchor, a difficult job, the launch now close to the cliffs. It was a very near thing.

At Atlas Cove they got the men and gear on board, then started out for the ship, the winds now sharp with snow. The return would normally have taken forty minutes. Under these conditions it took eighty, but by 11.00 a.m. everyone was on *Discovery*. Mawson noted in his diary, 'Davis had the impudence later to ask me whether I did not realise what a fool I had been in taking such a risk. The fact is he drove me to it.'[11]

Making south-east from Heard Island on 4 December, *Discovery* pioneered the echo-sounding of the long undersea ridge running from Kerguelen past Heard Island to Gaussberg in Antarctica, which Mawson named the Banzare Rise. Along the way, full plankton and hydrographic stations were regularly run, and meteorological balloons released and tracked by theodolite to measure wind velocities at high altitudes. By noon on 12 December the ship was in heavy pack-ice, at lat. 65°18' S., long. 80°12' E. On the 14th, with coal down to 270 tons and little slack water about, Mawson decided to abandon his plan to reach the vicinity of Gaussberg and then work west, instead trying directly for more navigable waters to the west in the hope of getting through to Enderby Land some 600 miles away. First, though, they were compelled to make north and, only after 17 December, slowly south-west. By Christmas Day they were close to the Antarctic Circle but just 150 miles west of their 16 December position, and nowhere near land.

Tensions rose and fell. One source of annoyance for Davis was the way Mawson 'messes about with everything from the food to the stowage of the holds'. On 9 December, after Mawson had worked with the scientific staff for hours on the big winch, Davis told him 'You make yourself into a regular boatswain. Why don't you get someone else to do that?', but soon gave up on this front as Mawson continued to regard almost every aspect of the ship as his own business.[12] One might distrust Davis's view that the scientific work lacked clear organisation, that 'it is all so hopelessly muddled; no system or method but just impulse rules here'.[13] Yet among Mawson's staff there was criticism too: 'He's not absolutely the best organiser', R. G. Simmers, the meteorologist, observed,

—beforehand, yes, as, for instance, in the minute detail in which we have been equipped—but in carrying out things oh no. If he tells one man some arrangement re programme that seems to suffice to his mind, for the whole group. And so far it hasn't. All the same I wouldn't rather have a different leader for any money as he is so capable himself, looks after everyone, and is such a continual cheerful inspiration . . . Wine, cigar, chocolate or sweets at every dinner.[14]

Phillip Law, who knew him well in the 1950s, also claims that 'He was a bit of a muddler and a messer administratively.'[15] However, in fairness it should be stressed that on BANZARE Mawson was almost as old as Edgeworth David had been on the BAE, and that when Law knew him Mawson was into his late sixties and seventies.

On 14 December, with the ship's passage blocked by a floe but open water further ahead, Mawson proposed using ice-chisels to break off the corner of the floe on the port bow. Davis went into a rage—'If you do that then you can go up onto the bridge and run the ship, I shall have nothing to do with it'.[16] To Mawson he seemed 'sulky, pigheaded, damned rude, uncouth and has no physical strength or stamina'.[17] There were regular disagreements over which direction offered best prospects of advance. Commander Morton Moyes, the cartographer, who had been meteorologist at the Western Base on the AAE (and who, like Davis, would not be on the second BANZARE voyage), wrote in his diary, 'all are heartily tired of the bickering which goes on over courses to be steered, speed & such matters. It makes things very unpleasant.'[18] The ship would often be stopped in its tracks while Davis, exhausted, took a daytime nap, not always trusting his Chief Officer, K. N. MacKenzie, to take charge in the ice conditions.

By 16 December a frustrated Mawson had actually convinced himself that Davis was criminally insane: 'It is a crime that we are going so slowly when all conditions are favourable. But the Captain's mental state is so serious that I have to restrain my actions in regard to him, else things may be much worse.' He decided to try to get the medical officer, Dr W. W. Ingram, to pronounce Davis insane, in which case he could be dismissed at once and MacKenzie, for all his lack of experience, appointed in his place, but Ingram, unsurprisingly, demurred. Mawson recorded,

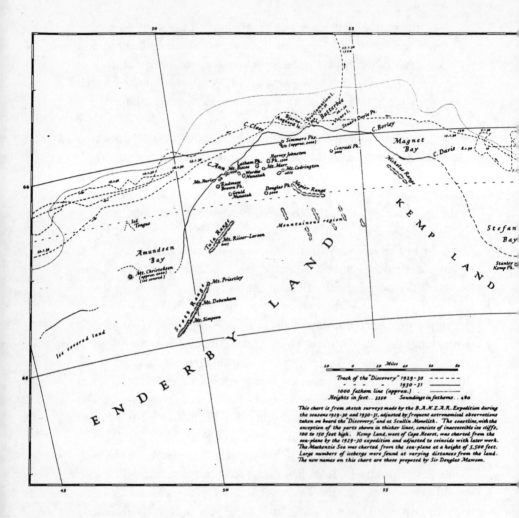

The track of the *Discovery* along the coasts of Enderby, Kemp and
Mac–Robertson lands during the two voyages of the BANZARE.
Original map prepared under Mawson's supervision

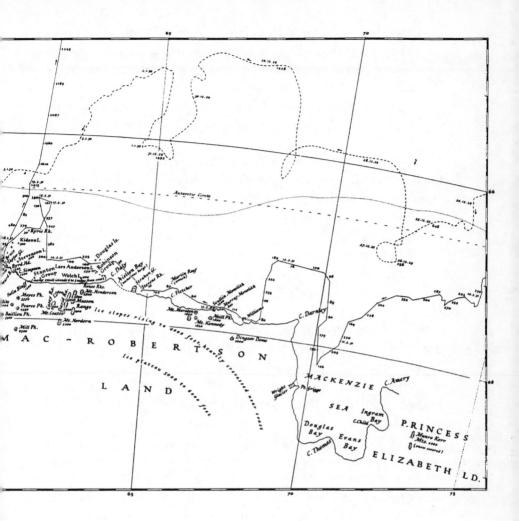

Have had a long talk with the Doctor who agrees that the Captain has lost mental balance and is on verge of insanity. He, however, cannot take action until the case is more clearly defined. In the meantime we are wasting opportunity and coal and are not doing all that is possible for Mr MacRobertson or the Committee. This worries me and depresses me seriously.[19]

Mawson was undoubtedly depressed, Davis was far from insane, and Dr Ingram was displaying admirable diplomacy. The simple truth about Davis is that his spirits were up and down just like Mawson's—each would drift to the edge of the reasonable. Just above Mawson's desk as he wrote those extraordinary entries, attached to the panelling of his cabin wall, staring at him, was a framed photograph of Mac-Robertson. 'Just what are you doing to merit my lavish patronage?' the man in the frame seemed to ask, every day, every night.

It was becoming imperative to get the Gipsy Moth set up and flying, but circumstances, the weather, fogs and pack kept it shipboard until 31 December when at last, with the ship at 66°10' S., 65°10' E., Flight Lieutenant Stuart Campbell and Eric Douglas made a flight to 5000 feet. They reported mostly solid pack ahead of the ship to the south for at least 40 miles, a few possible islands in the pack, and further away, on the horizon, just maybe, land. To the west the pack appeared broken and navigable. No reason for celebration here, and Mawson's diary records none, but it *was* New Year's Eve, and the end of the 1920s, and that evening, at 7.00 p.m., Mawson suggested to Davis, whom he found in bed, that they break out some wine. 'No, certainly not', Davis replied testily, 'what do you take me for? I'm not going to give them anything of that kind to make a row about in the night', then added, more calmly, 'If I do anything of that kind it will be for their dinner tomorrow'.[20] So the men were disappointed that night, and Mawson saw the decade out in solitude:

Midnight. At 11.30 pm the ship was steaming north in a perfectly placid sea, with the full disc of the sun above the south horizon. It was a marvellous scene—the rafts of ice, limned on the horizon, seemed unreal. Opal colouring in sea and sky, purplish-blue colour of some of the ice rafts. An open sea about us. I went up to the main truck to judge the nature of the pack ice to west and found it all broken ice with navigable waterways between. There seemed no reason whatever why we should not be running NW.[21]

He wished to drive north-west and then west in order to find a way south towards the 'land' seen by Campbell and Douglas, or failing that, to push further west to Enderby Land where the Norwegians were likely to be making. But when he awoke at 8.00 a.m. on New Year's Day, the ship was stationary with consolidated pack to the west.

He waited until 10.00 a.m. for Davis to emerge from his cabin, then knocked on the door and entered. Davis was sitting in his chair. Mawson, who wrote down the whole conversation later that day from memory, asked him what he was waiting for, thinking that Davis seemed 'in some ways not unlike Jeffryes was, prior to his dementia—he sits for hours in that chair and stares into vacancy'. Only rarely would the Captain say a word throughout a meal, and always had breakfast sent to his room.

Davis looked up and glowered. As far as he was concerned, he declared, he would stay there for a week and not worry. By waiting, there was a prospect that the ice pack to the west would blow away, allowing them to proceed in that direction.

Mawson begged to differ. That prospect was slim, he argued, especially as the present breeze from the north-west was tending to compact the ice. They were burning up two and a half tons of coal per day. Whatever they did now must be in accord with their obligations in regard to Enderby Land, where they should make their most concerted effort to reach land and raise the flag. They had to move west without delay. Since the pack prevented this, they would have to edge north to *get* west. Mawson thought the pack was probably loose enough to traverse to the north-west, judging by the sky, if a westerly course was in fact impossible.

This blithe assumption of expertise sent Davis into a tirade. Mawson, he said, was 'nothing but impatience', wanting to do everything at once. The ship had been 'a bedlam' ever since he came on board at Cape Town. He rushed everybody about, doing too many things at once, until everyone was 'heartily sick of things'. He would soon wake up and find that the staff would no longer put up with it—they were complaining amongst themselves, it would soon burst out, and then he would realise what a 'fool game' he had been playing. On any expedition Davis had been on before, he remonstrated, holidays like Christmas 'were always kept sacred and no work was done'. If Mawson interfered with regular holidays on expeditions he must expect to get all the staff against him. One of the most foolish things he did was 'to overwork everybody'. Unlike Shackleton, he never thanked the men for their efforts. Davis had 'slaved' himself almost to death in London arranging for the expedition, and all Mawson could do was to criticise the fact that he had bought the motor launch in Australia when it could have been purchased in Britain. Nor had Mawson 'properly congratulated' him for his achievement in taking them to the sub-Antarctic islands they had visited—'a most onerous job'. He was left to wear himself out in a service for which he received no thanks.

Unfortunately, Davis went on, Mawson could not help himself, it was his nature, and Davis should have been wiser 'in view of the past'. All he had got out of the AAE was £400 per year—'I got nothing more, and I *wanted* nothing more'. Spurious honours like the OBE were 'no good' to him, he despised such things. All he wanted was 'to get out of this show'—get ashore in Melbourne and have nothing more to do with it. It had been a hopeless thing from beginning to end. The AAE would have been a fiasco but for Davis. 'You owe everything to me. I made you. But I get no thanks for that.' The early part of the AAE, when Mawson had been aboard, had been 'a pandemonium'. All went well after he got off the ship.

Mawson, standing there through all of this, stared back, thinking 'The man is quite unsound mentally.' Then he calmed things down with a pleasantly modulated sentence which brought them both back to normality: 'Could you take the ship a couple of miles west to the edge of the pack so we can view it at close hand and decide on the next move?'[22]

Later, around midday, there was a fine New Year's dinner with Yalumba port wine, and in the evening a two-tier cake, iced and inscribed 'Doc and Davis' ('Doc' being Mawson). All was good cheer and normality.

But Davis's words stuck. Before he went to bed Mawson spoke to some of his staff—AAE veterans Morton Moyes and Frank Hurley, his University of Adelaide colleague Professor Harvey Johnston, and Dr Ingram—saying that he hoped they were not over-worked, that rumours had reached him that he was pushing them all too hard, and that if so he could arrange matters better. They laughed this off, saying they would be happy to work twice as hard, and that 'their only complaint was that the ship was dawdling and wasting too much valuable time'.[23] Harold Fletcher later observed that 'if Mawson wanted somebody to do a particular job and he sort of half refused . . . Mawson would say, "All right, I'll do it myself", and away he'd go. . . . He would always find that the expedition member would follow him and do the job or help him do it.'[24]

Next morning Mawson noticed that Davis had 'improved a great deal, and I judged his bitterness has been chiefly that he has wanted my company all this time, but his remarks to me early on the voyage had not been calculated to cause me to have more to do with him than at all necessary'.[25] But Davis's gloom continued. 'He is the world's super pessimist', Mawson observed in his diary. 'The fact that the first thing he bought for the expedition equipment was 2 pairs of handcuffs illustrates this.'[26]

There was a radiogram that night from Casey: back on 22 December the Norwegians had claimed land between Enderby Land and Coats Land further west. This was beyond the British and Australian arc of interest and caused no consternation. It did, however, cause another argument between Captain and Commander, publicly, over lunch on 3 January. 'Of course the Norwegians have every right to try and anticipate us at Enderby Land', Davis declared, 'and we've been most disgracefully secret about our plans'. Mawson, who had revealed his secret instructions only to Davis, objected weakly 'Ours is a scientific expedition'. Davis laughed. 'That's all eye-wash. We're out to grab land!'[27]

Hurley was up in the Crow's Nest early on the morning of 4 January and thought he discerned two peaks to the west-south-west. That evening Mawson climbed up there himself, and using his Zeiss binoculars he clearly saw the Antarctic plateau 30 or 40 miles to the south, with dark rocky peaks further inland rising out of the ice. No one had ever seen this land before. The next day, with the ship at 66°30' S., 61°07' E., Campbell took Mawson (in the front seat) up to 4000 feet, though he did not leave the general area of the ship, anxious lest they be forced to land somewhere inaccessible to *Discovery*. This flight gave them their first extensive sighting of what Mawson would name Mac-Robertson Land— 'a trade name of chocolates & lollies', as Harold Fletcher and others on board contemptuously called it.[28] Mawson recorded the event that night:

> As we rose, a wider and wider view of the land unfolded. A black, rugged mountain appeared to the east of the rising plateau slopes. Tips of peaks rose from the plateau elsewhere. Rock mountain outcrops appeared at intervals right around to even north of west. A few dimly seen black mountain masses showed up to extreme W, even beyond what had previously appeared to be the end of field of vision. . . .
>
> We flew about 10 miles over pack towards land. Peak on plateau to S of ship probably 15 miles inland and probably only 500 ft high above, so that evening mirage greatly elongates it in vertical. Height of plateau where rise may be 3000 ft, so total height of peak 3500 ft. The black mountains to east probably from 2000 to 3500 ft high.
>
> Were in air just over 1 hour.[29]

He had seen the Framnes Mountains (later named by the Norwegians), inland of what is now Mawson Station, Australian Antarctic Territory.

A violent hurricane blew up out of the east the following day and continued through the 7th and 8th, drifting the ship far to the west, past Kemp Land (unseen) towards Enderby Land. On the 9th, at 8.00 a.m., Mawson was handed a cable from Dr Henderson of External Affairs: the land discovered—and actually landed upon—

by the Norwegians back in December had not been between Coats and Enderby Lands at all but between Enderby Land and Kemp Land, in fact just east of where *Discovery* now lay. They had claimed 100 kilometres—62 miles to the Australians—of coast. 'This is most exasperating', Mawson noted,

> for they have evidently made a direct voyage here to raise their flag, and they knew this was in our itinerary. This sort of thing is not helpful to science, for it means to compete with such 'explorers' an expedition should not arrange any organised programme of detailed scientific work but just rush to most likely points of coast to make landing and raise flags.[30]

But this is precisely what Mawson had been instructed to do by his Prime Minister. Canberra had put flag-raising at the top of its priorities and Mawson, with all his regular tow-nettings, hydrographic stations and so on, had badly compromised the primary goal. He had just drawn up a proclamation claiming Mac-Robertson, Kemp and Enderby Lands—now this! Here one has the fruits not only of hopeless division in the command structure but of unswerving devotion to the goddess Science. Add in the days spent at the Crozets and Heard Island and one sees the inevitability of this Norwegian coup. It was a smile of Fortune beyond Mawson's deserving when Norway soon disclaimed what Riiser-Larsen had recently claimed. In the interests of British–Norwegian relations Mawson was to be allowed to claim the Enderby and Kemp Lands coasts, as well as Mac-Robertson Land (which was his by sighting, though he had not landed there), despite the fact that he had been beaten to the first two by three weeks already, was yet to sight them, and would not reach them on this voyage. Important the scientific work undoubtedly was, urgent it was not. Davis acutely observed after watching one of the many tow-nettings, 'We laboured in the last expedition to get such work done and it was supposed to be of great importance. Yet the results of that work are still in the lumber room somewhere after sixteen years!'[31] As already seen, the sea-spiders would spend twenty years in the 'lumber room'.

The next morning it was snowing. Frustrated by the continu-ous pack to the south, Mawson visited Davis in his cabin and put it that they could well advance slowly east along the pack edge looking for breaks to the south. With the current and wind they were drifting to the west. They needed to land on Kemp Land or Mac-Robertson Land, not on the Norwegian discovery in Enderby Land.

Davis raised his eybrows. Mawson was 'quite wrong', he said, in supposing that the ship was west of Kemp Land. If he wanted to know where the ship was, he should ask Davis, and not ask Moyes about his 'sights' or where *he* thought the ship was.

This was acute of Davis—Mawson had done just that, and he now had to protest that as Leader he had every right to ask any officer a question. Mawson knew perfectly well that Davis was relying on dead-reckoning for the ship's position. In any case Davis did not think much of Mawson's idea of pushing east. Even if they did manage to find a break in the pack, he argued, they could be caught and crushed in it. He said he was 'not going to take any risks for that bloody rubbishing business of raising the flag ashore'.

To Mawson, noting it all down later, Davis was talking 'a lot of rubbish' as well as blaspheming far too much—standard fare from him, and something Mawson hated. 'All the time he was in the wrong.'

The next day he tried the same argument again, but Davis was very clear. He did not want to be bothered listening to Mawson's arguments, he said, he wanted a definite order to do one thing or another.[32]

Though Mawson enjoyed quoting Dr Ingram's assessment of the narrow-skulled Davis's 'great cranial deficiency',[33] this Captain was not dumb. If Mawson wanted to set directions, let him take the responsibility. As Davis put it in his Private Journal, 'If I say yes and we get into a mess he simply says "Oh, Captain Davis said it was O.K."'.[34] In any case Mawson abruptly changed his mind by 180 degrees that very afternoon: 'The fact that the Norwegians are somewhere about this neighbourhood trying to claim territory is a factor which decides us to move west without further delay, or we shall be forestalled in everything'.[35]

Soon they were off the coast of Enderby Land, and on 12 January travelled along west in full sight of it. On the morning of the 13th they found themselves close by a black rock or island (the expeditioners use both words in their diaries), sighted the previous evening. As the nearby mainland was inaccessible, a landing party went ashore on the island and Mawson led them to the summit, 850 feet up. Here a flagpole was erected, a tablet placed at the foot, and at noon a proclamation read in which Mawson claimed for the Empire 'the full sovereignty of the territory of Enderby Land, Kemp Land, Mac-Robertson Land together with off-lying Islands as located in our charts constituting a sector of the Antarctic Regions lying between Longitudes 73° East of Greenwich and 47° East of Greenwich and South of Latitude 65°'—all without landing on the mainland. Though everyone gave three cheers, not everyone was impressed. The young biologist Harold Fletcher wrote that night, 'We claimed a huge tract of land which we had not landed on & had not even seen all of it—the idea being to get in early. And then the Norwegians are abused for doing less things than that!'[36]

Back on *Discovery* again they moved further west, with a good view of Mt Codrington, named by Captain John Biscoe in 1831. On the following day, the 14th, they met up with the *Norvegia*. Fletcher's diary describes her well:

Imagine a ship about 100 ft. or so long—scarred along the water level with ice fighting—and loaded with coal to the gunwale level. Between the foremast & the bridge a huge "Lockheed Vega" cabin plane was stowed and on the only other vacant space aft—was a Norwegian Naval Seaplane with ⅔rds of her hanging overboard. The wings of the Lockheed Vega extended about 20 ft. on either side of the ship and she rolled alarmingly even in the slight heave we were experiencing in that calm sea. We thought of our worries— or at least the Skipper's worry—for our "Moth" was, compared to their moorings, as safe as a bank, and we blushed with shame for him, he being too hard-boiled to blush for himself.[37]

After mapping Bouvet Island, Captain Hjalmar Riiser-Larsen had set out for Enderby Land. Whereas Campbell and Mawson had not flown far from their ship for fear of being forced down, Riiser-Larsen and his aviator, Commander F. Lützow-Holm, had boldly flown their seaplane to the mainland, 90 miles from their ship, mapping the coasts of Enderby Land in the area of Cape Ann (named by Biscoe), then landed near the shore where the outlying, snow-covered surface was just half a foot above the level of the sea. Lützow-Holm had taken the seaplane up to the edge of this compacted snow, then, gunning the engine, had forced it directly up the slope onto the surface, 'skiing' it on its floats a good distance towards the shore. Then they had donned skis and headed inland 5 miles towards a protruding rock peak or nunatak. Daring deeds.[38]

Dressed in black flying suit and scarf, Riiser-Larsen now came on board *Discovery*. The two commanders had an amicable meeting, Riiser-Larsen hearing out Mawson's argument that the Norwegians should concentrate their work to the west of long. 40°E., the Australians to the east. In any case, Riiser-Larsen said, they had finished their land work in this region and were now devoting their attention to whaling matters and the drift of the pack. He indicated that coal could be supplied to *Discovery* from one of the Norwegian factory ships processing whales in the vicinity, but Mawson was not prepared to put himself in their debt. It would have looked bad at home.

For the time being *Norvegia* continued east, *Discovery* to the west. Two days later they passed each other heading in the reverse directions. The Norwegian commander had made a huge impression on Mawson's men: 'A wave of hero worship is sweeping over the ship', Fletcher wrote the day after the encounter, 'everyone is talking about him—what a wonderful leader he is & what physique etc. etc. until we had raised him on such a pinnacle of fame—that he ranked as the world's most intrepid explorer'.[39]

While Mawson had been talking with Riiser-Larsen, Moyes had handed him a decoded message from Australia: Henderson and the Committee wanted the flag planted definitely on the continent proper, as often as possible. Mawson read it, handed it back and tried to forget it, successfully enough to leave it out of that day's diary entry.[40]

The next day, with land out of sight but presumed to be trending south-west or south, and *Discovery* being forced west-south-west away from it by the dense edge of the pack, Mawson decided they would turn back. 'I should have thought you would have done so', Davis responded helpfully. 'We will only be wasting time going on.' First, however, they stopped to run a full plankton and marine station. It seems extraordinary that Mawson was still using up valuable hours and coal in this way, for when the ship was stopped, coal was of course still being consumed.

Proceeding east on the 16th, Davis enthused over the Norwegians, particularly their flying activities. Mawson diverted the attack to the marine side of things: 'Maybe they can put it over us in matters of seamanship too—you can judge that, Davis. But in other departments we are equal to them or better.'[41]

Davis laughed at the idea. 'It's nothing but a cinema show!' He intensely disliked Hurley, who was always joking and clowning about, cine camera in hand, filming the expedition's work for commercial release back home.

Nothing significant occurred over the next few days if one excepts the scientific work, marine stations, dredgings and so forth, which of course went on as usual. Conditions were unsuitable for flying and Mawson was talking about returning to the somewhat unimaginatively named 'Proclamation Rock' or 'Island'. Squabbling continued unabated over things like direction and whether or not to have the ship hove to in storms that drove them far to the west. Davis reported on 19 January that just 147 tons of coal remained. He required 120 tons to reach Kerguelen (obviously including 50 tons he would have been counting as ballast), so they had just 27 tons left for use down here. With the storm past they made east and on the 23rd passed within 10 or 12 miles of Mt Biscoe and Cape Ann, seen a century earlier and of course by the Norwegians. Air surveys at last got underway on the 25th, back in the vicinity of Proclamation Island. This time Mawson made sure they flew over the continent. At 3000 feet he passed back to Campbell a little flag with attached mast. Campbell dipped the Moth to the side and dropped it. In the front seat Mawson solemnly intoned the proclamation again, 'claiming once more all the land discovered and this time including the newly discovered slice at our furthest west', that is, adjacent to Cape Ann.[42]

Back on board again, he tried to persuade Davis to take the ship through the two miles of storm-battered, very loose pack to the mainland shore, past and between intervening islands. Everyone was 'heartbroken', as Mawson put it, that Davis would not try to get in so that they could actually set foot on Antarctica. 'Capt D's attitude now and always on this expedition has been that of one in charge of a passenger steamer in regular service', Mawson remarked. 'On no account will he take what may be even a slight risk. It is evident that he should not be sailing an exploring expedition.'[43] Next day, Australia Day, Davis again declined to risk it. Riiser-Larsen called him 'the Nestor of Antarctic skippers'.[44] Nestor's virtue lay not in boldness but wisdom. In all justice, Davis should be allowed to put his view, jotted down on the 25th:

> To approach a point of land between islands with a boat ahead sounding [for depth, rocks, etc.] is a dangerous business in uncharted waters, but to push into pack in such circumstances as Mawson suggests would not be justified on any grounds whatever. The object of this being to plant a flag on the mainland where it would be about 5 miles from the position on P. Island that the flag was raised on Jan. 13th. It is unpleasant to have to decline to meet the wishes of the leader of the expedition but when so little sense of responsibility is manifested one must put the safety of those on board first.[45]

These words can be judged by those qualified by marine experience. Prima facie, they seem reasonable.

Mawson and Davis had now been reduced to communicating by notes. Davis wrote to Mawson, 'I have to report that the amount of coal remaining on board at noon today will be 120 tons. This is the minimum amount with which I consider it will be possible to make Australia via Kerguelen. Will you please furnish me with instructions accordingly.' Mawson did so, admitting in the process that 'In arriving at this conclusion you have had to bear in mind the possibility of the vessel, on account of its poor sailing qualities and the prevailing boisterous weather, not being able to make Royal

Sound [at Kerguelen] and accordingly having to make Australia without any replenishment of coal supplies'.[46] These notes, copies of which Davis later sent to the Committee, were selectively ignored by Grenfell Price in writing the BANZARE Geographical Report in the early 1960s, though Lady Mawson had given him access to all Mawson's papers, and this omission led Davis single-handedly to end his long and close friendship with Lady Mawson. Davis was perfectly right to think the notes should be noticed.[47]

Discovery now headed north. 'I have left the Antarctic coast with great regret', Mawson wrote in his diary that afternoon. 'Another week here with aeroplane would have completed mapping MacRobertson Land and added detail of Scott Mountains [south-west of Cape Ann]. I am sure we could have spared another 20 tons of coal for this; in fact, if I was in full authority over the handling of vessel, I would not leave these shores until down to 80 tons.'[48] In his diary, in conversations with his staff, and back in Australia, Mawson represented this departure of 26 January as a grossly, even perversely over-cautious proceeding on Davis's part, especially seeing that they reached Kerguelen with sixty tons of coal. Subsequent writers have repeated this line, including Grenfell Price.[49] Davis is never allowed to testify in the matter.

The key factor is the possibility of *Discovery* missing Kerguelen because of exceptionally bad weather and having to sail home non-stop, but there is another factor. As we have seen, Davis had informed Mawson as early as 12 March 1929 that this ship required a minimum of 50 tons of coal as ballast on top of stores, equipment and so on '*when returning from Enderby Land*'[50]—and he was certainly not discounting this by reference to the weight of geological specimens he and Mawson knew the ship would then be carrying. Even fully loaded, as all the surviving diaries attest, this ship handled woefully—'rolls like a tub and sails like an old barge', as Commander Moyes had noted after leaving Cape Town.[51] Taking all this into account, *Discovery* reached Kerguelen with just 10 tons of coal in excess of ballast requirements, and if she had been forced past Kerguelen her return to Australia would have been a fraught thing.

This first BANZARE cruise was a great disappointment to all concerned, though a positive spin was put on it at home for the populace. A divided command was just one factor. In retrospect Mawson, knowing in advance of *Discovery*'s limited coal-carrying capacity and ballast requirements, should have sailed directly from the Cape to Kerguelen, thence to Antarctica, and (as required of him in his secret instructions from the Prime Minister) with territorial aquisition always as his chief objective. The Crozets and Heard Island were left 'at discretion', and though the scientific work was built into the instructions, obviously and almost literally at Mawson's dictation, it was meant to be secondary. Not only would he have arrived in the Antarctic over two weeks earlier, he would have been able to spend at least two weeks longer there than he did, weeks that may have provided additional possibilities for access to the mainland through the fortuities of weather and endlessly shifting pack.

The return voyage saw the continuation of a regular marine programme, and further scientific activity at Kerguelen, including additions to the tons of geological specimens Mawson had already collected. He was still hopeful that more might be done in the Antarctic on this cruise. Even on the return to Kerguelen he had entertained hopes of recoaling from the South African whaler *Radioleine*, 300 miles west of them, and returning south. The almost constant north-westerly swell in those latitudes would have made this hazardous. Then, with the ship fully re-coaled at Kerguelen, he again wondered whether they might not return to Australia *via* Queen Mary Land. Davis was not sure whether he was serious, but pointed out that they would reach Antarctica in the autumn, that the days would be short, and that in 1902 the *Gauss* had been frozen-in off Queen Mary Land as early as 22 February.[52]

Relations between the two continued bad, and Mawson's accounts of their rows make depressing reading. On one occasion in March, for instance, Davis was insisting that Mawson would 'drive everybody mad', 'screwing' everything he could out of people and getting away with it. What was the whole expedition for?—'for your aggrandisement!' Mawson was the only one who got anything at all out of it, and he was only too happy to 'work everybody to death and take the lot.' Mawson told him he was talking rubbish, and Davis stamped down the ladder, calling out

'Who got everything out of the last expedition?' Mawson countered that he had certainly got plenty of work out of it, and Davis shot back 'And not a penny less than £10 000!' That was a lie, Mawson retorted—he never had a penny out of it but debts. To Davis, who hated stopping for hours at a time so that marine stations could be run, the scientific work was 'rot' and 'worth nothing'. Meeting with land and mapping were vital; 'all the rest is eye-wash'.[53] And so it went, all the way home. Mawson had developed sciatica and lumbago and they were now very noticeable, making matters worse.[54] At one point Davis threatened to take the ship into Albany, Western Australia, cause a scandal, resign and send it back to England, cancelling any possibility of a second cruise.[55]

Fortunately he was dissuaded from this, the ship finally reaching Port Adelaide for a public welcome as planned on the morning of Tuesday, 1 April. Paquita and the children had gone on board the previous day as *Discovery* lay at anchor off the suburb of Semaphore. Among those who inspected her at Port Adelaide were the Governor-General, Lord Stonehaven, and the Governor of South Australia, Sir Alexander Hore-Ruthven. On the following day there was a civic reception at the Adelaide Town Hall at which Lord Stonehaven informed the crowd that the achievements of the BANZARE 'rank with anything that so far has been accomplished'.[56] Precisely where they 'ranked' was not spelt out, but his Lordship struck the right note for a nation in steep decline, where accomplishments of any kind were welcome.

15 SIEGE OF THE SOUTH

THE AUSTRALIA TO which Mawson had returned was depressing, with jobs blowing away like so much dust and scraps in the streets. Business activity had slumped so fast that unemployment would soon exceed 20 per cent, heading for 30. Inside another year beggars would be wandering the cities, tramps or 'swagmen' along country roads. 'Depression without parallel' it was called by the new Labor Prime Minister, James Henry Scullin, who held the poisoned chalice after defeating Stanley Melbourne Bruce's Nationalists at the election of 12 October 1929, a fortnight before Wall Street crashed. The new Government, retrenching wherever possible, was unsympathetic to a second year's cruise of the BANZARE, and Mawson had to appeal again to Mac-Robertson, who offered another £6000, provided the Government assisted equally.[1]

Mawson's earliest plans for the BANZARE had envisaged only one cruise and the Bruce Government had endorsed this concept in January 1929, but when at the same time *Discovery* became available for two years, Mawson had begun to think in terms of a two-year programme.[2] Dr Henderson of External Affairs had found it hard to sell this idea to a Government so recently sold on the one-year programme by Mawson himself, and it had been left unresolved.[3] The Scullin Government was persuaded partly by the arrival of four Norwegian factory ships in Australian and New Zealand ports in March 1930, heavy with whale oil worth a total of over £1 300 000. Mawson had always advocated developing a strong Australian whaling industry to harvest the seas to the south, with internationally agreed limits on the kill.[4] By the time his report on the first cruise was tabled in Parliament on 21 May 1930, the second cruise had been agreed, and was announced the following day.

In his report his achievements were duly set forth and Davis blamed for the shortcomings. The early return to Kerguelen when coal reserves had fallen to 120 tons 'was a great disappointment to me, for earlier in the voyage we had arrived at a verbal understanding that a limit of 80 tons would suffice'. But the only conceivable reference to this 'understanding' in Mawson's diary comes on 16 January 1930 when Davis asks Mawson his views on the coal situation and Mawson says he thinks they will need '25 or 30 tons as emergency in case of bad weather off Kerguelen'. Davis sounds Mawson out here but is not reported by Mawson as saying anything himself. In his report Mawson does not mention the word 'ballast'. He blames Davis, in effect, for the fact that the 'proposal' to take coal from the *Radioleine* had to be 'abandoned' because Davis 'took a very serious view of the difficulties of coaling the *Discovery* at sea'. After returning to Kerguelen, 'Captain Davis was averse to making another short visit to the Antarctic coast, en route to Australia (a call at Queen Mary Land having been in view)'—nothing here about the inherent difficulties and dangers of autumn reconnaissance in the Antarctic, and with the phrase 'in view' wrongly suggesting that Davis had also entertained this idea and then backed away.[5]

Immediately on return, Davis had told Henderson at Port Adelaide that he would not go south again. In a draft resignation dated 15 June 1930 he pointed out that 'a marine expedition under the leadership of a layman . . . will not work'.[6] On 22 May a reporter from the *Register* asked Mawson, 'Are you prepared to go south again under the same conditions of leadership?', putting his finger on the structural problem of command rather than the merely personal.

'I am not prepared to answer that question yet', Mawson replied, 'the time has not arrived for it. . . . I did not know that there was any intention of publishing the report, otherwise the wording might have been more carefully revised, so that no unwarranted construction could be placed upon certain paragraphs.'[7]

The additional Mac-Robertson money came with an understood condition: Mawson would do his best to secure the
confectioner a knighthood. This was not as easy as it sounds. The
new Labor Government would not recommend anybody for
honours. They were not, however, opposed to other parties making
recommendations direct to Whitehall. Mawson wrote to Casey in
London, asking him to 'move as best you can in England to bring
under notice Mr MacRobertson's princely help in the prosecution
of our Antarctic programme', and adding that 'his merit does not
rest there only, for he has for years distributed at Christmas in
Australia ten or twelve thousand pounds to charities. I am writing
also a note to Mr Bruce. . . . I should like you to bring this letter
under notice of Sir Harry Batterbee' (of the Dominions Office).[8]
As a consequence, Mac-Robertson received his first knighthood in
1932. Subsequent gifts to the State of Victoria in its centenary year,
1935, would gain him a second. And on Mawson's recommendation he was elected an FRGS in 1931.

Between April and November of 1930 Mawson was kept busy
with teaching duties and organizing the second cruise. Meanwhile
the first of the BANZARE films was worked up by Hurley for
commercial release as *Southward Ho! with Mawson*—a disastrous
mistake. By releasing this they killed the market for the main film
covering both cruises, *Siege of the South*, which appeared the
following year. Hurley wrote to Mawson in early May,

> I have rolls of packice, miles of ice bergs and scenery—sub Antarctic
> galore, but of Antarctica beyond glimpses of Proclamation Island
> taken from the ship and Cape Anne from 20 miles range, there is
> nothing to show. . . Two hours on Proclamation Island would have
> solved the debacle I am now trying to solve.[9]

The American film of Byrd's South Polar flight was coming—they
would have to try to delay its release. Mawson became depressed,
complaining that Hurley was not devoting enough time to the film.
Hurley countered that

> If I had got what I wanted in the South, I would not have been
> reduced to glueing my eye to a rotten magnifying glass for nearly

six weeks to produce a set of coloured slides. Nor would I have been put to the extreme of faking sections and begging ancient scenes from the 1911 film. . . . Please do not write letters which have the suggestion that I have 'exploited' the expedition or are [*sic*] not doing my best for it.[10]

He thought the film would net £3000 over a short three-month season. Hurley always was an impossible optimist. In a new age of talkies, this film was silent. It opened at the Sydney Lyceum Theatre on 9 August, and its antique feel was actually enjoyed by one nostalgic reviewer—'like a visit to the country after a series of hectic city binges'. He also praised Hurley's live voice-over: 'a resonant Australian voice' with 'racy, Digger-like wit'. The faking was not detected.[11] In Sydney the film returned £1300 to the BANZARE, but it flopped elsewhere and was not widely shown.

When Hurley suffered what the BANZARE's hydrologist, Alf Howard, recalls was termed a 'physical breakdown' ('whatever that might mean'), Howard was called in to do the live voice-over from Hurley's script.

> I would appear on the stage, introduce myself, apologise for Hurley's absence and indicate that I would conduct the lecture from the control box. While on my way back to the box a still of Mawson was shown accompanied by a message from him from a disc. This was followed by a series of coloured stills to the accompaniment of music and by then I was ready to talk to the film with Hurley's script and the assistant dubbing in music and sound effects.[12]

Thus each screening of this film was labour-intensive at a time when cinemas, thanks to soundtracks, had been labour-light for a year or two.

Meanwhile Mawson had appointed K. N. MacKenzie ship's captain and the expedition's second-in-command. With *Discovery* being refitted, MacKenzie had little to do during the winter months. In December 1932, travelling on the *Strathnaver* for England, Mawson met the daughter of the woman who was

MacKenzie's landlady in the Melbourne suburb of St Kilda through that 1930 winter. She remembered MacKenzie very well, telling Mawson 'she did not like his "shifty" eyes but that some Melbourne girls were greatly taken with him. Said he spent most of the 1930 winter in tow of Melbourne girls. No wonder the ship's stores were stolen!! and the crew drunk!! Well his guns are spiked now.'[13] MacKenzie had a rugged face, trim beard, thick dark eyebrows over slightly tired-looking eyes. Judging from his photograph he was not one who would follow his leader to hell and back—half-way, perhaps.

This cruise was to take in Macquarie Island, a sanctuary for wildlife thanks partly to Mawson's frequently expressed concern for the conservation of sub-Antarctic fauna. Thence they would proceed 700 miles south to the vicinity of the Balleny Islands to trans-ship 100 tons of coal from the *Sir James Clark Ross*, a factory ship, then sail to Commonwealth Bay to revisit the AAE's Main Base, reoccupying the magnetic station and measuring the movement of the land ice since 1914. From here they would proceed to Queen Mary Land following *Aurora*'s old route around to Gaussberg, and further if possible. Then home. Regular marine stations would be run.[14] The staff were largely unchanged. Morton Moyes and J. W. S. Marr, cartographer and hydrologist respectively on the first voyage, dropped out, and the AAE veteran A. L. Kennedy (cartographer) and Lieutenant K. Oom RAN (hydrographic surveyor) replaced them.

The expedition left Hobart on 22 November 1930, sounded the Mill Rise (an elevated undersea plateau) south of Tasmania, and reached Macquarie Island on 1 December. Sea elephants were thriving there—Mawson estimated their numbers at 30 000. One had even occupied a deserted sealer's hut, licences for the island not having been renewed after 1916. The AAE's hut was intact but dilapidated, the masts on Wireless Hill long ago blown down (or perhaps toppled by earthquake, as they had fallen towards the prevailing wind), but the AAE's field magnetic station was reoccupied. Rabbits, quite tame, hopped about everywhere. In the fog and misty rain Mawson collected large quantities of rock and soil specimens, while other staff busied themselves in their own fields.

They were at sea again on 9 December, and coaled as planned from the *Clark Ross* on the 15th, far to the east, near the 180th meridian. While the coaling proceeded, Hurley went off in a chaser boat to film a catch. Another 50 tons of coal was taken from the Norwegian whaler *Kosmos* on 29 December. Loose pack was everywhere—they had been in it since Macquarie Island. Then on 2 January, as Mawson recorded,

> At 3 am pack suddenly commenced to close; closed before could get out. Heavy glaciers, large elements—very bad, dangerous. At 3.30 propeller struck at high rate of speed, stopped engines. By miracle did not break propeller. Got out after bad bumping. Big seas.[15]

This incident doubtless made MacKenzie more cautious.

They entered Commonwealth Bay after passing through a hurricane, and landed at Cape Denison on 5 January, staying until the 6th. The weather smiled on them, with two exceptionally still, sunny days. R. G. Simmers, the meteorologist, recorded that 'the hut which was surrounded with a litter of cases yet which seemed still in first class order showed that after all it was filled with ice. So without delay everyone got down to work. . . . An entrance was effected through the skylight.'[16] Mawson noted that 'Remarkable effects of snow-blast erosion were everywhere evidenced on the exposed timbers. In many places the planks had thus been reduced in thickness by more than half an inch. Inside . . . great masses of delicate ice crystals hung in festoons.'[17] At a formal ceremony on a nearby rocky point, a flag was hoisted and Mawson claimed possession of King George V Land, defined as lying between 142° and 160°E.

Steaming west on the 6th, uncharted features of the Adélie Land coast were recorded. The aeroplane was test-flown on the 7th at long. 138°E. Given the heavy pack conditions it would be a vital resource. It was in the Moth, from 8000 feet, that an extent of coast (to be named Banzare Land) was sighted on the 15th, near long. 124°E., some 100 miles south-east of the ship, its nearest point being named Cape Goodenough after the President of the RGS. The next day Eric Douglas went up again to 8000 feet, in lat. 64°49' S., long.

120°36' E., and sighted to the south-east more of this coastline trending south-west. The pack between the ship and the land was far too dense to navigate. Mawson went up with Stuart Campbell on the 18th, in lat. 64°21' S., long. 117°E., but only to 3000 feet because of cloud, and thought he discerned land to the south-south-west, tentatively naming it Sabrina Land. Capt. J. Balleny had reported land in this vicinity and so named it in 1839. With the ship continuing west, weather prevented further flights until 27 January when Mawson and Douglas went up to over 5000 feet, the ship then in lat. 65°7' S., long. 107°22' E. Undulating, brightly sunlit land ice was discerned far to the south—this was probably what the American Charles Wilkes had named Knox Land in 1840. Unfortunately, on its retrieval by the ship the Moth was badly damaged.

Conditions made any survey of the Queen Mary Land coast impossible. This had been mapped by the AAE's Western Base party, but Mawson had wanted to raise the flag here. The Moth was repaired by 6 February and tested on that date, near long. 84°E., while *Discovery* took on another 20 tons of coal from the whaler *Falk*, Captain Lars Andersen. Hurley, getting no footage of Antarctica and blaming Mawson for 'weakness' in not compelling MacKenzie to take greater risks with the ship, was venting his frustration in his diary, contrasting Mawson's leadership with the 'high standard' set by Shackleton. He noted disparagingly that they had actually found the *Falk* and its companion, the *Listris*, to the *south* of them—and with stewardesses aboard:

> One was attired in a garment which exhibited bare arms to the shoulders, & the other in a muslin dress. It made us feel very ridiculous. Our thick woollen attire, the exploring purpose, our ice-navigation & so on. Here were two ancient iron vessels, leisurely coaling side by side & two women aboard further south than us! Here was pathetic comedy indeed![18]

Other large Norwegian and British ships were passed during the following days as the pack cleared to the west and gave way to open water. It was a veritable highway. Simmers noted on 6 February that according to Lars Andersen, 'there are this year forty two factory ships in the Antarctic and the chasers if distributed evenly around the [Antarctic] circle would be at fifty mile intervals. So there can't be much not known these days . . . there are now no less than eight [floating] factories off Enderby Land.' And two days later he wrote, 'We have lost count of the number of chasers we have met belonging to three separate factory ships all of which we have seen.'[19]

Not only were the Norwegians whaling, they were busy charting these coasts. R. A. Swan has pointed out that through January and February 1931 four whalers belonging to Lars Christensen, the *Seksern, Bouvet II, Bouvet III* and *Thorgaut* made numerous sightings along the Mac-Robertson Land coast between long. 60°E. and long. 75°E., naming it Lars Christensen Land, though not claiming it for Norway. Meanwhile the Norwegian whalers *Antarctic, Thorshavn, Thorshammer* and *Hilda Knudsen* were off Enderby and Kemp Lands, observing and charting. The result, as Swan points out, was that 'Norwegian and English names were given to many identical features, to the great confusion of later students of Antarctic history and of workers in the field'.[20]

Mawson was airborne again on 9 February (lat. 66°30' S., long. 76°E.), and at 5200 feet could see land ice on the horizon from the south-east to the south-west. This sighting was confirmed a few days later and the region named Princess Elizabeth Land. Making south-west, the ship now entered what was named the MacKenzie Sea, another flight revealing its coastal features. From here they mapped the coasts of Mac-Robertson Land, named on the first cruise. This time the improved conditions allowed of closer approach to the coasts. New features were charted, and known features charted more accurately. Striking mountain ranges were observed, and parties were able to reach the mainland on 13 February. At Murray Monolith it was too dangerous to jump from the boat onto the slippery rocks, so they touched an oar against a rock and threw a canned proclamation and an inscribed plate, which inconsiderately fell back into the sea. At Scullin Monolith on the same day they managed to get ashore and raise the flag, Mawson repeating the ritual of taking possession. His cartographer,

Lieutenant Oom, was kept busy inserting names on the maps, including the Masson, David, Casey and Henderson Ranges.

On 18 February there was a ceremony in a valley at Cape Bruce, named after the Prime Minister who had authorised the BANZARE. Simmers was one of the party:

> Dux jumped ashore and ran up the valley waving a flag and looking as pleased as punch. . . . We forthwith proceeded [with] building a cairn, hoisting the flag, reading the same proclamation as on the 13th, God Save the King, and cheering. . . . In the confined space of the valley our voices seemed very loud and cheerful compared with the previous efforts which have been on the tops of hills where the voices seem thin and are easily lost in space.

Then they drank champagne, pouring some of it over the cairn. Among the flags sequentially flown was an Air Force Ensign brought by Stuart Campbell, a New Zealand flag brought by R. A. Falla (the ornithologist), and an Australian Ensign belonging to A. L. Kennedy which had been with him through the AAE, World War I, and two Carnegie Institute expeditions.[21] A Union Jack was also flown, and another Australian Blue Ensign, carried by Mawson. Twenty-seven years later this same Blue Ensign would drape his coffin and accompany him to his grave at St Jude's Anglican Church in Brighton.

Discovery's coal reserves were by now around 100 tons, and the next day a course was set for Australia, over the Banzare Rise, where soundings additional to those taken on the first cruise were obtained, more accurately delineating this shallow stretch of the seabed.[22]

Mawson's relations with MacKenzie were an improvement over those with Davis on the first cruise, but conflicts occurred. Things worsened on the voyage home. Mawson had been told on 10 March that coal would soon be down to 40 tons. On 12 March he decided to check for himself. He poked about in the various coal bunkers, asking the firemen to estimate how much remained in each. They reckoned the main bunker held 25 tons, with quite a few additional tons in the starboard and port bunkers. Then he mentally added to all this the coal in three of the holds: starboard 4 and 5, and port 5—another 40 tons, he thought. That would make at least 75 tons. He then went to MacKenzie and asked whether they might not proceed directly to Melbourne rather than to Hobart. 'I did not say', he confided to his diary, 'that I had discovered a discrepancy in the amount of coal on board compared with the coal sheets daily supplied by the Chief Engineer. He agreed that Melbourne was only 60 miles further than Hobart but held that with the ship as it is (light) there is a danger trying to make Melbourne.'

In Mawson's view this was 'all rather disgusting as we evidently had more than 100 tons when we turned back. He must have had 50 tons more than he reported.' (Mawson seems to be in error here—by his own figuring, this 50 should read 35.) MacKenzie was 'evidently somewhat strained. . . . He refers to [*Discovery*] as being very light, with practically no ballast.' Yet, Mawson estimated, there were almost 80 tons of stores, rock specimens, weights, gear and so on in the holds—'In all quite 150 tons. Now when Scott brought this ship back from the Ross Sea in 1904 she arrived in the Auckland Islands. . . with only 10 tons of coal, and she had transferred practically all her stores and specimens to the relief ships before leaving Hut Point.'[23] (After this experience, Scott refused to take *Discovery* south again.) Here one sees 'Captain' Mawson at his theoretical best. He includes as 'ballast' all stores, gear, bags of cinders, specimens and so on, which is perfectly valid—theoretically. In short, *Discovery*'s notorious need of ballast applied only when she was totally empty! He would sail her as Scott had intrepidly sailed her back to the Auckland Islands, at the limits of her instability, with no margin for error or capricious fortune.

This second BANZARE cruise ended in Hobart on 19 March 1931. The expedition's extensive discoveries and claims, strongly augmenting the superb geographical achievements of the AAE, provided the grounds for the *Australian Antarctic Acceptance Act* of 1933. This became law in 1936, establishing (with British agreement) the Australian Antarctic Territory, that vast slice of the Antarctic 'cake' running from long. 45°E. around to 160°E., with the sole exception of the French Terre Adélie. Since the late 1950s, however, all national claims have been 'in abeyance' by international agreement. Neither the United States nor the Soviet Union had ever recognised them in any case.

The greatest scientific contribution of these cruises was that, as a result of the oceanographical programme, a continuous undersea land-platform around a third of Antarctica was clearly demonstrated, establishing the continuity of land of continental dimensions beneath the ice plateau, in contradistinction to a series of islands cemented by the polar ice cap. This left unresolved whether there were not two continents beneath the ice, riven by a channel from the Weddell Sea to the Ross Sea, a question then being answered by the work of Richard Evelyn Byrd.

Hurley had excellent film footage of the second cruise, and he and Mawson now set about to exploit it. There had been considerable public interest in both cruises. Stuart F. Doyle, Chairman of the Australian Broadcasting Company and Managing Director of Union Theatres Ltd./Greater Union, had even wanted to install broadcasting equipment on the ship, the idea being to send weekly half-hour reports by short wave, to be relayed around Australia on the broad band, but Mawson had been unable to provide them with a separate operating cabin and the idea lapsed.[24] There was reason to think the new film would do well. It had a continuous sound-track, printed on during production (no sound recordings had been made in the Antarctic). Still, there were worries. The Byrd film had flopped in Australia, a bad omen, and from Hurley's point of view Mawson had fed the press the wrong kind of news: 'Your press reports concerning storms, packice difficulties and coal shortages were bad publicity. The difficulties encountered have—after reading all the press clippings—entirely eclipsed the work done.'[25]

The new film included the first cruise, cannibalising *Southward Ho! with Mawson*, so Hurley had to fake important sections including the scene on Proclamation Island, for he only had silent footage of the island taken from the ship. He was a practised faker, however, and was able to write in April 1931,

A brief note to let you know that our escapade on the cliffs at Bondi has been quite successful. The visual part is splendid and the voice much better than I had hoped for—seeing that the conditions were so unfavourable for recording. Every word is clear and distinct and the synchronisation 100%. It will be a 'telling' section.[26]

They hoped Stuart Doyle, as Managing Director of Greater Union, the film's marketers, would cover the cost of the sound-tracking: 'I have . . . advised him that we have placed his name on our charts', Mawson told Hurley.[27] Meanwhile Hurley was paying close attention to the little details:

> Can you lend me a Union Jack, same size as those which were used when 'Proclamation' Ceremonies [at Cape Bruce, second cruise] took place? Can you get me made (without cost) a tablet similar in size to those carved roughly by me[:] The British flag was raised and British sovereignty asserted on the 18th Day of February 1931.[28]

Slowly, everything was coming together.

The hoped-for profits were intended to fund the scientific reports, but Mac-Robertson wanted to go halves. 'I am becoming a little disappointed in him', Mawson told Hurley. 'At the last Committee meeting, I found him extremely anxious to make a lot of money out of the showing of the film.' Hurley endorsed these sentiments: 'Under no consideration whatsoever should the old rascal be permitted to share in the film. What next!! He has received more publicity already than his fortune could buy.' Mac-Robertson also wanted to appear at the beginning of the film and say a paragraph. 'I don't see how it can be done decorously', Hurley complained.[29]

Siege of the South opened to a capacity audience in Brisbane at the beginning of October,[30] and also in Melbourne, then later in other cities and towns. Hurley sometimes said a few words at the initial screenings, even in country towns, to give a personal touch. Yet by December he thought they would be lucky to make £4000 from it in Australia and New Zealand, since 'the film holds no great highlights of adventure like Scott or the Endurance film'.[31] This was wildly optimistic, as gradually became clear in early 1932. Meanwhile Mawson was falling out with Hurley over the latter's failure to provide promised negatives to accompany Mawson's article on the BANZARE for the *Geographical Journal*, which was also to be read to the RGS by Professor Frank Debenham. Request after request went unanswered. 'I am getting pretty wild at not receiving those negatives from you', he wrote in February. 'There was just the same trouble, you will remember, after the 1911–14 Expedition.'[32] Hurley always had more projects in hand than he could easily manage.

At the same time as the film was about to be released in Sydney, in February 1932, Stuart Doyle was reporting poor returns from screenings in places where the earlier film had been shown. This augured badly for Sydney. Mawson thought Doyle was not pushing the film, and told him so.[33] Greater Union, he believed, were content to make their money from gloom-busters like *On Our Selection*.

By late September the final returns were in, and the shocking bottom line was a net loss to the BANZARE of £8 0s 0d. It was all Doyle's fault, and Hurley's too. 'I am tremendously disappointed with the whole thing', Mawson told Hurley. 'The result is utterly different from what you yourself had expected as revealed in conversations with myself and advice given on the matter of exploitation of the film.' School children, conducted by their teachers, had attended 'in bodies' and there had been 'crowded houses in Brisbane and Adelaide', yet the net return to the BANZARE after expenses, including Hurley's editing, print costs, sound work and so on, was an £8 bill. 'How any sound business concern could handle film . . . under these circumstances and return a negative result, I fail to understand.' To cap it all off, the New Zealand release was now uncertain.[34]

Two months later, in the first half of December 1932, Mawson left for England on the *Strathnaver*, principally to sell the film rights there. Three or four weeks' inactivity on the water was welcome— he needed a holiday. Unfortunately the company looked unpromising. 'We have on board a Dr. and Mrs. Barlow of Adelaide?' he wrote, somewhat puzzled, to Paquita, who had stayed in Australia with the children. 'I think he must be a suburban doctor. I don't remember seeing him at any time. They don't look at all impressive—but she is an unusually good tennis player. . . . Dr Barlow has a remarkably big head.' Then there was the St Kilda landlady's daughter, lounging in her deck chair, applying lipstick, and telling him all about 'shifty-eyed' MacKenzie's girlfriends.[35]

Things looked up after Port Said. Strolling on the deck, he spied Francis Bickerton, who had been in charge of the 'air-tractor' on the AAE. Over drinks Bickerton related how he had sold his Newfoundland farm and invested in a new golf club in California. It was almost ready to open when the Crash came. Down on his luck, he was offered $3000 a year and all expenses by a rich Californian if he would take the man's twenty-year-old son around the world—anywhere to keep him away from a girl with whom he had become infatuated. They shot grizzly bear in the Canadian Rockies and big game in the Congo and Kenya. The 'job' over, Bickerton had flown from Nairobi to Cairo and caught the *Strathnaver* at Port Said for England.[36]

In London Mawson put up at the Royal Societies Club and set about trying to sell the film rights. It was depressing work. He was told that the market had been saturated by Herbert Ponting's new Scott film coming on top of the Shackleton and Byrd films, that there was a slump in the picture industry, that Hurley's strident Australian voice was particularly off-putting. Mawson replaced the voice with another, but he wanted too much for a film that had made a net loss in its country of origin, and found to his chagrin that 'with the film industry all in the hands of foreign Jews, I was not able to secure a guarantee of £5000 on a 50/50 exploitation basis'.[37] He cut a deal with Gaumont but it was tentative, and there was no guaranteed sum. They strung him along for a year.

On 6 March, in the evening, he addressed the RGS on the Kerguelen Archipelago. (The previous week they had had a private screening of *Siege of the South*.) The President, Sir William Goodenough, concluding the meeting, praised Mawson's concern for Antarctic fauna. 'One realized, as Sir Douglas talked, how much he really cares for the preservation of life of all kinds in the Southern Seas that he has sailed so long and which he knows so well.'[38] This highlighted an important aspect of Mawson's work. He had long advocated an international agreement to control the whaling industry. For instance, in the 1920s he had told Sir James O'Grady, Governor of the Falkland Islands, at a meeting of the AAAS in Hobart, of 'the need of some drastic control of whaling', in Sir James's words, 'to prevent the certain obliteration of the whale from the Antarctic. I now *know* Sir Douglas is right, there are 12 Whaling Companies, mostly Norwegian, operating within the jurisdiction of this Colony [the Falkland Islands Dependency] and you can imagine the enormous "kill" each season.' With the huge tonnages being taken in the early 1930s and consequent slump in the price of whale oil, he went on, there was 'a devilish process being tried out aboard the mother-ship, or factory, that is, the "canning" of whale meat with tomato pulp for the China Market. And so the slaughter goes on.'[39] The 1933 declaration of Macquarie Island as a flora and fauna sanctuary was largely due to Mawson's advocacy. Following the AAE he had used his influence with Sir Ronald Munro Ferguson, Lord Novar, Governor-General of Australia from 1914 to 1920, in Mawson's words 'co-operating [with Novar] in efforts to secure the maintenance of that Island as a sanctuary' following the non-renewal of sealing licences in 1916. The Tasmanian Government, however, which had the jurisdiction, 'proved very mean' even after 1933, and in the 1950s 'their sheep, goats, etc.' would be roaming the island, making a mockery of the 'ideal of the Island . . . as an inviolable sanctuary'.[40]

Before leaving for home Mawson was approached by the well-known portraitist Henry James Haley to sit for him, and agreed. The portrait shows the sitter in his doctoral gown, and years later was purchased by his widow.

In the depressed atmosphere of the mid-1930s the Australian Government failed to follow up on the BANZARE cruises. It would not be until 1939, and then largely due to Mawson's influence, that the Government would entertain the idea of a regular Antarctic research programme. World War II would send the proposal into deep freeze, and in 1947 it would re-emerge as ANARE.

16 THE DOMESTIC WORLD

∽

Though Mawson worked intensely hard, sometimes on too many projects at once, family life was not sacrificed when he was in Adelaide. This was because he did not generally spend his evenings with friends or at parties but at home. His scientific work, his chairmanship of South Australian Hardwoods, and Harewood absorbed his energies, and the evenings were for quiet relaxation, reading or writing.

The family home in King Street, sketched out during the AAE and designed on American principles, sat well back on its large block, approached by a drive, with a small 'forest' along the street frontage, fruit trees further in, and a tennis court. It was thus secluded from the street, a very private world.

Though he enjoyed spending time with his daughters Pat and Jessica, he never talked down to them, even when they were very small, in the fond way many parents do. Instead he was ceaselessly explaining things. The garden provided lessons in horticulture, its bird-life in ornithology. Regular visits to the farm taught the children about animals—Paquita Mawson recalled the girls 'walking down the road hand-in-hand carrying a milk can which they had been filling . . . There was a stream for them to paddle in, with frogs. There were cows to see milked and bullocks to watch when they moved logs for the timber mill.'[1] Their father was always 'very patient', the daughters recall, 'unless you did stupid things. For instance, he was furious with the children who carved their initials in the trees along King St.'[2]

He would read to them, but his choice of books was that of a man of action, not a romantic—*Robinson Crusoe* and *Swiss Family Robinson* were staple fare, and he taught *them* to read Dickens to *him*. One day, in the garden, he found Jessica weeping over Charlotte Brontë's *Villette*. 'Why are you crying?' he asked affectionately. 'If the book makes you cry, why read it?—silly thing!'

In the family's interests he was concerned to provide against unforeseen eventualities, perhaps because as a child he himself had not had much family back-up, but also because university pensions then were not very generous. Following his return from World War I he took out two life insurance policies with the AMP Society, with annual premiums of twelve guineas and £17 2s 11d respectively, and regularly bought shares, particularly BHP, generally in packets of a hundred. Expenses were kept low. Going through the accounts from the 1920s one sees how frugal he was. This is how his daughters remember him. 'He wouldn't take a cab, even when sick', they point out. 'He went by tram.' At least in the early 1920s, his suits were not made for him but bought from stores like Miller Anderson. Telephone calls averaged only two a day. An enthusiastic photographer, he continued to use glass plates into the 1940s long after they had ceased to be available, because he had a large supply of them, and in the early years at Brighton he had his own developing room. He bought good furniture but often at a discount. When he bought a Pleyel grand piano (No. 51855), in burr walnut, it was second-hand (£150 0s 0d).[3]

The children's education was physical as well as intellectual, as befitted the daughters of an explorer. Pat was just six and Jessica not yet four when they started taking dancing lessons.[4] Mawson followed every step in their schooling. They attended Woodlands Church of England Girls Grammar School in nearby Glenelg, an excellent establishment at the upper end of the market. In the early 1920s he wrote a revealing letter to the headmistress, of which only the undated draft survives:

Please excuse the absence of my children at yesterday's church function. They spent the day, on my instructions, doing school work at home. It is with great regret that I find Woodlands school devoting so much time during the week to church matters. I have made full provision for their religious training and am anxious for them to devote the week days between 9.30 am & 4 pm to the ordinary educational subjects.

Furthermore I am strongly adverse [*sic*] to such small children being taken to the city unless absolutely essential. I am of course in agreement with a preliminary prayer in the morning and reasonable instruction in biblical history.[5]

His religious views were vague. He paid pew rent (£11 0s 0d annually) at St Jude's Church of England, Brighton, but did not normally attend, according to his daughters, who recall, though, that in his lectures on geology he would admit 'that *something* created this world'. And this world reflected its divine origin. Bryan Forbes, a 'Cadet' student of Mawson's in the 1940s, remembers him saying 'I worship God through Nature'.[6] As already seen, before and during the AAE he believed in a benevolent, superintending Providence. Essentially he was, and remained, a theist of a classical-stoicist kind, like his favourite philosopher, the second-century Roman emperor Marcus Aurelius, whose *Meditations* he had read to his men during the AAE. No religion, not even Christianity, could circumscribe God. Alan Wilson, a lecturer under Mawson in the 1940s, sometimes spoke with him about religious matters and confirms these observations.[7] The girls should learn about their historical culture and religion, but the central requirement was a sound modern education with science to the fore. As for Paquita, though she taught the children to pray, she was an agnostic. When Sir Robert Menzies was suffering from periodic strokes in the early 1970s she wrote, 'I would pray for you, Sir Robert, if I could'.[8]

Throughout their marriage Mawson and his wife were frequently separated by her visits to her parents in Melbourne or to her wider family in Holland and elsewhere, or by his absences interstate and abroad, but the children generally had at least one parent with them and there was always a maid to help out. In late January 1926 he was on his way home from examining the forests of New Zealand, and Paquita, back in Adelaide, sent a letter to reach him in Melbourne. She had not been feeling well. This was nothing new— she had heart and thyroid problems which often sent her to Melbourne for rest and recuperation. The children had been saying their evening prayers. Pat had prayed, 'And please God make Mummy better tomorrow'. Then Jessica had added, 'And please Lord make Mummy better the day *after* tomorrow', explaining, 'He's got to have time!' Paquita had been nervous in the secluded house, a burglar's dream, but soon lost her fears. 'I've got over being nervous', she wrote. 'Your pistol is handy. . . . I sleep without qualms and . . . last night couldn't be bothered to see if the bathroom window is locked! How's that for bravery?'[9]

Whenever he was overseas he sent carefully thought-out letters to the girls. During his time in England in 1928 promoting the Sounds scheme (see Chapter 12) he wrote to Pat, who had been staying at Victor Harbour with the family of John (later Sir John) Cleland, Professor of Pathology at the University of Adelaide, a keen botanist and ornithologist.

> So you enjoyed yourself at Victor Harbour with the Clelands . . . I am glad, my young minx, that you took note of natural phenomena such as the morning star, etc. I only wish I had been there to give you a more accurate explanation than you appear to have got from the fishermen. I note by your sketch that you know quite a lot of the local geography. There is one point I should mention, that is, that what you call Petrol Cove is Petrel Cove. I suppose that long ago it was a haunt of Petrels (a sea bird). Perhaps they came ashore to lay eggs there. The mineral you got from the Clelands was Galena not Galina. My little love, a naturalist is just what I do want to make of you—or rather *not make* you but I wish you to see how very interesting it all is. Unfortunately in order to do well in science you need to first get a good knowledge of mathematics—to be able to write presentably—to be able to compose good accounts of things in English. Then if you can also read in foreign languages so much the better. But to be a decent intelligent citizen, as of course we

must all be we need to learn some history, some geography, some music, etc. as well . . .

I am glad you noticed that I 'had not written for ages'. I thought perhaps you did not care—and that would break what is left of my heart. . . . Well just heaps and heaps of love from Dad, the most faithful friend you will ever have.[10]

The letter shows the quality of Mawson's bond with this child. His unrestrained affection, his revealed view of the world, his evident ambition for this child are all interesting.

At the same time he was writing to Paquita pointing out that she had neglected the children's safety at the farm:

Many thanks for the photos taken at Harewood. They are interest-ing reminders. One shows children with bare feet at the spring. We know that there are black snakes living at the spring—it is unwise for them to paddle in that water or poke about in the reeds there. They can bare themselves down to the waist if they like but not the feet in snaky country. This is my advice. The children *must* be careful of snakes—I know the danger and I don't fear it myself because I have the snake sense—they have not and may get bitten.[11]

The tone is well judged—'We know', 'This is my advice', rather than complaint and admonition.

The headmistress at Woodlands organised the girls to prepare Christmas presents for the first BANZARE cruise, but this did not win her Mawson's automatic complaisance when it came to the school's educational policies. In May 1931, when Jessica was thirteen, her father wrote asking that she be given instruction in Arithmetic in addition to the Mathematics she was already studying. Dora Gillam, the headmistress, did not want to upset Jessica's syllabus, but she caved in and agreed to allow the child to take extra work in Arithmetic in the periods normally devoted to Sewing, Preparation and Art.[12]

Like most Australian children then whose parents owned a farm, the girls were taught to shoot, by a father who had rated 'Marksman' in the Sydney University Rifles. Without her father's knowledge, 14-year-old Jessica assumed the role of instructor herself, showing a small friend how to load and fire the rifle, but the instruction was poor, the friend shooting Jessica through both her legs. 'She has just come back from the hospital', Mawson told Hurley at the end of September 1932, 'and we are hopeful that the left leg, over which she still has no proper control, may eventually be completely restored to usefulness'. Fortunately it healed itself.[13]

A revealing outsider's view, as a child, of life in the Mawson home in the early 1930s is provided by Mrs W. N. Hoerr, the daughter of Mawson's colleague and AAE comrade Cecil Madigan. During one of her visits the Mawson girls showed her presents they had received, including a box with coloured lights that lit up if the correct answer was given to particular questions. She had never seen anything like it. 'Maids in uniform served the soup', she recalls. Later she and the Mawson children went to the beach for a swim. 'Pat and Jessica . . . scooped up jellyfish from the sea and talked about them in what seemed to me to be scientific terms which impressed me, as I had never thought of jellyfish as anything other than just plain jellyfish.'[14]

As first Pat, then Jessica, went through their degrees at the University of Adelaide the intellectual bonds with their father strengthened. Pat graduated at the end of 1936, at the annual Commemoration ceremony, on a day when the clouds burst over the city—'the heaviest rain I remember in Adelaide', Mawson observed. In the procession, he watched with pride as she took her science degree. During the summer vacation she accompanied him to a conference in New Zealand, and on her return to Adelaide took up a Research Scholarship for 1937 with a stipend of £100.[15] Later, when she helped him edit the BANZARE reports, she was to all intents and purposes her father's colleague. Jessica's interests led her into medical work—in 1940 she took up a position at the Institute of Medical and Veterinary Science at the Adelaide Hospital, 'preparing', as Mawson told Davis (a friend once more) 'for the expected epidemic of pneumonic influenza which may follow the war, as it did last time'.[16]

As students at school and then at the University, the girls frequently stayed with friends of the family who had similarly aged daughters—the Clelands, the Bagots (Walter Hervey Bagot, architect to the University and designer of its Bonython Hall), the de Crespignys (Constantine Trent—later Sir Trent—Champion de Crespigny, eminent doctor and Dean of Medicine at the University), and others. Mawson sometimes took them with him to the Flinders Ranges, or interstate. When Paquita was touring Persia for several months, from late 1938 to early 1939, father and daughters travelled together by car from Adelaide by way of Mallacoota and Sydney to Canberra for the meeting of the Australian and New Zealand Association for the Advancement of Science, ANZAAS, successor to the AAAS, almost an expeditionary trip for its time, when cars were less reliable. And in February 1941 he took Jessica with him to Hobart, staying with Sir Ernest and Lady Clark at Government House, climbing Mt Mawson, visiting Tasmania's west coast and the Mt Lyell Mining Company at Queenstown, and looking over the Tarraleah hydroelectric works.[17]

Paquita Mawson had her own busy life in Adelaide. She was an enthusiastic worker for the Mothers and Babies Health Association (MBHA) and gave garden parties for them at Brighton. She belonged to two clubs, the Queen Adelaide and the Lyceum, and in May 1934 wrote to Mawson from Melbourne to sound him out on her becoming President of the Adelaide Lyceum. 'Re your letter, Lyceum Club', he replied, 'you know what it will cost—I know you would like the job so do so if it won't strain us too much. We are overdrawn £200 now.'[18] She was elected President at the next Annual General Meeting. Mawson generally deferred to her on matters of mutual interest. She was a large woman with a strong personality, and Alan Spry, one of Mawson's students in the 1940s, recalls her turning up at the Department on rare occasions. 'She would walk into the old Geology building and if he wasn't in his room she'd yell at the top of her voice, "Doug-*LASSS!!*"'

For his part, moves were afoot to secure his election to the Adelaide Club, but this took time. In February 1936 Paquita asked him how it was progressing and he replied, 'Re Club—*festina lente*—can't hurry it',[19] even though he knew plenty of prominent and long-standing members—de Crespigny, Bagot, Sir William Mitchell the Vice-Chancellor, Sir George Murray the Chancellor and many others, as well as more recent members like John Rymill, pastoralist and explorer. Whoever was behind this first move to get him in, nothing happened, and the following January he was telling Paquita, 'I wrote Mitchell suggesting he put me up for Club'.[20] This paid dividends on 3 April 1939 when he was elected by ballot, his Proposer and Seconder being Murray and Mitchell respectively.[21] He regularly used the Club though he was not a 'clubbable' personality, in fact shy and somewhat uncomfortable in social situations.

Mawson was always honoured in what he by now regarded as his home town, but though he and his wife were prominent in their different spheres they contrived, through the 1920s and 1930s, to give their children a close and private family life, the best possible supervision in their education, and the knowledge that in their parents' eyes they came second to nothing.

17 Relations with Byrd, Ellsworth and Wilkins

Mawson's affinity for the United States is epitomised by his offering himself as Australian minister to Washington during World War II (see Chapter 18), and was the product of visits, lecture tours and professional friendships. He was particularly friendly with Richard Evelyn Byrd and Lincoln Ellsworth. With Sir Hubert Wilkins, born in South Australia, there was a hint of rivalry. These relationships illuminate the men's individual characters and ideals. Wilkins and Ellsworth were vital in the pre-history of the Australian National Antarctic Research Expeditions (ANARE). Byrd, Ellsworth and Wilkins were the foremost polar flyers in the golden age of flight—heroic American icons. American by 'adoption', Wilkins was based there and regarded by Americans as one of theirs, witness his major entry in the *American Dictionary of Biography* and his 'state funeral', as it effectively was, when his ashes were scattered at the North Pole in 1959 by the nuclear submarine USS *Skate*.

As already seen, Byrd and Mawson met in November 1928 in Wellington. Commander Byrd was on his way south, already famous as the first to fly, or claim to have flown, over the North Pole, on 9 May 1926. He had also flown across the Atlantic in 1927. Like Mawson, Ellsworth and Wilkins, he contributed to *Problems of Polar Research* ('Polar Exploration by Aircraft'). Invalided out of the

Navy at a young age, he retained Naval rank, his exploits advancing him to Commander and then Rear-Admiral. He came from an old Virginian family, politically active then as now, and was directly descended from the Elizabethan composer William Byrd. Knowing Mawson would be in town, he had telegraphed suggesting a meeting.[1]

They were introduced by Leigh Hunt, the entrepreneur behind the Sounds project and founder of the New Zealand Antarctic Society, in Hunt's office. Byrd suggested all three have dinner at the hotel. He booked a private room, and after the final course they retired there for coffee and cigars, in company with some of Byrd's men. He had never been to Antarctica and needed advice. Byrd's early books are replete with references to and quotations from Mawson. In *Skyward* (1928) Sir Douglas had just been cited as 'a great expert on Antarctica' and, with Scott and Shackleton, 'the inspiration' behind Byrd's forthcoming expedition. In *Little America* (1931) he would refer to Mawson as 'perhaps the greatest living authority on the Antarctic' and 'my friend'.[2] Byrd's chief objective was to solve the major problem as set forth in Mawson's article in *Problems of Polar Research*: was Antarctica one continent, or two, riven by a channel from the Weddell Sea to the Ross Sea? But he also needed answers to mundane questions. He planned to lay his depots on the Great Ice Barrier (Ross Ice Shelf) at regular intervals in anticipation of forced landings, and sought Mawson's advice on the nature of the Barrier surface and appropriate distances.[3]

Byrd appreciated Mawson's balanced position on the American nineteenth-century explorer Wilkes. Davis's voyages in *Aurora* during the AAE, like Scott's earlier, had thrown doubt on some of Wilkes's Antarctic sightings. To some Americans, like Mawson's friend W. H. Hobbs, this was outrageous, and any contorted arguments were justified to defend all of Wilkes's claimed sightings. Mawson had never impugned Wilkes's integrity and had gone out of his way to express admiration, writing that in his view Wilkes had undoubtedly sighted the mainland. In Wellington he reiterated the point for Byrd.[4] Their balanced attitudes on Wilkes helped cement their friendship, whereas Hobbs's extreme nationalism would corrode his friendship with the Australian.[5]

The fact that Wilkes was an American actually predisposed Mawson in his favour. As he told Hobbs's rebellious graduate student Mary E. Cooley, who also had balanced views, 'In my review, "Wilkes's Antarctic Landfalls", I discussed his achievements in a more friendly spirit than I should have done had Wilkes sailed under the Union Jack'.[6] That sentence says a lot.

From Wellington Byrd moved his ships (with four aircraft including a Ford tri-motor) south to Dunedin, thence to the Barrier where he established a wintering base he named Little America, close to Amundsen's old base. A year later, on 28 November 1929, he (with his aircrew) became the first to fly over the South Pole. Mawson was impressed by him—'a charming personality and a very able organiser . . . a great Virginian'. Believing that the United States should claim its own Pacific quadrant in unexplored western Antarctica, he agreed with Byrd's repeatedly raising the Stars and Stripes in these regions on his various expeditions, claiming possession of new lands for his country, actions never followed up in Washington, which consistently declined to recognise Antarctic claims.[7]

When Byrd, at Little America, learned that Canberra had backed the BANZARE he telegraphed the press agencies: 'My friend Sir Douglas Mawson is great scientist as well as explorer and there is none who has greater knowledge of Antarctic than he'; all assistance would be provided if needed. Byrd's nine-hour flight over the South Pole was 'magnificent' in Mawson's view.

The expedition was no stunt. Scientists were heavily represented, some chosen on the advice of Hobbs, who had led expeditions to Greenland, and it was Hobbs who persuaded Byrd to establish a secondary meteorological station far to the south of Little America.[8] This was the Bolling Advance Weather Base, which Byrd manned, alone, for five months through the Antarctic winter night of 1934 during his next expedition, 'in the dark immensity of the Ross Ice Barrier, on a line between Little America and the South Pole. It was the first inland station ever occupied in the world's southernmost continent.'[9] This was an existential and romantic act. Its meteorological results aside, it perhaps had value for the science of Antarctic psychology, though most of his friends thought it crazy. He went half mad and almost died as a result of his heating system slowly and insidiously gassing him, and recorded his frightening decline in his diary. It was his expedition, not some government's, he could do as he pleased provided he did not endanger his men unduly. It was a chance 'to live exactly as I chose, obedient to no necessities but those imposed by wind and night and cold, and to no man's laws but my own'.[10]

In 1932 Mawson had written to Gordon Hayes, 'You will find Byrd an extraordinarily nice fellow. Don't believe any adverse criticism made against him', though in 1934 he was 'out of sympathy' with Advance Base. 'My own plan would have been to install two juniors in that job. It is rather like the general leaving the army in the middle of an engagement, with the object of conducting a scouting operation.' To Hobbs it seemed 'incomprehensible'.[11] What Mawson most admired about Byrd was his independent leadership—like Mawson, he raised the money for his ventures and ran them largely on his own terms. The great landmarks named by both pay tribute to the private fortunes which backed them—Mac-Robertson Land, the Rockefeller and Ford Mountains. One of Mawson's complaints against the ANARE expeditions of the 1940s and 50s would be their state control. He would write to John Abbottsmith in 1950,

> I observe you were not happy the way things were managed at Heard Island. I can see room there for a strong man in charge . . . A Government run show of that kind lacks much that is a feature of private enterprise. In the latter, the Leader, above all others, is anxious to secure the best results. Hence he is determined that all shall be doing their best for the mutual benefit.[12]

This is attractive philosophically, and sound in its logic, but by the late 1950s the American and Soviet Antarctic expeditions had assumed a scale beyond the scope of private money. Already in Operation Highjump (1946–47) Byrd would lose control to the Navy.[13]

This friendship would last to the end. In 1947, following Operation Highjump, Byrd wrote,

I just received a copy of the National Geographic Magazine for October, which contains an article I wrote on our last Antarctic Expedition.

I find a mistake in that article which concerns you . . . There is a statement there to the effect that scientifically speaking [Paul] Siple [Byrd's right-hand man] knows more about the Antarctic than anyone else. I recall correcting the galley proof to the effect that this was true with the exception of Sir Douglas Mawson.

Somehow or other this correction never got into the final proof . . . I very much regret this error, since I have always held a very great admiration for you as a man, an explorer, and a scientist.

I want to take this opportunity to thank you most sincerely for what you did for Siple when he came through Australia.

With high regard and admiration . . . Richard E. Byrd[14]

Mawson was Byrd's direct link with the heroic age of polar exploration. Though just six years separated them, Byrd was a pioneer of the mechanical age, looking to Mawson almost as a mentor from a lost world. Yet Byrd died first, in 1957. Their correspondence, continuing to that year, became political in focus. Mawson's anxiety about the growing Soviet presence in Antarctica led him to urge Byrd to press Congress to claim western Antarctica. Byrd hedged in his replies—he held the sensitive post of Officer in Charge, Antarctic Programs—but showed Mawson's letter 'to some of the top people in government concerned with the Antarctic'.[15] Shortly before his death he contemplated a trip to Australia *en route* to the Antarctic but was forced to call it off. He had wanted to 'discuss the several vital matters which you touched on in your letter of last summer'.[16]

Their greatest contributions to the science of Antarctic geography were complementary. Mawson demonstrated, to a degree next to proof, the continentality of eastern Antarctica, Byrd the connected continentality of western Antarctica. Between them they thus answered the greatest of all questions over the physical geography of the sixth continent.

A year before Byrd's North Polar flight of 1926, Lincoln Ellsworth and Roald Amundsen had tried for the Pole but drifted off course, their two aircraft forced down and imprisoned in the pack for twenty-five days. In 1926, with Colonel Umberto Nobile in the Italian airship *Norge*, they succeeded, three days after Byrd had claimed the same goal.[17] It was a few months after this flight that Amundsen pointed Mawson out to Ellsworth at the Old Waldorf. Ellsworth filed the face away. He was restless, with money to burn, most of it made by his father in the Ellsworth coal mines south of Pittsburgh. He could have lounged around in his club, the Metropolitan in New York, and given parties for the international set at his grand Swiss berghof, but 'Desire nagged me continually until I was able to settle on the last great adventure of South Polar exploration—the crossing of Antarctica'.[18] This goal had seduced Shackleton, no one had achieved it, and now Ellsworth proposed to fly across, answering in the process the great unanswered question: one continent, or two?[19]

To this end he needed the most advanced aircraft money could design, one which did not yet exist, so he went to Jack Northrop at El Segundo in California and Northrop built him the Gamma, an all-metal, low-wing monoplane with 600-horsepower engine, cruising range of 5000 miles, and top speed of 230 miles per hour (much slower as finally configured with skis). Ellsworth named it *Polar Star*. He bought a ship built in Norway of pine and oak, then sheathed the hull in additional oak and armour plate, for use in ice. It had a cruising radius of 11 000 miles, made 8 knots and ran on a Diesel-type engine. He named it *Wyatt Earp* after the marshal of Dodge City and Tombstone whose gunbelt he carried on board. This ship would later take the ANARE on its first expedition south.

For his manager and right-hand man Ellsworth chose Sir Hubert Wilkins, as eminent a polar flyer as himself, and at that time the only Australian rival to Mawson's status as an explorer. A war correspondent and photographer of rare distinction who actually insisted on photographing the real fighting on the front lines (MC and bar), explorer, aviator, geographer, climatologist and naturalist, his greatest feat, for which he was knighted and received the Patron's Medal of the RGS, was his 2500-mile flight with Karl Ben Eielson from Point Barrow in Alaska east over the Arctic to Spitsbergen in April 1928.[20] He was second-in-command on Stefansson's disastrous Arctic expedition of 1913–18 and on J. L. Cope's unsuccesssful Graham Land expedition of 1920–21, and naturalist on Shackleton's final expedition of 1921–22. Wilkins ardently promoted the concept of a ring of meteorological stations on the Arctic ice, an idea, as R. A. Swan has said, 'of great value as the future was to show'.[21] He argued the concept for the south too. He was the first to explore the Antarctic by air, in 1928 and 1929, though one or two of his 'discoveries' were in error, and in 1930 he planned to reach the North Pole from beneath the ice in his submarine *Nautilus*, bought from the U. S. Navy—though he never actually took it beneath the ice. This was another concept vindicated by time but ridiculed then.

Mawson and Wilkins could not avoid each other, for Wilkins made periodic visits home to South Australia. He would be interviewed, and like Mawson he sought the ear of government. Swan describes his 1925 proposal for an Australasian Polar Pacific Expedition as 'both ambitious and daring'—the unknown coast of King Edward VII Land all the way to Graham Land would be aerially surveyed with a view to setting up a chain of stations sending out daily weather reports.[22] There was great enthusiasm in South Australia but Wilkins was unable to raise the funds.

Mawson's view of Wilkins was influenced by Hobbs, an 'aerologist' with definite views on the relation of ice masses and winds, and with the tenured scientist's distrust of the gifted amateur. Hobbs thought Wilkins's meteorological schemes 'crazy'.[23] Mawson took up the cry, but with adjectival slippage—Wilkins's schemes were *generally* crazy. Hobbs had to bring things back into balance: 'You do less than justice by Wilkins', he told Mawson. Wilkins's flights were of great value, and his meteorology crazy only because he failed to understand the aerological relation of ice masses to wind.[24] Hobbs was hobby-horsing. Actually, as *Flying the Arctic* (1928) shows, Wilkins was well aware of the need to take glacial topography into account.

Mawson told J. P. Thomson of Queensland that 'Wilkins knows nothing about science . . . The scheme that appeared under his name for concentre [*sic*] Meteorological Stations was that of

Dr. Mosman formerly of the Scottish Antarctic Expedition, . . . now of the Argentine Meteorological Service. It is unthinkable that the Federal Government should ever make arrangements for Wilkins to direct Meteorological work in the Antarctic.'[25] Yet on the first BANZARE cruise, while Mawson and Davis were running Wilkins down, Mawson's own meteorologist, R. G. Simmers, was actually reading Wilkins's *Flying the Arctic*: 'From the book one gets a better opinion of him than Sir D or Commander entertain. Their gibes at his taking all the credit for flying sound rather hollow in the face of his remarks in his book giving the piloting credit to Eielson.'[26] Indeed Wilkins had even been invited to contribute to *Problems of Polar Research*, though not on meteorology ('Polar Exploration by Airplane')—the most prestigious collection of articles on its subject and a seal of academic approval.

To make matters worse, Wilkins, though a quiet man like Mawson, outshone him in the tawdry world of show business. He was unembarrassed by hyperbole and aimed at the broad bottom end of the market, as the naivety of this advertisement for his film clearly shows:

[Picture of racing aeroplane]
With
SIR HUBERT WILKINS
to the
Antarctic
The Arctic
by
Submarine & Aeroplane
Personal Appearance of
SIR HUBERT WILKINS
On no account miss this
outstanding picture.
Thrills above and beneath the Ice—The North Pole—
The South Pole—Polar
Bears—Eskimo Walrus—Whales—The Famous Submarine
'Nautilus'—The Aeroplane 'Southern Cross'
= 6000 FEET OF THRILLS! =

Who cared or even knew that Wilkins had never been to the North or South Pole? Who bothered to ask what an 'eskimo walrus' might be? This picture promised more thrills per minute to Depression audiences buying their two-hour escape than were dreamed of in the cold philosophy of BANZARE and its middle-brow offshoot, *Siege of the South*.

Now Wilkins was working with Ellsworth, someone Mawson instinctively trusted—the latter two had corresponded, and Ellsworth had purchased BANZARE equipment through Wilkins in London. The first two attempts at the Trans-Antarctic flight had to be abandoned but in November 1935 they tried again, from Dundee Island off Graham Land. Wilkins was in charge on the *Wyatt Earp*. Following Ellsworth's departure with his pilot Herbert Hollick-Kenyon, Wilkins proceeded to the Bay of Whales to pick them up. But *Polar Star*'s radio broke down after 1000 miles, and to the outside world they were 'lost'. Instead of taking fourteen hours the flight took twenty-two days because of weather problems, with three intermediate landings, across 350 000 square miles of previously unknown land, to within 16 miles of the shack at Little America on the Bay of Whales where they arrived by foot on 15 December. There they awaited the ship, which would duly arrive. There was no need of rescue.[27]

To the outside world, though, radio silence spelt distress or disaster. Mawson suggested to the Australian Government that the Royal Research Ship *Discovery II*, cruising south of the Indian Ocean, be diverted to the Ross Sea to search for the 'missing' men, and within a day she was made available by the Colonial Office.[28] The Australian Government virtually chartered her complete with officers and crew. Under Davis's eye she was loaded at Melbourne with special stores and equipment, two short-range aircraft and Air Force officers under Flight Lieutenant Eric Douglas, sailing on 23 December for the Bay of Whales. Mawson wanted to go himself but his offer was declined on grounds of space and because extensive land-work was ruled out. However, he supplied sledges from his stock at the University, instruments, finnesko, tents and so on, in case land work proved necessary.[29] He had been cabled by Ellsworth's wife requesting details of search activities, and kept her informed, not raising hopes.[30] The aircraft sighted Hollick-Kenyon on 15 January 1936 outside the shack at Little America (Ellsworth was inside with an infected foot). *Polar Star* was shipped home, and Ellsworth sailed on *Discovery II* for Melbourne.

Mawson travelled by the Melbourne Express to meet him at the Williamstown docks, but there was such an ovation it was impossible to talk for long. He made a brief speech, calling the flight 'an undertaking of the first magnitude—full of hazard and rich in geographical interest'.[31] Later he called at the Oriental but Ellsworth was out, so he left a card and took the train home. Ellsworth wrote a grateful letter, relating his first sight of Mawson in 1927.[32]

It is probable that Ellsworth's example—he was well into his fifties—inspired Mawson to renew his own Antarctic activities. Another South Australian, John Rymill, was achieving successes in his leadership of the British Graham Land Expedition (1934–37). Mawson had said publicly in 1935 that he had merely 'postponed' plans to lead another expedition.[33] His Presidential Address to the Melbourne meeting of ANZAAS in January 1935, 'The Unveiling of Antarctica', urged an international administration of Antarctica and controlled whaling, and predicted 'summer pleasure cruises amongst the pack-ice' and the generation of wind power on the Antarctic coast.[34]

During the Imperial Conference of June 1937 in London, Wilkins told Casey (now Federal Treasurer) that Ellsworth planned to fly in the Australian quadrant, from Enderby Land to the Ross Sea or, alternatively, to make a triangular flight deep into Enderby Land. He suggested the Government consider establishing meteorological stations in Antarctica, purchasing Ellsworth's equipment following his flight. Ellsworth, he said, was spending around £20 000 all up, including aircraft.[35] Casey, heading the Conference's Polar Committee, accepted Wilkins's concept of meteorological stations, and Mawson was reduced to voicing support. In June 1938 Wilkins was touted in the press as a possible leader of the proposed expedition, and Rymill was also expressing interest. In September Wilkins, with Lady Wilkins, passed through Adelaide on his way south to join Ellsworth, and on the 16th he and Mawson discussed the idea of the Government purchasing *Wyatt Earp* and its two aircraft. Mawson thought the Government would smile on a reasonable offer.[36] Then in early November Ellsworth cabled Davis and Mawson, 'My ship and two airplanes one Northrop Delta and one Aeronca for sale total twenty thousand'—dollars, that is.

By now Mawson was champing at the bit for one last southern venture. He wrote off to Davis seeking his support for a geological-cum-meteorological expedition using Ellsworth's equipment. Davis turned it down flat: any expedition should be a Navy thing. Rymill's had been a private show, but he had been 'of the right age', had strong British Government backing, and his expedition was 'not in the nature of a summer vacation . . . I have no intention of taking further part in any Antarctic exploration'. It was up to 'younger men'.[37]

This hit home. Mawson was now fifty-six. In 1934 he had contracted influenza, 'the worst attack of any sort of infection I have had and it seems to have troubled my heart a good deal', he told Hobbs.[38] This was just after the death of Sir Edgeworth David from lobar pneumonia. In the autumn of 1936 Mawson was afflicted with acute sciatica and his general condition that year was in decline.[39] 'I have got into rather poor health', he told one correspondent in August. 'The doctors cannot find anything specifically wrong . . . and recently thought that I may be benefitted by the extraction of a few teeth. This has now been done.'[40] His trip to New Zealand with his daughter Pat in January 1937, he told Leigh Hunt, 'will have to be in the nature of a complete holiday, else I shall break down. My activities in connection with the Science Congress are being reduced to a minimum . . . to survive the meeting.'[41] He had been similarly exhausted after World War I, suffering an extended case of neuritis.[42] His restless mind was his body's curse. To top it all he was seriously troubled by arthritis.

By late 1938 he was thinking in terms of a permanent research station at Cape Freshfield, George V Land, north of where Ninnis had died, close to the magnetic Pole, to be manned over ten or fifteen years by the universities, each providing one or two men every summer to relieve those of the previous year. He brought this scheme before the Australian Vice-Chancellors' Conference on

28 February 1939 and it was endorsed.[43] At the same time he was pressing the Government to accept Ellsworth's offer.[44] Ellsworth became impatient on the matter, cabling Mawson from the Antarctic in early January 1939, 'leaving the Antarctic January 20 is there a sale for my ship'.[45]

Suddenly, on 13 January, Canberra's attitude changed. A report in the *Canberra Times*, direct from Ellsworth in Antarctica, declared that 'eighty thousand square miles of land never before seen' had been flown over and that 'following the precedent set in earlier discovery, I claim the area for the United States'.[46] Ellsworth named the vast region American Highland. It was deep within what Mawson had named Princess Elizabeth Land and powerfully challenged the shaky sector principle on which the Australian Antarctic Territory had been established.

It has been assumed, on the basis of no evidence whatsoever, that Ellsworth's claim was encouraged by Washington to challenge unjustified sector claims by other nations. There is a better, more human explanation. Ellsworth was impatient over the sale of his ship and aircraft. Just days earlier Wilkins, from the *Wyatt Earp*, had made several landings, one at the western side of the Vestfold Hills, flying the Australian flag. 'Have found excellent harbour', he cabled External Affairs in Canberra on 13 January (probably the same hour Ellsworth sent his cable from the same transmitter), 'centre of a promising geological area suitable as a meteorological base' (site of ANARE's Davis Station in the 1950s). In these tandem cables Wilkins and Ellsworth knowingly combined to push Canberra into a quick decision, Ellsworth playing bad guy, Wilkins good guy.

In Wilkins's cable, which interestingly mentions geology, something he had little interest in, he urged the Government to accept Ellsworth's offer of his equipment in the interests of con- solidating Australia's claims in the Antarctic, suggesting the question be referred to Mawson. The Secretary of External Affairs, W. R. Hodgson, did exactly this on 16 January. Fortuitously Mawson was in Canberra at the time, attending the Science Congress there, and he endorsed the sale at once. It was then formally referred to the Department of the Navy and publicly

Wedding group, 31 March 1914, outside Linden, the Delprat house in Toorak, Melbourne. From left, Hester Berry (bridesmaid), J. K. Davis (best man), William Mawson, Douglas Mawson, G. D. Delprat (bride's father), Paquita Mawson (Delprat), Henrietta Delprat (bride's mother), Elizabeth (Carmen) Delprat (bride's sister, bridesmaid), T. W. Edgeworth David, G. D. Delprat jr (bride's brother, groomsman)

Stereoscopic pair: the drive at Harewood, Mawson's farm in the Adelaide Hills, lined with the deciduous trees he planted

BANZARE: geopolitics in process. Mawson in his cabin on *Discovery*,
Macpherson Robertson watching from the wall

BANZARE: the regular playing-out of the dredge wire, and other marine-biological, oceanographic and meteorological activities, scientifically valuable, consume time. Meanwhile the intrepid Norwegian, Hjalmar Riiser-Larsen, is already exploring the coasts of Enderby Land, December 1929.

BANZARE: Mawson with some of the scientific personnel

BANZARE: Mawson (in front seat), about to ascend in the Gipsy Moth
with pilot Stuart Campbell

With daughters Jessica (left) and Patricia, at home in Brighton,
Adelaide, 1930

Stereoscopic pair: overlooking a section of Harewood, developed by Mawson from the 1920s to the 1950s

BANZARE: cheering the King on Proclamation Island,
Enderby Land, 13 January 1930

BANZARE: Scullin Monolith, in Mac-Robertson Land,
where Mawson landed and raised the flag, 13 February 1931

Mawson with American trans-Antarctic flyer Lincoln Ellsworth and
Sir Hubert Wilkins (right) at the Australian Club, Macquarie Street, Sydney,
2 March 1939. The discussions at this meeting are detailed in the text.

Same day, same people,
leaving the same place.
Wilkins, nicely attired,
has *not* secured
Mawson's support for
a proposed Australian
Antarctic expedition,
for Mawson has plans
of his own.

Mawson in the field in South Australia in 1948, still using a large-format glass-plate camera for the ultimate in fine definition, is shaded by Don Bowes, who became Professor of Geology at Glasgow.

BELOW Members of the University of Adelaide's Department of Geology, which now included a chair of Economic Geology, in 1949. From left, back row: John Hawke, Peter F. Howard, Alan Spry, Kevin Parkinson, Allan Wilson, A.P. (Lon) Wymond; front row: Hector Brock, Mawson, Ngaire Dolling, Eric Rudd, Alf Kleeman

The Mawsons in the family car, early 1950s. Mawson was not rich: the car is a Vanguard.

With Soviet Antarctic personnel from the *Lena* at the Department of Geology, University of Adelaide, early April 1956

From left, Phillip Law, Director of ANARE, Mawson,
General Hjalmar Riiser-Larsen, and Captain J. K. Davis, *c.* 1956, Melbourne

Mawson with Sir Raymond Priestley, veteran of expeditions under
Shackleton and Scott, and sometime Vice-Chancellor of the University of
Melbourne, and J. K. Davis (right), at the rooms of the Royal Society of
Victoria in Melbourne, 3 December 1956, for a meeting on Australia's role
in the forthcoming International Geophysical Year

Rare Kodak colour print of Mawson at the beach, south of Adelaide,
early 1950s

Behind, from left, Mawson, daughter Patricia Thomas, Paquita Mawson, son-in-law Ifor Thomas, daughter Jessica McEwin, with the grandchildren in front, and Peter McEwin behind the camera, mid-1950s. Kodachrome

Mawson visiting pine plantations, South Australia, mid–1950s.
Kodachrome

Mawson (right) at Mt Stromlo Observatory near Canberra, mid–1950s.
At left, the ever-elegant Sir Ian Clunies-Ross, Chairman, CSIRO,
with Dr D. F. Martyn. Kodachrome

Carrington Smith's 1955 portrait of Mawson. The strange circumstances of its completion are described in Chapter 20.

announced on 8 February. The finally agreed sum was £4400.[47] Casey subsequently told the press that *Wyatt Earp* would be used to set up meteorological stations in Antarctica, with Mawson as adviser.

Now it was up to Mawson to find an expeditionary leader, for even if he were to go south in the first year, he accepted that another man should be appointed for the longer term.[48] He turned first to Rymill, who declined because of his responsibilities on Penola Station.[49] Wilkins, Mawson knew, would be interested, but would have to be paid. Ellsworth, with whom Mawson had been in continuing contact by cable and telegram, had offered to co-operate in Antarctic work.[50] What did he mean by this? He had said he would be sailing from Sydney for California on 3 March on the *Monterey*, so Mawson travelled to Sydney and on 1 March was shown over the *Wyatt Earp* by Wilkins and Ellsworth.

The following day they met at the Australian Club, where they sat in black leather armchairs at a small table against windows hung with cedar venetian blinds.[51] Mawson found Ellsworth 'an extremely nice man socially' and 'an exceedingly pleasing personality', but quickly realised he had little knowledge of science. Ellsworth reiterated his willingness to co-operate with Australia in Antarctic exploration and Mawson tried to draw him out, but he was vague. He made no offer to back a joint venture financially, and Mawson was too proud to insert the suggestion, suspecting that Ellsworth's chief interest was in 'conducting some stunt that would fit in with a scientific programme on the first expedition'.[52]

So after the first fifteen minutes Mawson turned his attention to Wilkins. Knighted by George V, befriended by the dashing Italian aviator and Air Minister Italo Balbo and the *Duce* himself, married to Suzanne Bennett, a glamorous actress, Sir Hubert had substance and presence. Not many months earlier he had led the search for Sigismund Levanevsky, the Soviet flyer who had vanished on a polar flight from Moscow to Fairbanks. In a Lockheed Electra Wilkins flew a long series of complex patterns from the Canadian far north almost to the Pole itself, over frozen, unknown seas, pioneering techniques for navigating by moonlight. Personally decorated by Stalin for these efforts, Sir Hubert was now volunteering his services to his homeland, but his bank account was modest, and he needed Mawson's support, for whatever proposal he might make to the Government, he well knew, would be referred to that source for advice.

The aircraft the Government had just purchased along with the *Wyatt Earp* were, Mawson had found, 'extraordinarily good'.[53] Given strong Government backing, Wilkins could have used them to the full in surveying vast interior stretches of the Australian Antarctic Territory at the expense only of aviation fuel, operating from a meteorological base on the coast or from the ship, giving real substance to Australia's Antarctic claims, but Mawson does not seem even to have considered the idea of extensive aerial surveys such as Ellsworth had just flown, though this must have been in Sir Hubert's mind.

Mawson asked him how interested he was in doing further work in the south. Wilkins said he was extremely interested, and hoped the Government would finance him and lend him the *Wyatt Earp*. Mawson then suggested that if Wilkins could raise £10 000 from outside sources, and put up a reasonable proposition for a wintering station on the western side of the Dependency, he would not stand in his way, in fact he would be favourable to the Government's lending the ship for a year—just so long as Wilkins could offer a reasonable programme of work. He added that he would give Wilkins a couple of months to sound out the possibilities and find the money. Mawson would not put anything up on his own behalf in the meantime.

He was telling Wilkins, loud and clear, that he could only expect the Government to provide the ship, not even to match any private funds as in the case of the BANZARE.[54] He made nothing in the way of an encouraging gesture to Sir Hubert, who sat there glum.

The drinks waiter appeared—a photographer from the *Sydney Morning Herald* was at the desk, could he take a photograph? Mawson consented. By the time the photographer was in action Mawson had turned his attention back to Ellsworth. The two clearly had a great rapport and the photograph shows it, and shows Wilkins's feelings too as he sat there, on the outside, in a homeland that has so often viewed its greatest expatriates with suspicion. As they walked down the front steps into the street the photographer took another. Mawson's grin shows his satisfaction, Ellsworth looks complacent, Wilkins forces a smile.[55]

Mawson knew that his own scheme could be run on a shoestring budget. The universities would supply and pay the men, for a start. 'When Wilkins has done his best and proved either that he can or cannot obtain the £10 000', he told Rivett, 'I can again come into the picture'.[56] Even if Wilkins's plans were entertained by the Government 'they would need to be carefully investigated'.[57] Mawson would obviously be one of those investigating, but he did not expect things to get that far. 'I know this', he told Rymill, 'that in Government circles at least, Wilkins does not carry very much weight. So I think it most likely that he will be giving up the idea of conducting an Australian expedition to the south.'[58] Wilkins, however, did not give up. He worked out a thorough programme and put it to the Government a few months later. In early August they rejected his offer, not because the proposal was flawed, but because of financial constraints. A month later German troops crossed the Polish frontier and all Antarctic schemes were off for the interim.

Wilkins offered his services to the Government for war work but this offer too was rejected. The United States, though, saw his value and employed him on various government missions in the Middle East, the Aleutians and South-east Asia. He held a variety of defence-related posts, his advice was sought on rations and equipment for units fighting on sub-Arctic fronts, and he served in the United States Weather Bureau and the Arctic Institute of North America. It is natural and right that Americans claim him as their own. After his death his enemies in Australia still found ways to slight him. Lady Wilkins told J. K. Davis that

> They even suggest that I . . . was a mere nothing in Wilkins's life. The reverse is understating the truth. . . . They are writing him up but with a patronising air, and if not damning him with faint praise, they're coming close to it. I was told at the funeral that there was a lot of jealousy towards him, and I can see that . . . There seems to be

outright hatred for me . . . I suppose they resented his being married, but I never hindered him as some wives would have, especially American ones.[59]

Since then, however, historians of Australian Antarctic history including R. A. Swan have done justice to him, laying many of the slurs.

Mawson's attitude to Wilkins was less than generous, less than fair, and can be attributed to the scientist's instinctive distrust of the gifted amateur. An element of territoriality was in play too. Australia was Mawson's political turf, he had the ear of government in R. G. Casey, but then Wilkins would breeze in, seduce the press, interest people in his latest proposals, and be on his way to somewhere more exciting than Australia. He was probably looking for a way to come home for good in 1939, but the doors were closed.

18 THE GEOLOGIST IN THE FIELD

PRIOR TO THE 1930s Mawson's South Australian field work, conducted mainly in the Flinders Ranges and noted in previous chapters, was not very systematic. Essentially it was a series of 'reconnaissance operations', establishing foundations for his more co-ordinated approach through the 1930s and 1940s.[1] Significant papers in the late 1920s included his study of the igneous rocks around Wooltana on the eastern escarpment of the Flinders Ranges, with their evidence of late Cambrian glaciation, and his Presidential Address to the AAAS in Perth in August 1926, a comprehensive study of the igneous rocks of South Australia. 'By discussing them region-by-region in their structural and stratigraphic context', David Corbett points out, 'he produced what was essentially a geology of the State'.[2]

Then, with Cecil Madigan, he made a trip to the western McDonnell Ranges in Central Australia in November 1927, driving out where motor vehicles had never travelled, investigating a deposit of potassium nitrate reported to Madigan at the University. This proved uneconomic. On the way Mawson noted the long succession of exposed sedimentary beds, ran traverses at a number of points heading west and measured over 10 000 feet of strata from a Precambrian basement. He was able to make correlations with similar sequences in South Australia and provide evidence of 'cryptozoal limestones' like those Precambrian examples he had identified in 1924 in the Flinders Ranges (see Chapter 10). Mawson and Madigan published these findings in London in 1930.³ As a result of this trip Madigan became fascinated with the geology of Central Australia and would make his major contribution in that field.⁴

Madigan had sacrificed two years of his life to the AAE, staying on through the second winter. Then came the war, so that his career only got going in the 1920s. Tall and handsome, devoted to his wife and children, he was popular with many of his students. He was also patient, for he was the last man with whom Mawson settled up after the AAE. Pressed by debts and the responsibilities of marriage, he finally wrote in February 1920,

> Dear Mawson,
> I find myself deucedly hard up for cash, having been almost cleaned out after paying for this house. I wonder if you could settle up the balance of my expedition acct. It wd. be most accept-able at the moment. The balance owing is £8.17.11, and with £4.15.0 for the slides this totals £13.12.11. Very sorry to have to ask for it. Hoping to see you later in the week.
> Yours ever, C. T. Madigan⁵

Lee Parkin, a student of both men in the mid-1930s and Mawson's Cadet (fees paid in return for assisting the professor), recalls that

> One of the excursions I went on was down to Murray Bridge. We were up on the level, up above the river height. Mawson was telling the students how the heaps of shells proved that the sea level had been over that area. Two of us walked back to the Madigan camp and Madigan was saying, 'The heaps of shells here just proves that the ocean's never been up here. That's where the natives had all their feeds.' The fellow with me said, 'That's not what Professor Mawson is saying, sir', and Madigan just replied, 'If you want to join the bloody opposition go and join him'.⁶

Madigan's somewhat military manner did not please everyone.⁷ His relationship with Mawson was tense at times, but not totally unfriendly.

Meanwhile Mawson's friendship with Edgeworth David, derailed over the Sydney Chair but now shakily back on track, was threatened again by David's 'discovery' of Precambrian 'fossils' when poaching on one of Mawson's preserves, the Adelaide Hills. A long silence ensued from Mawson's side, David fearing he had lost the friendship again.[8] It was restored, however, Mawson even driving him up to his sites.

In 1936 Mawson delivered a State Centenary address to the Royal Society of South Australia on 'Progress in Knowledge of the Geology of South Australia', a ten-page historical and bibliographical survey, generous in its assessment of the work of such geologists as Ralph Tate, Howchin, David, W. G. Woolnough and Madigan, and very modest in regard to his own. By now his national reputation as a scientist was reflected in his Presidency of ANZAAS (1935–37). He was consolidating his work in the Flinders Ranges, around Mt McKinlay in 1937, at Parachilna Gorge in 1938, in the Wirrealpa Basin in 1939, at Wilpena Pound in 1940–41, and in other areas of the north, but also working in the Mt Lofty Ranges investigating the first stage of the Adelaide Series at Mt Magnificent south-east of Adelaide.

On these excursions, often in remote and difficult country, he was accompanied by senior students. On one occasion, recalled by two of them, Reg Sprigg and Lee Parkin, the expedition had got off to a bad start when Sprigg damaged Mawson's camera. A few days later Sprigg forgot that the portable radio had been placed, during a stop, on the running board of the departmental utility truck. Told by the 'Old Man' that he could drive, Sprigg set off at speed, the radio falling to the ground at the first bend. Mawson's fury was increased when, after surveying the bits and pieces, he climbed back in and sat on his spectacles, breaking them.[9] Generally, though, he was relaxed with students in the field, and cooked the meals, which were high in fat (as they had had to be in Antarctica). 'He was a very good camp cook', Ralph Segnit, his Cadet from 1942 to 1945, insists. 'He made excellent Irish stew in half a kerosene tin.'[10] Informality had its limits, though—driving back into Adelaide from one of these trips he declared, 'Now I must become Sir Douglas Mawson again!'[11]

The late Eric Rudd was his student from 1928. Rudd wished to participate in the Intervarsity Sports in Melbourne and asked if he might miss the last week's lectures. The answer was 'No'. Mawson saw sport as an unproductive expenditure of energy. Rudd decided to go anyway, but found Mawson in the same compartment of the train, travelling across for a BANZARE-related meeting and returning the next day, perhaps, to give his lectures later in the week, or even cutting them himself. Rudd stayed in Melbourne the whole week. Nothing was said, but later, on an excursion, ten miles from camp, Mawson declared: 'Rudd, I want that granite boulder carried back to the camp'. Rudd picked it up and staggered along with it, and almost seventy years later he recalled the scene as though it had happened the day before:

> Every time one of the other students would say, 'We'll give you a bit of a rest, we'll carry it for a while', Mawson'd say 'No, I want Rudd to carry that'. Next morning I got up and was about to put it in the back of his car. 'Look, Rudd,' he said, 'I don't think it's as good as I thought it was. Leave it here.' It was never mentioned again—we were great friends. I thought it was the nicest way, because the boys didn't ever know what it was about. I didn't ever say, and he never mentioned it. And he certainly didn't take it out on the exam papers. Behind it all, he was a pretty humane person.[12]

Years later he would back Rudd for the Chair of Economic Geology.

The results of his field work through the 1930s appeared in individual papers on the areas studied, and in 1942 they were synthesised in a landmark article, 'The Structural Character of the Flinders Ranges'. This was accompanied by a map of the central area of the Ranges, co-ordinating several cross-sections of parts of the area treated in earlier papers and showing their relation to the overall structure. Through the 1940s he continued to publish landmark papers of this kind. One of these returned to a topic of long-standing interest, on 'The Nature and Occurrence of Uraniferous Mineral Deposits in South Australia', delivered to the local Royal Society on 12 October 1944, and should be seen as a contribution to the war effort. It represented his accumulated knowledge of a field he had pioneered, assessing the known uranium deposits and their recoverability. Unmentioned 'circumstances' had arisen, he said, which deemed it 'expedient' to bring the facts together. These circumstances were obviously the Manhattan Project and its development of the atomic bomb, about which he may have had confidential information, perhaps from Sir David Rivett at CSIR. The Americans would soon be complaining about lack of security in that institution.

In 1947 he supplemented his paper of 1942 on the Flinders Ranges with another major synthesis, 'The Adelaide Series as Developed along the Western Margin of the Flinders Ranges'. Two important papers in 1949 identified previously unknown glacial events, the findings based on field work since 1938 at Elatina in the northern Flinders Ranges and at the Bibliando Dome 42 miles east of Hawker.[13] His analysis of the Precambrian sedimentary record of the Dome, amounting to nearly 50 000 feet in all, clearly showed that the glacigene section had accumulated 'in two main divisions separated by a notable inter-glacial epoch'.[14] By now he was making use of aerial photography in his field work and analyses.

Meanwhile he had paid a number of visits to the lower southeastern areas of South Australia, investigating granitic and other igneous rocks of the region with Lee Parkin, W. B. Dallwitz and E. Ralph Segnit.[15] He also investigated the nature of the bituminous 'coorongite' on the east of the southern Coorong around Salt Creek with a British petroleum expert, Washington Gray, who thought there might be oil below. This was in the 1930s and nothing came of it, but Gray, later Managing Director of Commonwealth Oil Refineries (which became BP), continued his contacts with Mawson—Paul Hackforth-Jones, who worked with Gray, recalls them having lunch as Mawson's guests at the Adelaide Club in the early 1950s and being struck by Mawson's 'charm, integrity, stature, modesty'.[16]

His geological field work, and (after BANZARE) his enhanced reputation as an Antarctic explorer, brought him further awards: the Gold Medal for Oceanographic Research from the Geographical Society of Paris, 1927; the Nachtigall Medal of the

Geographical Society of Berlin, 1928; the Polar Medal, bronze, with clasp, 1929–31; the Founder's Medal of the Royal Geographical Society of Queenland, 1929–31; the Ferdinand von Mueller Memorial Medal, 1930; the Sir Joseph Verco Medal of the Royal Society of South Australia, 1931; the Clarke Memorial Medal of the Royal Society of New South Wales, 1936; the John Lewis Medal of the Royal Society of South Australia, 1950; and the Galathea Medal, 1950–52. Within the Australian scientific world his prominence was further recognised when he became a foundation fellow of the Australian Academy of Science (AAS)—he was one of the ten members of its Provisional Council who personally received the Academy's Charter from the Queen in Canberra on 16 February 1954.

Mawson was generally less impressive in the lecture theatre than in the field. He would present a solid lecture backed by handouts, with information set out systematically, but his delivery was formal and uninspired—except when lecturing on Antarctica with slides, as Ralph Segnit points out. 'Then he was very exciting to listen to.'[17] He had little sense of humour when the joke was on him, as it was when a student deliberately arranged his slides in the wrong order for his last first-year lecture, in 1952. 'The thing became pretty hilarious', Lee Parkin remembers. 'Mawson couldn't take that.'[18] When Alan Spry, as a junior student, blew a trombone in a lecture he was naturally thrown out. He points out that Mawson had a tremendous memory for each of the rocks in his vast Departmental collection: 'Just after lunch, north of the creek, at the end of January 1941—that sort of thing'.[19]

His office was a shambles. 'Any letter you wrote to him', Eric Rudd recalled, 'you went back three months later, he'd scratch through the heap and find it, he was going to reply to it'.[20] He kept up a massive correspondence, filing away carbons of most of the letters he sent. The number preserved, inbound and outbound, must run to five figures. They provide a week-by-week, often day-by-day record of his work, interests and friendships across his entire adult life.

David Corbett has pointed out that when Mawson entered the University of Sydney in 1899 'the scientific world-view was of a cooling, shrinking earth not more than one hundred million years old . . . Mountain belts were seen as a crustal adjustment to a cooling interior and most geologists accepted the relative permanence of the continents and oceans.' The two biggest developments from 1900 to 1950 were 'the application of the discovery of radioactivity to the dating of rocks, and Wegener's hypothesis of continental drift'.[21] Mawson was extremely interested in the first, though his university was too small to be able to afford the age-dating equipment. The latter, which did not achieve orthodox status until after Mawson's death, was a theory he declined to accept, 'citing the rigidity of the ocean floors and the lack of any known mechanism that could power the process'.[22]

His contribution to South Australian geology, however, was outstanding, and his 102 papers, which have stood the test of time, provide the proof.[23] He inspired a significant number of his senior students to become distinguished geologists, men like Rudd, Parkin, Sprigg, Segnit, Forbes and others, and his own output continued almost to the end of his life. If there was one thing lacking it may have been the ability to think three-dimensionally about structural problems, at least in the view of one or two who worked with him. Spry puts it down to his lifelong concentration on Precambrian stratigraphy.[24]

His crowning achievement at the University was the Mawson Laboratories, a long and spacious three-storey building of impressive quality, largely to Mawson's own designs. It was completed in 1952, shortly before his retirement, and more than compensated for decades of sub-standard accommodation and unsatisfactory laboratories. Construction started in late 1948 and the final cost ran to £120 000. As he told Hobbs at the end of 1948, 'Chiefly through my own activities the Broken Hill Mining companies have contributed £50 000 to endow a Chair of Mining and Economic Geology in our School of Geology'. Eric Rudd had just been appointed to it.[25] This was a major victory, second only to the building itself. By the early 1950s Geology had a faculty of five permanent appointments and included, besides Mawson and Rudd, the palaeontologist Martin Glaessner, Alan Wilson and Alf Kleeman. The offices were spacious, the lecture theatre acoustically superb, the halls and corridors wide and elegant, and there was (and still is) a large room devoted to Antarctic petrology with row upon row of beautifully crafted display cabinets. In 1933 they cost £600.[26]

Only once after 1925 was he tempted by another academic post. This was in March 1937. 'Applications for the Professorship of Geology at Oxford University close on the 6th this month', he wrote to Paquita (in Melbourne looking after her parents). 'I am not applying but might have done so—had you been keen on it. I have had several notices of it posted to me by anonymous folk.' Five days later he wrote again. He could still cable them, and his chances would be 'first class', but was it worth it? There were better geological opportunities in South Australia, there was the timber company, there was the farm. Oxford were offering £1200 per year, the same as at Adelaide, with more perquisities. 'But of course there is to be a war within 2 years'. There would be less chaos for the family in staying, 'so I have done nothing'.[27] There were also Paquita's parents to consider. Both were slowly dying of cancer, G. D. Delprat's case being furthest advanced. None of the Delprats' other children were there to look after them, and Paquita Mawson was a caring daughter, as well as a caring wife and mother. She was particularly worried that her father might take his own life. 'With respect to the revolver', Mawson advised her, 'it would probably be better to leave it with him but replace all cartridges with blank cartridges'.[28] G. D. Delprat died in March 1937 with an estate valued at £60 000, some of which went to Paquita. Her mother, Henrietta Delprat, died in December. Free of responsibilities, the Mawsons began to plan a holiday to Europe, even letting the Brighton house in 1939 in anticipation of this. When war broke out they were forced to take a flat at Ruthven Mansions in the City.

There was one other position he considered, and in this case he put his name forward. In late 1941 he had sought to make a contribution to the war effort, writing without effect to Essington Lewis, who was in charge of munitions.[29] Then a few months later he learned that his friend Dick Casey was leaving his post as Australian minister in Washington. By now the United States was in the war. On 23 March 1942 he wrote to Labor Prime Minister

John Curtin offering himself as Casey's replacement. Just four days later Curtin replied:

> Dear Sir Douglas Mawson,
>   I am indeed grateful to you for the intimation of your willingness to make your services available to the Commonwealth as conveyed in your letter of 23 March. Your offer is greatly appreciated and you may be assured that it will receive the fullest consideration.
>   I am most anxious that we should have an appointment made which would ensure the maintenance of the standard set by Mr. Casey and meet the existing understanding between the United States and the Commonwealth and at the same time be in accord with the standing we have in the British Commonwealth of Nations.
>   Yours sincerely,
>   John Curtin
>   Prime Minister[30]

Mawson seems not to have kept a carbon of his letter to Curtin, and the relevant file at Australian Archives in Canberra appears to have been destroyed.[31] What made him think he had a chance? He knew distinguished Americans in his field and had wide knowledge of the United States. He was an eminent Australian. The man selected was Sir Owen Dixon, the greatest lawyer Australia has produced, who had to be pressured to take the position. Alongside Dixon Mawson may seem inadequate, but he might have done well in the position. He knew and understood America a lot better than Dixon, and Dixon had little more political experience than him. Unlike Dixon, who despised the vulgarities of America, he identified with the country's free-wheeling spirit.

Insight into his feeling for the United States is provided by a letter he wrote in 1943 to Mary Cooley, Hobbs's dissenting student, then at Mt Holyoke College in Massachusetts, on the war contribution of her 'great country':

> I cannot say too much for the keen and conscientious bearing of members of your Military forces whom I have contacted here . . .

Your great nation has it in its power to prevent any future recurrence of international armed strife . . . merely by joining a compact
with other peace-loving peoples to enforce arbitration in international disputes. All peoples within the British Commonwealth
would be parties to such an agreement. There is also no doubt that
all the smaller countries of Europe would join in. Others would then
have to follow.[32]

He managed to make his own small contribution to the war
effort. Following the collapse of France he wrote to External Affairs
suggesting they do something about the French possessions of New
Caledonia and Kerguelen Island before Germany could step in. He
was told that moves were afoot to encourage the 'Free French'
element on New Caledonia. On Kerguelen he heard nothing until
February 1941, when he and Jessica were staying with Sir Ernest
and Lady Clark at Government House in Hobart. At a party one
evening a naval officer introduced himself. 'You will be interested
to learn', he said, 'that we received your advice regarding
Kerguelen, and a visit paid to the Island revealed that the enemy
were making use of it'. Mawson then sent the Navy a copy of the
map he and Davis had produced of the island during the
BANZARE, drawing the Navy's attention to the useful character
of Port Jeanne d'Arc as an enemy supply base.[33]

His civic virtue in these years is epitomised in a letter of
February 1943 to the Liquid Fuel Control Board in Adelaide:

> Dear Sirs,
>   I enclose licence recently granted to me for 8 gallons of petrol
> to replace some stolen petrol.
>   Ultimately I was able to carry on vital deliveries from my farm
> without using enclosed so am returning it unused.
>   With thanks,
>   Yours faithfully[34]

For a geologist to whom motor transport is the *sine qua non* of field
work, this seems to go beyond the call of duty. To Mawson, though,
the national interest was paramount, and his probity was absolute.

19 MAWSON AND ANARE

No SOONER WAS the war over than Mawson was again advocating an Australian Antarctic programme.[1] This time, however, it would not be of his devising and not always to his liking.

In July 1946 R. G. Casey, as interested as ever in Antarctic matters, spent a week in Adelaide. Mawson saw him over cocktails at Government House and organised for him to address the Commonwealth Club. Although Casey's party was in Opposition, he had influence with bureaucrats at External Affairs in Canberra and there can be no doubt that Mawson asked him to use it.[2] The relevant minister was H. V. Evatt, but the key person was William E. Dunk, Secretary of the Department, who had worked closely with Casey when he was Treasurer in 1939. Mawson may have seen Evatt himself. In any case, a few months later Mawson received an invitation from Dunk to attend a meeting in Melbourne on 2 December at the Victoria Barracks. It's purpose was to formulate recommendations for Cabinet on the 'development and use of the Australian Antarctic Territory' and 'greater continuity of effective occupation', without which Australia's claims had no international legal validity.

This meeting involved interested departments—External Affairs, Navy and Air—as well as CSIR, and its recommendations formed the basis of a Cabinet Agendum on a proposed expedition, approved on 16 January 1947.[3] Mawson had suggested the establishment of a base at Cape Freshfield, 200 miles east of Cape Denison (which was considered too windy). After the Melbourne meeting he wrote to Dunk recommending Group Captain Stuart Campbell, RAAF, chief pilot on the BANZARE, as leader of any expedition. He had already contacted Campbell, who was keen.[4] Rymill, on the other hand, was not.[5]

The next meeting, in Melbourne on 24 January 1947, constituted itself the Executive Committee on Exploration and Exploitation, indicative of an economic as well as political motive. Mawson recommended that Ellsworth's old ship, the *Wyatt Earp*, be supplemented by a Naval auxiliary ship for transport of supplies. They should also have at least two twin-engined aircraft. At this early stage the Committee were considering an expedition for the 1947–48 summer. A transitory summer party would concentrate on biology and geography, while a wintering party would consist of physicists and meteorologists.[6]

Evatt attended the afternoon meeting on 5 May, where a less ambitious preliminary expedition was agreed on. This was because Mawson was finally unable to vouch for the suitability of Cape Freshfield. 'I've seen it', he told them, 'but I can't definitely state that the rock under the covering ice is above sea level or sufficient to provide foundations for huts. It's essential that any scientific station be on hard rock, given the movement of the surface ice.'[7] In fact Mawson had only seen Cape Freshfield from 20 miles away, on 11 December 1912, and the AAE's Eastern Coastal Party had not got much closer.[8] So *Wyatt Earp* was to sail south with limited personnel and search for potential continental sites so that in 1948–49 another expedition might establish itself without delay; at the same time a Naval auxiliary ship would proceed to sub-Antarctic islands with scientific staff. The Committee also resolved to co-opt the Director of Navigation, J. K. Davis, as a member at future meetings. Evatt took a liking to Mawson (it was not mutual), inviting him onto an advisory committee to make recommendations on a comprehensive Japanese settlement including the educational, economic and cultural fields—meetings were held in Canberra and included members of Parliament from both parties and experts in constitutional law.[9]

Stuart Campbell was in the chair at the next meeting, on
9 July, and became Chief Executive Officer of what was from now
on called the Australian National Antarctic Research Expedition
1947 ('Expeditions' after 1947)—ANARE. Phillip Law, a lecturer in
Physics at the University of Melbourne, attended for the first time
as ANARE's Senior Scientific Officer.

This is not the place to rehearse the well-recorded history of
ANARE, but Mawson's part in its inception was important and he
continued to play a strong guiding role. In addition to his membership of the Executive Planning Committee he was also on the
Scientific Advisory Committee and later the Biological Sub-
Committee. Briefly, *Wyatt Earp* sailed south on 26 December 1947
but had to return to Melbourne with mechanical problems (her
tail-shaft was in danger of snapping). Though she sailed south again
on 8 February 1948 she was unable to reach the Antarctic mainland
owing to pack-ice and the lateness of the season. A Naval landing
craft, LST 3501, had earlier left Fremantle on 28 November 1947
for Heard Island and landed a wintering party of fourteen men. A
meteorological station was set up and a scientific programme
initiated. This expedition was led by Campbell, who did not stay
with the wintering party, returning with the ship to Melbourne in
January 1948. In March 1948 LST 3501 landed a party of thirteen
on Macquarie Island for a planned period of fifteen months,
another meteorological station being set up there. Thus ANARE
was underway, in a sub-Antarctic fashion, less than a year after
the preliminary meeting organised by Dunk. From May 1948 its
activities would be overseen by a special Antarctic Division of the
Department of External Affairs. The focus here will be Mawson's
continuing input and his assessment of ANARE's development.

His view of the first year of ANARE's work under Campbell
was highly favourable. Campbell, however, only lasted as Director
of the Antarctic Division until January 1949, when he was replaced
by Phillip Law who would continue in the post until 1966, with
great achievements to his credit, including the establishment of
several continental bases. Mawson's attachment to Campbell was
close and personal and he was sorry to see him go. He told
J. S. Cumpston that External Affairs 'does not realise how much

they owe him. I did learn from Burton [Dr J. W. Burton, then Secretary of the Department of External Affairs] that Campbell cut some of the red tape (in order to get something done) and did incur Burton's ire: but who would not?'[10] He told Paul Siple, Byrd's right-hand man, that Campbell's departure was partly political—he had crossed swords with Burton 'who turned out to be a socialist tinged with Red'—and 'partly because the Antarctic programme was temporarily in abeyance'.[11]

As these letters suggest, Mawson disliked the fact that ANARE was controlled by the Government. His remarks to John Abbottsmith in 1950 on the advantages of private over state-run expeditions have been quoted already (see Chapter 17). He told Robert Dovers, 'I suspect that being in charge of a Government expedition, as you will be, is not quite the same as would be the case if it were a private undertaking. There will be sure to be limitations and restrictions. When things go wrong you alone will be the loser.'[12] It was not just ANARE—the CSIR was threatened with precisely the same thing, he told Eric Harrison, Deputy Leader of the (Liberal) Opposition, at the end of 1948, and the pernicious process had to be resisted: all sections of the CSIR not seconded for defence purposes should 'be maintained as at present constituted and not gradually broken down and incorporated as adjuncts to existing Government departments. . . . I view with the deepest concern the new Public Service Bill which will give power to the Government to place, at any time, the control of the whole of the work of the [CSIR] in the hands of the Commonwealth Public Service Board.'[13]

He effectively constituted himself as a waste-watch committee in defence of the taxpayer at the Executive Planning Committee meeting on 3 June 1949. Phillip Law, in the chair, addressing himself to matters arising out of the minutes, was saying that negotiations over the purchase of a new ship were proceeding and that there was nothing to add. At this point Mawson asked a startling question. Was it the Government's intention to pursue the present Antarctic research indefinitely? He felt there should be some limit to the activities of ANARE—unless, of course, it could be made to pay for itself. Before any decisions were taken to commit large sums for scientific exploration in the Antarctic, he said, a critical analysis should be made in order to discover if the money might be more usefully expended elsewhere.

There must have been disbelief around the table at this. Such committees are not accustomed to dispute their right to public money—their very existence, as it were. The silence was broken by the Chairman. He pointed out that the Government was already committed to an Island programme of at least five years. It had set up a permanent Antarctic Division in Melbourne to carry on this programme, and to prosecute plans for establishing a base on the Antarctic continent. Whether or not a ship could be purchased would have a strong bearing on the Government's attitude.

To Mawson this was beside the point. It was the whole philosophy he was worried about. He said he wished to make something clear. When he first suggested an Antarctic expedition to the Government, he had not contemplated the present large expenditure. He had considered that part of the cost should be met by proceeds from associated commercial undertakings such as whaling. It had always been his view that Australian activity in the southern regions should be allied with the fisheries industry, more especially whaling. If Australia persisted with the present plans, his proposals regarding whaling should be carefully borne in mind. Whaling expeditions could finance an Antarctic programme, and in addition, their ships could take with them aircraft capable of surveying large areas of the interior. If attention were not paid to the commercial side, then in his opinion it would be too expensive to maintain base camps indefinitely.

There was the Mawson philosophy in a nutshell. ANARE should pay for itself. Exploration and development, meaning exploitation of resources, properly managed, should go hand in hand to the benefit of both.

Law countered this by arguing that recommendations to the Government regarding the setting up of a whaling industry lay outside the functions of the Committee. At that point Dr F. W. G. White, representing the Commonwealth Scientific and Industrial Research Organisation (CSIRO), successor to the CSIR, weighed in on Mawson's side. At their last meeting, he reminded the

Committee, members had been unhappy at the prospect of having to recommend a purely scientific programme with concomitant expenditure, and had passed a resolution. He then asked the Secretary to read it out. It stated that the Committee 'requests direction from the Government as to its future policy on the exploration and development of the Antarctic' and 'does not consider that . . . scientific work alone could justify the dispatch of a major expedition'. White then asked whether External Affairs had given a reply to the resolution.

Law replied that they had not. He presumed that they realised the position, though—they had been given all possible information. But in Law's opinion the question of the period of operation of ANARE was a matter for his own Department, and in any case he felt that further consideration of this matter should be postponed until near the end of the five-year period to which the Expedition was committed.[14]

Law was a strong Chairman and Director and he pushed ahead with his five-year programme, but he heard what Mawson and White were saying, and would soon be contemplating such developments as a controlled sealing industry,which would not deplete numbers, on Macquarie and Heard Islands. He would be prevented from implementing these ideas by conservationists of a more radical cast than himself or Mawson.[15] Although Mawson was defensive of the sanctuary status of Macquarie Island and opposed introduction of foreign elements such as dogs and horses, he had nothing against limited culls of the fauna with the exception of endangered species like the King Penguins.

By mid-1950 ANARE's Executive Planning Committee were considering chartering ships to establish continental bases, but it was not until late in 1953 that these plans were realised. Mawson generally supported Law's initiatives, though there were bound to be disagreements. Casey, now Minister for External Affairs and Law's political chief, had to work hard to convince Cabinet that a continental base was worthwhile when the Government was trying to reduce expenditures and inflation. Casey himself wavered, and Mawson backed up Law, defending his choice of Mac-Robertson Land for the proposed Mawson Station. Casey had thought a site that far west weakened the meteorological argument, but Mawson was able to overcome these doubts.[16]

Mawson's occasional criticisms, not always well founded, were either expressed to Law himself or privately to Davis and others. For instance, in early 1953 he wrote to Law opposing his plan to take horses to Macquarie Island—they would damage the herbage, their forage would have to be taken there with them and would spread alien seeds through the island, and diseases carried by horses might cross to native species. A small tractor should be taken instead.[17] He was also critical of the failure to eradicate rabbits and cats introduced decades earlier[18]—though Law had in fact issued orders for this to be done, and it was no easy task.

Law's great strength was his ability to get his own way with bureaucrats and run ANARE with a good degree of autonomy. Mawson should have liked this quality, given his antipathy towards Government enterprises of this kind, but he probably saw Law as part of the Government, in distinction to the field commanders with whom he identified more. To his credit, he never displayed any resentment at Law's having all the funding he needed, in contrast to his own expeditions for which he had had to fight for every penny. As already seen, though, he could be critical of what he saw as excessive expenditure.[19] In general it should be said that Mawson was supportive of Law. There were many meetings of the Executive Planning Committee, and a great variety of discussions and decisions in which Law found Mawson's support most valuable. On many occasions Mawson dined at Law's house to discuss points.

Something that did worry both Mawson and Davis was a clause in Law's *Operations Manual—Antarctic Continent*, p. 26, to the effect that 'the leader of the Expedition is to carry out instructions from the Director'. Davis and Mawson both felt that the field commander, Robert Dovers, should have had more autonomy, as well as a say in the selection of his men, or at least the right to object to anyone he thought unsuitable.[20] On the other hand Davis had nothing but praise for Law's chartering of the *Kista Dan* for the new continental undertaking.[21] The criticism of Law in respect of the field commander's autonomy was unjustified—Dovers was encouraged by Law to use his initiative to the full. At the end of

June 1954 there were articles in the press about Dovers's exploits on a winter excursion from Mawson Station to the Scullin Monolith—a motorised vehicle and equipment had been lost, and men injured. 'I would like to know whether Law asked Dovers to go to Scullin Monolith at that time of year', Mawson wrote to Davis. 'Actually it is the last place he should have visited, for its position has been fairly well fixed and we got our geological specimens from there in 1931.'[22]

In fact Law had not ordered this trip. 'These are adventurous blokes', he points out. 'They want their own achievements. The winter is the only time you *can* go to the Scullin Monolith—across the sea-ice (it's badly crevassed inland).'[23] Robert Dovers himself later made the same points in reply to a letter from Mawson, and defended the Director in the strongest terms:

> I feel that you expect a little too much of Mr. Law. He is without doubt an excellent organiser, and has considerable experience— particularly in ship work. He lacks experience in certain directions but on my own experience, learns very readily. Perhaps his greatest misfortune is that he has had excellent fortune in all his ventures and as a result rates the Antarctic a little too lightly. He is always an enthusiast and that is a hard thing to be over a long period. I do not think it fair that you expect also of him to be a highly experienced traveller as well. I should think it would be very difficult to find anyone to replace him.[24]

Even so, Mawson reserved the right to criticise. For instance, there was too much concentration 'on fancy physics laboratories at the Bases instead of facilities to get about the country for geography & geology' (Law was a physicist).[25] This amuses Law: 'In fact I was pushing like hell for geography and exploration!'[26]

In 1957 Mawson was strongly opposed to the proposal to take over Wilkes Station in Wilkes Land from the Americans following the International Geophysical Year, 1957, at the expense of the second Australian mainland station at Davis in Princess Elizabeth Land which had only recently been set up. 'The Davis area is geologically unexplored and I'd be loath to close the station there', he told the Executive Planning Committee on 25 November 1957. 'There's nothing geologically interesting at Wilkes, though it might be valuable meteorologically.'[27] He was unable to attend the meeting in April 1958 when the go-ahead was given, but mailed his views to Casey (who was now often chairing these meetings), with copies to Law. They were disregarded. He told Robert Dovers a few days later, 'they have gone quite haywire and taken over the Wilkes Base. Where it will all end I don't know.'[28] In Davis's view it had been a political decision pure and simple, 'to please the Americans' (Davis had been at the meeting).[29] In Law's view it was important to continue the geophysical work the Americans had done at Wilkes, and to extend Australian territorial occupation.[30] This was Mawson's last battle on the Executive Planning Committee and he had lost it. His health had long been failing, and the trips to Melbourne were becoming an impossible strain.

The opinions, off-hand in the main, expressed by both parties in the correspondence between Davis and Mawson, two old men no longer at the centre of Antarctic affairs, should not be taken as representative of their general attitude to ANARE. In most meetings, and on most issues, Mawson backed the Director. He took the Executive Planning Committee very seriously indeed, regularly travelling across by air on ANA or TAA, leaving Adelaide by the early-morning DC6B or Viscount service and returning the same night. This meant rising at 5.15 a.m. and getting home again at 9.30 p.m., too long a day given the state of his heart after 1954 (see Chapter 20). There was a sound reason why, in the final year or two, he could no longer stay overnight in Melbourne. His chronic arthritis in the shoulders, arms and knees made it hard for him to dress himself. In July 1958 Casey kindly offered to pay Paquita's fares and expenses so that she could accompany her husband on these trips, and this meant that they would be able to stay in Melbourne overnight, for, as Mawson put it to Casey, 'I would have no trouble dressing'.[31] Sadly, circumstances dictated that this arrangement would remain theoretical.

20 TO THE
LAST HORIZON

MAWSON'S RETIREMENT WAS scheduled for December 1952, during his seventieth year, but he expected to go on working without salary on his geological projects. He had plenty in hand— papers that existed in his head and wanted writing up, specimens awaiting analysis, sites to revisit. He assumed he could continue to use a room in the new Mawson Laboratories, and that the rocks on which he was working would continue to be stored in the crypt. How else was he to complete his life's endeavour? But he reckoned without a *bête noir* in the shape of the 'Abominable Rowe-man'.

This was the Vice-Chancellor, Professor A. P. Rowe. Whatever his achievements for the University of Adelaide, human management was not among them. Of earnest mien, with sour eyes under formidable black brows, he was widely disliked for his dictatorial and implacable manner. When gigantic stencilled footprints appeared in the University grounds one morning, coming out of Rowe's on-campus 'flat', heading in the direction of the Bonython Hall, and then proceeding directly up the wall to the roof, instead of laughing it off and offering a reward for the capture of the Abominable Rowe-man, he called in the detectives and fumed and fulminated, as intended. Rowe had a colour film made of the University to attract overseas staff, and when it premiered to the home audience, whose morale was low, someone asked aloud 'Where is this wonderful place?'[1]

By mid–1952 things were at a crisis. 'I find that there is now an overwhelming majority of Professors antagonistic to Rowe', Mawson told Paquita. 'They are preparing something like a mutiny.'[2] Any rebellion, however, was unlikely to come from the Education Committee or similar bodies which Rowe had tyrannised into obedience. The secure knowledge of this fact, and a delight in his own unreasonableness, shines darkly through his letter refusing Mawson's request to be allowed to continue to use a room in the new building after retirement:

> I know that some who are not versed in these problems may think it unreasonable not to give you a share in the new building. But your very distinction and your untiring labours in connection with the building of the new laboratories makes it particularly desirable that, after retirement, you should have a room in another building.[3]

Over the following months Rowe remained adamant on the point, and Mawson had to go over his head to Sir George Ligertwood, the Chancellor, who presided over the University Council. Mawson explained that he needed to work on the large collection of specimens in the crypt, which could not readily be moved, certainly not to some little office elsewhere, and that the only appropriate place for him to work was in the new building. 'I should be greatly surprised' he told Ligertwood, 'if the Council decreed that my life's work should be suppressed . . . without the Council making a full enquiry at which I would be present to give a full explanation'.[4] That was the way to handle Rowe (and Ligertwood). As a result of this letter Rowe backed down. The affair is important because it caused Mawson much distress through the second half of 1952.

His retirement was marked by a farewell party and a special presentation by his colleagues. Several months earlier, to mark his seventieth birthday, he had been presented with the *Sir Douglas Mawson Anniversary Volume* of papers on geology by colleagues and friends, edited by Eric Rudd and Martin Glaessner, a tribute to the esteem in which he was held by others in his field. And a few months after his retirement he was honoured with the D.Sc. by his *alma mater*, the University of Sydney. He was made Professor Emeritus and continued to attend meetings of the Faculty of Science. His rooms were on the lower floor of the Mawson Laboratories, and he went in most days, writing up papers on the Willunga Basin, South Australian glaciology and other topics, and finding time in 1953 to assist palaeontologists from the University of California investigating the remains of extinct marsupials at Lake Callabonna, 150 miles north of Adelaide.[5]

Social and domestic life in these years revolved around daughters and sons-in-law (Jessica had married Captain Peter McEwin in 1944, and in 1946 Pat had married Ifor Thomas, Reader in Zoology), seven grandchildren, and a relatively small circle of close friends—Trent de Crespigny, the Huxleys, the Hicks, the Heckers, the Neills, the Jeffares, the Robsons, the Rudds and a few others. De Crespigny and Rudd have been introduced earlier. Leonard (later Sir Leonard) Huxley was Professor of Physics, Kenneth Neill and his wife were neighbours, and Sir Stanton Hicks was Professor of Physiology—the Mawsons never ceased to be amused at how his young second wife called him 'daddy' in front of their friends. A. N. ('Dery') Jeffares was Professor of English. Stewart Hecker was Mawson's doctor at Brighton, Hugh Robson was Professor of Medicine and honorary physician at the Royal Adelaide Hospital. Of these, de Crespigny, Neill and Robson were fellow members of the Adelaide Club. Other close friends included a neighbour, Lorna Todd, daughter of Sir Charles Todd, and Jeanne Proctor, daughter of Sir Lancelot Stirling of Strathalbyn. With Paquita occasionally away interstate or overseas, Mawson would find himself reliant on these friends for evening company. There were numerous others interstate or overseas, some introduced in earlier chapters, and far too many to list.

One Sunday afternoon in April, 1954, driving back from the Adelaide Hills, he felt an unfamiliar pain in his chest. It was not particularly intense. He had planned to fly to Canberra the following afternoon, and next morning rose as usual and packed his suitcase. Paquita suggested they take an hour to see Hugh Robson at the Royal Adelaide Hospital, and Mawson consented. They had hardly driven a mile before he was hit by intense chest pains. Later that morning he was hospitalised. It was a standard heart attack. Ever since 1934 he had had doubts about his heart, and now they were resolved. In Ru Rua Hospital he lay immobile for a month, though after three days his cardiogram was normal and within a fortnight he was dictating letters. His prognosis was positive—'am told that provided I do not take on heavy physical work . . . I might have no further trouble for years'.[6] After a further period of sitting up and moving about he was allowed home, where Paquita had arranged a wing of the house that took in the winter sun, cosy and convenient, lined with books and warmed by a fire.

Unfortunately the heart attack was followed by chronic arthritis. Nevertheless, just two months after the heart attack he was flying to Melbourne for the 16 June meeting of ANARE's Planning Committee. This may have been a step too far too soon—for whatever reason, it was not repeated for some time. He reduced his regime of work and sold Harewood to his friend and business partner Charles Phillipson, although he would continue his interest in South Australian Hardwoods which he had chaired for so long.

The surviving men of the AAE and BANZARE would gather annually in Sydney or Melbourne to revive their old spirit and reminisce. Though he usually missed these reunions, Mawson would sometimes send messages and was regarded as present in spirit. When the news of his heart attack got abroad he received long letters from several of these men—men who had lost the diffidence of youth and wanted him to know what he meant to them. George Dovers, cartographer, Western Base, AAE:

> I do not see why I should not at this stage of our lives (we are both old men and shortly to set out on the greatest exploration trip of all) take this opportunity of telling you, that I consider that I was a most privileged person to have had the opportunity as a young man of serving under your leadership. . . . I do not think there is any doubt that the experience and example we had as young men under your command had a most tremendous effect for good on our characters and through us to our children.[7]

Charles Laseron, taxidermist and collector, Main Base, AAE:

> The years 1911–13 are still the chief milestone of my life, and ever since then I have always felt the urge to do something which would be a credit to the Expedition. I think you would like to know that while writing my three books, it is your approbation as our old leader, that I have wanted more than anything else. It is for this reason that the first of my author's copies has always been sent off post haste to yourself.[8]

John Hunter, biologist, Main Base, AAE:

> The 1911–14 days will ever take pride of place in my memories, and the example you set in leadership has always inspired me over the years.[9]

The enforced rest continued through the winter of 1955— long, idle days and evenings, with Paquita briefly interstate, the hail battering at the windows and things going wrong: 'The *Advertiser* was delivered in a puddle of water and hopeless. Mrs Chivers went off in her car and bought another one.' He would do some writing up, a bit of reading, correspondence, the same old routine. Mrs Chivers could never co-ordinate her chores, 'continuing to burn the toast bringing morning tea, pure tannic acid and without sugar . . . really old in mind. She gets up about 6 am and makes herself coffee—at 7 am she makes me tea—then gives the cat a week's meat in one helping. By 10.30 she may have washed up. It is lucky she was not passed to Jessica.'[10]

On good days he would take the tram to town, do a bit of work or sit for his portrait to Carrington Smith. The University Council had commissioned this and it was to be hung in the Bonython Hall. Rowe, who was still around, walked in on the day it was to be completed.

'It's very dark', he observed sourly, examining it from different angles, beetling his brows. 'Especially the face—the *face* is too dark.' The painter was a humiliated irrelevance as Rowe pondered the implications. 'It seems . . . it seems to represent you as of a *coloured* race, Sir Douglas!'

Carrington Smith, acknowledging the fault, spent the rest of the day lightening the complexion. Late in the afternoon Rowe reappeared with a couple of others. '*Much* better! Now it represents you as a medieval *alchemist!*'[11] The painting hung in the Bonython Hall until it was replaced by another by Ivor Hele, when it was relegated to the Mawson Laboratories.

Sometimes during these weeks when Paquita was away he would go out. Lorna Todd, across the street, celebrated her seventy-eighth birthday that winter of 1955, a living connection to the deep past, her father Sir Charles Todd, of telegraph fame, having been born in 1826. Mawson was invited for drinks at 5.00 p.m., and found a party of her old friends seated around a big fire, in sofas and armchairs. The sweet sherry was being served and the sandwiches, and later the coffee and the tea, with the cream puffs and the birthday cake. Clara Serena was there, the famous soprano who had sung in the great opera houses of Europe—famous at least in her home town, though forgotten now. Mawson had known her and her husband for years and in 1933 had presented her with a photograph that had appeared in *Home of the Blizzard*. 'Go on, Clara!' they were saying, 'Sing something for us. Sing "Silver Threads Among the Gold".' So she went over to the piano where someone was already striking up the chords and obliged them all. Then Mawson called for a toast to celebrate the occasion.[12]

By 1956 he was feeling strong enough to travel to his ANARE meetings. In April of that year two Soviet ships, returning from the Antarctic where the Russians had established bases deep within the Australian Antarctic Territory, called at Port Adelaide—the *Lena* early in the month and the *Ob* three weeks later. Mawson showed the officers around Adelaide and the Hills and arranged for them to visit the University. Their geologists, led by Professor O. S. Vialov, were especially interested in the evidence of glaciation in the Inman Valley, but were more impressed by Mawson himself. To them he was a living legend and they felt honoured by his attentions.[13] He was shown over the ships with their sophisticated scientific equipment, and there were several dinners at Mawson's home and aboard the ships, where caviare and Volga sturgeon, Russian wines and vodka were lavishly laid on. He was particularly upset that nobody from External Affairs visited the ships and that the Mayor refused to see them. This seemed mean. Convinced by these visits that Russian activities in the Antartcic were of great scientific value, he still wondered about the strategic implications and possible territorial claims. A political conservative, he distinguished between these officers and scientists and their government. 'They are very open', he told Casey. 'Should not Australia show such a contingent of visiting scientists some recognition? I think [W. C.] Wentworth's views regarding Russians are extreme.'[14]

Towards the end of 1956 Melbourne hosted the Olympic Games. They were opened by the Duke of Edinburgh, whom the Mawsons had met during Queen Elizabeth's visit in March 1954, just before Mawson's heart attack. The Duke stayed on in Melbourne for a symposium hosted by the Royal Society of Victoria on Australia's contribution to the forthcoming International Geophysical Year. This was held on 3 December and speakers included (besides the Duke), Mawson, Law, Marc Oliphant and Dr D. F. Martyn. Mawson's address, a survey of Australian expeditionary work, had archival significance, for it was televised. Television footage of Mawson is extremely rare, perhaps nonexistent, for in this case it was evidently destroyed by the ABC.[15]

In early 1957 he turned down the Presidency of the Geological Society of Australia on the grounds of health, but was still reasonably active. Then in May he became the victim of one of those trains of consequences fate or Providence sometimes arranges. He attended a meeting of ANARE's Executive Planning Committee at Parliament House in Canberra, where Casey was in the chair. It was a long meeting, Mawson's input was major, and he appeared to win all his points.[16] But he was tired and still recovering from a cold. He flew home, sitting on the other side of the aisle from Phillip Law for the flight to Melbourne, then transferring to the Viscount service to Adelaide. Both Law and Mawson were lean men and felt the cold. Law reached up and turned off the cooling nozzle—these things annoyed him, and he had written to the airlines suggesting that at the end of each flight the cabin crew go around and turn them off, so that at the beginning of a flight one had the option of turning them on. Mawson was seated next to someone whose nozzle was pointed sideways, focused directly on him. Being gentle and unobtrusive, rather than reaching over and turning it off he put up with it for the entire flight. As a result he developed pneumonia, and consequently his heart began giving trouble again. Things were very worrying throughout the rest of May and early June, and he had not fully recovered in early August.[17]

Still, he managed to lead a deputation to Premier Thomas Playford in late June to press for an Oceanographical Institute in Adelaide. After the others had departed he asked Playford, whom he knew well, 'Why on earth did you encourage Rowe to hold on to his job?' (Rowe had announced his intention to resign but then, to everyone's dismay, had changed his mind.)

Playford replied, 'Well, after the Honours List came out, Rowe sailed in here, obviously very upset, and wanting to know why Mark [Mitchell, Deputy Vice-Chancellor] had been knighted and he not. He didn't think it right that his *assistant* be knighted, and not he. I told him, "Look, Mark's had a long period of good works to his credit—it might be possible for you also to build up such a record, if you keep doing your best for the community." '[18]

This had been a perfectly just response on Playford's part. Whereas Mitchell, in addition to his distinguished academic career, had served as President of the South Australian Council of Social Services since 1954, providing assistance to the needy, Rowe had served only the goals and purposes of the Vice-Chancellorship, which may be a worthy office, but is hardly philanthropic.

Mawson's letters are now full of arthritis and the latest varieties of cortisone. He thought he would be unable to travel to Melbourne for the launching of Paquita's biography of her father, *A Vision of Steel*, on 23 May 1958. At the last minute he decided to go 'by train tonight to attend with her a launching party. . . I cannot stay over in Melbourne', he wrote to John Bechervaise.[19] It was a select affair, according to Ann Blainey, who with Geoffrey Blainey was among the guests. They included Essington Lewis. The Blaineys knew nobody, so Lady Mawson made a point of talking to them. Mawson had read and enjoyed Blainey's first book, *The Peaks of Lyell*. 'He was very approachable', Blainey recalls, 'rather frail—though you wouldn't have guessed he would be dead within months'.[20]

There were few consolations that final year. With Paquita he attended a dinner at Government House in honour of the Queen Mother which he enjoyed, as the former Duchess of York vividly remembered his showing her over the *Discovery* in 1929 and wanted to talk to nobody else.[21] And in August there was an ANZAAS conference in Adelaide at which he attended a number of papers. During that week they entertained visiting scientists every night— unwise, for it seems to have resulted in exhaustion.[22] Then in September he had a stroke, not particularly severe, but it affected his speech for several days.

Soon he was corresponding again. The letter of latest date read for this biography was written on Friday, 11 October 1958, to John Bechervaise, who had led a series of ANARE expeditions. It conveys no intimations of mortality.[23] Arthur Alderman, Mawson's successor in the Chair of Geology, came to dinner the following night. They discussed Mawson's unfinished projects and he handed across all his working papers, explaining their geological contexts so that someone could take them over—as in a relay race, which science and civilisation are, in a sense. Sunday was warm and bright. Some friends paid a visit and everyone sat outside on the cool, springy buffalo-grass lawn.

The next morning he suffered a severe stroke and lost con- sciousness. The family gathered around as he was not expected to last long, and it was better he die at home than in some hospital ward. His heart held out till the evening of the next day, Tuesday, 14 October 1958, then stopped at 9.00 p.m. It was fifty years to the day since he had set out, with David and Mackay, heading magnetic south, from his first-ever continental landing at Butter Point, South Victoria Land, on 14 October 1908, with the Ferrar Glacier on his left and cloud-capped Mt Erebus on the right horizon. Now he was outbound on George Dovers's 'greatest exploration trip of all', beyond horizons.

There was a Commonwealth state funeral, suggested by Prime Minister Menzies—normally these are reserved for political figures. It was held at St Jude's in Brighton, which was also the place of burial, on 16 October. Mourners in their hundreds filled the church, as they would fill St Peter's Cathedral four days later for the memorial service organised by the University. St Jude's bell tolled the seventy-six years of his life, and masses of floral tributes were laid out in the form of a magnificent cross on the church lawn.

The Blue Ensign draping the coffin was particularly significant, for it was the one Mawson had hoisted in Antarctica on the second BANZARE cruise, when he had stood, as his body now lay, under that white cross of stars that points south, to the polar centre of the turning sky.

Notes

Chapter 1: South

1 For the *Ellora* and other details here see the London *Times*, 14 and 21 June 1884 (shipping news); the Melbourne *Argus*, 27 August 1884 (shipping news); Ian Nicholson, *The Log of Logs*, I and II; and R. Scot Skirving, 'Recollections of the Emigration Service to Australia in Sailing Ships in Long-Past Years', pp. 689–97, an account by a surgeon who was medical officer on the *Ellora* in 1883—the name of the ship is disguised as *Palomar*. The *Times* indicates that *Ellora* stopped at Hamburg before proceeding south. Note that details of *Ellora's* tonnage and captain as given in Paquita Mawson, *Mawson of the Antarctic*, are incorrect.

2 Transcribed letters from Joseph Mawson of 3 Upper Park Road, Hampstead, NW, 1911–17, and extracts from the Parish Registers of Kirkby Overblow, 1655–1782, in the possession of Mr Gareth Thomas of Adelaide. It is interesting that Joseph Mawson cites a John Mawson of Rigton who was mentioned in Thomas Lord Fairfax's will of 1671—Fairfax was Cromwell's greatest general. See also Paquita Mawson, *Mawson of the Antarctic*, pp. 19–20.

3 Marriage certificate of Robert Ellis Mawson and Margaret Ann Moore, dated 7 October 1879, Robert's age not given on the certificate but deduced. Paquita Mawson gives Margaret Ann Moore's father's name incorrectly as Thomas. The certificate was witnessed by Thomas Moore and Mary E. Moore.

4 Melbourne *Argus*, 27 and 30 August 1884 (shipping news); *Sydney Morning Herald*, 1 September 1884 (shipping news).

5 Photocopy of petition dated 3 November 1888 provided by Mary McPherson, History Information Officer, NSW Department of School Education.

6 Information from Iris Hanna, 1997, former resident of Hyatt Road, Plumpton, sent to the author by Mary McPherson. See also James Hanna, 'Sir Douglas Mawson, Distinguished Pupil of Plumpton Primary School'.

7 The *Fortian*, 4 May 1909, pp. 47–9, 51; L. E. Gent, *The Fort Street Centenary Book*, pp. 98–9; R. S. Horan, *Fort Street—the School*, pp. 140–42, 160–61; R. S. Horan, 'History of the Fort Street Unions', pp. 40, 41, 48, 112–13. References provided by R. S. Horan.

8 Paquita Mawson, *Mawson of the Antarctic*, p. 23.

9 William Mawson to Douglas Mawson, 21 October 1926. Private papers in the possession of Mr Gareth Thomas of Adelaide.

10 See T. Griffith Taylor's biographical sketch, *Douglas Mawson*, p. 1.

11 Results from University of Sydney Examination Registers, G3/135, items 5 and 6, and other information supplied by Andrew Wilson, Archives, University of Sydney.

12 Mawson to Lt-Gen. Sir John Cowans, 8 December 1916, in MAC, 10 DM. Records of the Corps were destroyed in a fire. Lt. Col. Alan B. Lilley, *The Sydney University Regiment*, p. 14.

13 University Registrar to Mawson, 16 April 1902, in MAC, Biographical File; Paquita Mawson, *Mawson of the Antarctic*, p. 25, reproduces David's reference.

14 T. Griffith Taylor and D. Mawson, 'The Geology of Mittagong'.

15 The sources for the following account are Mawson's New Hebrides diaries and notebooks in MAC, 66 DM, the most detailed of which is the large notebook headed 'Bibliography' and (half-way through) 'Field Notes—Geology of New Hebrides'; Mawson, 'Preliminary Note on the Geology of the New Hebrides'; and Mawson, 'The Geology of the New Hebrides', which systematises Mawson's findings and is not chronologically arranged in the way of the 'Preliminary Note'.

16 Mawson, 'The Geology of the New Hebrides', p. 415.

17 Mawson, 'Preliminary Note', p. 214.

18 HMS *Archer*, 1770 tons, first of her class, completed 1888, was 225 feet long and had a full complement of 176. Further details in *Conway's All the World's Fighting Ships 1860–1905*, p. 81.

19 Mawson, New Hebrides diaries, large notebook, ' . . . Field Notes', 13 June 1903.

20 Paquita Mawson, *Mawson of the Antarctic*, pp. 26–7, where the recovery is said to have taken 'some weeks'. This source, however, is not always reliable. The incident is not described in Mawson's report or even in his field notebooks but he mentions it in correspondence (e.g., Mawson to Edgeworth David, undated draft, late 1924, beginning 'On return to office . . .', in MAC, 67 DM). It perhaps occurred during the first half of July, when there is a two-week gap in the geological notes (though he was taking photographs during that period), or even during one of the six-day gaps.

21 Mawson and T. H. Laby, 'Preliminary Observations on Radio-Activity and the Occurrence of Radium in Australian Minerals'.

22 See Griffith Taylor, *Douglas Mawson*, p. 1, and Paquita Mawson, *Mawson of the Antarctic*, pp. 27–8.

23 Quoted in Paquita Mawson, *Mawson of the Antarctic*, p. 30.

24 See Herbert M. Hale, *The First Hundred Years of the Museum, 1856–1956*, for a number of references to Mawson's work with the South Australian Museum.

25 Mawson to S. B. Dickenson, 26 September 1956, in MAC, 40 DM; the Adelaide *Register*, 4 and 5 May 1906; Mawson, 'On Certain New Mineral Species Associated with Carnotite in the Radio-Active Ore Body near Olary'.

26 Published as 'Geological Investigations in the Broken Hill Area' in the *Memoirs of the Royal Society of South Australia*.

27 Model type Minimum Palmos, ser. no. 3887. Account from Carl Zeiss, Jena, to S. P. Bond Ltd., 51 Rundle Street, receipted 5 February 1906 by Bond for £9 12s 0d, in MAC, 57 DM.

[28] Mawson, 'Geological Investigations in the Broken Hill Area', pp. 211, 212, 220, 224.

[29] Mawson to Edgeworth David, 28 September 1907, David Correspondence, Mitchell Library, in MSS 3022/1.

[30] Mawson to Margery Fisher, 18 August 1956, and an undated draft, almost certainly late-1956, in MAC, 48 DM.

[31] Mawson to Edgeworth David, undated, David Correspondence, Mitchell Library, in MSS 3022/1.

CHAPTER 2: MAGNETIC SOUTH

[1] Mawson to K. Graham Thomson, 24 June 1952, in MAC, 48 DM.

[2] Ronald McNicoll, *Number 36 Collins Street: Melbourne Club 1838–1988*, p. 143.

[3] See Ernest Shackleton, *The Heart of the Antarctic*, 1, pp. 27 ff.; and Roland Huntford, *Shackleton*, pp. 192 ff.

[4] Eric Marshall, diary, 9 January 1908, Royal Geographical Society, cited in Huntford, *Shackleton*, p. 198.

[5] John King Davis, *High Latitude*, p. 71.

[6] Mawson to Margery Fisher, 18 August 1956, and Huntford, *Shackleton*, p. 204.

[7] Illustrated in Shackleton, *Heart of the Antarctic*, 1, facing p. 222.

[8] Edgeworth David, diary, 14 and 17 June 1908, Mitchell Library MSS 3022.

[9] See Mawson to Paquita Mawson, 4 February 1915, Mawson Papers, Mortlock Library, in PRG 523/3, and chapter 8 below.

[10] For a more detailed account of the ascent of Erebus see Shackleton, *Heart of the Antarctic*, 1, pp. 170–93—essentially Edgeworth David's account in *Aurora Australis*, the book produced by the expedition in Antarctica; see too David's diary, Mitchell Library, MSS 3022. Mawson kept no diary on the climb.

[11] Frank Wild, typescript memoirs, p. 34, Mitchell Library, MSS 2191/1.

[12] Instructions to Edgeworth David, David Correspondence, Mitchell Library, MS 3022/1, also printed in *Heart of the Antarctic*, 2, pp. 73–6.

[13] Mawson, Antarctic Diaries, Notebook 1, 8 October 1908, in MAC, 68 DM.

[14] Mawson, Antarctic Diaries, Notebook 1, 23 October 1908. Mawson had originally been given the task of prospecting in Dry Valley by Shackleton before David invited him to join the Northern party—see Antarctic Diaries, Notebook 1, 24 November 1908.

[15] Mawson, Antarctic Diaries, Notebook 1, 9 November 1908.

[16] Mawson, Antarctic Diaries, Notebook 1, 23 November 1908.

[17] Alistair Forbes Mackay, BAE diary, 1908–9, Royal Scottish Museum, Edinburgh; typed transcript in MAC.

[18] Mackay, BAE diary, 14 December 1908.

[19] Mawson to William Mawson, 14 December 1908. Private papers in the possession of Mr Gareth Thomas of Adelaide.

[20] *Heart of the Antarctic*, 2, p. 162.

[21] Mawson, Antarctic Diaries, Notebook 2, 24, 25 and 27 December 1908.

[22] Mawson, Antarctic Diaries, Notebook 2, 31 December 1908.

[23] David papers, University of Sydney Archives, Series 5, BAE 1907–9: Field Notebooks, 1908–9, South Magnetic Pole journey, 31 December 1908.

[24] David, South Magnetic Pole journey notebook, 22 January 1909.

[25] David, South Magnetic Pole journey notebook, 8 and 11 January 1909; Mackay, BAE diary, 8 January 1909.

[26] Mawson, Antarctic Diaries, Notebook 2, 16 January 1909.

[27] Mackay, BAE diary, 16 January 1909.

[28] David, South Magnetic Pole journey notebook, 19 January 1909.

[29] Mawson, Antarctic Diaries, Notebook 2, 31 January 1909.

[30] Mawson, Antarctic Diaries, Notebook 2, 2 February 1909.

[31] Mawson, Antarctic Diaries, Notebook 2, 3 February 1909. See also Mackay, diary, 3 February 1909.

[32] Mackay, BAE diary, 3 February 1909.

[33] Mawson, Antarctic Diaries, Notebook 2, 4 February 1909.

[34] Mackay, BAE diary, 6 February 1909.

[35] *Sydney Morning Herald*, 31 March 1909. Fridtjof Nansen was at this time the most renowned of Arctic explorers.

[36] The *Fortian*, 4 May 1909, p. 51.

[37] The *Advertiser*, 22 April 1909.

[38] On G. D. Delprat see Paquita Mawson, *A Vision of Steel*, and the entry in *ADB*; on the meeting and courtship of Mawson and Paquita Delprat see Paquita Mawson, *Mawson of the Antarctic*, pp. 47 ff. Nancy Flannery of Adelaide is currently completing a biography of Paquita Mawson.

[39] Edgeworth David to Mawson, 7 September 1909, in MAC, 24 DM.

CHAPTER 3: GOLD-DIGGERS OF 1910

[1] Dates in this first section are those given in Mawson's diary notes, 'Round the World 1909–10', in MAC, 8 DM. One or two of them, including date of departure from Adelaide, differ by a couple of days from the less contemporary 'Abbreviated Log: Australasian Antarctic Expedition 1911–', in MAC, 54 AAE. I have preferred the former.

[2] Mawson to Edgeworth David, 16 January 1910, David Correspondence, Mitchell Library, in MSS 3022/2.

[3] Mawson to Edgeworth David, 16 January 1910.

[4] Mawson, diary notes, 'Around the World 1909–10'.

[5] Mawson to Edgeworth David, 16 January 1910.

[6] Edgeworth David to Mawson, 8 February 1910, David Correspondence, Mitchell Library, in MSS 3022/2.

[7] Mawson, 'Abbreviated Log: Australasian Antarctic Expedition 1911–'.

[8] Mawson, 'Abbreviated Log'.

[9] Mawson, 'Abbreviated Log'.

[10] Edward Wilson to Edgeworth David, 24 February 1910, David Correspondence, Mitchell Library, in MSS 3022/2.

[11] Mawson, diary notes, 'Around the World 1909–10', and 'Abbreviated Log'.

[12] Mawson, 'Abbreviated Log'.

[13] Mawson to Shackleton, undated ms., typed on BAE paper, with map, in MAC, 11 AAE.

[14] Mawson to Shackleton, undated ms. on BAE paper, MAC, 11 AAE.

[15] Undated draft cable, Shackleton to Thomas Barr Smith, BAE stationery, in MAC, 11 AAE; reply quoted in Mawson, 'Abbreviated Log'.

[16] Mawson, 'Abbreviated Log'.

[17] John King Davis, *High Latitude*, p. 138

[18] Shackleton to Mawson, 19 March 1910, in MAC, 8 DM.

[19] Certificate of Assay, 17 March 1910, in MAC, 8 DM.

[20] Mawson to Shackleton, 15 April 1910, in MAC, 8 DM. The file includes Mawson's report, progress of negotiations, etc.

[21] See Davis, *High Latitude*, pp. 139–40.

[22] Robert Mawson to Douglas Mawson, 12 June 1909, in MAC, 53 DM.

[23] Robert Mawson to Douglas Mawson, 13 March 1910, in MAC, 53 DM.

[24] Mawson, 'Summary and Suggestions', in MAC, 8 DM.

[25] Mawson, 'Abbreviated Log'.

[26] Mawson, 'Shackleton's Contract and Promise / 1910 / Omaha / Private', dated 16 May 1910, in MAC, 8 DM.

[27] Letters of early December between Mawson and G. D. Delprat, part of a collection of intimate correspondence between Mawson and Paquita Delprat, in the possession of Mr Gareth Thomas of Adelaide, currently being edited for publication by Nancy Flannery of Adelaide. There are also letters from Paquita Delprat to Mawson held in a closed collection at MAC, also being edited by Flannery, and read for this book.

[28] Mawson, 'Abbreviated Log'.

[29] For the cable see MAC, 8 DM. See also the letter from Alfred Reid to Mawson, 2 September 1910, same file.

[30] Mawson to T. H. Laby, 14 September 1910, Laby Papers, University of Melbourne Archives. Mawson was referring to the following papers: 'Chiastolites from Bimbowrie, South Australia', 'Pre-Cambrian Areas in the North-Eastern Portion of South Australia and the Barrier, New South Wales', and 'Geological Investigations in the Broken Hill Area' (his D.Sc. thesis).

[31] Mawson to J. K. Davis, 19 October 1910, Davis Papers, La Trobe Library, Box 3270/9.

[32] Mawson to S. B. Dickenson, 26 September 1956, in MAC, 34 DM.

[33] Undated eight-page typescript, 'Mt. Painter Minerals', in MAC, 34 DM.

[34] Mawson to Dickenson, 26 September 1956.

[35] Alfred Reid to Mawson, 2 September 1910.

[36] Mawson, 'Abbreviated Log'.

Chapter 4: Australasian Antarctic Expedition

[1] Mawson, 'The Proposed Australasian Antarctic Expedition, 1911'.

[2] Draft cable, David Orme Masson to Shackleton, 14 January 1911. Masson pre-paid for Shackleton's reply (seven words). MAC, 11 AAE.

[3] Mawson, 'Abbreviated Log'.

⁴ Mawson had already cabled Shackleton on 26 January, 'Leaving Adelaide tomorrow please enquire fully into available ships'. Draft cable, in MAC, 11 AAE.

⁵ Mawson to T. H. Laby, 10 March 1911, Laby Correspondence, University of Melbourne Archives.

⁶ Paquita Mawson is delicate on the matter (*Mawson of the Antarctic*, p. 45), but Mawson's press interview, which she quotes, makes his anger clear.

⁷ Mawson to Gerald Lysaght, draft letter, undated, in MAC, 11 AAE.

⁸ Mrs Lysaght to Mawson, 26 March 1911, in MAC, 11 AAE.

⁹ Mawson to Margery Fisher, draft letter, late 1956, in MAC, 48 DM.

¹⁰ Mawson to H. R. Mill, 18 July 1922, H. R. Mill Papers, Scott Polar Research Institute.

¹¹ Mawson to Laby, 10 March 1911.

¹² Mawson, 'The Plans of the AAE 1911', in MAC, 11 AAE.

¹³ See MAC, 135 AAE.

¹⁴ David Orme Masson to Mawson, 3 April 1911, following up a (lost) cable, in MAC, 11 AAE.

¹⁵ Mawson to Mme Delprat (in Holland), 4 April 1911. Private papers in the possession of Mr Gareth Thomas of Adelaide.

¹⁶ Mawson, 'Abbreviated Log'.

¹⁷ Mawson to Biedermann, 18 April 1911, in MAC, 13 AAE.

¹⁸ Ian Cameron, *To the Farthest Ends of the Earth: The History of the Royal Geographical Society 1830–1980*, p. 198.

¹⁹ Mawson, 'The Australasian Antarctic Expedition', the text of his 10 April address.

²⁰ 'The Australasian Antarctic Expedition', pp. 618–20.

²¹ Mawson to Paquita Delprat, 12 April 1911, quoted in *Mawson of the Antarctic*, p. 48. As will later be seen, Mawson's royalties were less generous than indicated there.

²² For a description of *Aurora* see Mawson, *The Home of the Blizzard*, 1, pp. 12–15. See also Mawson to W. S. Bruce, 28 March 1911, at SPRI, copy at MAC.

²³ This is merely a deduction, however, from the fact that there are none among the Lady Kennet Papers at the Cambridge University Library.

²⁴ Lady Kennet (Kathleen Scott), *Self-Portrait of an Artist*, p. 93.

²⁵ Mawson, 'Abbreviated Log'.

²⁶ H. E. Watkins to Mawson, 18 April 1911, in MAC, 13 AAE.

²⁷ Kathleen Scott to Mawson, 25 April 1911 (and also see letter of 3 May), in MAC, 13 AAE.

²⁸ See *l'Aerophile*, 15 April 1911; *l'Auto*, 14 April 1911; Jean Devaux and Michel Marani, 'Le Mystérieux "REP" Type D du Musée de l'Air et de l'Espace', and Brian Elliott, 'Le "REP" Polaire', both in the Bibliography. See also *Flight*, 29 April 1911.

²⁹ These figures are for Mawson's machine. See C. F. Andrews, *Vickers Aircraft Since 1908*, p. 42.

³⁰ Invoice, in MAC, 137 AAE.

³¹ Had it been intended only to use the machine as an air-tractor, as Mawson, after the Adelaide crash, implied, there would have been no point in hiring Watkins for the Antarctic trip, and he was clearly intended to accompany the machine to Antarctica.

³² *Flight*, 5 August 1911, p. 681.

³³ Cable, Walter Hall to Mawson, 12 May 1911, in MAC, 13 AAE, with other decliners mentioned here.

[34] Draft letter, Mawson to P&O managers, 2 May 1911, in MAC, 13 AAE.

[35] For a good account of the history of the *Aurora* see John King Davis, *With the 'Aurora' in the Antarctic 1911–1914*, pp. 5–11.

[36] Itemised costs submitted to Commonwealth Government, August 1911, in MAC, 11 AAE. This figure only appears not to square with figures published in Mawson's *Home of the Blizzard*, 2, pp. 311–12, where the itemising is done differently.

[37] 'List', with 'Davis collected for appeal' in Mawson's hand, in MAC, 11 AAE.

[38] For details of the cameras and other equipment here see MAC, 132 AAE and 136 AAE.

[39] The AAE's library is itemised in MAC, 43 AAE.

[40] Alfred Reid to Mawson, 22 September 1911, in MAC, 141 AAE., and Mawson, *Home of the Blizzard*, 1, p. 20.

[41] Paquita Mawson, *Mawson of the Antarctic*, p. 51.

[42] On Mawson's friendship with Way at this time see his letter to Way's biographer, A. J. Hannan, 20 June 1956, in MAC, 49 DM.

[43] George C. Henderson to Mawson, 28 November 1911. Private papers in the possession of Mr Gareth Thomas of Adelaide.

[44] On Henderson see *ADB* and M. R. Casson, *George Cockburn Henderson*.

[45] Mawson to Alfred Reid, 22 June 1911, in MAC, 13 AAE.

[46] Alfred Reid to Mawson, 29 September 1911, in MAC, 141 AAE.

[47] See the legal correspondence on this matter in MAC, 141 AAE.

[48] Mawson to H. E. Scrope, 16 March 1956, in MAC, 23 DM.

[49] H. E. Watkins to H. F. Wood, 10 October 1911, in MAC, 137 AAE.

[50] Frank Wild, typescript memoirs, Mitchell Library, MSS 2191/1, p. 64.

[51] J. K. Davis, Private Journal (14 August 1911–15 March 1913), 17 August 1911, Davis Papers, La Trobe Library, 3232/5.

[52] Mawson, *Home of the Blizzard*, 1, pp. 22–3.

[53] Archibald Lang McLean, introduction to a typescript version of his AAE diaries, Mitchell Library, in MSS 382.

[54] Charles Francis Laseron, *South with Mawson*, p. 12.

[55] McLean, introduction to typescript diaries.

CHAPTER 5: SACRED ANTHEM

[1] Francis H. Bickerton, typescript of 'Western Sledging Journey', p. 1, Scott Polar Research Institute.

[2] Mawson, *Home of the Blizzard*, 1, pp. 27–8.

[3] J. K. Davis, Private Journal, 12 December 1911.

[4] Arthur J. Sawyer, AAE diary, 15 December 1911, Mitchell Library, MSS 383.

[5] Davis, Private Journal, 26 December 1911.

[6] Archibald Lang McLean, diaries, 2 December 1911–26 February 1914, undated early entry, Mitchell Library, MSS 382/1–2.

[7] J. K. Davis, *With the 'Aurora' in the Antarctic 1911–1914*, p. 23.

[8] Davis, Private Journal, 14 January 1912.

[9] Morton Henry Moyes, AAE diary, 27 December and undated, Mitchell Library, MSS 388/1.

[10] Walter Henry Hannam, AAE diary, 2 January 1912, Mitchell Library, MSS 384.

[11] McLean, AAE diaries, undated early entry.

[12] Alec L. Kennedy, AAE diary, 29 January 1911, in MAC, 80 AAE.

[13] Kennedy, diary, 1 January 1912.

[14] Dr Alf Howard, private communication to the author, 17 March 1998.

[15] George H. S. Dovers, AAE diaries, small diary, entry for New Year's Eve, Mitchell Library, MSS 3812/1b.

[16] Charles Turnbull Harrisson, AAE diary, 27 December 1911, Mitchell Library, MSS 386/1.

[17] Alf Howard, private communication to the author, 24 June 1997.

[18] Moyes, diary, 1 January 1912.

[19] Kennedy, diary, 6 January 1912.

[20] See Mawson, *Home of the Blizzard*, 1, pp. 61–2.

[21] Kennedy, diary, 21 January 1912.

[22] Mawson to K. Graham Thomson, 24 June 1952, in MAC, 48 DM.

[23] Harrisson, diary, 17 January 1912.

[24] Charles Francis Laseron, *South with Mawson*, pp. 45–6; Frank Hurley, *Argonauts of the South*, pp. 46–7; Mawson, *Home of the Blizzard*, 1, pp. 88–90.

[25] McLean, diary, 19 January 1912.

[26] Harrisson, diary, 19 January 1912.

[27] Kennedy, diary, 19 January 1912.

[28] McLean, diary, 19 January 1912.

[29] Eric Webb, 'An Appreciation', in Lennard Bickel, *This Accursed Land*, pp. 202–3.

[30] Hurley, *Argonauts of the South*, p. 51, quoting his diary.

[31] Hurley, *Argonauts of the South*, p. 121.

[32] Charles Francis Laseron, AAE diary, 18 February 1912, Mitchell Library, MSS 385.

[33] Xavier Mertz, typed transcript of AAE diary, 1–2 March 1912, here translated from the German, copy at MAC.

[34] McLean, diary, 18 February and 28 May 1912.

[35] See 'Notes on the Conduct of 'Wireless' Operations, AAE', in MAC, 39 AAE.

[36] Hannam, diary, 10 September 1912.

[37] Mawson, small slip of paper with series of detailed, undated observations on the conduct of Leslie H. Whetter, surgeon, in MAC, 43 AAE.

[38] Mertz, diary, 6 October 1912, translated from the German; Mawson, Antarctic Diaries, Notebook 4, 3 October 1912.

[39] Mawson, Antarctic Diaries, Notebook 3.

[40] Mawson, Antarctic Diaries, Notebook 4, 3 October 1912. Direct speech given by Mawson.

[41] Mawson, small slip of paper with observations on the conduct of Leslie H. Whetter, surgeon.

[42] Bickerton, typescript, Western Sledging Journey, p. 21, Scott Polar Research Institute.

[43] Mawson, Antarctic Diaries, Notebook 3, 18 May 1912.

[44] Moyes, diary, 30 December 1911.

[45] Mawson, Antarctic Diaries, Notebook 4, 21 October 1912.

[46] T. W. Edgeworth David to Clinton Coleridge Farr, 18 February 1912, which quotes from Farr's letter to David, in MAC, 159 AAE; Edgeworth David to Mawson,

25 May 1925, in MAC, 24 DM. See also David to Farr, 1 February 1912, David Correspondence, Mitchell Library, MSS 3022/2.

[47] Quoted in Paquita Mawson, *Mawson of the Antarctic*, p. 77.

[48] Mertz, sledging diary, 10 November 1912, in MAC, 70 AAE, translated.

CHAPTER 6: DEATH AND DELIVERANCE

[1] Mawson to Paquita Delprat, 15 April 1913. Private papers in the possession of Mr Gareth Thomas of Adelaide.

[2] Xavier Mertz, sledging diary, 19 November 1912, translated.

[3] Mertz, sledging diary, 23 November 1912, translated.

[4] Mertz, sledging diary, 9 December 1912, translated.

[5] Mertz, sledging diary, 13 December 1912, translated.

[6] Mawson, Antarctic Diaries, Notebook 5, 13 December 1912.

[7] Mertz, sledging diary, 14 December 1912, translated.

[8] Mawson gives the furthest distance out as 315½ miles at the higher point to which he and Mertz went for ground observations and magnetic azimuth after Ninnis's death. Antarctic Diaries, Notebook 5, 14 December 1912.

[9] Mawson, Antarctic Diaries, Notebook 5, 14 December 1912.

[10] Mertz, sledging diary, 14 December 1912, translated.

[11] Mawson, *Home of the Blizzard*, 1, p. 240.

[12] J. Gordon Hayes, *Antarctica: A Treatise on the Southern Continent*, p. 293.

[13] Mawson, 'Out of the Jaws of Death', Part 1, p. 211.

[14] Mawson, pencilled 'Instructions to the Captain of the *Aurora*', in MAC, 43 AAE.

[15] Mertz, sledging diary, 16 December 1912, translated.

[16] As well as his diary Mawson continued to keep other records on the return, including full meteorological logs. These latter are in MAC, 69 AAE.

[17] Distances and other details here follow Mawson's diary rather than *Home of the Blizzard*, which sometimes differs.

[18] Mertz, sledging diary, 17 December 1912, translated.

[19] Mertz, sledging diary, 17 December 1912, translated.

[20] Mawson, *Home of the Blizzard*, 1, p. 251.

[21] Mertz, sledging diary, 23 December 1912, translated.

[22] Mawson, Antarctic Diaries, Notebook 5, 26 December 1912.

[23] Mawson, Antarctic Diaries, Notebook 5, 27 and 29 December 1912.

[24] Mawson, Antarctic Diaries, Notebook 5, 30 December 1912.

[25] Mertz, sledging diary, 30 December 1912, translated.

[26] Mawson, Antarctic Diaries, Notebook 5, 6 January 1913. Immediately preceding quotations from the same source, dates indicated.

[27] Mawson, Antarctic Diaries, Notebook 5, 7 January 1913.

[28] A. Leigh Hunt, *Confessions of a Leigh Hunt*, p. 127.

[29] Mawson, Antarctic Diaries, Notebook 5, 7(–8) January 1913.

[30] Mawson, *Home of the Blizzard*, 1, p. 260.

[31] Mawson, Antarctic Diaries, Notebook 5, 9 January 1913.

[32] Phillip G. Law, interview with the author, May 1997. Law's close knowledge of Mawson is reflected in his three-part article, 'The Mawson Story'.

[33] Mawson, Antarctic Diaries, Notebook 5, 11 January 1913.

[34] Mawson, *Home of the Blizzard*, 1, p. 261.

[35] Mawson, *Home of the Blizzard*, 1, p. 261.

[36] Mawson, Antarctic Diaries, Notebook 5, 11 January 1913.

[37] Mawson, Antarctic Diaries, Notebook 5, 17 January 1913.

[38] *Chicago Sunday Tribune*, 14 February 1915.

[39] Mawson, rough-draft meteorological notes taken on far-eastern journey, entry for 18 January 1913, in MAC, 69 AAE.

[40] J. Cleland and R. V. Southcott, 'Hypervitaminosis A in the Antarctic in the Australasian Antarctic Expedition of 1911–14: A Possible Explanation of the Illnesses of Mertz and Mawson'; R. V. Southcott, N. J. Chesterfield, and D. J. Lugg, 'The Vitamin A Content of the Livers of Huskies and Some Seals from Arctic and Subantarctic Regions'; and D. J. C. Shearman, 'Vitamin A and Sir Douglas Mawson'.

[41] Phillip Law, interview with the author, May 1997.

[42] Mawson, Antarctic Diaries, Notebook 5, 29 January 1913.

[43] Note preserved in MAC, 48 AAE.

[44] Mawson, Antarctic Diaries, Notebook 5, 8 February 1913.

[45] Eric Rudd, interview with the author, July 1997, reconfirmed August 1998. Madigan's diaries exist, owned by one of his sons, David Cecil Madigan of Hobart. However, I was not given access to them.

CHAPTER 7: MADNESS ALL AROUND

[1] Bill from J. B. Ellerker, Customs, Shipping & Commission Agent, in MAC, 143 AAE.

[2] Letters of 6 February from Eitel and his solicitors to Australasian Wireless Co. Ltd., Sydney, in MAC, 143 AAE.

[3] Florence Eitel to Mawson, undated but *c.* July 1916, in MAC, 143 AAE.

[4] Conrad Eitel, draft letter to J. K. Davis, 11 November 1912, in MAC, 143 AAE.

[5] Edgeworth David to Conrad Eitel, 7 November 1912, in MAC, 143 AAE.

[6] Conrad Eitel, draft letter to Edgeworth David, 14 November 1912, in MAC, 143 AAE.

[7] Bertram Clive Lincoln, diary, 29 January 1913, in MAC, recent accession, unfiled.

[8] Hannam, diary, 2 February 1913; Stillwell, diary, 27 January 1913; Laseron, diary, 4 February 1913.

[9] Hannam, diary, 6 February 1913. Expletive deleted in ms. Indirect speech in ms.

[10] See Davis, *With the 'Aurora' in the Antarctic*, pp. 97–9; related material in MAC, 44 AAE; and Hannam, diary, 9 February 1913.

[11] C. J. Hackworth, diary, entry for 9 February 1913, copy of Mr Phillip Law of Melbourne.

[12] Phillip Law in conversation with the author, November 1998.

[13] Mawson, *Home of the Blizzard*, 2, p. 131.

[14] McLean, diary, 17 March 1913.

[15] Mawson, *Home of the Blizzard*, 2, p. 136.
[16] Paquita Mawson, *Mawson of the Antarctic*, p. 92.
[17] Mawson to Paquita Delprat, 15 April 1913. Private papers in the possession of Mr Gareth Thomas of Adelaide.
[18] Most of the wireless messages that passed through Macquarie Island are in MAC, 28 AAE and 29 AAE, with others in 30 AAE.
[19] Mawson, draft letter, undated, to Kathleen Scott, in MAC, 177 AAE.
[20] Mawson, Antarctic Diaries, Notebook 5, 26 May 1913.
[21] McLean, diary, 4 July 1913.
[22] Mawson, Antarctic Diaries, Notebook 5, dates as given.
[23] Mawson, undated pencilled speech, in MAC, 177 AAE.
[24] Phillip Law believes that Mawson 'got Jeffryes out of proportion'—conversation with the author, November 1998. I disagree. Mawson had read of analogous cases, and the precedents were worrying.
[25] Mawson, Antarctic Diaries, Notebook 4, second part, 2 September 1913.
[26] Transmission in MAC, 28 AAE.
[27] Transmission in MAC, 28 AAE.
[28] Mawson, Antarctic Diaries, Notebook 4, second part, 22 september 1913.
[29] Mawson, Antarctic Diaries, Notebook 6, 11 December 1913.
[30] Mawson to William Bragg, 1 November 1913, in MAC, biographical file.
[31] See Davis, *With the 'Aurora' in the Antarctic*, pp. 133–46.
[32] Mawson to Norma Jeffryes, draft of letter dated 1 November 1913 and sent on arrival in Adelaide, in MAC, 177 AAE.
[33] Norma Jeffryes to Mawson, 21 March 1914, in MAC, 177 AAE.
[34] Sidney Jeffryes to Mawson, 13 March, 6 June, and 20 August 1915, in MAC, 177 AAE.
[35] Norma Jeffryes to Mawson, 21 March 1914. Jeffryes was not necessarily culpable in reapplying for a position for which he had been turned down by a leader unable to say no a second time. Norma Jeffryes cited a letter from Mawson to her brother of late 1911 in which he reputedly said he would have preferred Jeffryes but had already appointed his wireless people.
[36] J. Gordon Hayes, *Antarctica: A Treatise on the Southern Continent*, p. 210.
[37] Hayes, *Antarctica*, p. 257.
[38] Phillip G. Law, 'Some Antarctic Leaders', address to the Library Dinner of the Melbourne Club, 11 July 1996. See also Law's three-part series of articles, 'The Mawson Story'.
[39] W. S. Bruce to Mawson, 6 February 1914, in MAC, 183 AAE.
[40] Mawson to Edgeworth David, undated draft *c.* January 1925, in MAC, 67 DM.

CHAPTER 8: FAME WITHOUT FORTUNE

[1] Paquita Mawson, *Mawson of the Antarctic*, pp. 102–3.
[2] Mawson to A. J. Hannan, 20 June 1956, in MAC, 49 DM.
[3] Shackleton to Mawson, telegram of acceptance, 18 March 1914, in MAC, 183 AAE.
[4] 'Request that the Commonwealth Government take over the *Aurora* ...', in MAC, 183 AAE.

⁵ See the Melbourne *Argus*, 1 April 1914, and the *Age*, same date. The *Argus* coverage is better, and illustrated.

⁶ London *Times*, 4 May 1914.

⁷ Grosvenor Hotel account, in MAC, 27 AAE.

⁸ See Mawson to Edgeworth David, long undated draft of *c*. January 1925 in MAC, 67 DM. This letter is a partisan defence by Mawson of his right, as he saw it, to the Sydney chair of geology.

⁹ Archie L. McLean to Mawson, 13 December 1916, in MAC, 178 AAE.

¹⁰ Mawson had written to Paquita Delprat on 12 April 1911 that over dinner in Paris Heinemann had offered £1000 down and 60 per cent of the published price (Paquita Mawson, *Mawson of the Antarctic*, p. 48), but as we have seen, the first was a loan, and the 60 per cent seems to have been wishful thinking.

¹¹ Distribution lists and reviews in MAC, 150 AAE; the publisher's regular statements to Mawson, correspondence, etc. in MAC, 151 AAE. Production numbers quoted are careful inferences based on these files, the firm's 1915 print-run records apparently having been destroyed by the fire. Correspondence with the present-day firm of the same name has elicited no response—they would appear to be completely uninterested in their history.

¹² The *Times*, 4 May 1914. Paquita Mawson gives the date as 12 May.

¹³ The *Times*, 1 June 1914.

¹⁴ The *Times*, 23 May 1914.

¹⁵ The *Times*, 11 June 1914.

¹⁶ Mawson, 'The Australasian Antarctic Expedition, 1911–1914'.

¹⁷ Kathleen Scott to Mawson, 22 May 1914, in MAC, 51 DM.

¹⁸ Kathleen Scott to Mawson, 8 March [1915], in MAC, 51 DM.

¹⁹ Mawson to Frank Hurley, 18 June 1914, in MAC, 6 DM.

²⁰ Mawson to Herbert Ponting, 19 July 1914, AAE: Sundry Papers, Mitchell Library, MSS 171/18.

²¹ Paquita Mawson, *Mawson of the Antarctic*, p. 117.

²² See Mawson to Edgeworth David, 22 June 1914, in MAC, 24 DM.

²³ The *Ruahine* sprung a leak after leaving port and had to return, undergoing repairs before sailing once again. For the farcical circumstances see Paquita Mawson, *Mawson of the Antarctic*, pp. 119-21.

²⁴ See Mawson to Erich von Drygalski, 19 July 1914, in MAC, 153 AAE.

²⁵ Mawson to Cecil Madigan, 19 July 1914, AAE: Sundry Papers, Mitchell Library MSS 171/18

²⁶ See Paul-Emile Victor, *Man and the Conquest of the Poles*, p. 149. For a contemporary account see W. S. Schley and J. R. Soley, *The Rescue of Greely*, which includes the evidence of cannibalism.

²⁷ General Adolphus W. Greely to Mawson, 5 January 1915, in MAC, 51 DM.

²⁸ The theory is set out in a letter from Greely to Mawson of 9 November 1916, in MAC, Accessions, MI 40.2. A large lake has recently been discovered deep under the ice by remote sensing equipment at Vostok station, which lies far inland. This lake has not yet been entered by drilling equipment for fear of introducing pollutants, but some scientists hope to find archaic life forms in the lake, surviving from the time when Antarctica formed part of the great continent of Pangaea some 225 million years ago. Information from Robert Headland and Phillip Law

in conversation with the author, October and November 1998.

[29] Quoted in Paquita Mawson, *Mawson of the Antarctic*, p. 123.

[30] Mawson to Paquita Mawson, 4 February 1915. Mawson Papers, Mortlock Library, in PRG 523/3.

[31] See F. S. Dellenbough to Mawson, 18 March 1915; and Theodore Roosevelt to Mawson, 23 March 1915, both in MAC, 51 DM.

[32] Mawson to Paquita Mawson, 4 February 1915. Mawson Papers, Mortlock Library, in PRG 523/3. See also William Laird McKinlay, *Karluk*.

[33] William Herbert Hobbs to Mawson, 21 October 1914, in MAC, 21 DM.

[34] Recalled by Hobbs in a letter to Mawson of 17 February 1944. Private papers in the possession of Mr Gareth Thomas of Adelaide.

[35] Hobbs to Mawson, 17 February 1915, in MAC, 21 DM.

[36] Sir William Mitchell, Foreword to *Sir Douglas Mawson Anniversary Volume*, ed. Glaessner and Rudd.

[37] Gaumont correspondence, in MAC, 169 AAE.

[38] This script is in MAC, 181 AAE.

[39] See correspondence between Mawson and Hurley in MAC, 6 DM.

[40] Statements in MAC, 171 AAE, Mawson–Lee Keedick correspondence.

CHAPTER 9: THE MILLS OF WAR

[1] Mawson to W. H. Hobbs, 23 August 1915, Hobbs Papers, University of Michigan.

[2] Mawson was very proud of this campaign and gave its details in a long curriculum vitae for the years 1910–20, in MAC, Biographical File.

[3] Letters of reply, Department of Defence to Mawson, dated 23 September and 22 October 1915, in MAC, 10 DM.

[4] In MAC, 10 DM.

[5] Brig. Gen. H. J. Foster to George Murray, 4 March 1916, copy in MAC, 10 DM.

[6] The Licence to Import Arms, issued to Mawson on 10 May 1916 on his arrival in Britain, covers the pistol and fifty cartridges. Documents in MAC, 10 DM.

[7] Paquita Mawson puts his arrival in England two days later, taking it to be the date of his first letter from London, but the licence to import the pistol clearly reveals the date of entry as 10 May.

[8] Relevant documents are in MAC, 9 DM.

[9] Paquita Mawson, *Mawson of the Antarctic*, p. 128.

[10] Mawson, draft letter to Kathleen Scott, 20 May 1916, Mawson Papers, Mortlock Library, in PRG 523/6.

[11] Lady Kennet (Kathleen Scott), *Self-Portrait of an Artist*, p. 143.

[12] Mawson to Paquita Mawson, 2 June 1916, Mawson Papers, Mortlock Library, in PRG 523/3.

[13] In MAC, 10 DM.

[14] In MAC, 10 DM.

[15] For a good overview of Mawson's work for Moulton, see Roy Macleod, '"Full of Honour and Gain to Science": Munitions Production, Technical Intelligence and the Wartime Career of Sir Douglas Mawson, FRS'.

[16] See, and compare, Mawson's draft letter of Tuesday evening, 27 June 1916, to

Kathleen Scott, and his undated letter to his wife from the Royal Societies Club written a few days earlier, Mawson Papers, Mortlock Library, in PRG 523/6 and 523/3.

[17] Mawson to Paquita Mawson, undated, from Royal Societies Club, Mawson Papers, Mortlock Library, in PRG 523/3.

[18] Mawson to Paquita Mawson, 23 June 1916, private papers in the possession of Mr Gareth Thomas of Adelaide.

[19] Admiralty to Mawson, 3 July 1916, in MAC, 10 DM.

[20] Mawson, draft letter to Kathleen Scott, 27 June [1916], 'evening'. Mawson papers, Mortlock Library, in PRG 523/6.

[21] Letter of appointment dated 27 July 1916 from Exhibitions Branch, Board of Trade, as representative of the CIR at Liverpool on £400 per annum, Mawson Papers, Mortlock Library, in PRG 523/6.

[22] Mawson to Paquita Mawson, 19 July 1916, Mawson Papers, Mortlock Library, in PRG 523/3.

[23] Mawson to Paquita Mawson, 25 July 1916, Mawson Papers, Mortlock Library, in PRG 523/3.

[24] Memorandum Relating to the Carriage of Dangerous Goods and Explosives', in MAC, 10 DM.

[25] See Mawson's draft letter, first or second week of October 1916 but undated ('Saturday 1916'), to Kathleen Scott, Mawson Papers, Mortlock Library, in PRG 523/6.

[26] Mawson, draft letter to Kathleen Scott, 4 September 1916, Mawson Papers, Mortlock Library, in PRG 523/6.

[27] Mawson to Kathleen Scott, 6 October 1916, Mawson Papers, Mortlock Library, in PRG 523/6.

[28] Mawson to Kathleen Scott, undated but first or second week in October 1916, Mawson Papers, Mortlock Library, in PRG 523/6.

[29] Paquita Mawson, *Mawson of the Antarctic*, p. 136.

[30] Mawson to Charles Hodge, 17 October 1916, in MAC, 10 DM.

[31] Thomas Cook & Son to Mawson, 4 November 1916, with detailed itinerary, in MAC, 10 DM.

[32] See Paquita Mawson, *Mawson of the Antarctic*, p. 136.

[33] Correspondence with Vickers Ltd. over the account, in MAC, 137 AAE; Sir Trevor Dawson to Mawson, 21 November 1916, in MAC, 183 AAE.

[34] Mawson, draft letter to Lt. Gen. Sir John Cowans, 8 December 1916, in MAC, 10 DM.

[35] Walter Runciman to Mawson, 9 February 1917, in MAC, 10 DM.

[36] Walter Runciman to Mawson, 12 February 1917, in MAC, 10 DM.

[37] On Russian production of chemical weapons at this time see L. F. Haber, *The Poisonous Cloud: Chemical Warfare in the First World War*.

[38] See Mawson's letter to T. H. Laby on the subject, 30 November 1917, Laby Papers, University of Melbourne Archives.

[39] See the list of 'Reports furnished upon the following Plants', sent with Mawson's letter to Essington Lewis, 17 January 1942, in MAC, Biographical File.

[40] Mawson to David Orme Masson, 3 October 1917, Mawson Papers, Mortlock Library, in PRG 523/6.

[41] Mawson to Laby, 30 November 1917.
[42] Mawson to Essington Lewis, 17 January 1942. Reg Sprigg is in error in claiming that Mawson visited Russia in connection with war work—*Geology Is Fun*, p. 87. As Sprigg says on p. 1, 'Never spoil a good story for the sake of unconfirmable fact.'
[43] See Mawson to Sir Edmund Wyldbore Smith, 16 March 1918, Mawson Papers, Mortlock Library, in PRG 523/6.
[44] Mawson, draft letter to Sir Edmund Wyldbore Smith, 16 March 1918; draft letter of thanks for promotion, 20 March 1918. Mawson Papers, Mortlock Library, in PRG 523/6.

CHAPTER 10: THE SYDNEY CHAIR

[1] The *Argus*, 30 April 1919.
[2] Lady Kennet (Kathleen Scott), *Self-Portarit of an Artist*, p. 172
[3] Mawson to Paquita Mawson, undated ('Thursday'), Mawson papers, Mortlock Library, in PRG 523/3.
[4] Mawson to Paquita Mawson, 11 May 1919, Mawson Papers, Mortlock Library, in PRG 523/3.
[5] G. D. Delprat to Mawson, 17 June 1919, from London, in MAC, 54 DM.
[6] On Walter Howchin see the obituary notice by C. Fenner in *TRSSA*, LXI (1937), v–viii, and the *ADB* entry.
[7] Eric Rudd, interview with the author, July 1997.
[8] Walter Howchin to Mawson, 9 December 1916, in MAC, 67 DM.
[9] Mawson, undated draft letter to Howchin, in MAC, 67 DM.
[10] Howchin to Mawson, 30 April 1917, in MAC, 67 DM.
[11] Though there is no record of an offer from the University of Liverpool, Sir William Mitchell later referred to such an offer in his Foreword to the *Sir Douglas Mawson Anniversary Volume*.
[12] Sir Henry Miess to Mawson, 29 January 1919, in MAC, 183 AAE.
[13] Mawson to Paquita Mawson, undated ('Monday'), Mawson Papers, Mortlock Library, in PRG 523/3.
[14] Mawson to Paquita Mawson, 5 May 1919, Mawson Papers, Mortlock Library, in PRG 523/3.
[15] Mawson, 'Pre-Cambrian Areas in the North-Eastern Portion of South Australia and the Barrier, NSW'.
[16] Mawson, 'Igneous Rocks of the Mount Painter Belt'.
[17] Mawson, 'Evidence and Indications of Algal Contributions in the Cambrian and Pre-Cambrian Limestones of South Australia', p. 186; and see D. W. Corbett, 'Douglas Mawson: the Geologist as Explorer', pp. 119–22.
[18] See MAC, 57 DM.
[19] *Reports of the AAAS*, XV (1921), pp. 151, 154, 159.
[20] The *Argus*, 13 January 1921.
[21] J. K. Davis, 'Future Exploration: the African Quadrant of Antarctica'.
[22] See Paquita Mawson, *Mawson of the Antarctic*, p. 144.
[23] Full programme, annotated by Mawson, in MAC, 46 DM.

[24] W. H. Hobbs to Mawson, 29 May 1923, 27 March 1924, and 13 January 1949, in MAC, 21 DM.

[25] Mawson, draft letter to W. A. Selle, 10 July 1924, in MAC, 24 DM.

[26] W. H. Hobbs to Mawson, 14 August 1924, in MAC, 24 DM.

[27] 'Application for the Chair of Geology . . . by Leo A. Cotton . . . June 1924', in MAC, 24 DM.

[28] Edgeworth David to Mawson, 15 July 1924, in MAC, 24 DM. Nine days later David wrote again, saying how surprised he had been by Mawson's interest in the Chair, but that Mawson would of course be very much 'persona grata' if he were to come back to the University of Sydney. Letter of 24 July 1924 in the possession of Mr Alun Thomas of Adelaide.

[29] Hobbs to Mawson, 14 August 1924.

[30] See Edgeworth David to Mawson, 31 January 1925, in MAC, 24 DM.

[31] See Geoffrey Serle, *John Monash: A Biography*, p. 371

[32] Edgeworth David to Mawson, 10 September 1924, in MAC, 67 DM.

[33] Mawson to W. A. Selle, 11 September 1924, in MAC, 67 DM.

[34] See, e.g., telegram, Sir Henry Barraclough to Mawson, 10 September 1924, and his letter of 30 September 1924, both in MAC, 67 DM.

[35] Edgeworth David to Mawson, 25 September 1924, in MAC, 67 DM.

[36] Edgeworth David to Mawson, 16 November 1924, in the possession of Mr Alun Thomas of Adelaide.

[37] The withdrawal is discussed in David's letter to Mawson of 16 November 1924, in a letter from Selle to Mawson of 5 December 1924 (see below), and in Mawson to Selle, undated draft, c. mid-January 1925, in MAC, 67 DM.

[38] Edgeworth David to Mawson, 16 November 1924.

[39] Selle to Mawson, 5 December 1924, in the possession of Mr Alun Thomas of Adelaide.

[40] Telegrams, Selle to Mawson, 19 December 1924, Lawson (?) to Mawson, 20 December 1924, Mawson to Selle, 21 December 1924, all in MAC, 67 DM.

[41] The fullest details of this meeting are in David's letter of 31 January 1925 to Mawson, in MAC, 24 DM. The Archives of the University of Sydney could find no records of the Senate meeting.

[42] Mawson to Selle, undated draft, c. mid-January 1925, in MAC, 67 DM.

[43] Mawson to David, undated draft, c. mid-January 1925, in MAC, 67 DM.

[44] Mungo W. MacCallum to Mawson, 28 May 1925, in MAC, 24 DM. Italics mine.

[45] MacCallum to Mawson, 19 June 1925, in MAC, 24 DM.

[46] Edgeworth David to Mawson, 14 February 1926, in MAC, 24 DM.

[47] Sir William Mitchell, Foreword to *Sir Douglas Mawson Anniversary Volume*. The Archives of the University of Sydney say they have no records relating to the 1925–6 processes for appointing a new Vice-Chancellor (July 1998).

[48] H. S. Carslaw to Mawson, 30 January 1925 (direct speech as given by Carslaw), in MAC, 24 DM. See also Carslaw to David, 1 January 1925, in J. T. Wilson Family Archives, Series 4, Miscellaneous Personal Correspondence, University of Sydney Archives.

[49] Mawson to David, undated draft, c. mid-January 1925, in MAC, 67 DM.

[50] David to Mawson, 31 January 1925, in MAC, 24 DM.

[51] David to Mawson, 19 March 1925, in MAC, 24 DM.

[52] David to Mawson, 1 April 1925, in MAC, 24 DM.

CHAPTER 11: 'A CONTRACT IS A CONTRACT'

1 For a complete listing of these reports see Margaret Innes and Heather Duff, *Mawson's Papers—A Guide*, Mawson Institute for Antarctic Research (Adelaide, 1990), pp. 8/1–8/7.

2 Mawson, 'Reply to a speech by Dr Stirling ... on the Occasion of his [Mawson's] approaching Marriage', in MAC, 52 DM.

3 Andrew Fisher to Mawson, 28 October 1914, in MAC, 153 AAE.

4 T. H. Smeaton to Mawson, 10 November 1915, in MAC, 153 AAE.

5 South Australian Premier's Office to Mawson, 25 July 1919, in MAC, 153 AAE.

6 E. H. Stoney to Mawson, 29 May 1919, in MAC, 153 AAE.

7 Mawson to Paquita Mawson, 30 May 1919, Mawson Papers, Mortlock Library, in PRG 523/3.

8 Mawson's copy of the Agreement is in MAC, 153 AAE.

9 Mawson, copy of letter to the Committee on Printing of Records of the AAE, 27 March 1923, replying to theirs of 5 March, in MAC, 153 AAE.

10 A. J. Kent to Mawson, 26 November 1924, in MAC, 153 AAE.

11 Mawson to William Davies, 15 July 1931, in MAC, 153 AAE.

12 A. J. Kent to Mawson, 11 November 1925, in MAC, 153 AAE.

13 Kent to Mawson, 19 March 1929, and Mawson's pencilled 'answer' for his secretary's use, in MAC, 153 AAE.

14 Correspondence in MAC, 153 AAE, July–October 1931.

15 Mawson, *Home of the Blizzard*, 2, p. 292.

16 Mawson to Harold Hamilton, 21 February 1924, in MAC, 164 AAE.

17 Harold Hamilton to Mawson, 22 March 1924, in MAC, 164 AAE.

18 Mawson mentions this trip to secure the notes for the *Birds* report in a letter to Thomas Iredale of 8 October 1931. It may have been in January 1926 when Mawson was in New Zealand inspecting forests (see Chapter 12).

19 Mawson to Thomas Iredale, 15 July 1931, in MAC, 164 AAE.

20 Mawson to Iredale, 8 October 1931, in MAC, 164 AAE.

21 Mawson to Iredale, 14 December 1931, in MAC, 164 AAE. This mentions the letter to Anderson.

22 Mawson to Iredale, 30 November 1932, in MAC, 164 AAE.

23 A. Grenfell Price, *The Winning of Australian Antarctica*; and his BANZARE *Geographical Report*.

CHAPTER 12: POLITICS AND POWER

1 For an overview see R. A. Swan, *Australia in the Antarctic*, pp. 113–14.

2 Melbourne *Argus*, 13 January 1921.

3 See Swan, *Australia in the Antarctic*, p. 171.

4 Sir David Orme Masson to Mawson, 17 May 1925, in MAC, 34 BZE.

5 See Swan, *Australia in the Antarctic*, p. 171.

6 Mawson to S. M. Bruce, 16 June 1925, in MAC, 67 DM.

7 See Chapter 8, and also Paquita Mawson, *Mawson of the Antarctic*, p. 144.

8 Mawson to Paquita Mawson, 11 and 17 January 1926, Mawson Papers, Mortlock Library, in PRG 523/3.
9 Kathleen Scott to Mawson, 26 April 1920, in MAC, 51 DM. Her reference to the controversial Stefansson is interesting. In *My Life with the Eskimo* (1913) he had publicised his view that the wilderness could be benign, but after the disaster of his subsequent Arctic expedition his ideas were regarded with scepticism.
10 Kathleen Scott to Mawson, 11 November 1926, Mawson Papers, Mortlock Library, in PRG 523/6.
11 Mawson to Paquita Mawson, 8 December 1926, Mawson Papers, Mortlock Library, in PRG 523/3.
12 Vilhjalmur Stefansson to Mawson, 12 January '1926', error for 1927, in MAC, 23 DM. The letter indicates that Stefansson was given the room number and date by the hotel.
13 Paquita Mawson, *Mawson of the Antarctic*, p. 160.
14 Dennis Rawlins, in a recent study of Byrd's diary/logs for his 1926 North Polar flight, found an incriminating erasure and suspect entries. As a result the Byrd Archive at Ohio State University plans to publish the diary/logs.
15 Lincoln Ellsworth to Mawson, 28 February 1936, in MAC, 22 DM. Mawson asked Amundsen to dinner that month, but Amundsen had a prior engagement. Amundsen to Mawson, 14 January 1927, in MAC, MI 40/5.
16 In addition to Mawson and Ellsworth, there were Fridtjof Nansen, Vilhjalmur Stefansson, Erich von Drygalski, Raymond Priestley, Griffith Taylor, Richard E. Byrd, Hubert Wilkins, Umberto Nobile and many more. W. L. G. Joerg, ed. *Problems of Polar Research: A Series of Papers by Thirty-One Authors*.
17 Leaflet, and interviews with the *Ann Arbor News* and *University of Michigan Daily*, in MAC, 21 DM.
18 Details of the tour in MAC, 171 AAE.
19 Percival Edgar Deane to Sir David Orme Masson, 21 March 1927, in MAC, 34 BZE.
20 Sir David Orme Masson to Mawson, 8 April 1927, in MAC, 34 BZE.
21 Mawson to Masson, 2 May 1927, in MAC, 34 BZE.
22 Lady Masson to Mawson, 28 June 1927, Mawson Papers, Mortlock Library, in PRG 523/6.
23 See Mawson to Essington Lewis, 17 January 1942, in MAC, Biographical File; and Mawson to Sir Robert Horne, 31 January 1933, in MAC, 36 DM.
24 Paquita Mawson, *Mawson of the Antarctic*, p. 192.
25 Arthur Leigh Hunt, *Confessions of a Leigh Hunt*, p. 95.
26 Mawson to Paquita Mawson, 6 and 10 April 1928, private papers in the possession of Mr Gareth Thomas of Adelaide.
27 Mawson to Paquita Mawson, 4 May 1928, substantially Mawson's description. Mawson Papers, Mortlock Library, in PRG 523/3.
28 See Mawson's 'Outline of Mission to Europe', in MAC, 36 DM.
29 Mawson to Paquita Mawson, 3 July 1928, private papers in the possession of Mr Gareth Thomas of Adelaide.
30 Mawson, 'Outline of Mission'. This contradicts Hunt, *Confessions*, p. 96.
31 W. Henderson to Mawson, 2 and 8 October 1928, in MAC, 34 BZE.
32 Mawson to J. K. Davis, 6 November 1928, Davis Papers, La Trobe Library, in 3238/4.

[33] Mawson to Essington Lewis, 17 January 1942, in MAC, Biographical File; and Paquita Mawson, *Mawson of the Antarctic*, pp. 161–2.

[34] Mawson to Sir Robert Horne, 31 January 1933, in MAC, 36 DM. Paquita Mawson in *Mawson of the Antarctic* makes no connection between Mawson's alunite leases and the Sounds project.

[35] Mawson to Paquita Mawson, 24 November 1928, private papers in the possession of Mr Gareth Thomas of Adelaide.

[36] Mawson to W. Henderson, 1 March 1929, in MAC, 34 BZE; and R. G. Casey to Mawson, 30 January 1929, in MAC, 33 BZE.

[37] Quoted in Paquita Mawson, *Mawson of the Antarctic*, p. 159.

CHAPTER 13: DIVIDED COMMAND

[1] Ernest Shackleton, diary, 16 August 1901, quoted in Huntford, *Shackleton*, p. 47.

[2] Harold Fletcher, *Antarctic Days with Mawson*, p. 38.

[3] J. K. Davis to Mawson, 12 March 1929, in MAC, 1 DM.

[4] Mawson to J. S. Cumpston, 24 March 1953, in MAC, 23 DM.

[5] Phillip Law, in conversation with the author, November 1998, has pointed out that it was standard practice on ANARE expeditions during his time as director of the Antarctic Division, though he admits that there is an advantage in having a Naval officer in charge.

[6] Mawson to Cumpston, 24 March 1953.

[7] Mawson, draft unaddressed letter, 29 May 1930, written on the Melbourne Express, in MAC, 1 DM.

[8] Mawson to J. K. Davis, 21 February 1929, in MAC, 1 DM.

[9] In MAC, 30 BZE.

[10] Davis to Mawson, 12 March 1929; Mawson to Davis, 7 March 1929; MAC, 1 DM.

[11] Davis to Sir David Orme Masson, 5 June 1929, Davis Papers, La Trobe Library, in 3237/9.

[12] Davis to Mawson, 13 and 19 June 1929, in MAC, 1 DM.

[13] Mawson to Davis, 2 September 1929, in MAC, 1 DM.

[14] Mawson to Davis, 27 June 1929, in MAC, 1 DM.

[15] Cable received 10 June 1929, in MAC, 30 BZE.

[16] Mawson to Davis, 27 June 1929, in MAC, 1 DM.

[17] In MAC, 1 DM.

[18] For details of Mac-Robertson's involvement in the BANZARE see the Macpherson Robertson Papers, Royal Historical Society of Victoria, especially 'Mawson Expeditions: Statements of Accounts from Commonwealth Treasury'. Mawson had first approached Mac-Robertson for £10 000 by letter, on 31 January 1929 while sailing to England on the *Orama*. Two weeks earlier he had written similarly to Sir Langdon Bonython, without success.

[19] See photograph of Masson with Mac-Robertson in the *Otago Witness*, 4 June 1929, reproduced in this book; and George Taylor, *Making It Happen: The Rise of Sir Macpherson Robertson*, pp. 197–8.

[20] Smaller private donations came from A. M. and G. R. Nicholas, aspirin manufacturers (£600), businessmen W. L. and C. L. Baillieu and W. S. Robinson (£500),

Sir Samuel Hordern (£250), Mawson's friend Sir George Murray (£100), A. A. and F. N. Simpson, South Australian manufacturers of domestic appliances (£100), J. J. Rouse, head of Kodak Australasia (£100), and others including Dr Isaiah Bowman, Director of the American Geographical Society and a good friend of Mawson's (£100).

21 J. Gordon Hayes to Mawson, 12 March 1929, in MAC, 28 DM.
22 Mawson to J. Gordon Hayes, 17 March 1932, in MAC, 28 DM.
23 W. H. Hobbs to Mawson, 29 June 1929, in MAC, 21 DM.
24 A. Grenfell Price, BANZARE *Geographical Report*, p. 18.
25 Quoted by Paquita Mawson in a draft letter to Grenfell Price, *c.* 1960. Private papers in the possession of Mr Gareth Thomas of Adelaide.
26 'Realization Value of Estate', Mawson Papers, Mortlock Library, in PRG 523/3
27 A. Grenfell Price, BANZARE *Geographical Report*, pp. 25–7.
28 Mawson, private list of five complaints against Davis, headed 'Davis', in MAC, 1 DM.

CHAPTER 14: THE FRUITS OF DIVISION

1   Cmdr Morton H. Moyes, BANZARE diary, 19 October 1929, copy in MAC.
2   Quoted by Grenfell Price, BANZARE *Geographical Report*, p. 29.
3   See Mawson, 'The Antarctic Cruise of the "Discovery", 1929–30', p. 538; 'The B.A.N.Z. Antarctic Research Expedition, 1929–31', pp. 103–5; and 'The Kerguelen Archipelago', pp. 18–29.
4   Mawson, 'The Antarctic Cruise of the "Discovery", 1929–30', p. 537. The term 'Pleistocene' embraces the past two million years.
5   Copy in MAC, 30 BZE. Reproduced in Grenfell Price, BANZARE *Geographical Report*, pp. 22–3.
6   Minutes in MAC, 31 BZE.
7   Harold Fletcher, BANZARE diary, 3 December 1929, in possession of Ian Fletcher of Sydney.
8   John K. Davis, Personal Journal, entry for 2 December 1929, Davis Papers, LaTrobe Library.
9   Mawson, Antarctic Diaries, Notebook 7, 3 December 1929.
10 Mawson to W. Henderson, 3 December 1929, private papers in the possession of Mr Gareth Thomas of Adelaide.
11 Mawson, Antarctic Diaries, Notebook 7, 3 December 1929.
12 Davis, Personal Journal, 5 March 1929; Mawson, Antarctic Diaries, Notebook 7, 9 December 1929.
13 Davis, Personal Journal, 5 March 1930.
14 R. G. Simmers, BANZARE diary, 8 November 1929, copy in MAC.
15 Phillip Law, interview with the author, May 1997.
16 Mawson, Antarctic Diaries, Notebook 7, 14 December 1929.
17 Mawson, Antarctic Diaries, Notebook 7, 9 December 1929.
18 Moyes, BANZARE diary, 1 January 1930.
19 Mawson, Antarctic Diaries, Notebook 7, 16 December 1929.
20 Mawson, Antarctic Diaries, Notebook 7, 31 December 1929. Direct speech in source.
21 Mawson, Antarctic Diaries, Notebook 7, 31 December 1929.

[22] Mawson, Antarctic Diaries, Notebook 7, 1 January 1930. Mixture of direct and indirect speech in source.

[23] Mawson, Antarctic Diaries, Notebook 7, 1 January 1930.

[24] Harold Fletcher, interview with Tim Bowden, 12 May 1993.

[25] Mawson, Antarctic Diaries, Notebook 7, 2 January 1930.

[26] Mawson, Antarctic Diaries, Notebook 7, 3 January 1930.

[27] Mawson, Antarctic Diaries, Notebook 7, 3 January 1930. Indirect speech in source.

[28] Fletcher, BANZARE diary, 12 January 1930.

[29] Mawson, Antarctic Diaries, Notebook 7, 5 January 1930. According to Mawson the flight took place 'After lunch'. According to the aircraft's log, it took off at 0830. Copy of log supplied to the author by Edward Fletcher, Aviation Heritage Museum, Western Australia.

[30] Mawson, Antarctic Diaries, Notebook 7, 9 January 1930.

[31] Davis, Personal Journal, 10 March 1930.

[32] Mawson, Antarctic Diaries, Notebook 7, 10 and 11 January 1930. Mixture of direct and indirect speech in source.

[33] Mawson, Antarctic Diaries, Notebook 7, 12 December 1929.

[34] Davis, Personal Journal, 3 February 1930.

[35] Mawson, Antarctic Diaries, Notebook 7, 11 January 1930.

[36] Fletcher, BANZARE diary, 13 January 1930.

[37] Fletcher, BANZARE diary, 14 January 1930.

[38] Hjalmar Riiser-Larsen, 'The "Norvegia" Antarctic Expedition of 1929–1930', pp. 555–73, especially pp. 562–4.

[39] Fletcher, BANZARE diary, 15 January 1930.

[40] Fletcher's diary provides the information: entry of 14 January 1930.

[41] Mawson, Antarctic Diaries, Notebook 7, 16 January 1930. Indirect speech in source.

[42] Mawson, Antarctic Diaries, Notebook 7, 25 January 1930.

[43] Mawson, Antarctic Diaries, Notebook 7, 25 January 1930.

[44] Riiser-Larsen, 'The "Norvegia" Antarctic Expedition', p. 565.

[45] Davis, Personal Journal, 25 January 1930.

[46] These notes are in MAC, 1 DM.

[47] Correspondence between Davis and Paquita Mawson, especially Davis's of 28 September 1963 and 19 September 1964 refusing to see her in Melbourne, and an (unsent) explanatory note in response to hers of 21 September 1964. Davis Papers, LaTrobe Library, Series VII, in 3270/10. Lady Mawson made several attempts to restore the friendship and the whole affair is very sad.

[48] Mawson, Antarctic Diaries, Notebook 7, 26 January 1930.

[49] Grenfell Price, BANZARE Geographical Report, p. 83, and in The Winning of Australian Antarctica.

[50] Davis to Mawson, 12 March 1929, in MAC, 1 DM.

[51] Moyes, BANZARE diary, 23 October 1929.

[52] Davis, memo to Dr Henderson, 27 May 1930, Davis Papers, LaTrobe Library, Series VII, in 3270/10.

[53] Mawson, Antarctic Diaries, Notebook 7, 17 March 1930. Direct speech in source.

[54] Mawson, Antarctic Diaries, Notebook 7, 3 February 1930.

[55] Mawson, Antarctic Diaries, Notebook 7, 20 March 1930.

[56] Reported in Harold Fletcher, Antarctic Days with Mawson, p. 224.

CHAPTER 15: SIEGE OF THE SOUTH

[1] Mawson to J. B. Borley, 16 July 1930, in MAC, 35 BZE.

[2] R. G. Casey to Mawson, 30 January 1929, and Mawson to Dr W. Henderson, 1 March 1929, in MAC, 33 BZE and 34 BZE.

[3] See Henderson to Casey, 20 March 1929, in MAC, 33 BZE.

[4] See R. A. Swan, *Australia in the Antarctic*, pp. 197–8.

[5] Copy of report in Davis Papers, LaTrobe Library, 3270/10. It was read into the Parliamentary record.

[6] Davis Papers, LaTrobe Library, in 3237/8.

[7] Adelaide *Register*, 23 May 1930.

[8] Mawson to R. G. Casey, 15 August 1930, in MAC, 34 BZE.

[9] Frank Hurley to Mawson, 5 May 1930, in MAC, 6 DM.

[10] Hurley to Mawson, 1 July 1930, in MAC, 6 DM.

[11] *The Bulletin*, 20 August 1930.

[12] Dr Alf Howard, private communication to the author, 17 March 1998.

[13] Mawson to Paquita Mawson, 13 December 1932, Mawson Papers, Mortlock Library, in PRG 523/3.

[14] Plans as outlined by Mawson in the *Sydney Morning Herald*, 10 December 1930.

[15] Mawson, Antarctic Diaries, Notebook 8, 2 January 1931.

[16] R. G. Simmers, diary, 5 January 1931, copy in MAC.

[17] Mawson, 'The B.A.N.Z. Antarctic Research Expedition, 1929–31', p. 115.

[18] Hurley, diary, 6 February 1931, National Library of Australia, MS 883, Series I, Item 17.

[19] Simmers, diary, 6 and 8 February 1931.

[20] Swan, *Australia in the Antarctic*, p. 201.

[21] Simmers, diary, 18 February 1931.

[22] For thorough analysis of the geographical results of BANZARE see Grenfell Price, BANZARE *Geographical Report* and *The Winning of Australian Antarctica*.

[23] Mawson, sheets of notes for 12 March 1931 supplemental to Notebook 8.

[24] Correspondence with Stuart F. Doyle, in MAC, 6 DM.

[25] Hurley to Mawson, 24 March 1931, in MAC, 6 DM.

[26] Hurley to Mawson, 7 April 1931, in MAC, 6 DM.

[27] Mawson to Hurley, 16 April 1931, in MAC, 6 DM.

[28] Hurley to Mawson, 19 May 1931.

[29] Mawson to Hurley, 2 July 1931; Hurley to Mawson, 6 July 1931, and undated (July 1931); all in MAC, 6 DM.

[30] Telegram, Hurley to Mawson, 3 October 1931, in MAC, 6 DM.

[31] Hurley to Mawson, 2 December 1931, in MAC, 6 DM.

[32] Mawson to Hurley, 18 February 1932, in MAC, 6 DM.

[33] Mawson to Stuart Doyle, 18 February 1932, in MAC, 6 DM.

[34] Mawson to Hurley, 30 September 1932, in MAC, 6 DM.

[35] Mawson to Paquita Mawson, 13 December 1932, Mawson Papers, Mortlock Library, in PRG 523/3.

[36] Mawson to Paquita Mawson, 4 January 1933, Mawson Papers, Mortlock Library, in PRG, 523/3.

[37] Mawson to Mac-Robertson, 30 October 1933, Macpherson Robertson Papers, Royal Historical Society of Victoria.

[38] Mawson, 'The Kerguelen Archipelago', pp. 18–29, quoting p. 29.

[39] Sir James O'Grady to Sir Elliott Lewis, Governor of Tasmania, 14 August 1931, sent by Lewis to Mawson on 2 November 1931, in MAC, 22 DM. See also Grenfell Price, BANZARE *Geographical Report*, pp. 166–7, and Swan, *Australia in the Antarctic*, pp. 202–4.

[40] Mawson to J. S. Cumpston, 14 September 1953, in MAC, 23 DM.

CHAPTER 16: THE DOMESTIC WORLD

[1] Paquita Mawson, *Mawson of the Antarctic*, p. 146.

[2] This section is based on a long interview with Pat Thomas and Jessica McEwin in May 1997.

[3] Accounts, in MAC, 57 DM.

[4] Payment to Miss J. Whitby, 12 September 1921, in MAC, 57 DM.

[5] Mawson Papers, Mortlock Library, in PRG 523/3.

[6] Bryan Forbes, interview with the author, July 1997.

[7] Alan Wilson, interview with the author, August 1998.

[8] Information from Nancy Flannery of Adelaide, biographer of Paquita Mawson.

[9] Paquita Mawson to Mawson, '31 Jan Wed.', in MAC, 52 DM.

[10] Mawson to Patricia Mawson, 4 July 1928, private papers in the possession of Mr Gareth Thomas of Adelaide.

[11] Mawson to Paquita Mawson, 3 July 1928, private papers in the possession of Mr Gareth Thomas of Adelaide.

[12] Dora Gillam to Mawson, 30 May 1931; Mawson to Dora Gillam, 3 June 1931. Both in MAC, 52 DM.

[13] Mawson to Hurley, 30 September 1932, in MAC, 6 DM.

[14] W. N. Hoerr, *Clipped Wings, or Memories of my Childhood and Youth*, p. 122.

[15] Mawson to Paquita Mawson, 17 December 1936, Mawson Papers, Mortlock Library, in PRG 523/3.

[16] Mawson to J. K. Davis, 20 November 1940, Davis Papers, LaTrobe Library, in 3270/9.

[17] Mawson to Paquita Mawson, 1, 5 and 10 February 1941, Mawson Papers, Mortlock Library, in PRG 523/3.

[18] Mawson to Paquita Mawson, 14 May 1934, Mawson Papers, Mortlock Library, in PRG 523/3.

[19] Mawson to Paquita Mawson, 6 February 1936, Mawson Papers, Morlock Library, in PRG 523/3.

[20] Mawson to Paquita Mawson, 18 January 1937, Mawson papers, Mortlock Library, in PRG 523/3.

[21] Documentation from the Adelaide Club supplied by the Manager, Mr Stephen H. Williams.

CHAPTER 17: RELATIONS WITH BYRD, ELLSWORTH AND WILKINS

[1] Mawson, notes for a Byrd obituary broadcast on the ABC, in MAC, 23 DM.

[2] Richard E. Byrd, *Skyward*, p. 306; *Little America: Aerial Exploration in the Antarctic & the Flight to the South Pole*, pp. 13 and 43.

[3] Typescript notes by A. Leigh Hunt, in MAC, 36 DM, later compressed for *Confessions of a Leigh Hunt*.

[4] Byrd, *Little America*, p. 43.

[5] See for instance Hobbs's letters to Mawson of 5 December 1931, 7 March 1932, and 26 May 1932, all in MAC, 21 DM, and even 'reconciling' letters like that of 17 February 1944, in possession of Mr Gareth Thomas of Adelaide. And see Mawson to Hobbs, 13 January 1932, 20 April 1932, and 30 October 1934, all in MAC, 21 DM. See also Mawson, 'Wilkes's Antarctic Landfalls'.

[6] Mawson to Mary E. Cooley, 19 May 1939, in MAC, 21 DM. See also his letter to the same correspondent, 8 November 1943, in reply to hers of 1 October 1939, both in MAC, 21 DM.

[7] Mawson, notes for a Byrd obituary.

[8] Hobbs to Mawson, 31 December 1928, in MAC, 21 DM.

[9] Richard E. Byrd, *Alone*, p. 3.

[10] Byrd, *Alone*, p. 7.

[11] Mawson to J. Gordon Hayes, 17 March 1932 and 16 October 1934, in MAC, 28 DM; Hobbs to Mawson, 19 April 1935, in MAC, 21 DM.

[12] Mawson to John Abbottsmith, 1 February 1950, in MAC, 3 ANR.

[13] See Lisle A. Rose, *Assault on Eternity: Richard E. Byrd and the Exploration of Antarctica, 1946–47*, pp. 247–8.

[14] Byrd to Mawson, 21 September 1947, Byrd Papers, Folder 2212, Byrd Polar Research Center, Ohio State University.

[15] Mawson to Byrd, 14 April 1956; Byrd to Mawson, 17 August 1956. Byrd Papers, Folder 2212, Byrd Polar Research Center, Ohio State University. There is also an important letter on Antarctic geopolitics, particularly the American attitude to claims, and Mawson's attempts to change this, in Mawson to R. A. Swan, 27 January 1956, collection of the author.

[16] Byrd to Mawson, 23 February 1957, Byrd Papers, Folder 2212, Byrd Polar Research Center, Ohio State University.

[17] Roald Amundsen and Lincoln Ellsworth, *Our Polar Flight* and *The First Crossing of the Polar Sea*; and Ellsworth, 'Arctic Flying Experiences by Airplane and Airship', in Joerg, ed., *Problems of Polar Research*.

[18] Lincoln Ellsworth, 'My Flight Across Antarctica', p. 1.

[19] Ellsworth, 'My Flight Across Antarctica', p. 1.

[20] George Hubert Wilkins, *Flying the Arctic*. On Wilkins generally see Lowell Thomas (compiler), *Sir Hubert Wilkins*.

[21] R. A. Swan, *Australia in the Antarctic*, p. 169.

[22] Swan, *Australia in the Antarctic*, pp. 168–9.

[23] Hobbs to Mawson, 10 February 1926, in MAC, 21 DM.

[24] Hobbs to Mawson, 29 June 1929, in MAC, 21 DM.

[25] Mawson to J. P. Thomson, 1 July 1929, in MAC, 22 DM.

[26] R. G. Simmers, diary, 21 November 1929, copy in MAC.

[27] See Ellsworth, *Beyond Horizons*, and 'My Flight Across Antarctica'.

[28] Mawson to Lincoln Ellsworth, 6 January 1936, in MAC, 22 DM.

[29] Mawson to J. W. S. Marr, undated draft, late-1935, in MAC, 1 DM.

[30] Mawson to May Louise Ellsworth, 6 January 1936, in MAC, 22 DM.

[31] Mawson, speech notes in MAC, 22 DM.

[32] Ellsworth to Mawson, 28 February 1936, in MAC, 22 DM.

[33] The Adelaide *Advertiser*, 5 February 1935.

[34] Mawson, 'The Unveiling of Antarctica', especially pp. 33–7.

[35] W. R. Hodgson, External Affairs, to Mawson, 16 January 1939, in MAC, 6 ANR.

[36] Mawson to Sir David Rivett, CSIR, 22 December 1938, in MAC, 6 ANR; *Advertiser*, 17 September 1938.

[37] Davis to Mawson, undated but November 1938, in MAC, 1 DM.

[38] Mawson to Hobbs, 30 October 1934, in MAC, 21 DM.

[39] Mawson to Frank Hurley, 26 May 1936, in MAC, 6 DM.

[40] Mawson to J. F. Green, 1 August 1936, in MAC, 22 DM.

[41] Mawson to A. Leigh Hunt, 2 December 1936, in MAC, 36 DM.

[42] Davis to Mawson, 22 December 1919, in MAC, 1 DM.

[43] Full details in Mawson to John Rymill, 29 March 1939, in MAC, 23 DM.

[44] Mawson to Casey, 14 November 1938, in MAC, 6 ANR.

[45] Ellsworth, cable to Mawson, 3 January 1939, in MAC, 6 ANR.

[46] *Canberra Times*, 13 January 1939.

[47] Joseph Lyons, Prime Minister, to Lincoln Ellsworth, 7 February 1939, Ellsworth Papers, RG 401/36, National Archives, College Park, Maryland.

[48] 'I had thought to take a hand in establishing the said shore station and leave it for others to carry on.' Mawson to L. C. King, 9 May 1944, in MAC, 23 DM. See also the *Advertiser*, 3 March 1939, and Mawson to Rymill, 29 March 1939, in MAC, 23 DM.

[49] Mawson to Rymill, 24 February 1939; Rymill to Mawson, 7 March 1939. In MAC, 23 DM.

[50] See Mawson to Ellsworth, 16 February 1939, Ellsworth Papers, RG 401/36, National Archives, College Park, Maryland.

[51] The setting is based on photographs in the possession of the author. The account of their discussions is based on Mawson to Rivett, 9 March 1939, in MAC, 6 ANR; and Mawson to Rymill, 29 March 1939, in MAC, 23 DM.

[52] Mawson to Rivett, 9 March 1939.

[53] Mawson to Rymill, 29 March 1939.

[54] Indirect speech in the two sources.

[55] Photographs in possession of the author.

[56] Mawson to Rivett, 9 March 1939.

[57] Mawson to Rivett, 20 March 1939, in MAC, 6 ANR.

[58] Mawson to Rymill, 29 March 1939.

[59] Lady Wilkins to J. K. Davis, 25 July 1959, Davis Papers, LaTrobe Library, in 3271/7.

CHAPTER 18: THE GEOLOGIST IN THE FIELD

[1] See D. W. Corbett, 'Douglas Mawson: The Geologist as Explorer', the best account of Mawson's geological work. All of Mawson's geological papers were read for the present biography.

[2] Corbett, 'Douglas Mawson: The Geologist as Explorer', p. 123; Mawson, 'The Wooltana Basic Igneous Belt'; and Mawson, 'A Brief Resumé of Present Knowledge Relating to the Igneous Rocks of South Australia'.

[3] 'The Pre-Ordovician Rocks of the McDonnell Ranges, Central Australia'.

[4] Cecil Madigan, *Central Australia,* summarises much of his work.

[5] Cecil Madigan to Mawson, 4 February 1920, in MAC, 27 AAE.

[6] Lee Parkin, interview with the author, July 1997.

[7] Ralph Segnit, interview with the author, October 1998.

[8] Edgeworth David to Mawson, 18 and 28 October 1928, in MAC, 24 DM.

[9] Lee Parkin, interview with the author; and Reg Sprigg, *Geology Is Fun* (Adelaide, 1989), pp. 131–2.

[10] Ralph Segnit, interview with the author.

[11] Dr Robin Oliver and Bryan Forbes, interview with the author, July 1997.

[12] Eric Rudd, interview with the author, July 1997.

[13] Mawson, 'The Elatina Galciation: A Third Recurrence of Glaciation Evidenced in the Adelaide System'; and 'The Late Precambrian Ice-Age and Glacial Record of the Bibliando Dome'.

[14] Mawson, 'The Late Precambrian Ice-Age', p. 172.

[15] Mawson and Lee Parkin, 'Some Granitic Rocks of South-Eastern South Australia'; Mawson and W. B. Dallwitz, 'Palaeozoic Igneous Rocks of Lower South-Eastern South Australia'; and Mawson and E. R. Segnit, 'Granites of the Tintinara District'.

[16] Paul Hackforth-Jones, conversation with the author, 1998.

[17] Ralph Segnit, interview with the author.

[18] Lee Parkin, interview with the author.

[19] Alan Spry, interview with the author, August 1998.

[20] Eric Rudd, interview with the author.

[21] Corbett, 'Douglas Mawson: The Geologist as Explorer', p. 133.

[22] Corbett, 'Douglas Mawson: The Geologist as Explorer', p. 134.

[23] For a complete listing see Margaret Innes and Heather Duff, *Mawson's Papers—a Guide*, pp. 8/8–8/12. The AAE and BANZARE Reports are listed on pp. 8/1–8/7.

[24] Alan Spry, interview with the author.

[25] Mawson to W. H. Hobbs, 31 December 1948, in MAC, 21 DM.

[26] Mawson to Paquita Mawson, 27 September 1933, Mawson Papers, Mortlock Library, in PRG 523/3.

[27] Mawson to Paquita Mawson, 3 and 8 March 1937, Mawson Papers, Mortlock Library, in PRG 523/3.

[28] Mawson to Paquita Mawson, 2 October 1935, Mawson Papers, Mortlock Library, in PRG 523/3.

[29] Mawson to Essington Lewis, 24 December 1941 and 17 January 1942, in MAC, Biographical File.

[30] John Curtin to Mawson, 27 March 1942, Mawson Papers, Mortlock Library, in PRG 523/6.

31 C703/3, series A461. Information from Gay Hogan, Australian Archives, Canberra, 28 April 1998.
32 Mawson to Mary E. Cooley, 8 November 1943, in MAC, 21 DM.
33 Mawson to J. K. Davis, 17 October 1942, in MAC, 1 DM.
34 Mawson to Liquid Fuel Control Board, 1 February 1943, Mawson Papers, Morlock Library, in PRG 523/2.

CHAPTER 19: MAWSON AND ANARE

1 See, for example, the Melbourne *Argus*, 24 October 1945.
2 Mawson to Paquita Mawson, 4 July 1946, private papers in the possession of Mr Gareth Thomas of Adelaide; and 19 July 1946, Mawson Papers, Mortlock Library, in PRG 523/3.
3 William E. Dunk to Mawson, 20 January 1947, in MAC, 11 ANR.
4 Mawson to Dunk, 10 December 1946, in MAC, 11 ANR.
5 Mawson to Rymill, 9 December 1946, and Rymill to Mawson, 12 December 1946, in MAC, 23 DM.
6 Minutes of Australian Antarctic Executive Committee on Exploration and Exploitation, 24 January 1947, in MAC, 1 ANR.
7 Minutes of Australian Antarctic Executive Committee, 5 May 1947, in MAC, 1 ANR.
8 Mawson, *Home of the Blizzard*, 1, pp. 237, 333, and maps at the back of Vol. 2. Mawson's sledging diary does not actually mention Cape Freshfield.
9 Discussed briefly in Paquita Mawson, *Mawson of the Antarctic*, p. 202.
10 Mawson to J. S. Cumpston, 24 March 1953, in MAC, 23 DM.
11 Mawson to Paul Siple, 16 April 1956, in MAC, 23 DM.
12 Mawson to Robert Dovers, undated draft, in MAC, 23 DM.
13 Mawson to Eric J. Harrison, 19 November 1948, in MAC, 67 DM.
14 Minutes of ANARE Executive Planning Committee meeting, 3 June 1949, in MAC, 1 ANR. Indirect speech in minutes, and substantially as here in all verbal details.
15 Phillip Law to Mawson, 24 March 1952, in MAC, 3 ANR, and interview with the author, May 1998. The proposed sealing industry would only have killed 1600 bulls a year at each island, and would have raised £40–60 000 from each site every year for ANARE.
16 R. G. Casey to Mawson, 12 June 1953; Mawson to Casey, 22 June 1953. Both in MAC, 4 ANR.
17 Mawson to Law, 16 January 1953, in MAC, 3 ANR.
18 Mawson to B. W. Taylor, 5 March 1953, in MAC, 3 ANR.
19 Mawson to Davis, 25 December 1953, Davis Papers, LaTrobe Library, in 3270/9.
20 Davis to Mawson, 1 January 1954, in MAC, 1 DM.
21 Davis to Mawson, 18 March 1954, in MAC, 1 DM.
22 Mawson to Davis, 17 July 1954, Davis Papers, LaTrobe Library, in 3270/9.
23 Phillip Law, interview with the author, May 1998.
24 Robert Dovers to Mawson, 14 May 1956, in MAC, 23 DM.
25 Mawson to Robert Dovers, 7 May 1958, in MAC, 23 DM.

26 Conversation with the author, November 1998.
27 Minutes of ANARE Executive Planning Committee meeting, 25 November 1957, in MAC, 1 ANR.
28 Mawson to Davis, 25 April 1958, in MAC, 1 DM; Mawson to Robert Dovers, 7 May 1958, in MAC, 23 DM.
29 Davis to Mawson, 29 April 1958, in MAC, 1 DM.
30 Conversation with the author, November 1998.
31 Mawson to Casey, 10 July 1958, replying to Casey's of 3 July, both in MAC, 4 ANR.

CHAPTER 20: TO THE LAST HORIZON

1 Mawson to Paquita Mawson, 2 April 1950, Mawson Papers, Mortlock Library, in PRG 523/3.
2 Mawson to Paquita Mawson, 28 July 1952, Mawson Papers, Mortlock Library, in PRG, 523/3.
3 A. P. Rowe to Mawson, 20 May 1952, in MAC, 67 DM.
4 Mawson to Sir George Ligertwood, 30 October 1952, in MAC, 67 DM.
5 See Paquita Mawson, *Mawson of the Antarctic*, pp. 204–6.
6 Mawson to J. M. Bechervaise, undated draft, April 1954, in MAC, 23 DM.
7 George Dovers to Mawson, 20 July 1954, in MAC, 49 DM.
8 Charles Laseron to Mawson, 9 December 1954, in MAC, 49 DM.
9 John Hunter to Mawson, 31 January 1957, in MAC, 49 DM.
10 Mawson to Paquita Mawson, 1 June 1955, Mawson Papers, Mortlock Library, in PRG 523/3.
11 Mawson to Paquita Mawson, 1 June 1955.
12 Mawson to Paquita Mawson, 12 June 1955, Mawson Papers, Mortlock Library, in PRG 523/3; and correspondence with Clara Serena, 12 December 1933, in MAC, 48 DM. The details here are essentially based on the letter to Paquita Mawson.
13 Subsequently a brief biography of Mawson was published in Moscow as part of a series on the great explorers: E. M. Suzyumov, *A Life Given to the Antarctic: The Antarctic Explorer Sir Douglas Mawson.*
14 Mawson to R. G. Casey, 6 and 22 April 1956, in MAC, 4 ANR. W. C. Wentworth was a Liberal backbencher who represented Parliament's Foreign Affairs Committee on ANARE's Executive Planning Committee. He had a zealous antipathy towards the 'international communist conspiracy'.
15 According to information given to the author by ABC Television Archives in October 1998, the film footage cannot be found.
16 Minutes of ANARE Executive Planning Committee, 6 May 1957, in MAC, 1 ANR.
17 Phillip Law, interview with the author, May 1997. Mawson refers to this bout of pneumonia and heart trouble in a letter of 12 August 1957 to Geoffrey Dutton, in which he says he is still on a slow recovery. Letter in MAC, 48 DM.
18 Mawson to Paquita Mawson, 21 June 1957, Mawson Papers, Mortlock Library, in PRG 523/3.

[19] Mawson to John Bechervaise, 22 May 1958, in MAC, 23 DM.

[20] Geoffrey and Ann Blainey, conversation with the author, 1998. In a letter of 24 February 1955 to J. K. Davis, Mawson says 'Yes, I was very glad indeed to read *The Peaks of Lyell*. Am glad all that data has been put on record.' Letter in Davis Papers, LaTrobe Library, in 3270/9.

[21] See Paquita Mawson, *Mawson of the Antarctic*, p. 219.

[22] ' . . . he was tired now and we finished the month quietly.' Paquita Mawson, *Mawson of the Antarctic*, p. 220.

[23] In MAC, 23 DM.

BIBLIOGRAPHY

ABBREVIATIONS OF DEPOSITORIES of unpublished materials:

AT   Alun Thomas Collection, Adelaide
BPRC   Byrd Polar Research Center, Ohio State University, Columbus
GT   Gareth Thomas Collection, Adelaide
LaT   La Trobe Library, Melbourne
MAC   Mawson Antarctic Collection, University of Adelaide
ML   Mitchell Library, Sydney
Mort   Mortlock Library, Adelaide
NACP   National Archives at College Park, Maryland
NL   National Library of Australia, Canberra
RGS   Royal Geographical Society, London
RHSV   Royal Historical Society of Victoria
SPRI   Scott Polar Research Institute, Cambridge
TBL   Alexander Turnbull Library, Wellington
UAdelA   University of Adelaide Archives
UMelA   University of Melbourne Archives
UMichA   University of Michigan Archives, Ann Arbor
USA   University of Sydney Archives

MANUSCRIPT SOURCES
Diaries, Journals, Logs and Memoirs

Bickerton, Francis H. AAE Sledging Journal, at SPRI, copy at MAC.
Blake, Leslie R. AAE Diary, at LaT.
David, T. W. Edgeworth. *Nimrod* Diaries, BAE Field Notebooks, South Magnetic Pole Journey Notebook, all at USA; Miscellaneous Manuscripts and Diaries, at ML.

Davis, John King. Journals and Diaries, at LaT; Davis Papers in general, at LaT.

Dovers, George H. S. AAE Diaries, at ML.

Fletcher, Harold. BANZARE Diary, Mr Ian Fletcher of Sydney.

Hackworth, C. J. AAE Diary, copy of Mr Phillip Law of Melbourne.

Hannam, Walter Henry. AAE Diary, at ML.

Harrisson, Charles Turnbull. AAE Diary, at ML.

Hunter, John G. Notes and Papers, AAE-related, at NL.

Hurley, J. Frank. BANZARE Diaries, at NL.

Kennedy, Alec L. AAE Diary, at MAC.

Laseron, Charles Francis. AAE Diary, at ML.

Lincoln, Bertram Clive, AAE Diary, copy at MAC.

Mackay, Alistair Forbes. BAE Diary, at Royal Scottish Museum (Edinburgh), copy at MAC.

McLean, Archibald Lang. AAE Diaries, at ML.

Marshall, Eric. BAE Diary, at RGS.

Mawson, Douglas. Antarctic Diaries (BAE, AAE, BANZARE), at MAC; Geological Field Diaries, at MAC; New Hebrides Diaries and Notebooks, at MAC; Miscellaneous other diaries and logs, Mawson Papers in general, at MAC.

Mertz, Xavier. AAE Diary, Sledging Diary, copies at MAC.

Moyes, Morton Henry. AAE Diaries, at ML, NL. BANZARE Diary, copy at MAC.

Sawyer, Arthur J. AAE Diary, at ML.

Simmers, R. G. BANZARE Diary, copy at MAC.

Stillwell, Frank L. AAE Diary, at Basser Library, Australian Academy of Science, Canberra.

Wild, Frank. Memoirs, at ML.

Letters and Other Manuscript Sources

AAE Papers, various, at MAC, ML, LaT.

Adelaide Club. Ballot book, at Mort.

Admiralty, British. Correspondence, at MAC.

Agreement between the State Government of New South Wales and Sir Douglas Mawson on the printing of the AAE Scientific Reports, drawn up 22 August 1919, copy at MAC.

Ainsworth, George F. AAE papers, at MAC.

Amundsen, Roald. Correspondence, at MAC.

Antarctic Committee (BANZARE). Correspondence, at MAC.

ANARE Executive Planning Committee minutes and other ANARE papers, at MAC.

BAE Papers, various, at MAC, ML, SPRI, USA.

Bage, Robert. AAE papers, at MAC.

BANZARE Papers, various, at MAC, LaT.

Barraclough, Henry. Correspondence, at MAC.

Blake, Leslie R. AAE papers, at MAC.

Board of Trade, United Kingdom. Correspondence, at MAC.

Bragg, William Henry. Correspondence, at MAC.

Bruce, W. S. Correspondence, at MAC, SPRI.

Byrd, Richard Evelyn. Correspondence, at BPRC, MAC.

Carslaw, H. S. Correspondence, at MAC, USA.

Casey, R. G. Correspondence, at LaT, MAC.

Commonwealth Department of Defence. Correspondence, at MAC.

Commonwealth Department of External Affairs. Correspondence, at MAC.

Commonwealth Department of the Prime Minister. Correspondence, at MAC.

Cooley, Mary E. Correspondence, at MAC.

Cotton, Leo. 'Application for the Chair of Geology. . . June 1924' (University of Sydney), at MAC.

Cowans, John. Correspondence, at MAC.

Curtin, John. Correspondence, at Mort.

David, T. W. Edgeworth. Correspondence, at AT, MAC, ML, USA.

Davis, John King. Correspondence at LaT, MAC. Davis Papers in general at LaT.

Dawson, Trevor. Correspondence, at MAC.

Deane, Percival Edgar. Correspondence, at MAC.

Dellenbough, F. S. Correspondence, at MAC.

Delprat, G. D. Correspondence, at GT, MAC, NL.

Discovery Committee (BANZARE). Correspondence, at MAC.

Dovers, George. Correspondence, AAE papers, at MAC.

Dovers, Robert. Correspondence, at MAC.

Doyle, Stuart F. Correspondence, at MAC.

Drygalski, Erich von. Correspondence, at MAC.

Dunk, William E. Correspondence, at MAC.

Eitel, Conrad. Correspondence, at MAC.

Eitel, Florence. Correspondence, at MAC.

Ellsworth, Lincoln. Correspondence, cables, at MAC, NACP.

Examination Registers, University of Sydney, at USA.

Fisher, Andrew. Correspondence, at MAC.

Fisher, Margery. Correspondence, at SPRI, MAC.

Foster, H. J. Correspondence, at MAC.

Flight Logs of Gipsy Moth VH–ULD, Aviation Heritage Museum, WA.

Gaumont Co., London. Correspondence, at MAC.

Gillam, Dora. Correspondence, at MAC.

Greely, Adolphus Washington. Correspondence, at MAC.

Hackett, Winthrop. Correspondence, at MAC.

Hall, Walter. Correspondence, at MAC.

Hamilton, Harold. Correspondence, AAE papers, at MAC.

Hannam, Walter Henry. AAE papers, at MAC.

Harrisson, Charles Turnbull. AAE papers, at MAC.

Hayes, J. Gordon. Correspondence, at MAC.

Heinemann, William. Correspondence, at MAC.

Heinemann, William, Ltd., London. Correspondence, at MAC.

Henderson, George C. Correspondence, at GT.

Henderson, W. Correspondence, at MAC.

Hobbs, William Herbert. Correspondence, at GT, MAC, UMichA.

Hodder & Stoughton Ltd. Correspondence, at MAC.

Hodgson, W. R. Correspondence, at MAC.

Horan, R. S. 'History of the Fort Street Unions', 1994, with R. S. Horan.

Howard, Alfred. Correspondence, at MAC, and with the author.

Howchin, Walter. Correspondence, at MAC.

Hunt, Arthur Leigh. Correspondence, at MAC.

Hunter, John G. Correspondence, AAE papers, at MAC, NL.

Hurley, J. Frank. Correspondence, at MAC.

Jeffryes, Norma. Correspondence, at MAC.

Jeffryes, Sidney. Correspondence, at MAC.

Johnston, T. Harvey. BANZARE papers, at MAC.

Jones, S. E. AAE papers, at MAC.

Keedick, Lee. Correspondence, at MAC.

Kennedy, A. L. AAE papers, at MAC.

Kent, A. J. Correspondence, at MAC.

Laby, T. H. Correspondence, at MAC, UMelA. Laby Papers in general at UMelA.

Laseron, Charles. Correspondence, AAE papers, various, at MAC.

Law, Phillip. Correspondence, at MAC. 'Some Antarctic Leaders', Library Dinner Address, Melbourne Club, 11 July 1996, with the author.

Lewis, Essington. Correspondence, at MAC.

Lloyds Film Agency, London. Correspondence, at MAC.

Lyons, Joseph. Correspondence, at NACP.

Lysaght, Mrs Gerald. Correspondence, in MAC.

McLean, Archibald Lang. Correspondence, AAE papers, at MAC.

MacCallum, Mungo W. Correspondence, at MAC.

MacKenzie, K. N. Correspondence, at MAC.

Madigan, Cecil. Correspondence, AAE papers, at MAC.

Masson, David Orme. Correspondence, at MAC, UMelA. Masson Papers in general, at UMelA.

Masson, Mary. Correspondence, at Mort.

Mawson, Douglas. Correspondence, at BPRC, GT, LaT, MAC, ML, Mort, NACP, NL, RGS, RHSV, SPRI, TL, UAdelA, UMelA, UMichA, USA, the author. Mawson Papers in general at GT, MAC, Mort.

———. Personal Accounts and Receipts, at MAC.

———. Geological Investigations in the Broken Hill Area, D.Sc. thesis, University of Adelaide, at MAC.

Mawson, Joseph. Correspondence, at GT.

Mawson, *née* Delprat, Paquita. Correspondence, at GT, LaT, MAC, Mort. Mawson Papers in general, at Mort.

Mawson, Robert. Correspondence, at MAC.

Mawson, William. Correspondence, at GT, MAC.

Miess, Henry. Correspondence, at MAC.

Mill, H. R. Correspondence, at MAC, SPRI.

Moyes, Morton Henry. AAE papers, at MAC.

Newman & Guardia Ltd., London. Correspondence, at MAC.

NSW Committee on Printing of Records of the AAE. Correspondence, at MAC.

O'Grady, James. Correspondence, at MAC.

Parish Registers, Douglas, Isle of Man.

Parish Registers, Kirkby Overblow, Yorkshire

Petition to Minister of Education, NSW, 3 November 1888, at Archives, NSW Department of School Education.

Premier's Office, South Australia. Correspondence, at MAC.

Price, Archibald Grenfell. Correspondence, papers, at MAC.

Registrar's Office, University of Sydney. Correspondence, at MAC.

Reid, Alfred. Correspondence, at MAC.

Rivett, David. Correspondence, at MAC.

Robertson, Macpherson ('Mac-Robertson'). Correspondence, at MAC, RHSV. Macpherson Robertson Papers in general, at RHSV.

Roosevelt, Theodore. Correspondence, at MAC.

Rowe, A. P. Correspondnece, at MAC.

Runciman, Walter. Correspondence, at MAC.

Rymill, John. Correspondence, at MAC.

Sandell, Charles A. AAE papers, at MAC.

Scott, Kathleen. Correspondence, at MAC, SPRI.

Scott, Robert Falcon. Correspondence, papers, at MAC, SPRI.

Selle, Walter A. Correspondence, at AT, MAC.

Serena, Clara. Correspondence, at MAC.

Shackleton, Ernest. Correspondence, cables, papers, at MAC, ML.

Smeaton, T. H. Correspondence, at MAC.

Stefansson, Vilhjalmur. Correspondence, at MAC.

Stillwell, Frank L. AAE papers, at MAC.

Stoney, E. H. Correspondence, at MAC.

Swan, R. A. Correspondence, with the author.

Thomas Cook & Son. Correspondence, at MAC.

Thomas, Pat. Correspondence, at MAC.

Vickers Ltd. Correspondence, at MAC.

Watkins, H. E. Correspondence, at MAC.

Watson, Andrew D. AAE papers, at MAC.

Webb, Eric. Correspondence, AAE papers, at MAC.

Wild, Frank. Correspondence, AAE papers, at MAC, ML.

Wilkins, George Hubert. Correspondence, at LaT.

Wilkins, Suzanne. Correspondence, at LaT.

Wilson, Edward. Correspondence, at ML.

PUBLISHED SOURCES
Books

Amundsen, Roald, and Ellsworth, Lincoln. *Our Polar Flight*. Dodd, Mead, New York, 1925.

——. *The First Crossing of the Polar Sea*. Doubleday, Doran & Co., New York 1927.

Andrews, C. F. *Vickers Aircraft Since 1908*. Putnam, London 1969.

Australian Dictionary of Biography. Multiple volumes, in progress. Melbourne University Press, Melbourne 1966–.

Bickel, Lennard. *This Accursed Land*. Macmillan, Melbourne 1977.

Bonney, T. G. *The Story of our Planet*. Cassell & Co., London 1893.

——. *Volcanoes*. John Murray, London 1899.

Brown, Robert N. R. *The Voyage of the 'Scotia'*. W. Blackwood & Sons, London 1906.

Bruce, William S. See Brown, Robert N. R.

Byrd, Richard Evelyn. *Skyward*. Putnam's Sons, New York 1928.

——. *Little America: Aerial Exploration in the Antarctic & the Flight to the South Pole*. Putnam's Sons, New York 1930.

——. *Alone*. Putnam, New York 1938.

Cameron, Ian. *To the Farthest Ends of the Earth: The History of the Royal Geographical Society 1830–1980*. Macdonald, London 1980.

Casson, M. R. *George Cockburn Henderson*. Libraries Board of South Australia, Adelaide 1964.

Conway Maritime Press. *Conway's All the World's Fighting Ships 1860–1905*. Mayflower Books, New York 1979.

Cook, Frederick A. *Through the First Antarctic Night: 1898–1899*. William Heinemann, London 1900.

Davis, John King. *With the 'Aurora' in the Antarctic 1911–1914*. Andrew Melrose, London 1919.

——. *High Latitude*. Melbourne University Press, Melbourne 1962.

——. *Trial by Ice: The Antarctic Journals of John King Davis*, ed. Louise Crossley. Erskine Press, Norwich 1997.

Ellsworth, Lincoln. *Beyond Horizons*. Doubleday, New York 1938.

Fisher, Margery and James. *Shackleton*. Barrie, London 1957.

Fletcher, Harold. *Antarctic Days with Mawson*. Angus & Robertson, Melbourne 1984.

Gent, L. E. *The Fort Street Centenary Book*. Privately published, Sydney 1993.

Glaessner, M. F., and Rudd, E. A. (eds). *Sir Douglas Mawson Anniversary Volume*. The University of Adelaide, Adelaide 1952.

Haber, L. F. *The Poisonous Cloud: Chemical Warfare in the First World War*. Oxford University Press, Oxford 1986.

Hale, Herbert M. *The First Hundred Years of the Museum, 1856–1956. Records of the South Australian Museum*, Vol. 12. The South Australian Museum, Adelaide 1956.

Harker, Alfred. *The Natural History of Igneous Rocks*. Methuen & Co., London 1909.

Hayes, J. Gordon. *Antarctica: A Treatise on the Southern Continent*. The Richards Press, London 1928.

Hoerr, W. N. *Clipped Wings, or Memories of my Childhood and Youth*. Privately published, Adelaide 1995.

Horan, R. S. *Fort Street—the School*. Privately published, Sydney 1989.

Howchin, Walter. *The Geology of South Australia*. The South Australian Education Department, Adelaide 1918.

Hunt, Arthur Leigh. *Confessions of a Leigh Hunt*. A. H. & A. W. Reed, Wellington 1951.

Huntford, Roland. *Shackleton.* Hodder & Stoughton, London 1985 (2nd edn, Sphere Books, London 1989).

Hurley, J. Frank. *Argonauts of the South.* Putnam's Sons, New York 1925.

Innes, Margaret, and Duff, Heather. *Mawson's Papers—a Guide.* Mawson Institute for Antarctic Research, Adelaide 1990.

Joerg, W. L. G. (ed.). *Problems of Polar Research: A Series of Papers by Thirty-One Authors.* American Geographical Society Special Publication No. 7. Foreword by Isaiah Bowman. American Geographical Society, New York 1928.

Kennet, Lady (Kathleen Scott). *Self-Portrait of an Artist.* John Murray, London 1949.

Laseron, Charles Francis. *South with Mawson.* George G. Harrap, London 1947.

Lilley, Alan B. *The Sydney University Regiment.* Privately published, Sydney 1974.

McKinlay, William Laird. *Karluk.* Weidenfeld & Nicolson, London 1976.

McNicoll, Ronald. *Number 36 Collins Street: Melbourne Club 1838–1988.* Allen & Unwin/Hayes, Sydney 1988.

Madigan, Cecil T. *Central Australia.* Oxford University Press, London 1936.

Marr, J. E. *The Scientific Study of Scenery.* Methuen & Co., London 1900.

Mawson, Douglas. *The Home of the Blizzard,* 2 vols. William Heinemann, London 1915.

——. *Mawson's Antarctic Diaries,* ed. Fred and Eleanor Jacka. Allen & Unwin, Sydney 1988.

Mawson, Paquita. *A Vision of Steel.* F. W. Cheshire, Melbourne 1958.

Mawson, Paquita. *Mawson of the Antarctic.* Longmans, London 1964.

Mill, Hugh Robert. *The Siege of the South Pole.* Alston Rivers, London 1905.

Morgan, E. J. R. *The Adelaide Club 1863–1963.* The Griffin Press, Adelaide 1963.

Nicholson, Ian. *The Log of Logs.* Roebuck Society, Nambour, Qld, 1990.

——. *The Log of Logs, II.* Roebuck Society, Nambour, Qld, 1993.

Price, Archibald Grenfell. *The Winning of Australian Antarctica.* Angus & Robertson, Sydney 1962.

Rose, Lisle A. *Assault on Eternity: Richard E. Byrd and the Exploration of Antarctica, 1946–47.* Naval Institute Press, Annapolis 1980.

Schley, W. S., and Soley, J. R. *The Rescue of Greely.* C. Scribner's Sons, New York 1885.

Scott, Robert Falcon. *The Voyage of the 'Discovery'.* Macmillan, London 1905.

———. *Scott's Last Expedition*. Smith, Elder, London 1913.

Serle, Geoffrey. *John Monash: A Biography*. Melbourne University Press, Melbourne 1982.

Shackleton, Ernest H. (ed.). *Aurora Australis*. BAE, Antarctica 1908.

———. *The Heart of the Antarctic*, 2 vols. William Heinemann, London 1909.

———. *South*. William Heinemann, London 1919.

Sprigg, Reg. *Geology Is Fun*. Privately published, Adelaide 1989.

Stefansson, Vilhjalmur. *My Life with the Eskimo*. Macmillan, London 1913.

Suzyumov, E. M. *A Life Given to the Antarctic: The Antarctic Explorer Sir Douglas Mawson*. Foreign Languages Publishing House, Moscow 1960.

Swan, R. A. *Australia in the Antarctic*. Melbourne University Press, Melbourne 1961.

Taylor, George. *Making It Happen: The Rise of Sir Macpherson Robertson*. Robertson & Mullins, Melbourne 1934.

Taylor, T. Griffith. *Douglas Mawson*. Great Australians series. Oxford University Press, Melbourne 1962.

Thomas, Lowell (compiler). *Sir Hubert Wilkins*. McGraw Hill, New York 1961.

Victor, Paul-Emile. *Man and the Conquest of the Poles*. Hamish Hamilton, London 1964.

Wilkins, George Hubert. *Flying the Arctic*. Putnam's Sons, New York 1928.

Articles and Parts of Books

Alderman, A. R., and Tilley, C. E. 'Douglas Mawson 1882–1958', *Biographical Memoirs of Fellows of the Royal Society*, 5, London, 1960.

Cleland, J., and Southcott, R. V. 'Hypervitaminosis A in the Antarctic on the Australasian Antarctic Expedition of 1911–14: A Possible Explanation of the Illnesses of Mertz and Mawson', *Medical Journal of Australia*, Part 1 for 1969, pp. 1337–42.

Corbett, D. W. 'Douglas Mawson: The Geologist as Explorer', *Records of the South Australian Museum*, 30, 1998, pp. 107–36.

David, T. W. Edgeworth. 'The Ascent of Erebus', in Ernest H. Shackleton (ed.), *Aurora Australis*, BAE, Antarctica 1908.

———. 'Professor David's Narrative', in Ernest H. Shackleton, *Heart of the Antarctic*, 2 vols, William Heinemann, London 1909, Vol. 2, Chapters VI–XIII, pp. 73–222.

Davis, John King. 'Future Exploration: The African Quadrant of Antarctica', *Reports of the AAAS*, 16, 1923, pp. 488–92.

Devaux, Jean, and Marani, Michel. 'Le Mystérieux "REP" Type D du Musée de l'Air et de l'Espace', *Pegase: Revue de l'Association des Amis du Musée de l'Air*, 81, April, 1996, pp. 4–7.

Elliott, Brian. 'Le "REP" Polaire', *Pegase: Revue de l'Association des Amis du Musée de l'Air*, 81, April, 1996, pp. 8–16.

Ellsworth, Lincoln. 'Arctic Flying Experiences by Airplane and Airship', in W. L. G. Joerg (ed.), *Problems of Polar Research*, American Geographical Society Special Publication No. 7. American Geographical Society, New York 1928, pp. 411–17.

——. 'My Flight Across Antarctica', *National Geographic Magazine*, 70, 1, July, 1936, pp. 1–35.

Fenner, C. 'Walter Howchin, 1845–1937', *TRSSA*, 61, 1937, pp. v–viii.

Hanna, James. 'Sir Douglas Mawson, Distinguished Pupil of Plumpton Primary School', *Blacktown and District Historical Society Quarterly Journal*, 1, 1, January 1980.

Jacka, Fred. 'Mawson, Sir Douglas (1882–1958)', *ADB*, 10, 1986, pp. 454–57.

Law, Phillip. 'The Mawson Story', *Journal of the Royal Historical Society of Victoria*, 57, 1, March, 1986, pp. 3–13; 2, June 1986, pp. 13–18; and 3, September 1986, pp. 14–24.

Macleod, Roy. '"Full of Honour and Gain to Science": Munitions Production, Technical Intelligence and the Wartime Career of Sir Douglas Mawson, FRS', *Historical Records of Australian Science*, 7, 1989, pp. 189–201.

Mawson, Douglas. 'Preliminary Note on the Geology of the New Hebrides', *Reports of the AAAS*, 10, 1904, pp. 213–26.

Mawson, Douglas, and Laby, T. H. 'Preliminary Observations on Radio-Activity and the Occurrence of Radium in Australian Minerals', *Proceedings of the Royal Society of New South Wales*, 38, 1904, pp. 382–9.

Mawson, Douglas. 'The Geology of the New Hebrides', *Proceedings of the Linnean Society of New South Wales*, 3, 1905, pp. 400–85.

——. 'On Certain New Mineral Species Associated with Carnotite in the Radio-Active Ore Body near Olary', *TRSSA*, 30, 1906, pp. 188–93.

——. 'Bathybia', in Ernest H. Shackleton (ed.), *Aurora Australis*, BAE, Antarctica 1908.

——. 'Notes on Physics, Chemistry and Mineralogy: Ice and Snow', 'Mineralogy and Chemistry', 'Meteorological Optics', and 'Magnetic Observations. The Magnetic Pole and the Aurora', all in Ernest H. Shackleton, *Heart of the Antarctic*, 2 vols, William Heinemann, London 1909, Vol. 2, Appendix IV, pp. 334–8, 344, 345–7, 358–61.

——. 'Chiastolites from Bimbowrie, South Australia', *Memoirs of the Royal Society of South Australia*, 2, 3, 1911, pp. 189–210.

——. 'The Australasian Antarctic Expedition', *Geographical Journal*, 40, 1911, pp. 609–20.

——. 'Geological Investigations in the Broken Hill Area', *Memoirs of the Royal Society of South Australia*, 2, 4, 1912, pp. 211–319 and Plates.

——. 'Pre-Cambrian Areas in the North-Eastern Portion of South Australia and the Barrier, New South Wales', *Reports of the AAAS*, 13, 1912, pp. 188–91.

——. 'The Proposed Australasian Antarctic Expedition, 1911' *Reports of the AAAS*, 13, 1912, pp. 398–400.

——. 'The Australasian Antarctic Expedition, 1911–1914', *Geographical Journal*, 44, 1914, pp. 257–86.

——. 'Out of the Jaws of Death', *Strand Magazine*, 48, 1914, pp. 199–211 (Part 1), 311–23 (Part 2).

——. 'The Current Geographical Outlook', *Reports of the AAAS*, 15, 1921, pp. 145–60.

——. 'Igneous Rocks of the Mount Painter Belt', *TRSSA*, 47, 1923, pp. 376–87.

——. 'Evidence and Indications of Algal Contributions in the Cambrian and Pre-Cambrian Limestones of South Australia', *TRSSA*, 49, 1925, pp. 186–90.

——. AAE Scientific Reports, Series B, Vol. 2, Part 1: *Records of the Aurora Polaris*, Sydney, 1925.

——. 'The Wooltana Basic Igneous Belt', *TRSSA*, 50, 1926, pp. 192–200.

——. 'A Brief Resumé of Present Knowledge Relating to the Igneous Rocks of South Australia', *Reports of the AAAS*, 18, 1926, pp. 229–74.

——. 'Unsolved Problems of Antarctic Exploration and Research', in W. L. G. Joerg (ed.), *Problems of Polar Research*, American Geographical Society, New York 1928.

——, and Madigan, Cecil T. 'The Pre-Ordovician Rocks of the McDonnell Ranges, Central Australia', *Quarterly Journal of the Geological Society*, 86, 1930, pp. 415–28.

——. 'The Antarctic Cruise of the "Discovery", 1929–30', *Geographical Review*, 20, 1930, pp. 535–54.

——. *Commonwealth Parliamentary Papers, 1928–31*, 2, 1930, pp. 823–7 (Mawson's official report to the Prime Minister on the first cruise of the BANZARE).

——. 'The B.A.N.Z. Antarctic Research Expedition, 1929–31', *Geographical Journal*, 80, 1932, pp. 101–31.

——. 'The Kerguelen Archipelago', *Geographical Journal*, 83, 1934, pp. 18–29.

———. 'Wilkes's Antarctic Landfalls', *Proceedings of the Royal Geographical Society of Australasia* (SA Branch), 34, 1934, pp. 70–113.

———. 'The Unveiling of Antarctica', *Reports of the ANZAAS*, 22, 1935, pp. 1–37.

———. 'Progress in Knowledge of the Geology of South Australia', *TRSSA*, 60, 1936, pp. lvi–lxv.

———. AAE Scientific Reports, Series A, Vol. 2, Part 4: *Hydrological Observations*, NSW Government Printer, Sydney 1940.

———. AAE Scientific Reports, Series A, Vol. 2, Part 5: *Marine Biological Programme and Other Zoological and Botanical Activities*, NSW Government Printer, Sydney 1940.

———. AAE Scientific Reports, Series A, Vol. 4, Part 11: *Sedimentary Rocks*, NSW Government Printer, Sydney 1940.

———. AAE Scientific Reports, Series A, Vol. 4, Part 12: *Records of Minerals of King George V Land, Adélie Land and Queen Mary Land*, NSW Government Printer, Sydney 1940.

———. AAE Scientific Reports, Series A, Vol. 4, Part 13: *Catalogue of Rocks and Minerals Collected in Antarctic Lands*, NSW Government Printer, Sydney 1940.

———. AAE Scientific Reports, Series A, Vol. 1: *Geographical Narrative and Cartography*, NSW Government Printer, Sydney 1942.

———. 'The Structural Character of the Flinders Ranges', *TRSSA*, 66, 1942, pp. 262–72.

———, and Parkin, Lee. 'Some Granitic Rocks of South-Eastern South Australia', *TRSSA*, 67, 1943, pp. 233–43.

———. AAE Scientific Reports, Series A, Vol. 5: *Macquarie Island—Its Geography and Geology*, NSW Government Printer, Sydney 1943.

———. 'The Nature and Occurrence of Uraniferous Mineral Deposits in South Australia', *TRSSA*, 68, 1944, pp. 334–57.

———, and Dallwitz, W. B. 'Palaeozoic Igneous Rocks of Lower South-Eastern South Australia', *TRSSA*, 68, 1944, pp. 191–209.

———, and Segnit, E. R. 'Granites of the Tintinara District', *TRSSA*, 69, 1945, pp. 263–76.

———. 'The Adelaide Series as Developed along the Western Margin of the Flinders Ranges', *TRSSA*, 71, 1947, pp. 259–80.

———. 'The Elatina Glaciation: A Third Recurrence of Glaciation Evidenced in the Adelaide System', *TRSSA*, 73, 1949, pp. 117–21.

———. 'The Late Precambrian Ice-Age and Glacial Record of the Bibliando Dome', *Journal of the Proceedings of the Royal Society of New South Wales*, 82, 1949, pp. 150–74.

Mitchell, Sir William. Foreword to M. F. Glaessner and E. A. Rudd (eds), *Sir Douglas Mawson Anniversary Volume*, The University of Adelaide, Adelaide 1952.

Price, Archibald Grenfell. BANZARE Scientific Reports, Series A, Vol. 1: *Geographical Report*, Mawson Institute for Antarctic Research, Adelaide 1963.

Riiser-Larsen, Hjalmar. 'The "Norvegia" Antarctic Expedition of 1929–1930', *Geographical Review*, 20, 1930, pp. 555–73.

Scot Skirving, R. 'Recollections of the Emigration Service to Australia in Sailing Ships in Long-Past Years', *Medical Journal of Australia*, 1, 26, 27 June 1942, pp. 689–97.

Shearman, D. J. C. 'Vitamin A and Sir Douglas Mawson', *British Medical Journal*, Part 1 for 1978, pp. 283–5.

Southcott, R. V., Chesterfield, N. J., and Lugg, D. J. 'The Vitamin A Content of the Livers of Huskies and Some Seals from Arctic and Subantarctic Regions', *Medical Journal of Australia*, Part 1 for 1971, pp. 311–13.

Taylor, T. Griffith, and Mawson, Douglas. 'The Geology of Mittagong', *Journal of the Proceedings of the Royal Society of New South Wales*, 37, 1903, pp. 306–30.

Webb, Eric. 'An Appreciation', in Lennard Bickel, *This Accursed Land*, Macmillan, Melbourne 1977.

Newspapers

Advertiser, Adelaide

Age, Melbourne

Ann Arbor News

Argus, Melbourne

Canberra Times

Chicago Sunday Tribune

Daily Mail, London

New York Times

Otago Witness

Register, Adelaide

Times, London

Sydney Morning Herald, Sydney

University of Michigan Daily

Periodicals

Adélie Blizzard, Antarctica (AAE), at MAC
L'Aerophile, Paris
L'Auto, Paris
Bulletin, Sydney
Flight, London
Fortian, Sydney
Graphic, London
Illustrated London News
Strand Magazine, London

INDEX

Don